The film's coming attraction slide: such slides were printed on glass, and many were hand colored. *Courtesy of StartsThursday.com*

The Street of Forgotten Men:
From Story to Screen and Beyond

The Street of Forgotten Men:
From Story to Screen and Beyond

forewords by Kevin Brownlow & Robert Byrne

Thomas Gladysz

PandorasBox Press / Louise Brooks Society

2023

The Street of Forgotten Men: From Story to Screen and Beyond
A publication of the Louise Brooks Society™ / PandorasBox Press
www.pandorasbox.com

Cover design by Christy Pascoe
All images from the collection of the Louise Brooks Society
unless otherwise indicated

Copyright © 2023 Thomas Gladysz
Foreword by Kevin Brownlow © 2023 Kevin Brownlow
Foreword by Robert Byrne © 2023 Robert Byrne

All rights reserved. No part of this book may be reproduced or transmitted in any form or by any means, electronic or mechanical, including photocopying, recording, or any other storage and retrieval system without written from the author, except for the inclusion of brief quotations for a review.

ISBN-13: 979-8-218-20985-8

DEDICATION

To Christy Pascoe, with love and appreciation

This 1925 arcade card, tinted red and manufactured by the Exhibit Supply Co. of Chicago, Illinois, was printed on thicker stock than most postcards. Though meant to promote the film and its stars, Mary Brian's name is mistakenly given as Mabel Brian. *Author collection*

CONTENTS

	Acknowledgments	xii
	Foreword by Kevin Brownlow	xvi
	Foreword by Robert Byrne	xx
1	Introduction	xxiv
2	Author and Story	1
3	The Adaption	11
4	The Scenario	21
5	Making the Film	109
6	The Press Sheet	141
7	Entr'acte: A Musical Interlude	163
8	A Film History	177
9	A Legacy	239
10	*L'Ecole des Mendiants*	263
11	Around the World	279
12	Cast, Credits & Trivia	291
13	A Glossary	323
14	Further Reading	329
	Index	333

Studio clip art from 1925

Acknowledgments

First and foremost, I wish to thank Robert Byrne, film preservationist *extraordinaire*, who took on the task of restoring *The Street of Forgotten Men*. Without him and Jennifer Miko, this film would likely not have been given the second chance it deserves. I did my bit, and am credited in the acknowledgements of the restored print. It was an honor to have helped in a small way to bring this work back into circulation. And, it was a pleasure to have been present at the premiere of the restored film in San Francisco in 2022. Robert Byrne is to be thanked again. Not only did he restore the surviving film, he graciously consented to write a foreword to this book, and, he has been unfailingly helpful time and again.

Years ago, I spent an hour or so visiting with Kevin Brownlow in his London flat. He spoke enthusiastically of Herbert Brenon, and encouraged me to pursue my interest in *The Street of Forgotten Men*, a film he thought well of. I did, and this book is the result. My sincere thanks to Kevin Brownlow, not only for his encouragement, suggestions, and generosity in sharing information about the film, but also for writing a second foreword.

I also wish to acknowledge and thank Richard Koszarski (who I had the pleasure of meeting at the 2022 restoration premiere), Tim Moore, Barry Paris, Becca Pascoe, David Pierce, Ira Resnick, and Frank Thompson, each of whom, in some way, contributed to this project. Special thanks to my wife, Christy Pascoe, who designed the cover, assisted with images, and advised on the text. Without her considerable support, this book would not exist.

The following organizations, entities and websites (and associated individuals) also aided in the making of this book. My gratitude to each.

Ancestry.com

Cinema Treasures (cinematreasures.org)

Frances Howard Goldwyn – Hollywood Regional Library (Rudy Ruiz)
FultonHistory.com
George Eastman Museum (Nancy Kaufman, David Howe)
HathiTrust (www.hathitrust.org)
Internet Archive (archive.org)
JSTOR.org
Library of Congress Motion Picture Division
Louise Brooks Heirs, LC (Daniel Brooks)
Margaret Herrick Library, Academy of Motion Picture Arts and Sciences
Media History Digital Library (mediahist.org)
Mont-alto.com/PhotoplayMusic.html (Rodney Sauer)
Museum of the Moving Image
New York Public Library
New York Public Library for the Performing Arts
New York State Archives
New York State Historic Newspapers (nyshistoricnewspapers.org)
Newspapers.com
San Francisco Public Library (Ron Romano, Inter-Library Loan Department)
San Francisco Silent Film Festival
SilentHollywood.com (Kay Shackleton)
StartsThursday! (startsthursday.com)
Theatre Historical Society of America (historictheatres.org)
Vaudeville America (vaudevilleamerica.org)
Wisconsin Center for Film and Theater Research

The author also wishes to thank the following individuals who supported this project through GoFundMe: ALM Castermans, Eric Cohen, Kenneth Cone, William Kromm, David Dalimonte, Don Ferenci, Paul Gladysz, Thomas Gorman, Donna Hill, Amanda Howard, Kasia Kappes, Peter Knerr, Pamela Kirkpatrick, Paul Lutz, James Mason, Carol Morris, Channing J Nickell, Camille Scaysbrook, Susanne Sittig, Elizabeth Szabla, Amy Thomas, Frank Thompson, Andrew Weiner, Jimi Wilson.

Bits and pieces of this book were first tried out on my Louise Brooks Society blog (louisebrookssociety.blogspot.com), where anyone interested in *The Street of Forgotten Men* can find additional material which didn't make it into the book.

Two of a small number of generic newspaper ads available to exhibitors. These two-column supplementary ads come from the Paramount Press Sheet.

A pensive Easy Money Charlie (played by Percy Marmont), stands alone ...
Credit: Wisconsin Center for Film and Theater Research

FOREWORD
BY KEVIN BROWNLOW

Herbert Brenon - one of the giants of early cinema? Or a justly forgotten hack? He made films that fitted both categories.

When Thomas Gladysz emailed me that it was time to deliver this foreword, I reached for a venerable book called *A Million and One Nights*, which I knew to be full of stories as colourful as the man himself.

The volume fell open at a page with this declaration.

"Herbert Brenon – one of the motion picture's most spectacular and volatile personalities."

My own interest in the director began as a teenage film collector, with the acquisition of a rare but mild little thriller from 1921, *Chivalrous Charley*, not by Brenon but by Robert Ellis. In its cast appeared a young immigrant from Italy – omitted from the credits in the AFI Catalogue, by the way – called Rudolph Valentino. Realising this would be of value to my friend Leslie Flint, who ran the Valentino Memorial Guild, I took it round to show him. He was more interested in it than I was and an exchange was arranged; he showed me a superb historical film, *The Spanish Dancer* (1923), directed by Herbert Brenon. Valentino wasn't in it.

Fortunately, he had two copies, and he was happy to let one of them go. I was thrilled by the sheer scale of the picture. (I'd always been keen on epics.)

I found out that Valentino had been complaining about the lack of production values on the films he was making for Famous Players-Lasky, and so they had concocted this splendid vehicle. Its first title was *The Spanish Cavalier*, but when Valentino walked out anyway, it became *The Spanish Dancer*, with Pola Negri, something of a challenge for the director.

Irish–born Herbert Brenon did a splendid job. The film was full of humour, it was beautiful to look at – photographed by the great James Wong Howe * – and it had an impressive supporting cast; Adolphe Menjou, Wallace Beery, Gareth Hughes and Kathlyn Williams. It seemed that these players would do anything to work with Brenon, despite his reputation as a martinet.

Back in the 1950s, silent films were regarded by my generation as comical, even if they weren't meant to be. "Technically pathetic, badly acted, boring" – that's how my friends regarded them. Until I showed them a few of the films in my collection – like this one: technically impeccable, well acted and directed.

It was just the incompetently made copies that destroyed the reputation of early cinema – 'dupes' as duplicate copies were known – made by lab technicians who thought the same way as my friends. The standard excuse when I complained to the lab about their murky results, "It's an old film. You can't do a thing with it."

But my newly acquired copy of *The Spanish Dancer* was a Kodascope Library print, made for home viewing in the twenties and thirties. Kodak were anxious for people using cine cameras to have their films processed by Kodak. So they took enormous care over the printing. And the term 'an amber print' meant the best quality and finest tinting you could find on 16mm.

To make the films affordable, they were abridged – a seven-reeler was reduced to five. The Paramount release of *The Spanish Dancer* was ten reels, yet the Kodak people still reduced it to five. It worked well enough, though I always hoped to see what Brenon had done with that extra length. But the ten-reel Paramount release had been lost and the Kodascope Library abridgment was the only version in circulation – usually in poor dupes as film libraries were scarce and amber prints obsolete.

Not so long ago, I was asked to lend my print to the Eye Institute in Amsterdam, where curator Elif Rongen was working on a restoration. I agreed, but I felt nervous. Sometimes an abridgment works better than its original. But Elif had managed not only to find the missing footage, but also a cutting continuity, providing the original text of the titles, and the correct order for every shot. Equally important, she had found a lot of 35mm nitrate footage (you can't find better). The final result – as complete as in 1923 – was marvelous. She had brought back more of the humour and preserved the spectacle without any sense of excess.

In 1959, working as an editor for a London documentary film company, I needed an assistant, and they took on a young man called Peter Watkins (the future director of the 1966 anti-nuclear film *The War Game*). I was delighted to have someone so interested in films as an assistant. But from the start, he inspired argument. The first evening, I invited him to see *The Spanish Dancer*, hoping he might be instantly converted to silent films. The print sparkled on my screen, and I only regretted the lack of musical accompaniment. (Originally, at first-run theatres, the accompaniment would have been from live orchestra).

During a reel break, Peter said, "It's quite true, isn't it? Herbert Brenon's cinematic interpretation was negligible"

This annoyed me intensely, not only because I recognised the quote from Paul Rotha's book *The Film Till Now* – very anti-Hollywood – but also because I was showing him a film I felt protective about. I argued with him and then put on the next reel, and by the end he admitted that Brenon had a certain level of talent. (To his credit, when I later showed him Abel Gance's *Napoleon*, he was so impressed, he wrote a fan letter to its director.)

William K Everson, the New York-based doyen of film collectors and historians, was a particular enthusiast for Brenon; his favourite silent film was *A Kiss For Cinderella* (1926) and he always enthused about the beauty of the sole surviving original print, preserved in a famous archive. When it turned out to have decomposed in their care he was inconsolable, and directed a campaign against inadequate film conservation. The print had been acquired in 1936, but not preserved until 1967, by which time reels 8 and 9 had started to decompose – but only in certain spots and only briefly. Everson offered to pay for the preservation himself, but he was turned down and the film was copied on to 16mm reversal. "Not worth doing it on 35mm," he was told, the underlying message being, "It's just an old film. You can't do a thing with it."

The star, Betty Bronson, used to come from Hollywood to New York to introduce the film, and she must have felt a great sense of achievement, listening to the audience reactions afterwards. Everson attended a screening five years later and the entire reel had gone. "A real crime," he said.

Some years ago, I did an exchange with James Card for a 16mm print of *Peter Pan*, and emphasised that the print quality was all important. He was visiting London and he brought the print with him. He handed it over and I eagerly unwound a few feet and was delighted by what I saw. But when I put it on the projector, that quality lasted for five minutes and then it reverted to the usual soot-and-whitewash so common at the time. To quote Mary Pickford, I was madder than a wet hen, but to no avail.

Later, an expert on early cinema, David Pierce, heard that there was to be a restoration of *Peter Pan*. It didn't materialize, so he put his own money into the project. Pierce learned that the rights to *Peter Pan* had been sold by Paramount to Disney in 1939. "I licensed the film from Disney and TriStar (producers of *Hook*)," Pierce wrote me, "and received elements from Disney for release (through Kino) in 35mm, VHS, DVD and BluRay. The restoration work was performed by Scott MacQueen from the Eastman House nitrate, incorporating the intro titles (the ones signed by James Barrie) from a 16mm print held by Disney. Being able to license *Peter Pan* was a combination of knowing Scott MacQueen, him working on the film, and then having a few lucky breaks in reaching the right people in Disney legal. I funded the reissue of the film, though the restoration work was funded by Disney."

The result of Pierce's work, which is still available, is outstanding.

There's another vivid memory of Brenon's films, *Beau Geste* (1926). A stunning achievement, which was selected by D. W. Griffith as one of his Fifty Best Films, and won the *Photoplay* Medal of Honor for 1926. And while a tremendous success on release, its impact in more modern times was set to be ruined by terrible presentations. Not that the organisers didn't try hard.

At the first screening I attended, at the Queen Elizabeth Hall in London, a 35mm print had been sent from the United States, only to be impounded by Customs. The duty was too much for the organisers to pay. A London film collector happened to have a 16mm print and would have saved the day except that 16mm in a 800 seat theatre was woefully inadequate – and it was a miserable print to begin with. At the second, which I also attended, a local orchestra was hired and their vain efforts to cope with the epic images sounded like the first few minutes on Omaha Beach in 1944. Many of us held our hands over our ears. Yet what a tribute to Brenon – in both cases the underlying quality of the films still shone through. Both times the films still worked and were much admired.

Dancing Mothers (1926) was an elegant and adult film, with a surprise ending, but I have to admit it has no more cinematic interpretation than a television play. It's a silent talkie, with too many titles. Nonetheless, it boasts a wonderful performance by Clara Bow, not to mention Alice Joyce, and it is one of the treasures of my collection.

The Street of Forgotten Men was incredibly rare, and when I found a still, I sent a copy to Louise Brooks, whom I had recently interviewed.

She wrote back, "How sweet of you to send me the still from *The Street of Forgotten Men*. I never saw the picture and this is the first still I have ever seen of my bit part.

"Harold Rosson was the camera Man (sic) on *Street*. Unlike his brother Arthur, he was a dreary guy whose passion for beautiful women I found most depressing. He told me to get my left eye tooth capped (which I did); and always to wear black patent leather shoes like Norma Talmadge (which I didn't). **

"But I wouldn't have missed knowing Herbert Brenon.

"I think it was this first picture I made that disgusted me with films. Brenon was typical of that 19th century theatre direction which extracted emotion out of actors with personal insults. And since I cared nothing for films I told him to go to hell. This attitude he found so delightful (being an Irishman) that he asked me to go with him to the Kentucky Derby at Louisville. And to my surprise, I did.

"He was absolutely charming there, entertaining me and all the men from the local exchange and Paramount exhibitors in his suite at the hotel with the best bourbon and anecdotes in his Dublin accent."

Lon Chaney explained Brenon to a 15-year old Loretta Young, who had co-starred with him in Brenon's *Laugh Clown Laugh* (1928) and been given a hard time.

"You've got to figure Brenon can't help it. He rides you, the company rides him, and the public rides the company. It's all a merry-go-round."

* James Howe would not become James Wong Howe until 1925.

** Hal Rosson married Jean Harlow. He may have been a retiring sort of individual. [He refused to talk to me because most reporters who said they wanted to talk to him, really wanted to hear spicy tidbits about Harlow… And the magazine *Confidential* was going full blast in 1964.] However, he was among the most brilliant of all cameramen. He later photographed *The Docks of New York* (1928), *The Asphalt Jungle* (1950) and *The Red Badge of Courage* (1951).

... as Portland Fancy's funeral passes by on the street of forgotten men. *Author collection*

FOREWORD

BY ROBERT BYRNE

Ten years ago, more or less, we were talking between films on the mezzanine in San Francisco's iconic Castro Theatre. The conversation turned to the early films of Louise Brooks and our disappointment that so many of her early films are lost. *The American Venus* (1926), *Rolled Stockings* (1927), *Evening Clothes* (1927) … how amazing it would be to see those lost treasures. Those films may have been trash or they may have been treasures, but we will likely never be in a position to judge for ourselves. Who wouldn't give their right arm to see Brooks as "Snuggles Joy" in the hard-boiled *The City Gone Wild* (1927)? What must that have been like? And then there is her very first screen appearance in *The Street of Forgotten Men* (1925). The title intrigues. Undoubtedly that too is lost, along with all the others.

"Well actually," spoke up Thomas Gladysz, "the Library of Congress has a print. There is a reel missing but I believe it is mostly complete."

When it comes to Louise Brooks, Thomas knows where all the bodies are buried.

Thus began our quest to restore, preserve, and screen *The Street of Forgotten Men*. At that time the film was still under copyright, but not for much longer. With each passing year American films produced during silent era were (and are) passing into the public domain. We would have to wait, but Thomas had planted the seed.

On January 1, 2021, all American films released in 1925 shed their bonds of copyright and *The Street of Forgotten Men* entered the public domain – and we were prepared. The interim years had provided time for research, fundraising, and developing an approach for dealing with the missing reel. Research is generally the most time-consuming and least glamorous aspect of a restoration project, but most projects don't have the advantage of having Thomas Gladysz's decades of work at their disposal. Materials that would have taken years to track down: production records, trade press, stills, production images, censor records, newspaper clippings, advertisements, and promotional materials, everything we could hope for, were already in hand. The book you are reading is irrefutable proof that Thomas Gladysz leaves no stone unturned.

From a technical perspective, the most challenging aspect of the restoration were the decisions regarding how to deal with the missing second reel. The film was originally released in seven reels but the original 35mm nitrate negative preserved at the Library of Congress had only six. Chemical decomposition of nitrate film stock is an inalterable fact and the only known surviving copy of *The Street of Forgotten Men* was (and is) slowly wasting away. The nitrate negative had been duplicated and preserved in 1969 but by that time the second reel was already beyond salvation. Fortunately, if we were going to deal with a missing reel, this was the one we could most live without. For sure the absent footage includes important exposition but we could, and did, find a reasonably seamless way to combine stills with text from the script and created a visual bridge to smooth the narrative gap while filling in the missing information.

Meanwhile, a funny thing also happened during the restoration. We came to the realization that *The Street of Forgotten Men* is a really good film. We launched our restoration with the Holy mission of resurrecting Louise Brooks' first film but honestly gave little consideration to the quality of the film itself. The film's historical significance was all the incentive we needed. The film could have been terrible and we still would have done the work, but how wonderful that it is not. The film is directed by Herbert Brenon (*Peter Pan* (1924), *The Spanish Dancer* (1923), *Beau Geste* (1926), *Laugh Clown Laugh* (1928), and 120 other titles), boasts high production values and features a first-rate cast. The Bowery sequences and the "cripple factory" are extraordinary and the plot twists in interesting directions before ending up where you expect that it will.

And of course, there is Brooksie. There is danger in a "first screen appearance." There was every risk that she could have only appeared as a barely-recognizable extra perched on a barstool. Instead, there she is, fully formed, black helmet bob and all. She plays a bona fide role in the film's climactic sequence and even has a line of titled dialogue: "You're just wonderful, Whitey!" Tuck that away for your trivia contest.

Louise Brooks appears in 20 shots, precisely 2,085 frames, of *The Street of Forgotten Men*. Projected at 20 frames per second, she occupies one minute and 44.25 seconds of screen time. Within that brief span a star was born, though nobody, including the star herself, realized it at the time. And for the most part, film fans, or at least American film fans, probably never quite figured it out – at least not before her rediscovery and revival in the late 1950s.

A star is born: John Harrington as Bridgeport White-Eye with the uncredited Louise Brooks as his moll. *Courtesy of San Francisco Silent Film Festival*

And so here we are, almost 100 years later, celebrating the film, and the star, that we almost lost forever. It is no coincidence that we have Thomas Gladysz to thank not only for this fascinating volume but also for planting the seed that brought *The Street of Forgotten Men* back to life.

And now, Thomas, how about *The City Gone Wild*? I wasn't kidding about "Snuggles Joy" you know.

Early Paramount poster art, published in *Motion Picture News* on May 16, 1925. Notably, this pre-release poster describes the film as "The *Miracle Man* of 1926."

INTRODUCTION

Like other film buffs, I want to see every film featuring my favorite star. In my case, my favorite is Louise Brooks, the silent era actress with the distinct bob best known for playing Lulu in *Pandora's Box*.

I first came across the actress in the early 1990s, while browsing the shelves of a video rental shop. During one visit, I noticed *Pandora's Box* in the classics section; I was not familiar with the film, but its packaging drew my attention and I thought I would check it out. I watched the movie that evening . . . and was awestruck. I was spellbound. I had never seen any actress, any star, or anyone, like Louise Brooks.

After that, I was determined to see each of her films. Soon, I tracked down the other film Brooks made under G.W. Pabst's direction, *Diary of a Lost Girl*. And again, I was wowed. I also found *Prix de Beauté*, the movie she made in France, and *A Girl in Every Port*, an earlier American film which supposedly inspired Pabst to cast Brooks as Lulu. Those were the few films then available on home video.

Over the next few years, and through a slow trickle of classic and budget releases (some on VHS, some on laser disc, some on DVD), I managed to find *It's the Old Army Game*, *The Show Off*, *Love Em and Leave Em*, *Beggars of Life* and *The Canary Murder Case*, as well as each of the actress' talkies from the 1930s.

Altogether, there are 24 films in Brooks' somewhat slight filmography. At the time, six were considered lost. A couple survived incomplete, and a few others were rarely if ever shown in theaters or on television. Altogether, I had little hope of seeing a third of the actress' films, and instead had to content myself with merely reading about them. Such was the fate of many film buffs at the time.

Since first "discovering" the actress, I have found a great deal of pleasure in researching Brooks' film career, looking up articles in whatever vintage newspapers or magazines I could access. For a number of years, I made weekly trips to the San Francisco Public Library, where I would scroll through rolls and rolls of microfilm. I also put through hundreds of interlibrary loan (ILL) requests, systematically attempting to track down every possible review, article, and reference. I found Brooks' career, as well as the silent film era, endlessly fascinating. Research was my personal means of time travel.

Over time, my interest spread to Brooks' co-stars and contemporaries, to the films of the early sound era, and to the broader history of the period, the Jazz Age. I was a silent film buff – but also think of myself as an independent researcher & film historian (admittedly an *amateur film historian*). My interest in Brooks has continued for more than a quarter of a century.

One of the films in Brooks' filmography that had long eluded me was *The Street of Forgotten Men* (1925). The actress made her screen debut in this otherwise little-known film, playing a moll in an uncredited bit part. As one of Brooks' silent films, it has never received much attention, except for the fact that it marked the actress' first screen appearance. In other quarters, *The Street of Forgotten Men* is known as one of a number of movies directed by Herbert Brenon, the once acclaimed director who made the still revived *Peter Pan* (1924), *Beau Geste* (1926), *Laugh, Clown, Laugh* (1928) and other early classics.

The Street of Forgotten Men was once considered a lost film. (Kenneth Tynan described it as so in his 1979 profile of Brooks in the *New Yorker*.) It was also a film I had read about and researched but had never seen – until 2006, when I had the chance to spend a day at the Library of Congress in Washington D.C. At the time, the library held the only surviving print of *The Street of Forgotten Men*, albeit an incomplete one. During my visit, I arranged to see what remained. For my screening, I was escorted to a quiet back-room. There, I sat in a cubicle with a little hand-crank projector and ran the film for an audience of one – me. It was an unusual, intimate, and thrilling experience. As projectionist, I could start and stop the film whenever I wished. And I did just that, taking notes on most every scene, not knowing if I would ever see the film again. Despite Brooks' brief appearance, I found the film fascinating. Years later, I still hold that opinion.

There is much to recommend about *The Street of Forgotten Men*, which was both a popular and critical success at the time of its release. The film is based on a story by a noted writer of the time; it was made by a significant director, shot by a great cinematographer, and features a fine cast which includes a future screen legend at the very beginning of her career. Altogether, there are many points of interest.

The Street of Forgotten Men: From Story to Screen and Beyond is a deep dive into the history of one film – its literary source, its making, its critical reception, and its surprising, little-known legacy. It is the primary intention of this book to show how one film might be exemplary of filmmaking and film culture during the silent era.

However, there is more to this story…. One of John Donne's famous poems begins "No man is an island entire of itself; every man / is a piece of the continent, a part of the main". To me, what Donne's verse says about humanity is what I believe about significant works of art, including films. Everything is connected in some way, in that nothing is created in a vacuum. I have kept Donne's lines in mind while writing this book. If anything, this book achieves one thing – it places *The Street of Forgotten Men* in the rich cinematic and cultural context of its time. Does such a context elevate this particular film as a work of art, or as a cinematic achievement? Not necessarily. But then, that was not my goal.

I had long thought of writing a book about *The Street of Forgotten Men*, and have been unknowingly gathering material for years, if not decades – since, years ago, putting through all those ILL requests at the SFPL for the many NYC newspapers. The film's 2022 restoration – and the fact that published material from 1925 has come into the public domain gave me the incentive to complete this project. With the film's restoration, it should begin to make its way into the stream of available films. I hope this book prompts the interest of film buffs and film scholars alike, and acts as a companion work for those who have the opportunity to see the film.

I also wrote this book for another reason, because it is a book I would like to read about this or any film. Does it matter that *The Street of Forgotten Men* is a lesser film in the larger scheme of things, or in the history of film? No. Because, no film is an island.

STARTING THURSDAY
Return Showing of
**"The Street
of
Forgotten Men"**

The Morning News, Wilmington Delaware – December 2, 1925

The Street of Forgotten Men is very much a film of its time – aesthetically as a silent movie, and culturally as an artifact of America in the 1920s. The original story, various studio documents including the scenario and press sheet, as well as some of the articles and reviews which both preceded and followed the film's release, use language and reflect attitudes regarding the disabled, ethnicity, gender, or the homeless which today some might find inappropriate, or offensive (i.e., racist, sexist, classist).

"Cripple," for example, is a frequently used term which has rightly fallen into disuse. So has the notion – referring to immigrants, as "hordes of foreign born" entering the country. Other terms used in documents and articles from the time and reproduced in this book are "wop," "nigger," "fat," "bum," etc.… These terms, once thought acceptable or colorful and now considered discriminatory or offensive, have been retained, as their past use honestly, though unfortunately, reflects their times.

One of the purposes of art is to offer a window on the values of the past. It is not my intention to cause hurt by retaining such terms in documenting the history of this film, nor do I condone the use of such terms today. I also do not wish to rewrite history or censor the past, but rather learn from it.

Two fake beggars. (Top) Percy Marmont as Easy Money Charlie. *Author collection* (Bottom) John Harrington as Bridgeport White-Eye. *From the Core Collection Production files and the Paramount Pictures photographs of the Margaret Herrick Library, Academy of Motion Picture Arts and Sciences*

A newspaper ad for the magazine story – February 1925

AUTHOR AND STORY

In the early years of the 20th century, George Kibbe Turner (1869-1952) was a well-regarded writer who made his name as a muckraking journalist, and then as the author of a number of celebrated novels and short stories. Notably, between 1920 and 1932, nine of Turner's stories were made into thirteen films. At the time, his renown was such that movie studios sometimes included his name in their advertisements, noting that their film was made from one of his stories.

Turner first began writing for magazines in his early twenties, while working as a newspaper reporter at the Springfield *Republican* in Massachusetts. By 1899, he had placed a small number of pieces in *McClure's*, a popular magazine of the time which would go on to publish his first book, *The Taskmaster* (1902); Turner's debut novel, about goings-on in a company town, was described by *The Nation* as "thoughtful, eager, even impassioned." (2-5-1903) A few years later, in 1906, Turner was hired by *McClure's* as a staff writer. (Another hire, around the same time, was Willa Cather.) His first major assignment was to report on a new form of municipal government set up in Galveston, Texas following the devastating hurricane of 1900. Turner's widely read article, "Galveston: A Business Corporation," proved highly influential and helped secure his reputation.

During his more than ten years with *McClure's*, Turner made his name as one of the leading muckraking journalists. His reform-minded contemporaries included Lincoln Steffens, Ida Tarbell, Frank Norris, Jacob Riis, and most famously Upton Sinclair, author of *The Jungle*. Early on, Sinclair was a champion of Turner's work. In 1922, Sinclair devoted part of a column in E. Haldeman-Julius' weekly progressive newspaper, *Appeal to Reason*, to his muckraking friend. Sinclair wrote "Ten or fifteen years ago this man used to write for *McClure's*, and I think, for the *American Magazine*. At this time these magazines were honestly edited by independent and high minded men, and George Kibbe Turner was a 'coming writer.' I shall never forget some of his short stories, which were as good as anything published in the magazine in those days. There was a series of Wall Street stories, full of bitter, burning contempt for our money masters and their pride and pomp. There was another series called 'Butterflies,' dealing with the showgirls and artists' models, and other poor feminine waifs of the great Metropolis of Mammon. They were full of human feeling and sympathetic insight into the plight of frail human creatures struggling to keep decent in a world which starved them into indecency. I wrote Turner several letters of friendly sympathy, and tried hard to find a book publisher for those stories." (4-22-1922)

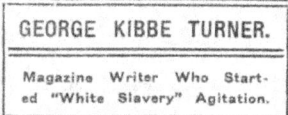

Photo by Marceau, New York.
George Kibbe Turner, magazine writer, is the man who is credited with starting the New York agitation against the "white slave evil." He has been writing since 1891.

Turner's journalism – which put a spotlight on the corrosive entanglement of government and vice – included a 1907 exposé of drink, gambling, and prostitution titled "The City of Chicago: A Study of the Great Immoralities," as well as piece from 1909, "The Daughters of the Poor: A Plain Story of the White Slave Trade Under Tammany Hall." Each were widely read, and each stirred calls for action. Notably, two months after the latter piece appeared, a judge charged a grand jury to investigate Turner's allegations, and appointed John D. Rockefeller, Jr. as its foreman. Turner would testify.

With the eventual decline in muckraking journalism, Turner turned once more to fiction. The stories and novels that followed – melodramatic and at times as provocative as his non-fiction, appeared in popular publications like the *Saturday Evening Post*, *Atlantic Monthly*, *Red Book*, and *Woman's Home Companion*. Others were serialized in newspapers across the country.

Turner's best-known novels include *The Last Christian* (1914), *The Biography of a Million Dollars* (1918), and *Red Friday* (1919) – the latter is an early red-scare novel which warns of the dangers of Bolshevism in America. There was also *Hagar's Hoard* (1920) – which centers on a greedy Confederate miser amidst an outbreak of yellow fever, and *White Shoulders* (1921), a society drama in which a mother tries to marry her daughter off to the highest bidder. The latter was made into a film, as were other of Turner's more sensational stories. Among them was *Held in Trust* (1920), a widely-seen

Metro release starring May Allison.

Another success came with "Those Who Dance" – Turner's 1922 story about a federal agent and a gang of bootleggers. First National adapted it into a film in 1924 starring Blanche Sweet, Bessie Love, and Warner Baxter. In 1930, Warner Bros. remade the story as a talkie starring Monte Blue, Lila Lee, William Boyd and Betty Compson. That same year, Warner also filmed "Those Who Dance" as *Der Tanz geht weiter*, a German-language version of the story shot in Hollywood with a German-speaking cast which included William Dieterle as director and star. A Spanish-language version, *Los que danzan*, was also made starring Antonio Moreno and Maria Alba. And, there was a French-language version, *Contre-enquête*, with Suzy Vernon.

Perhaps the best-known film adapted from a Turner story is *The Girl in the Glass Cage* (1929), which stars Loretta Young as a pretty young cashier at a movie theater who is stalked by a neighborhood thug. Also popular was Richard Dix's star-turn in RKO's *Roar of the Dragon* (1932), based on Turner's "A Passage to Hong Kong."

"The Street of the Forgotten Men" (with the determining article, *the*, prior to the word forgotten) appeared in the February 14, 1925 issue of *Liberty* magazine. Inspired by people and happenings from the turn-of-the-century, the story was described as a "Romance of the Underworld – The Strange Story of a Bowery Cinderella and a Beggar Who Lost Himself for Love." It was illustrated by Dudley G. Summers, one of the name illustrators of the time.

"The Street of the Forgotten Men" sketches incidents in the life of Easy Money Charlie, a "fake bandager" who feigns the loss of an arm in order to panhandle on the streets of New York. Charlie is one of a group of professional beggars, or con men, whose gathering place is Diamond Mike's Dead House, an old-time saloon with a back room known as the "Cripple Factory."

Despite his fraudulent life, Charlie is a decent sort at heart, and he is convinced by a denizen of the street to raise the child of another down-and-out local, the dying Portland Fancy. He does so, though removed from the squalor of life in the Bowery.

Like other of Turner's writings, "The Street of the Forgotten Men" caught the attention of not only the reading public, but also of a handful of movie studios who saw in its "strange story" the makings of a successful motion picture.

A ROMANCE OF THE UNDERWORLD—*The Strange Story of a Bowery Cinderella and a Beggar Who Lost Himself for Love*

"The Fancy wants to see you, over in her rooms," she told him.

The Street of the Forgotten Men

By George Kibbe Turner

Pictures by Dudley G. Summers

THIS is a story of Adolphe the Disguiser, of the double life of a man he knew. And he has known a plenty of them. For that is in the line of his business, the disguising of men and women. But no case like this, exactly. For this was the double life of a dead man—a faked dead man—and the woman he gave up his life for.

He ran across him in Diamond Mike's old Dead House, the old-time hang-out for the professional beggars along the Bowery, back in those days when the begging graft was going big.

For at that time Adolphe was in charge of the back room there—the old Cripple Factory, as they called it, where they fitted out these phony cripples to go begging. And this man was a fake bandager, as they called them. And the name he went by was Easy Money Charlie.

It was easy money, too, those days in the begging game—fifty, a hundred, yes, up into the hundreds of dollars on good afternoons—one of the biggest, steadiest grafts in New York for a good line. And this Charlie was working the fake right arm with a black stocking over it—a better stunt than just the plain usual plaster of Paris stump that you wiggle under your coat on the shoulder.

And his age helped him—for he wasn't much more than a boy—and his face and his smile! It got the women in the shopping district, seeing how bravely this kid was suffering in back of his plaster arm.

THEN back again in the evening, with his forty or fifty dollars in change, and have his real arm underneath unstrapped by Adolphe in the Cripple Factory, and out into that hard bunch in the front room of the Dead House, and out through them to the sidewalk, staring off over the street—that Street of the Homeless Men, wondering what he'd do that night; whether he'd drink himself to death, or what.

But this night he was going through the front room, between the stained, brown-topped tables, where the panhandlers, the cheap beggars who work without any makeup, sat before their beer with the women in the last year's hats, with their sharp eyes and their quick smiles, anxious to please, because this was the last stop going down—here in this Dead House—before the river. And he was almost through when this fat one they called Dutch Dolly held him up.

"The Fancy wants to see you, over in her rooms," she told him.

"Who? Me?" he said back, sore. For he kept clear of the women; they weren't in his line.

"Yes, you," said the fat Dutch.

"What ails her?" he asked, still talking hostile.

"She's dying," she told him.

"And she wants to see me?" he asked her again, slow and wondering.

"Yes. Go on over, Easy — that's a good skate," she said, grabbing him by the elbow. "You'll find out what for when you get there." And he took the address finally, and went out over and saw this woman — this Portland Fancy, as they called her. For they said she originally drifted in there, following a sailor from Portland, Maine.

When he went up the dim stairway with the

[CONTINUED ON NEXT PAGE]

[CONTINUED FROM PAGE SEVENTEEN]

maroon painted sides and the ruts in the old stairs' treads, Easy Money Charlie turned to the left into this back room and found her waiting for him, propped up on some cheap fancy pillows—her hair just fresh curled, all dolled up in her best pink wrapper. And she didn't look so bad as you might have thought, for she was high-colored and bright-eyed, the way these "con" patients are when they get excited. And on the wall across from her, he noticed especially, there was a crucifix, along with some pictures that weren't so good.

And he took her hand, with the phony diamond on the engagement finger, and gave her one of his easy-going, quick-firing smiles. And told her to cheer up—she was going fine. For he saw she was about done. And then he sat down and asked her what he could do for her.

"It's the kid," she said, between coughs.

"I didn't know there was one," said Easy Money Charlie.

"Six years old. They put her in an institution and made a number of her," she said, in a dry, harsh voice, and stopped, coughing. "A number and not a kid," she said, going on. "And you know what becomes of the majority of them after they go through one of those institutions. I do, if you don't. I was a graduate."

"I know," said Easy Money.

"And you're a good, free-hearted guy, Easy," she said, looking up at him, where he sat still and stiff and wondering, waiting for what she was going to spring on him. "And you make big money. You've got a wonderful graft. Ain't you ever lonesome in this dirty hole here for something that really smiles when it sees you coming?"

"You might say so!" said the faker.

"Didn't they tell me you had a dog once, in your room?"

"He died. A truck got him," said Easy Money Charlie, still looking out the window.

And then she started up—tried to—from the fancy pillow with the cheap lace on it, her string of dollar pearls showing against her best pink wrapper, talking fast, in a hurry to get through.

"Take her, Charlie. For God's sake, will you?" she said, in a hoarse, high voice. "You're a good kid. You've got the coin. And you're the only man down here that ever gave a woman a good, clean, decent smile. You're my last chance. For there's no woman here to hand her over to, you know that. Take her, will you, Easy?" she said, grabbing him.

And he stared away from her—out the window into the dirty night—not knowing what to say to her.

"It'll cost you not much more than the dog. And it'll be a lot more satisfaction," she said, pleading. "And she's a nice-looking kid. You won't be ashamed of her."

"A girl!" he said, without thinking. "Are you crazy in the head?" And jumped to catch her when she started falling over sideways.

"Here. I'll do it. Sure. I'll do it!" said Easy Money, laying her back on her fancy pillow. For he thought she might be passing out right there before his eyes.

AT that, Fancy made him swear it, turning her eyes up for him to get the crucifix off the wall. For she couldn't speak, after that spell she had when he refused her. And he got it down for her, for he couldn't oppose her, naturally, at that stage of the game. And when he shook hands with her, starting to go out, she kissed his hand, which made it worse. For he kept seeing it afterward, that look she gave him.

"Whatever you do—whatever you do——" she said, stammering and hurrying, as if the devil was after her, "keep her out—don't let the Dead House get her. Don't let the Dead House swallow her up—like it did me. Like it did the rest of them!" she said, calling out their names — Sue, Annie, Polly. "Dead—worse than dead—walking in and out that Dead House!"

And he saw how it was—the fever was getting her; and that name was beating on her brain—that old name that the panhandlers gave their place, to keep their courage up, and have one more laugh, anyhow, at the last thing a man laughs at—himself and his own misery. He knew that was it, no doubt—her fever. But it made him crawl, hearing it, just the sound of her raving on.

So he promised her everything in sight, and unhitched her from his sleeve. And got out and hurried down and told the girl, who was waiting down on the pavement till he came out, to go along up there quick.

And the next night, when he was changed out of his beggar's gear, and was coming out in his regular clothes—always spick and span those days—from the Cripple Factory, another one, the one with the gold tooth they called Sunshine Annie, came to him in the Dead House, and he knew from her eyes the news she had.

"She was speaking of you," she said. "Calling out your name up to the last minute. Telling what you were going to do for her kid—send her straight—keep her out of this!" she said, looking around.

AND he stood there without answering. For he could hear her raving on—about the Dead House, and her kid. He stood looking around the place, at those beggars and their women, watching and thinking. For he knew there was more truth than poetry to that name. There were a half dozen he knew himself, that were supposed to be dead—the place was full of them, and the whole street; dead men and missing women — dead ones walking

THEY were fighting over this girl—the one to drag her down, destroy her; the other to keep her up out of the mire.

"No doubt at last you'll marry her!" said Adolphe, going on with his little joking.

"Shut up," said the faker, ugly. "You've got a mean mind."

"I only asked what was natural," said Adolphe back. And he wasn't the only one asking it, either, naturally.

So, then, to make a long story short, for a dozen years this Charlie went on with that double life, that long masquerade of his, between that new home he had fallen into that crazy way and the Street of the Homeless Men and the Dead House down below; and the Avenue of the Women, the high-toned shopping district, where he got his living mostly.

Every morning he left about the time a man would start for business, and every night he would come home again—and nobody the wiser. And all the time he was showing her the best time a kid ever had—building up from the beginning, wiping out all the memory of everything that she really was; making her a kind of princess—or his idea of one, at least. For, like the rest of the big grafters, money flowed away from him like water, as easy as it came. And it was still coming pretty easy then, though not so easy as it had been once.

So year after year he kept her, playing around with her himself, keeping her off the streets, keeping her a kid as long as possible, putting off answering that question which everybody was always putting up: What was going to happen to her when she grew up?

II.

WHEN it came finally, it came with a bump. There were three or four of them sitting there in the Cripple Factory with Adolphe, as they did sometimes in the late afternoons—Humpy Johnson, the fake humpback; Blinn, the throw-out, he of the flexible joints; Legless Law, the biggest money maker in the game; and Bridgeport White-eye, the fake blind man—this last one a kind of enemy and rival of Easy Money Charlie and a sorehead generally. For his eyes were giving out finally from rolling them back up under his lids—the way they

[CONTINUED ON PAGE TWENTY-ONE]

around, laughing, drinking, forgotten, by God and man.

"You're going through with it, ain't you—with her kid?" said the girl. "You wouldn't be the rat to lie to her, and her dying?"

"How would I," he said, "when I swore it on the crucifix?"

SO he got him a housekeeper, an old Irishwoman, as neat as a pin; and he hired a flat away up on the Heights, as far as possible from the Dead House and the Cripple Factory; and got the kid and put her and the old woman in it, and started trying it out—living like a human being once more.

"How arrives it, as far as you've come?" Adolphe asked him, taking off his fake arm for him in the evening that next week.

"Can you imagine it? A home—after this!" he said, sweeping his hand out in front toward the Dead House and the Street of the Forgotten Men, where they stand in the bluish-white electric light before the twenty-five-cent lodging houses, milling around on the sidewalk after supper, staring out across the street, with nobody knowing or caring whether they're alive or not. "It's just a plain case of resurrection from the dead."

"And how is the baby—the kid?"

"You ought to see her, Frenchie," he said. "now I've got her dolled up out of that bluechecked asylum dress, and her hair growing out—curly. She's a little queen!" he said, waving his free arm some more. "And she's going to stay one, don't fret! She's brought me back to life. And there's nothing I've got that she can't have. She's going to live like what she is—a little queen, a princess!

"She's going to have a real childhood—fairy tales and everything! That old Irishwoman I've got is filling her full of good old Irish fairy tales right now. I'm going to show her the best time a kid ever had. And if she wants trained white peacocks and cream-colored ponies with three tails she can have them. She's started out to be a child, not a number!"

"And then what—after she is a child no longer?" asked Adolphe, joking. "What will you do with her then, your fairy-tale princess?"

"Forget it. Now is now," said the beggar, looking ugly.

[CONTINUED FROM PAGE NINETEEN]

do from working that trick after a while; and he had had to come down to smoked glasses and a sign, which had cut in half the money he took in.

"Who was that little queen I saw you stepping out with on the avenue this morning?" asked the White-eye. For Charlie had been taking a morning off, going shopping with her, helping her pick out some more expensive dresses.

He didn't answer anything — just stared back, still and ugly.

"So that's the one you're raising for yourself?" said the White-eye, taking his answer from his face. "Quite a kid. I guess I'll raise me one. I like them young, too," giving Easy the leer.

And the next minute they all thought they were going to see a beggars' free-for-all — the real thing. For a mixup in the Dead House was the rawest thing, always, in the Street of Forgotten Men. They fought there with everything they had — all over the floor, like dogs; nothing barred, without interference or mercy — sore, they claimed, from being looked down on and despised and pitied all day.

They had been waiting for these two to get at it. And they were well matched. For, though White-eye had forty pounds the better of it, yet he was soft and flabby, and the other man, they said, was quite a scientific fighter.

Easy did his share, anyway. He had the blind faker by the throat in a minute. But the blind faker quit and hollered right away.

"Don't, for God's sake, Charlie!" he croaked, his lard-colored face turning almost as red as his little red eyelids. "I didn't mean anything. Easy! Easy! I can't fight!"

"Why not, you fat oyster?" said the other beggar, shaking him.

"It's my eyes. Don't! Don't! The doctor says that anything — any blow might get me — strike me blind. Honest to God, he did," he said. "And I apologize, Charlie. I get down and roll over!"

"That's a new one," said the fake bandager, giving him a last shake, and letting him loose. And the crowd of panhandlers that had piled in from the front room of the Dead House set up a howl, seeing how scared he was. For he actually shook all over like a jelly.

WHEN he and all the rest of them were gone out of the Cripple Factory, except Adolphe and this Charlie, the beggar still stood there, staring as if somebody had just cracked him over the skull.

"She's a kid no longer. I've got to start her on her next step."

"What step is that?" said Adolphe. "But I can guess, no doubt. You will marry her."

"Are you all crazy?" he said back. "Or just low minded?"

"Why not? You are not so old yourself. Why not, if you should care — if you should love her?" said Adolphe, and stopped short, for the faker had him by the collar, looking down into his eyes with the look of a crazy man.

"If I should care!" he said. "If I should care! I'd kill her first, and be done with it, before I'd hitch her to this and me. That's how much I care. No; I've got different plans for her than me or the Dead House, if I can only put them through."

"What are those?" Adolphe asked him.

He smiled a little now — the kind of crooked smile he had when he was joking.

"As long as I can't kill her, I guess I'll have to pass away myself," he said.

"Pass away!" said Adolphe, getting excited. "You mean you would die — kill yourself?"

"Not entirely. No," he said, still with that crooked smile.

"Die — yet not entirely! What is this?" asked Adolphe, confused.

"You'll see that later," he said, leaving him now.

AND he did — about a month later. Adolphe was sitting in the Cripple Factory when the beggar came back in, smiling that curious, comical smile that he kept on his face so much after that.

"Meet the dead man," he said to Adolphe, holding out his hand.

"Who?" "What?" said Adolphe.

"Me. I died, as I said I would. My death took place two weeks ago, at sea, on a small steamer," he said, explaining. "So they had to bury me, right there in midocean. My lawyer just got the word."

"Your lawyer!" said Adolphe.

"Sure. I died right, under a lawyer's orders. So it will be all legal."

"But — but where is the girl?" asked Adolphe, stammering.

"She's on her way — out of all this! To be somebody. He's got her — my lawyer, my executor — into a big, swell finishing school, with the best and richest girls in the country. That's what a lawyer's for; they can pull the strings you can't, if you've got their price."

"A school of finishing! What, then, does it finish?" Adolphe asked.

"Girls — for marriage — and high society!"

"For marriage! For society!" Adolphe said after him.

"Sure," he said, with his crooked, joshing smile again; and went on and told him this scheme he had been working on for all these years, to get her in among these millionaires — meeting them, getting into their houses, marrying, through this school.

"Did you ever see what these young millionaires have to choose from among their own crowd — the scenery that steps out of the limousines on the avenue. That's why they break away so much and marry actresses, isn't it? All right, then; suppose you can bring one like her — a real looker — right in with them! There's only one answer, as far as I can see. And there's a big boys' college, too, just over in the next town from this school. I'm giving her all the chances."

"But how, then, will she live with all those wealthy others you describe to me?" Adolphe asked him next.

"From my estate — naturally," he said, smiling once more. "My fortune that I'm leaving her — now I'm stepping out of her way."

"Your estate! Your fortune! What, then is this?" said Adolphe.

"That's me," he told him, and went on and explained the entire scheme. "I can earn it, can't I? And the lawyer can pay it out to her, as the income from my estate. You can get a lawyer in New York for most anything. And I've got one of the trickiest in the business. And I've got the graft — about the only graft in New York that will stand up to that today. But believe me, Frenchie, what I've got to put up for her now is enough to bring the sweat out on the brow of any honest dead man. To say nothing of the way the old graft is going now!"

Meanwhile this Charlie, the fake bandager, or the dead man, as he always called himself now to Adolphe, kept going, making pretty fair money still — working the women in the shopping district.

"But it keeps me hustling," he said, grinning that crooked grin, "keeping up the income from my estate — feeding her the money to travel up in line with these girls from these big, rich families. For she's going in great shape now, just as I knew she would. It's enough to make a dead man laugh," he said, "to see the places she goes, the big houses she goes around to from that school, popular all over, as she would be! And they can't keep that boys' college down the road going — the place is deserted since they saw her."

"She will be married soon, no doubt," said Adolphe.

"She will if any number of them can make her," he told him.

"And you will then be glad?" Adolphe asked him.

"Why wouldn't I be?" he came back, sharp.

"Why not? Why not, unless you might wish yet to marry her yourself. For you are young yet," said Adolphe, smiling, and stopping when he saw his face.

"Will you stop singing that song — or will I kill you?" he said, looking black and ugly — and then smiling again when he saw how he had Adolphe scared. "I'm no Indian giver. It's no gentleman, Frenchie, that would give his life for a lady and take it back again. And there's nothing she can't have from me — and never was — don't forget that — not even a husband."

And then, an evening or two after that, he came in with his face all lighted up, for he had seen her on the avenue, laughing and enjoying herself "with the rest of the millionaires!" he said. "But in mourning for me," he went on after a minute. "In kind of half-mourning for me! What do you think of that?"

"Should she not know you, perhaps," said Adolphe, "seeing you? Is there not some danger there?"

"Would you think so, looking at me?" he said. "Even if I was out of my makeup?"

And Adolphe said nothing. For he was a different man entirely — twenty years older since he had left her and fallen back, another dead man in the Dead House, as he called himself.

"That isn't the danger now," he said.

"What is?" Adolphe asked him.

"That somebody might get after her — from down here. Hitch her back some way to this!"

"How would they? Who would know her?"

"That fat worm — that White-eye might, maybe," he answered. "If his eyes are not too far gone to recognize her. I'm keeping my eye on that bird. I'm a little leary of the way he's acting lately. He's ripe and ready for anything today, the way things are moving with him now; you know that!" And Adolphe nodded back at him.

III.

THE world was getting better, and the grafters sorer and uglier and more desperate every day. They were out after the big beggars strong now — driving them, hounding them off the streets. Even real cripples — like Legless Law, the biggest in the game — were getting cut down to almost nothing — not over ten or twenty dollars a day. And fake bandagers like Easy Money Charlie had to keep on the jump to keep out of jail — to say nothing of the cash he had to dig up somehow now for this girl to spend — through this phony estate.

And for plain fake blind men like Bridgeport White-eye, with nothing more than smoked glasses and a sign to guarantee him, the thing was getting hopeless; to say nothing of the fact — as Adolphe and this Charlie both figured out now — that he might really be losing his sight, finally — after all those years of that fak-

[CONTINUED ON NEXT PAGE]

[CONTINUED FROM PAGE TWENTY-ONE]

ing—rolling his eyeballs up under his eyelids, straining them.

And right after that this Charlie came in one evening, all excited.

"I had it right," he said. "He's after her!"

"Who?"

"The White-eye. He's been nosing around that school! I ran across his trail up there. I'd been suspecting this—his starting out to get her. But before he does!" he said, and stopped.

"What then?" asked Adolphe, prompting him finally.

"Do you think I'll let him get to her now? To blackmail her—and tell her everything! And drag her down, without a doubt, into the graft—before's he's through! Hitch her back, and drag her back, maybe, into this Dead House where her mother was. I'll kill him first!" he said, excited.

"How could you?" Adolphe asked him.

"Why couldn't I?"

"Then what of her? What of your estate? What would she live on—if you killed him—and they got you for it?" asked Adolphe, arguing.

"That's it," he said. "If it hadn't been for that; if she was safe and married, he'd have been lying with his fat paws crossed upon his chest long ago."

"Listen, then. Be calm," said Adolphe. "Let us think. It cannot be so bad as yet."

"Why not?"

"Or else you would have heard of him by now. He has found the school, perhaps. But what else does he know? Would he know her name?"

"No. You don't know that. Nor anyone here but me."

"No," said Adolphe. "Nor do I think now that he could tell her by sight—with his eyes as they go now—and the few past times he may have seen her out with you. So how can he act—choose her out—among so many? You see? Let us wait, then. Watch him."

So he did, finally trailing the blind faker, watching him, keeping track of all his movements. And no doubt he would have found him going up there again finally, and jumped him and maybe killed him, only in a day or two this new last turn came up. For one evening the fake bandager came back into the Cripple Factory, his face lit up now like a Chinese lantern.

"It's come out all right, after all! Everything's worked out, all right!" he said.

"What has?" asked Adolphe.

"She'll be married," he almost shouted, "this next week. I've worked it. I've pulled her through."

"Married? How? To whom?" said Adolphe, motioning to keep down his voice, for, although they were alone now, you could never tell who might be drifting in.

So he talked down low again, and told him all about it. And it seemed his calculations had been right—the competition was pretty small in that rich crowd of girls in the marriage game; and a girl of her looks was chased and hunted by the swells, until finally she was going to marry one—a brother of one of the girls at school, a millionaire easy.

"She's landed now, for life," said the fake bandager, all excited. "She's a little queen, a princess—and she'll be one now forever!" he said. "And now it's up to me to go out and finish up my job."

"What job?"

"I'm going to get that White-eye, for luck. Just so as to be sure."

"Wait," said Adolphe, holding him off. "I wouldn't start—not yet."

And then he told him what he had heard just lately, that this White-eye was out, laying in wait to get this man himself, when he could get him right.

"Yes. He's just that kind of a rat!" the beggar told him, sneering.

He had hardly finished saying it when they both looked up, and saw the phony blind man looking down at them, with his little red eyes, from the doorway. He stood there for a minute, eyeing them, and after a minute or so more he went over to the bar and got a drink. And then came back, and into the Cripple Factory with them.

AND Adolphe saw that he had been firing up considerably before. He didn't like White-eye's looks. He stood there with his white face and red eyes, like a great hog still, but one that had been driven into a corner and was set, fighting for its life. And he looked down then, and his face stiffened and his eyes grew redder yet. And Adolphe, looking down with him, saw what it was he had seen. For the fake bandager still stood there, just as he had come in, with his right arm strapped down under his fake one, and just one arm free to fight with.

So, sure of that now, the big one stepped over to the other, and looked him up and down.

"Listen," he said, his voice thick and ugly from the drink. "Am I in on this?"

"On what?" said the fake bandager, standing still, with murder in his eyes.

"On this big new graft of yours."

"What graft?"

"On this kid of yours. This plant you've put up at that school, hunting millionaires. Come across now. No bull. I'm all posted up. I've been listening in on you in here—for weeks now!"

"If you know so much, why haven't you done something?" asked the fake bandager, standing up to him, sneering; forgetting, evidently, all about his having but one arm to fight with.

And at that the other man became excited, giving himself dead away, proving Adolphe's idea that he had gone as far as he could alone—that he was up against it. And then he jumped for Charlie, grabbing him by his throat. "Her name! Give me her name. Will you give it to me? Or will I choke it out of you?" he shouted, and started clamping down on his throat.

So Adolphe saw that they were at it, at last; and that he had a murder on his hands, probably, before those two got through. And of all the strange things he had seen in this crazy Street of the Forgotten Men, this was the craziest. They were fighting over this girl—the one to drag her down, destroy her; the other to keep her up out of the mire; fighting like mad dogs to kill one another for this girl, who did not even know there were two such men alive or such a place as this Dead House, where they were tearing each other to pieces over her.

"Fight! Fight!" yelled somebody in the front room. And they all came piling in, all the panhandlers and their women—grafters out of luck, spoiling, starving for a good old-time beggars' fight.

Whang! The two were on the floor together. For the smaller man, the more scientific fighter, had tripped the other, using what he had to fight with, naturally—his feet.

"Atta boy. Easy! Kill him! Kill him!" yelled the beggars and their women, shouting crazy with their hunger after pain and cruelty, fed up with bad luck and begging, all the day long crawling the cold sidewalks, whining to be pitied and despised. And then nothing from it, those lean times, but moving on because a cop was coming.

"Choke him, White-eye. Hang his tongue out!" yelled one side. "The boots, Charlie! The boots!" the others howled.

For, of course, now—if he was going to save himself, to pry himself loose—the fake bandager, with his right arm still tied down, would have to do his fighting with what he had—his feet and legs. But could he? Could he pry him off in time?

"He's got him! He's got him!" called the yelling beggars, crazy with pleasure and excitement, craning forward from the circle they had made around them—panhandlers and fake sailors, throw-outs, high-heels, soap eaters, fit throwers, floppers, and fake bandagers—cheap beggars and good grafters all together. And on one of the old round tables a woman in a last year's hat, an old timer, was stamping with split yellow satin slippers, screaming, wild with joy.

For the big boy was killing Charlie now, it looked like—choking him, cursing him, saying to him in a low, husky voice where he had him in between his knees, "Will you give it to me now—her name? Or do I croak you?"

And the one underneath shook his head again, and the one on top clamped down. And the feet were up again; and they were all over the floor once more, like dogs, with the big dog on top—still with the throat grip that could not be shaken off.

"The boots. The boots, Charlie! Give him the boots!" his crowd kept yelling. For he was fighting with his feet and legs, prying, reaching up; trying, some claimed now, to clamp on what they call the scissors hold, with the legs around the waist, the clutch that pops their eyes out like marbles when a good man once sets it right.

"Hey! Clamp it. Clamp it down! Mash him!" yelled the beggars—yelled, and stopped off short, astonished!

For the phony blind man—though the other had not really set his hold yet—had quit now, all of a sudden—groveling, pawing, pushing the fake bandager away; and then bawling out, a hoarse, loud kind of bellow, louder than the yelling beggars:

"Stop. Stop. Easy. For the love of God. Easy, stop!" they heard him howl. "It's come. It's come!"

FOR the minute the other beggar on the floor beside him, hearing that voice, held back, breathing, choking, waiting, stiff and astonished—while the other man pushed up first one red eyelid and then the other, and peered forward. And then called out again to the silent beggars in that horrible, husky, frightened voice:

"I'm blind. I'm blind. I'm blind!"

And the other man drew away from him where he fell, face forward, on the black floor, blubbering. But the beggars around them all started laughing, shouting, and howling at him.

"Arrrr!" said the beggars, laughing fit to split. For that was a likely tale—a h ll of a way to quit!

"Arrrr!" they yelled, and stopped—looking behind them. For somebody was working in from the edges. And then a cop showed up—a young cop.

"What's going on here?" he asked. And they told him.

"Well, what do you think of that?" he said, and got up White-eye, the big one, who was still wallowing on the floor, weeping.

"Stand up," he said. "Let's look at you. A blind man, huh? A blind beggar hollering be-

He had seen her on the avenue, laughing and enjoying herself "with the rest of the millionaires!"

cause he's blind? That's a new one," he said, and laughed.

"And who's the other one?" he asked. And they told him.

"A one-armed man—fighting a blind man!" he said, with a comical look. "And what were they fighting about?"

"A woman—something about a woman's name!" said the beggars.

"Can you beat that! In the world?" said the comical young cop. It struck him so funny that it made him go easy with them.

"What would you do?" he said to them. "If I let you go?"

"I'll take him home—if he wants me to," said the one-armed man, speaking up finally—working anything, probably, to get loose. "Our quarreling is done—forever. I'll take him home."

"Yes. And kill him on the way!" said the cop.

"Why should I kill him?" he said again.

"He can't do me any harm now—for life. He's stone-blind!"

"Will you trust him?" said the young cop to the blind man. The latter bowed his head finally that he would, unable to speak yet—dead to everything but what had just happened to him.

"Is it far?" the young cop asked him.

And they told him no. Just up the street.

"Well, take him along," said the young cop. "And I'll be following, watching after you."

"Cracked! The half of them are cracked down here in this dead-and-alive hole," he said, looking after them, twirling his club. "And with more than one, let me tell you, there's a woman back of it," he said to himself again, and shook his head, getting a last glimpse of them as they passed, all friendly and peaceable, down the Street of the Forgotten Men—the small one keeping the big one going; and turned finally to go up into the blind man's lodging house.

"Cracked over some woman!" he said, shaking his head once more and moving on when he saw no more of them. "Like all the rest of us!"

But as for the woman they were fighting over—these beggars, these two dead men from the Dead House—she never yet—so Adolphe says—has learned that there were such men in the world, nor such a place as they fought over her in—the one to save and the other to ruin her.

She was married long ago to her millionaire. And if she ever even thinks of the Street of the Forgotten Men—which this man who saved her still goes muttering down—it is only in the amusing, comical words of an old, half-remembered song.

Another story of the underworld and its strange life, by George Kibbe Turner, will appear in an early issue.

Percy Marmont and Mary Brian. *Author Collection*

THE ADAPTION

Rights to "The Street of the Forgotten Men" were snapped up soon after Turner's story was published in *Liberty* magazine. According to *Motion Picture News*, "nearly every producing company in the business bid high to secure the screen rights" (5-16-1925), with Paramount taking the prized property. Quickly, the studio began to assemble a team around Herbert Brenon, the newly assigned director then riding a wave of popularity following the triumph of *Peter Pan*. With a spotlight on the director, Brenon's next film would be considered an important release.

Another early assignment went to John Russell, who was given the job of adapting Turner's "strange story." Russell reduced Turner's short fiction to 14 passages or key scenes, some of which were drawn directly from the story. Besides suggesting where each of the 14 scenes might be shot – either on set or on location – each were given a setting, for which Russell also provided a sketch within which dramatic action might occur. Notably, a few of Russell's suggestions were taken-up – these include visual touches like the black ribbon around the dog's picture in Easy Money Charlie's room, as well as a picturesque location for the wedding scene, specifically the Little Church Around the Corner.

Russell also provided "Notes on characters in *Street of Forgotten Men*." And likewise, Russell's suggestion to cast Mary Brian as Fancy (here given as Fannie) was adopted. Other of his ideas were not, such as Diamond Mike's excessive weight.

What follows is Russell's six-page adaption of Turner's magazine story, faithfully transcribed from the copy housed at the Hollywood Branch of the Los Angeles Public Library. Except for a reduction in the amount of space between lines and paragraphs, the adaption's formatting and punctuation has been preserved. (A few typos have been silently corrected.) This document has been transcribed because the photocopy obtained by the author some two decades earlier was, in parts, barely legible. Not so with Russell's notes on the characters in the film, which also follow.

John Russell......

THE STREET OF FORGOTTEN MEN

(Suggestions on set and location.... Following is a preliminary list, so far as possible to state at present.)

1. The street of Forgotten Men – (set)
2. Diamond Mike's Dead House – outer room – (set)
3. "   "   "   "   – Cripple Factory – (set)
4. "   "   "   "   – rear alley – (set)   **One big set.**
5. Portland Fancy's room – (set)
6. (About three small sets or locations, for Fancy's fade-backstory.)
7. Easy Money Charlie's room – (set)
8. Rural cottage, in grounds – (location)
9. Int. of same: living room – (set)
10. Fifth Ave. fashion parade – (location)
11. Lawyer's office – (set)
12. Garden party in grounds – night – (set)
13. Country road – (location)
14. Ext. fashionable N.Y. church, for wedding. – (location)

– – – – –

Notes on the above.

1. There is only one such street in N.Y. and that is the Bowery. We must show it as it was in 1912. I suggest it could be built as a composite of interesting bits taken from old photos. It will show

probably a somewhat heightened, even exaggerated picture of dives and resorts where the homeless men gather. Impressionistic. The dark shadow of the "L". The flaring lights of saloons, penny arcades and shooting galleries. There is still one remnant of this old color to be found today. It is just possible that something might be done here with an actual location.

2. This is a low-class beer-saloon of the old days:
A bar, a free-lunch counter and a barkeep armed with a bungstarter to rap the knuckles of those who try too freely to grab the eats without first buying the necessary scuttle of suds. Bare and greasy tables set further back, for such guests as have serious thinking to do. At the rear, a door into another room which is the cripple factory – (I suggest this might be a swinging door.)

3. The cripple factory itself is one of our most important sets. I see a room like the dirtiest, dingiest stage dressing room you ever saw, enlarged about four times. It must be a sizable set, to give room for the fights and for rather intricate business. At the center is a good sized makeup stand, flanked by broken old gas-jets with the usual bent-wire globes. Here Adolphe – the Disguiser – plies his trade: something like a barber at his mirror, well supplied with makeup material, grease paints, brushes, cosmetics etc. On the walls are hanging

every possible kind of prop for making fakes: crutches, artificial arms and legs, the steel frames of paralyzed limbs, wigs, black spectacles, etc. Perhaps a wheel chair standing in one corner. Also a collection of little printed signs for fake beggars to wear – "Help a Poor Man" – "I am Blind" etc.
It is important that one side of the room should be partly closed off with ragged hanging curtains, behind which Adolphe's clients may change their clothes at least in partial privacy. Inside this are a wash bowl, another lighted mirror, hooks on the wall etc. – for it is here that the clients prepare themselves to exit in their proper persons. The other side of the room extends to a rear door, giving on the rear alley. There are four or five chairs against the wall for waiting clients: again suggesting a barber shop. I suggest that for extra decorations there might be several pictures hanging on the walls showing Adolphe's particular triumphs in makeup – his particular pride – two or three phenomenally horrible looking cripples, all fakes. Against the wall, a row of rough lockers marked with the names of owners, "Easy Money Charlie," "Humpty Joe", "Legless Lew", etc.

4. We need only a glimpse of this alley, with room for a beer truck to stand backed up, from which beer kegs are being rolled down supposedly into Diamond Mike's cellar below. By opening the rear door of the cripple factory, we look directly down into this alley. It is dim and bare and need not be with cobbles for flooring. A blank brick wall behind it.

5. Just a bare bed room. A few little feminine touches in cheap curtains, a sentimental picture or two cut from illustrated papers and pasted on the wall: and in a prominent place, a hanging crucifix. Near it, a photo of the child. A tattered arm chair in which the sick girl is sitting.

6. These sets have not yet been worked out. They are used to tell Portland Fancy's pathetic story in quick flashes: probably they include a counter in a department store, where she is arrested: a court room scene: a jail cell: possibly also a flash of an orphan asylum, with the little girl orphans being drilled, in line.

7. The apartment where Easy Money Charlie has made his home. Somewhere in the Bowery, but it is clean and neat – very bare but comfortable: also masculine, with a few pictures of his dog with black ribbon around it, prize-fighters and sporting events on the walls. This man is prosperous in his way: probably he has one cozy old leather arm-chair in which he smokes, a box of good cigars, plenty of sporting papers to read. A bed and a center table.

8. This exterior should show a charming little rustic cottage, in upper Harlem, or L.I. – with plenty of grounds, trees, shrubs, grown with vines, etc. A child's swing on one of the trees. A path leading down to a gate on the public road. The place is not new but rather antiquated and old-fashioned: the sort of place such a man would pick out for a comfortable inconspicuous hideout.

9. The interior should carry out the same idea: it is old fashioned, Victorian, low-circled but with comfort verging on luxury. Good solid old furniture. A big comforting fireplace. Rather pretentious pictures on the wall: [one] of them religious. Flowers ion vase. This is the general living room off one side is the entrance to the kitchen – Fannie's room off the other side – at back, through the doorway, is Easy's own room, possibly to give depth to the set.

10. Fifth Ave. ad lib. I suggest a photographer should get actual on Easter Sunday.

11. Just the office of a first-class lawyer doing a first class practice: a big desk: a comfortable chair for clients: door in back.

12. This is to stage a garden party in the grounds of some fashionable suburban villa – at night. The effect is to be pictorial as possible, with shrubbery, rustic benches, summer houses, arbors, trellises, Chinese lanterns etc. Probably a jazz band in eccentric costume. At one side there must be a garden wall, partly shaded by overhanging trees and vines from which a hidden intruder can look down upon a summer house bench.

13. This is the other side of the garden wall – the outer side – along a road from which the intruder climbs. It should be partly masked with shrubbery so that with lighting we can get sinister and impressionist effect, of the creeping intruder.

14. Pictorial setting of a country road. This is our wedding set: fashionable church with awning and carpet. Room for many vehicles and quiet a crowd. We use the exterior only. At one side, some distance from the entrance, a wing or bastion of thew church structure gives partial shelter where a witness can stand unobserved. I suggest that pictures of an actual wedding of this kind might be taken in long shots, to be matched later for the closeup action. Perhaps the Little Church Around the Corner would be good for this.

- - - - - - - - -

Russell........

Notes on characters in "Street of Forgotten Men."

EASY MONEY CHARLEY....About 24 when we first see him: lithely built - lean jawed - sardonic expression, but not bad-looking. After the long time lapse he shows few changes - perhaps an added touch of gray and deepened facial lines. This man's antecedents are bad: he is at best a semi-criminal. But he has a streak of gold in his soul. After the time lapse we get his development - his nature has expanded, he is less shifty and suspicious in demeanor. In the early story we never see him laugh: and even his smile is grim and tight-lipped. But subsequently, in his life at home, he is actually happy. Remember that this man's emotional capacity is strong and deep, but strongly repressed: he has the cynical protection of his hard-boiled exterior. His business should always be very quiet, with controlled tenseness in the big moments.

FANNIE....Mary Brian - why say more?

WHITEY......A sturdy beggar: husky and muscular. In appearance and expression he should be sinister, but not repulsive. If he wears a patch over one eye it will help the actor to get over the assumed blindness of his one eye. The key note of his character is expressed as malignance: malignant envy, avarice and cunning. But he is no coward. After the long time lapse, his makeup should show more lines and whitened hair.

ADOLPHE.....A good character bit for a deft sympathetic, plausible, middle-aged Frenchman. We get good comedy touches from him in his artistic pride in his "art." He is shallow, but kindly. Choose him for plastic facial expression.

ADOLPHE'S ASST.....An obsequious, sallow-faced young wop: typical barber...who addresses ADOLPHE as "padrone."

DIAMOND MIKE.....A huge fat man with monstrous thick neck and a head sloping upward to a point, whereon a few thin hairs are carefully parted and plastered. The burlesque saloon-keeper: tough as they mak 'em.

PORTLAND FANCY......A frail, consumptive girl - very pale and sunken-eyed, but with the remnants of prettiness. Very sympathetic and appealing. She shows timidity and refinement.

DUTCH DOLLY.....A Bowery prostitute: fat, coarse and dripping with cheap sentimentality under her toughness. Has the brain of a hen but a good heart. Vulgar and horribly over-dressed, with feathers, gauds and cheap jewellry.

WIDOW M'GEE.......A stout, motherly, bustling Irish-woman, with a heart of gold and Irish characteristics. The perfect nurse and house-keeper: loyal and sentimental. At the same time, be careful she does not over-act: we are not interested in her mental reactions to the strange situation in which she is thrown. She is not prying or suspicious about it. In other words, keep her on the surface, keep her obvious.

PHILIP PEYTON.....A boy of intelligence, and character. Remember he is a successful lawyer in his father's firm. Member of an aristocratic family - but no suggestion of snobbishness. He is forceful and human.- boyish on his sentiment side: but with real brains and understanding.

OFFICER QUINN.....A wise, cynical, smiling cop.

BOWERY CHARACTERS.....As ragged, sinister, furtive and hopeless as wanted. The Bowery lodging houses are full of them. They are on the outer edge of failure and misery.

Among the fake beggars we characterize three or more: Humpty Joe, who wears a false hump: LEGLESS LAW, who straps one foot up behind him under a ragged overcoat: another uses crutches with a fake club-foot.

The women are generally the cheapest and most pathetic of trulls. The Dead House is their last stop on their progress to the River or Potter's field. We can hardly afford to be too realistic here. For the facts are too grim. We will have to show them rather flashy, over-dressed, painted: but not too unfortunate. Their clothes will be those far out of fashion even for 1921 - and poor and over-done at that. With the exception of DUTCH DOLLY and one other we can keep them pretty well in the background; make them appear merely tough atmosphere. DOLLY, of course, is one of those who has found her proper metier and is not unhappy in it - there are such. The other doxie is WHITEY's: with whom he plays the scene over the newspaper. Let her appear actually heavy: a hard-bony, sneering little rip of a woman, with a face like flint - frankly predatory, so that we hate her at sight.

##################

```
THE STREET OF FORGOTTEN MEN

By

George Kibbe Turner.

        Adaptation
           by
       John Russell


        Continuity
           by
       Paul Schofield


          --ooOoo--
```

FADE IN ON
                    Scene 1.

LONG SHOT OF THE BOWERY:

A general view of the "Street of Forgotten Men". There is only one such street in New York - The Bowery. We present a picture of that sinister thoroughfare, shadowed by the iron cloud of the "L" structure, and cut into it the title:

TITLE: "THE STREET OF FORGOTTEN MEN"--
                    THE BOWERY.

Run long enough to give the general atmosphere and color of the locale.

The first page of the scenario / screenplay of *The Street of Forgotten Men*.
Courtesy of New York Public Library

THE SCENARIO

A scenario can tell us things about a film which can't be found, or may not be apparent, in the film itself. That's the case with the scenario for *The Street of Forgotten Men*. Adapted by John Russell from George Kibbe Turner's story – with continuity by Paul Schofield – *The Street of Forgotten Men* scenario is an 111-page type written document which scripts a good deal more of a story than is found in the surviving film. For the director, this scenario suggests situations, settings and action for numerous scenes. For the cameraman, it suggests approaches to filming specific incidents. And for the actors, it suggests otherwise unseen motivation, thoughts and feelings for key characters.

The scenario not only reveals more story, but also more detail. For example, the scenario tells us Fancy's middle name, Claire – a trivial bit, to be sure. More significant are the circumstances around the time when baby Fancy was taken from her mother, Portland Fancy. In the scenario, Portland is caught shoplifting; it was a Mother's act of desperation and a pivotal scene in the film. The incident is depicted in stills as well as on a lobby card, which is surprising, as criminal acts, especially those by women, were not often depicted on posters or lobby cards (the "public face" of a film). As a result of her attempted theft, a judge orders her baby taken from her and placed in a home for children.

Also revealing is the significant role played by a minor character like Officer Quinn; in the scenario, he brokers a truce between Easy Money Charlie and Bridgeport White-Eye, and then delivers a few curt observations about their disreputable behavior. In the film, however, Officer Quinn is an unimportant figure. So much so, the character in the film is without a name and the actor who plays him not identified.

The scenario reveals other significant information about the film and its making which are not found in other documents, including the Press Sheet, the film's surviving six reels, or reportage from the time. For example, a note included in the scenario at the beginning of scene one suggests an approach to filming in New York City, and further suggests the director and cameraman look at another film. The scenario note reads: "NOTE:---Please look at material shot by Mr. Dwan for NEW YORK LIFE: with especial reference to results obtained by the use of the supersensitive stock, or Boston Tech stock; It may be possible with this stock to get same of these shots with a masked camera, on the Bowery, and in some of the places that would be unavailable with ordinary stock and the necessity for lighting equipment and the attention it draws to the work."

The movie the note refers to is likely Allan Dwan's *Night Life of New York* (1925), a now lost Paramount production filmed and released around the same time as *The Street of Forgotten Men*. Set and shot in New York City, this silent comedy stars Rod La Rocque and Dorothy Gish, and includes Riley Hatch (Diamond Mike, the bartender, in *The Street of Forgotten Men*) in a small role. Notably, its screenplay was co-authored by Paul Schofield, who contributed the continuity and the above-mentioned note to the scenario for *The Street of Forgotten Men*.

The scenario proves telling in other ways. Notably, it makes apparent something any serious film buff likely knows, that film-making during the silent era was image-centric, and story-telling was visual. It also suggests something less obvious, that film makers of the time were sometimes improvisatory. It should also be noted that the scenario only corresponds generally with the surviving film; however, according to film preservationist Robert Byrne, it proved valuable in reconstructing the action from the missing second real.

What follows is the scenario of *The Street of Forgotten Men*, faithfully transcribed from the sole known copy housed at the New York Public Library. Except for reducing the amount of space between lines and paragraphs, the scenario's original formatting has been largely preserved. A few obvious typos have been silently corrected, though unusual usages and punctuation have been retained. The following abbreviations are used throughout.

EXT. = exterior (outside) shot
f.g. = foreground
INT. = interior (inside) shot
TITLE: = intertitle, printed dialogue or narration shown between or during scenes

THE STREET OF FORGOTTEN MEN

By

<u>George Kibbe Turner</u>.

Adaptation
by
John Russell

Continuity
by
Paul Schofield

--ooOoo--

FADE IN ON **Scene 1.**

LONG SHOT OF THE BOWERY:

A general view of the "Street of Forgotten Men". There is only one such street in New York - The Bowery. We present a picture of that sinister thoroughfare, shadowed by the iron cloud of the "L" structure, and cut into it the title:

<u>TITLE</u>: "THE STREET OF FORGOTTEN MEN" -- THE BOWERY.

Run long enough to give the general atmosphere and color of the locale.

Scenes 2
       3
       4
       5

ATMOSPHERE SHOTS AD LIB:

To heighten the impression. The important idea is to give a distinct and colorful picture of a street probably without a parallel anywhere else in the world, with its distinctive denizens --- character shots that can be obtained only on the ground itself.

NOTE:---Please look at material shot by Mr. Dwan for NEW YORK LIFE: with especial reference to results obtained by the use of the supersensitive stock, or Boston Tech stock; It may be possible with this stock to get same of these shots with a masked camera, on the Bowery, and in some of the places that would be unavailable with ordinary stock and the necessity for lighting equipment and the attention it draws to the work.)

On the last of these shots - a QUICK FADE ---

TITLE: WHILE THE BOWERY, LIKE THE OCTOPUS BURIED IN THE MUD AND SLIME, SENDS ITS LEECH-LIKE TENTACLES OUT INTO THE CLEANER WATERS OF FIFTH AVENUE.

FADE QUICKLY INTO

Scene 6.

EXT. BEAUTIFUL HOTEL OR CLUB ENTRANCE:

Well-dressed people pass, and standing against one of the sides of the entrance, is "Easy Money Charlie". After just enough footage to establish the fashionable locale, LAP-DISSOLVE INTO

Scene 7.

EXT. HOTEL ENTRANCE: CLOSE SHOT ON CHARLIE:

As we see him first he is in his professional makeup; apparently a pitiful, one-armed beggar with a little tin cup presented for the charity of the passers-by. And a charitable passer-by, as we watch him, stops and regards him sympathetically -- then drops several coins into his cup. As Charlie mumbles his thanks -- introduce him:

TITLE: "EASY-MONEY CHARLIE" -- SO CALLED FROM THE SIZE OF HIS "EARNINGS".

He glances out of shot - and up a little, at----

Scene 8.

EXT. SIDEWALK CLOCK:

Showing exactly five o'clock;

Scene 9.

EXT. HOTEL ENTRANCE: MEDIUM SHOT ON CHARLIE:

Like any hard-working man, who has reached the union time for quitting work, he puts his cup away in his coat pocket, and as he ambles out of the shot, FADE OUT.

<u>TITLE</u>: DOWNTOWN IN WALLSTREET, PROSPEROUS MEN HAVE THEIR STOCK AND COTTON EXCHANGES -- THEIR CLEARING HOUSE……..

LAP DISSOLVE INTO SECOND TITLE:

<u>TITLE</u>: THE BOWERY HAS ITS CLEARING HOUSE… FOR PANHANDLERS, BEGGARS, WOMEN -- and WORSE; THE NOTORIOUS "DIAMOND MIKE'S DEAD HOUSE." -----------

FADE INTO

Scene 10.

EXT. THE "DEAD HOUSE"; FULL SHOT:

Getting the Bowery atmosphere outside. There is no sign, except a "CAFE" sign. The windows are screened off -- and behind the open heavy oak doors, is a pair of swinging door-gates higher than a man's head… Officer Quinn comes into the scene - sauntering and twirling his club, as we LAP DISSOLVE INTO

Scene 11.

INT. THE "DEAD HOUSE"; FULL SHOT:

Getting over the atmosphere of the place. It is a low-class fin-mill and beer cellar of the pre-prohibition days, with a bar and an adjacent free lunch counter. Diamond Mike himself presides behind the counter with a couple of assistants. He is a man shaped like a pyramid from his head to his waist, with the jet black, huge mustaches of his type. In his loud shirt front he wears the huge diamond which has given him his name, and his fame. He is drawing drinks at the bar, for customers and waiters, and at his right hand is a bungstarter which we shall see him use in a moment. The floor of the place is covered with sawdust. Further back, against the wall are a few tables for the convenience of such guests as have serious drinking to do. Two or three unkempt waiters with spotted aprons are attending to these favored clients. The center of the floor is cleared for dancing, at one side is a cheap piano. At intervals, one of the waiters seats himself at the piano and dashes off an old time waltz, at which time a couple of spielers sitting on the side of the floor do their stuff, as we shall show. There are various beer signs and a risqué lithograph or two, and in a prominent place is a rough painting of a huge foaming beer glass with this sign above it --- "The biggest schooner on the avenue for 5¢."

Run the long shot long enough to get over the place thoroughly, then cut to

Scene 12.

INT. THE "DEAD HOUSE"; CLOSE SHOT ON MIKE:

Get a good study of him, as he expertly draws schooners, carves off the foam, and slaps them on the bar. The bungstarter is at his right hand - on the side nearest the "free lunch", which is tipped in. A ragged client, who has not heretofore been near the bar, sidles into the shot, and furtively reaches for a sandwich. Like a flash, Mike grabs the bung-starter and slams him over the knuckles - then, pointing to the quartette of foaming glasses before him, gets over plainly that "No suds - no lunch!" Introduce Mike with the following title, cut into the first part of the shot ---

TITLE: "DIAMOND MIKE" --- HIMSELF.

Scene 13.

INT. "THE DEAD HOUSE": MEDIUM SHOT DANCE FLOOR AND PIANO:

As a waiter slams his tray on the top of the piano - sits down, and begins to play. The couple of spielers, sitting at a table, immediately get up and begin their dance. The boy in the old time "Bowery Boy" outfit, with short double-breasted jacket, tight trousers and billie-cock hat over his eye; the girl in a feathered hat, a tight jacket with leg of mutton sleeves and a short flaring skirt. With crooked elbows they do some old-time spieling. Enough of this for a laugh - then ----

Scene 14.

INT. THE "DEAD HOUSE": CLOSE SHOT ON TABLE:

At which are sitting Dutch Molly and Portland Fancy. They are bedraggled birds of the night; cheaply dressed, wearing big hats with ragged feathers. The waiter has just served them drinks - Molly a huge schooner of beer -- Fancy a big slug of cheap whiskey. The women have been watching the dance indifferently, but they brighten up a bit on the arrival of the drinks - grab them.

Scene 15.

INT. THE "DEAD HOUSE": CLOSEUP ON PORTLAND FANCY:

Get a good study of her - she is not the type of tough street-walker represented perfectly by Dutch Molly, but a much more refined and delicate type. We get strong pathos from her pale face and appealing eyes as well as from the greater reserve and gentleness of her manner. She looks sick - actually she is in the late stages of tuberculosis. She now raises the brimming slug of raw whiskey. She cannot control a shudder of distaste. Suddenly she is taken with a racking cough - a pitiful and painful cough which shows how far gone she is.

Cut into this scene the introductory title:

TITLE: SHE WHOM THE BOWERY KNOWS AS "PORTLAND FANCY" .... HER REAL NAME NO ONE HAS EVER BEEN ABLE TO WRING FROM HER ....

Scene 16.

INT. THE "DEAD HOUSE": CLOSEUP ON DUTCH MOLLY:

Watching Fancy with a certain amount of rough sympathy. She glances at the other shrewdly as we introduce her with the title:

TITLE: "DUTCH MOLLY" - WHO NEVER HAD ANOTHER NAME …..

She leans forward, with a sudden impulse to speak:

Scene 17.

INT. THE "DEAD HOUSE": MEDIUM SHOT BOTH WOMEN:

As Molly points to the slug in Fancy's hand, and referring to her foaming schooner, asks her:

TITLE: "What do you take that poison for?.. Why don't you stick to suds….it 'ud fatten you up."

Fancy controls her cough - and replies:

TITLE: "I hate the stuff! But it's the only thing that stops my cough!"

And with this she drains the glass at a single gulp, then shudders. Dolly watches her with casual good- nature.

Scene 18.

EXT. THE DEAD HOUSE: MEDIUM SHOT:

As Charlie enters. He no longer ambles. But strides along with the air of a prosperous and self-satisfied business man, in his own bailiwick - Officer Quinn is standing near the entrance, regarding the various characters that pass with a friendly and cynical eye. It is his regular beat. He knows Charlie by sight and gives him a quizzical and off-hand nod as he passes, a greeting which Charlie returns, as he turns into the Dead House....

Scene 19.

INT. DEAD HOUSE: MEDIUM SHOT ON TABLE:

As Molly tells Fancy:

TITLE: "If you keep on with that stuff, kid...it's gonna to git you!"

Fancy shrugs her shoulders and answers with a pitiful attempt at lightness:

TITLE: "What's the difference? I ain't got long anyway - and I wouldn't care much - if it wasn't for just one thing...."

Molly makes an awkward gesture of sympathy - then looks out of scene - while Fancy shows emotional weakness - she covers her eyes with her hand.

Scene 20.

INT. THE DEAD HOUSE: LONGER SHOT:

As Charlie enters - waves his hand at Mike - who greets him genially - and speaking to several of the "guests" comes down toward the table in f.g. at which the two women are sitting - Molly looks up at him - and it is evident that she knows him and he her. He gives her a careless nod of greeting as he passes on toward the rear door leading into the back room. As he passes - Molly reaches quickly across the table, grabs Fancy's arm - and calls her attention to Charlie - Fancy looks - then at Molly questioningly. Charlie stops before the door---

Scene 21.

INT. DEAD HOUSE: CLOSE SHOT DOOR TO THE "CRIPPLE FACTORY":

This door is either a small one, or perhaps we can get an added idea of secrecy about it if it is masked to resemble a part of the wall or paneling - the idea being that only clients who are in "the know" would find it. Charley finds the button - and the panel slides - showing a little hallway and another door. As he closes the panel behind him, cut back to----

Scene 22.

INT. THE "DEAD HOUSE": CLOSE SHOT ON WOMEN:

As Dolly leans across the table, the moment Charlie has disappeared, and nodding toward the door through which he has gone, tells Fancy:

TITLE: "There's a guy might help you.... they say he's kinda soft-hearted... and he makes more money than any other phony beggar in the joint!"

Fancy has started coughing again - a pitiful and wretched figure. She controls it - looks after Charley, then shakes her head timidly - evidently lacks the courage to accost him.

Scene 23.

INT. THE "CRIPPLE FACTORY"; FULL SHOT:

As Charlie enters:

A dingy, low-ceiled, dirty room, something between a low-class theatrical dressing room and a barber shop. At the center, against the far wall are two large mirrors before which stand large chairs with high backs, something like barbers' chairs. It is here that Adolphe plies his trade. The mirrors are flanked with many-jointed gas-jets of the old type, with bent wire globes about their flaring flamed. In front of the central mirror is Adolphe's make-up shelf, well supplied with grease-paint, brushes, cosmetics, etc. The walls on both sides of the mirror are hung with every conceivable sort of paraphernalia for making up fake cripples. Artificial legs and arms, crutches; wigs; patches for blind eyes; black goggles, and a collection of signs for beggars to wear about their necks; "Help a Poor man" "I am Blind!" etc; In a corner is a propelling wheel chair with hand levers such as a paralyzed beggar might use. On the wall are photographs – Adolphe's art gallery, which shows particular triumphs of his art: some especially horrible specimens of supposed cripples - all fakes. At one side of the room, back, is a sort of alcove, partly closed off by ragged curtains on sliding rings, which affords a sort of small dressing room. It is supplied with another smaller mirror and make-up stand, small chair and hand-wash-bowl. This serves as a retiring room for Adolphe's clients - it is here they remove the last traces of their make-up and resume their costumes of everyday.

Against the wall are several battered lockers in a row. They are something like the lockers of a gymnasium. Each of these bears a grimy paper label on which is scrawled the name of its owner: "Easy Money Charley"; "Humpty Joe"; "Legless Law"; etc. In these the clients of the place are accustomed to keep their clothes and property while engaged in their professional pursuit.

At the other side of the central mirrors against the wall, is a row of three battered, strong backed chairs for waiting clients; again as in a barber shop. In the far corner of the room is a rear door giving upon the back alley. An opening this door one would look down a foot or two directly into the cobble-paved alley, with a cellar window below and to one side.

At the moment we enter the place with Charlie, in this full shot, all the chairs are occupied. The day-watch of beggars are going off duty, and the night-watch is coming on. Adolphe himself is busy at a chair, making up "Humpty Joe's" face, while an assistant is strapping on Joe's back the fake hump which gives him his name. A couple of day beggars are removing their make-ups in the little dressing alcove.

Charlie, entering, is hailed by others, as he enters, and he returns the greeting and nods around the room.

Scene 24.

INT. THE "CRIPPLE FACTORY" CLOSE SHOT:

On Adolphe, as with the concentration of the artist, he draws a line on "Humpty's" face. He is a plausible, smiling little caricature of a Frenchman, very proud of his art, of course; sophisticated and even semi-criminal, but nevertheless keeping the pose of the true creative artist. He and his assistant are clad in ragged duck jackets. He finishes the line, and stepping back, inspects it and nods his approval. Then and then only - he looks up as Charlie enters the scene, and greets him in a friendly and effusive manner, as we introduce him with ---

TITLE: "ADOLPHE" - THE GENIUS BEHIND THE "CRIPPLE FACTORY"
…..

While this action is going on, the assistant is strapping to "Humpty's" back the fake hump. Adolphe proudly tells Charlie to look at the job he has done - indicates "Humpty's" face. Charlie looks, and nods approvingly, with a cynical smile. Just then, the assistant pulls too hard, and Humpty turns and snarls at him. Charlie is pulling the ragged coat carefully off of the false arm. The pockets are sagging, and Charlie lifts it tentatively, Adolphe watching, smiling, as Charlie hands him the coat, and tells him:

TITLE: "Pretty good today, 'Dolphe…. count it for me, will you."

Adolphe nods - hangs the coat up carefully, and indicates that he will attend to Charley's financial matters as soon as he is through with Humpty. Then he assists Charley out of the harness of his artificial arm - and Charley, with it in his arm exits scene, showing the two good arms. As Adolphe turns back to Humpty -----

Scene 25.

INT. "CRIPPLE FACTORY"; CLOSE SHOT ON CORNER:

In this corner is a small box, filled with straw, and fastened to a staple in the wall behind the box is a chain, which is stretched out straight as a little mongrel pup, fastened by the chain to his collar, is leaping and barking in a transport of delight such as only a puppy can give. Charlie, his false arm in his hand, enters the scene, and squats into the close shot, taking the wildly wriggling little pup in his arms, pets it tenderly. The pup responds with tail, nose and tongue. Then Charlie tells it "You just wait a minute, old top", and puts it gently down - exits.

INT. "CRIPPLE FACTORY": LONGER SHOT:

As Charley goes to his locker, opens it - and puts the false arm inside - bends down, and takes out a piece of manilla paper, wrapped around some puppy biscuit - goes back to the puppy which leaps in transports at his return….and as he plays with it and feeds it ---

Scene 27.

INT. DEAD HOUSE: FULL SHOT:

Shooting toward the door - with the table at which Molly and Fancy are sitting in f.g. as the doors swing open, and there enters the most sinister and most strongly characterized individual in our story - Bridgeport White-eye - he tap-taps with his cane as he comes - and just inside the door pauses.

Scene 28.

INT. DEAD HOUSE: CLOSE SHOT ON WHITEY:

Getting a good study of him. He is a sturdy, broad-shouldered individual, and even in the Dead-House, does not drop the pretense of being blind. One of his eyes is covered with a patch - the other half closed, and habitually squinted and walled. Introduce him with title:

TITLE: "BRIDGEPORT WHITE-EYE" - KNOWN TO THE DEAD HOUSE AS "WHITEY"

He now starts the tap-tap-ing ahead of him again, as he starts down---

Scene 29.

INT. DEAD HOUSE: FULL SHOT AS BEFORE:

He comes down with the air of one accustomed to command attention and respect in this place, and from the way in which everyone turns and looks at him, it is evident that he is a highly regarded and well-known figure to them all. But as the two women at the table, Molly and Fancy, observe him as he goes by, both show aversion and dislike tinged with fear at the sinister apparition. After he has passed, Dolly tells Fancy:

TITLE: "There's a guy that wouldn't do nothing for you… He's a bad 'un….That bozo wouldn't give you the right time!"

Fancy concurs in this heartily.

Scene 30.

INT. CRIPPLE FACTORY: FULL SHOT:

As Whitey opens the door and enters, he gets the same attention. By this time Humpty is all ready to go out, and Adolphe is finishing counting Charley's pile of change. Humpty, on his way out, greets Whitey, who nods in a surly way, and Whitey taps taps his way to the middle of the floor. Charley looks up and sees him - instantly leaves his pup, and coming over, he unceremonious dumps an occupant out of one of the waiting chairs and then turns around - takes Whitey's arm, and leads him to the chair. As he sits down, Adolphe leaves his shelf, and starts toward them, some clean new bills in his hand.

Scene 31.

INT. THE CRIPPLE FACTORY: CLOSE SHOT:

As Whitey looks up, and, his manner ungracious and curt, as he accepts the courtesy, growls:

TITLE: "That you, Charley?.....What d'ya make today?"

At this instant Adolphe enters the scene - and handing the bills to Charley tells him:

TITLE: "$152.27, Charley, minus my $1.52…..Ma foi…..how you get ze l'argent!"

At mention of the sum, Whitey throws down his cane angrily. The keynote of this man's character is envy and hatred. But one thing about him which makes him a really interesting and unusual type for a villain is --- that the man is an acting artist. Even his own associates believe him to be blind: Charley believes him to be blind: but the fact is, a fact that must soon be revealed to the audience - that he is not blind at all. Now the actor ego crops out, and he snarls indignantly; to Adolphe, as Charley, sticking the bills in his pocket, exits the scene---

TITLE: "Me—I'm the one artist in this business... and I can't make half of that!"

Adolphe looks down at him, and shrugs his shoulders.

Scene 32.

INT. CRIPPLE FACTORY: CLOSE SHOT ON CORNER:

Charley in, bends to play with the puppy, which greets him ecstatically again - and hearing this, he turns and shoots over his shoulder:

TITLE: "I guess it's because you're too much on the level, Whitey: A really blind man ain't got much show in this game!"

Back, as he turns again to the puppy, which grabs him by his crooked forefinger, growls and wrestles with it....

Scene 33.

INT. CRIPPLE FACTORY: CLOSE SHOT ON WHITEY AND ADOLPHE:

This remark of Charley's makes Adolphe cackle with glee; he is the only man in on Whitey's real secret. And now Whitey, with a snarl, kicks Adolphe viciously on the shin, and the caddie suddenly shifts to a wince of pain as Adolphe grabs his leg in both hands. Whitey turns his apparently sightless eye toward Charley, and asks him:

TITLE: "What you doin', Charley?... Foolin' with that pup of yours there?"

As he gets this over, he reaches for his cane - and finding it raises himself up to his feet. He starts out of scene.

Scene 34.

INT. CRIPPLE FACTORY: MEDIUM SHOT CORNER:

Door to alley tipped in, as Whitey comes in, and Charley, the dog up in his arms, looks up and tells him "Yes." Whitey looks down a second - then makes a proposition which must have been in his mind for some time:

TITLE: "I need some kind of a mutt to lead me around... it 'ud be worth a lot more money to me... What'll you take for it?"

Charley looks up - and the pup struggles to lick his face, as, smilin', he tells Whitey: shaking his head - "Nothing!"

Whitey snarls down at him:

TITLE: "I ain't asking you to give me the mutt... I'm askin' you to sell him."

Charley shakes his head - and comes back with:

TITLE: "That would be worse than givin' him away, Whitey... but I'm too fond of him!"

At which Whitey sneers again with malignant disappointment and envy. He watches as Charley puts the puppy gently back in the box, and gets up to exit scene... Then he goes over to the alley door, which is standing partly open - looks out...

Scene 35.

INT. CRIPPLE FACTORY: SHOOTING THROUGH DOOR INTO ALLEY:

Past Whitey's back – and showing a beer truck laden with heavy kegs, backed up, and discharging its freight. A pair of heavy keg skids leads from the rear of the truck down to the cellar window of Diamond Mike's cellar below. Two men in sacking aprons are rolling the kegs down the skids. Whitey looks back toward the pup...

Scene 36.

INT. CRIPPLE FACTORY: MEDIUM SHOT:

Shooting from Whitey toward the corner, and the little curtained alcove. Charley with a last look at the pup, goes on back, and disappears from sight behind the curtains of the alcove. Whitey moves swiftly. In two steps he reaches the puppy and picks it up, pretending to pet it. Then he moves back to f.g., by the door, and puts the puppy down on the floor near the door. He watches outside, while the pup stands, looking up at him trustingly.

Scene 37.

INT. CRIPPLE FACTORY: SHOOTING THROUGH DOOR INTO ALLEY:

Same angle as before. This shot shows the truck and the top of the skid - but not the bottom by the window. The helper on the truck places a keg on the skid - balances it a second - just as he is about to let it go, Whitey takes his foot, and kicks the puppy out of the door, unnoticed by Charley, who just then comes into scene behind Whitey… The keg rolls down the skid - and as it does the man on the truck registers his alarm and horror - he yells out. Charley whirls - and rushes to the door beside Whitey - looks down into the alley - and then turns a face on Whitey that is fiendish with rage. Whitey shrinks back. Charley, with a yell - jumps down ---

Scene 38.

EXT. ALLEY: CELLAR WINDOW: END OF SKID: CLOSE SHOT:

The poor little puppy is stretched out - limp and quite dead, as Charlie sinks into the close shot and picks it up; as he tries to revive it ---

Scene 39.

INT. CRIPPLE FACTORY: FULL SHOT:

Charley's yell has startled everyone, and they rush to the door to watch, while others run in from the outer room among them Dutch Dolly and Portland Fancy. They all crowd around the door. Whitey slinks back, afraid of the reckoning he fears is coming.

Scene 40.

EXT. ALLEY: CLOSE SHOT ON CHARLEY AND THE DOG:

Charley is openly crying as he tries to revive the dog. Then he realizes that the pup is beyond all help. He gets unsteadily to his feet, the little limp body in his arm - and turns toward the door.

Scene 41.

INT. CRIPPLE FACTORY: FULL SHOT:

The crowd at the door part, as Charley lays the pup's body on the floor - then jumps up and in. He pays no attention to anyone in the crowd - stoops and picks up the puppy, and carries it over to the box, lays it tenderly in. Then he turns viciously toward Whitey, sitting in the chair, and throws at him a threatening accusation - Whitey, as the others crowd close, makes a hurried denial, cringing back from Charley's black anger. The denial gets over, for Charley, still believing Whitey really blind, is not certain Whitey did the deed. He turns back - drops on his knees again by the box containing the puppy...

Scene 42.

INT. CRIPPLE FACTORY: CLOSE SHOT ON DOLLY AND FANCY:

As Dolly looks sharply at Fancy. The latter feels the gaze, and returns the look - Dolly nods slightly, her eyebrows raise a little - and then she jerks her head at Charley, as much as to say – "What did I tell you... there's a guy that would help you!" Fancy turns again to look at Charley...

Scene 43.

INT. CRIPPLE FACTORY: CLOSE SHOT ON CHARLEY:

As he covers the little pup with a piece of burlap sacking, and wipes the tears from his eyes —

Scene 44.

INT. CRIPPLE FACTORY: CLOSE SHOT ON DOLLY AND FANCY:

Both women are watching Charley, and it is plain that the incident has made a deep impression on Fancy; and she shows by her softened expression - a certain look of hope that has come into her tired eyes - a hope that almost makes her smile a little in the certainty that a man who can feel so keenly about the misfortune of a little dog may also be kindly toward an unfortunate woman or an unhappy child. And on this expression, softened - the suggestion of a hopeful smile, we FADE OUT.

TITLE: THE PASSING DAYS DID LITTLE TO SOFTEN THE ACHE IN CHARLEY'S HEART AT THE LOSS OF THE ONLY LIVING THING THAT HAD LOVED HIM...

FADE IN ON **Scene 45.**

INT. DEAD HOUSE: FULL SHOT:

Same action and types as before: Dutch Dolly is sitting alone at the same table, in f.g. But she is not drinking; she keeps glancing back at the concealed door; and when Charley finally appears - it is evident from her intentness as he comes down toward her that it is he she has been waiting for. She gets up - and as he starts past her, she braces him. Charley is now in his regular clothes. He is clean, dapper - almost to the point of foppishness. But he is surprised as Dolly stops him. She tells him earnestly:

TITLE: "Fancy wants to see you over at her room, Charley."

Charley frowns - he isn't interested in women. Dolly insists pleadingly, in pantomime indicating that Fanny's home is just a few steps away - it will be little trouble for Charley to run around for a moment. Charley hesitates before her insistence. Then he asks:

TITLE: "What ails her? She wants to see me?"

Dolly nods impressively, and takes Charley by the elbow as she continues her plea:

Scene 46.

INT. CRIPPLE FACTORY: CLOSE SHOT ON DOOR:

Whitey and Adolphe are alone, talking. Whitey opens the door into the Dead House - and stops short - looks (getting over once more that he can see perfectly). He smiles his sneering grin, as he motions for Adolphe to look: He indicates: Between their bodies, through the open door, we can see the action of the preceding shot - Dolly pleading with Charley: Whitey closes the door - and turns to Adolphe, as he growls, in his usual sarcastic, nasty way:

TITLE: "And he's the guy that never monkeys with the frails! He makes me sick!"

Adolphe, a diplomat to the core, only shrugs his shoulders in his exaggerated French way - while Whitey mutters on to himself.

Scene 47.

INT. DEAD HOUSE: CLOSE SHOT ON CHARLEY AND DOLLY:

Charley is weakening, and when Dolly pulls persuasively on his sleeve, and begs him - "Aw - come on, Charley… it won't hurt you to find out what she wants," he tells her "Aw - Hell, all right, then." And they start out of scene, with a QUICK FADE:

FADE IN QUICKLY ON
Scene 48.
INT. PORTLAND FANCY'S ROOM:

The set is a small bedroom, very plain, but exquisitely neat and clean, and with pathetic feminine touches, such as cheap curtains, a ribbon on the pillow, one or two sentimental or religious pictures on the wall; a bunch of poor withered flowers in a glass. Conspicuously placed, either on the wall or on a small bare table -- are a crucifix and a photograph. The photograph is that of our child character as subsequently used -- a pretty little ringletted girl of three years old. Portland Fancy, in a cheap crepe dressing gown, is lying back among pillows on a battered arm chair. There are medicine bottles beside her, to suggest that she has already had medical attention. Her abundant hair is loose about her shoulders. Her eyes are sunken, her face haggard. She is extremely weak, and plainly in a much more critical condition than when we last saw her. With pathetic suspense, she is watching the door. A gleam of hope, a little rigid leaning forward, registers her eagerness, as she speaks - "Come in."

The door opens - and Charley stands there - then enters slowly. He is not at all a willing visitor, but once more we get a touch of the man's innate human tenderness and sympathy toward anything helpless or unfortunate. Fancy speaks to him, timidly, and then he comes forward and takes the hand she offers him. He awkwardly says the conventional thing - hoping she will soon be better, as we go to ---

Scene 49.

INT. PORTLAND FANCY'S ROOM: CLOSE SHOT ON THEM:

As, the conventional over with, Fancy stops - frightened - not knowing how to begin. Charley hesitates, too; and finally very awkwardly - he asks her what he can do for her. Fancy starts to answer - and is seized with a violent coughing spell. She fights for control - and when she finally conquers the cough - she tells him, between tortured breaths:

TITLE: "It's the kid."

She indicates the photograph of the child. Charley looks at it - then tells her:

TITLE: "I didn't know you had one."

Fancy nods: "Three years old, she tells him, with pride in her breaking voice. Then she turns to Charley with pathetic appeal:

TITLE: "They put her in an institution and made a number of her!"

She goes on talking, with increasing emotion and pathos; as we FADE OUT ON THEM - but not until Fancy, talking, has held up her left hand - and shown Charley the wedding ring on her finger - and then the title:

TITLE: "After he died, things was tough… I guess I must have been nearly crazy… because one day…."

Then, as she goes on, FADE OUT SLOWLY - and into--

FADE INTO

Scene 50.

INT. DEPARTMENT STORE: CLOSE SHOT ON COUNTER:

Fancy, looking woe-begone and starved, comes furtively along the counter. Looking about her like a hunted animal, she suddenly takes up and conceals some expensive piece of wearing apparel from the counter. She is caught by the clerk, who grabs her arm - yells out of scene, and the store detective steps up to her, and at a word from the clerk, discovers the article she has taken. He lays his hand on her shoulder - QUICK FADE.

Scene 51.

FADE QUICKLY INTO: MEDIUM SHOT JUDGE'S DESK IN COURTROOM SUGGESTED:

At the rail at which prisoners are arraigned. The judge is presiding. The store detective and a policeman have Fancy in charge at the rail. Woman probation officer or Matron enters, carrying an infant wrapped in a shawl in her arms, and passed the child to Fancy, who receives it with extravagant affection. This can probably be played with a prop for a baby. The policeman and detective, as well as the Matron, regard the grief and love of the young mother with pitying gaze. But the judge sternly calls everyone to order - cuts short her appeal - and delivers her sentence. Fancy listens, appalled and stunned as she hears the punishment he metes out. QUICK FADE......

FADE QUICKLY IN ON

Scene 52.

INT. PRISON CELL:

Fancy is bidding goodbye to her baby. The woman officer is waiting - sympathetic, but manifestly impatient to end the agony, which Fancy, in her horror at letting go of the baby, is protracting. Finally the matron ruthlessly, because ruthlessness is necessary, takes the baby from Fancy, who is in a state of utter collapse. As the barred door closes behind the matron, and is locked by a turn-key, and the matron, with the baby in her arms, disappears, Fancy, with a wild cry of desperation, falls on her knees against the bars, as we FADE QUICKLY:

FADE IN SLOWLY ON

Scene 53.

INT. PORTLAND FANCY'S ROOM: CLOSE SHOT:

Resuming the action, as Fancy cries out:

<u>TITLE</u>: "I did it to save my baby... and they took her from me!"

When she finishes, both Fancy and Charley are emotionally wrought up - Fancy to the very highest pitch, and Charley in pity and sympathy. Fancy fights her cough again - then she tells Charley, with a half-sob:

<u>TITLE</u>: "The reason I'm telling you all this is... I ain't got long to live... and I'm asking you to save this kid of mine from that institution."

Charley regards her in amazement: She goes on hurriedly:

<u>TITLE</u>: "You kin afford to take her!" Then her voice changes - it is pleadingly that she asks him:

<u>TITLE</u>: "Ain't you ever lonesome for something that's glad when it sees you comin' home?"

This has its effect on Charley. He looks away from her, embarrassed - and touched to the quick. She sees it, and leaning desperately forward in her chair, she clutches his arm -- she cries out, an agony of entreaty in her face and eyes and voice:

<u>TITLE</u>: "Take her Charley... For God's sake, will you?"

She hesitates a second - then goes on:

<u>TITLE</u>: "I seen you that day when your dog was killed... a man who could be good

to a dog like that could learn to love a little child!"

Charley is weakening. But he still avoids her gaze - and is trying hard not to be carried away with his natural impulses, which are all for sympathy and kindness. Fancy shakes his arm, her weakness pitiable, but her passion and frenzy terrific, as she tells him:

TITLE: "I don't want my little girl to end up in that Dead House... like she will if she never has anyone to love her - and care for her!"

Her emotion is too much far Charley. He takes his both hands and covers her poor, emaciated one with them - half choking and unable to trust himself to speak, he nods a tentative acceptance of her plea. Eagerly she snatches at the ray of hope which she gets from him. She is rapidly weakening, and another paroxysm of coughing causes Charlie to try and get her back more comfortably in her chair. But Fancy pushes him back, in order to reach into a table drawer. She takes out a legal looking folded paper, and tells him:

TITLE: "I've signed her over to you... made you her guardian!"

She thrusts the paper into his hands; then she begs him:

TITLE: "Call her Fancy... then I'll feel.. wherever I'm goin'... that I still have some share in my little girl."

Scene 54.

EXT. HALLWAY: CLOSE SHOT ON DOOR:

And Dutch Dolly, listening with her ear at the door, smiles to herself, delighted at what she hears.

Scene 55.

INT. PORTLAND FANCY'S ROOM: CLOSE SHOT ON THEM:

As Before: Charlie is looking at her, wracked with pity as she fights another coughing spell. As she gets control of herself, he asks her:

TITLE: "Fancy -- what?"

Fancy looks at him hesitantly. She almost whispers:

TITLE: "I've never told anyone that before... Fancy Claire...

Charlie gets this -- and nods. Then, with a final effort, Fancy reaches over and snatches the crucifix. Holding it up before him, her hand trembling, she calls on him to swear that he will keep his promise. Charley raises his hand toward the emblem and pantomimes his solemn oath. A gleam of radiant happiness comes to the dying woman, as she clasps the crucifix to her breast and sinks back into her chair. Her eyes close - she is scarcely breathing. Charley looks at her in sudden alarm - leans over and speaks. Fancy slowly opens her eyes - smiles at him. At this instant Dolly enters the shot hurriedly, as though she had heard and entered. She bends quickly over Fancy, while Charley steps back, awkwardly fumbling his hat as he watches, his human emotion grimly visible in his face, as we FADE OUT.

FADE IN ON

Scene 56.

EXT. BOWERY STREET: LONG SHOT:

From the narrow door of a tenement house, four men - an undertaker and his assistants, with great difficulty are carrying out a cheap coffin to a waiting hearse. A few idle bystanders, such as always congregates at such events is standing by - a couple of bums, a Bowery character or two, a few ragged children. The hearse as it stands at the curb is facing away from us, so that between us and the hearse we see a single cheap hack, which is about to follow the unhappy Fancy to the grave. Four of the women typical of the Dead House, follow the coffin out, and start to enter this hack. The last is Dolly. She stops, and looking toward the camera, sees someone in the foreground, leaning against a lamppost - she comes down and speaks to him.

Scene 57.

EXT. SIDEWALK AND LAMPOST: CLOSE SHOT ON CHARLEY:

As Dolly enters from camera - speaks to him. He is in ordinary clothes, a cap pulled down over his eyes, leaning up against the post, and regarding the funeral proceedings with a grim and thoughtful eye. He is smoking a cigarette. His whole attitude is reflective and sardonically philosophical. Since that scene in Fancy's room, when he was carried away with emotion, he has had time to reflect - and now as he leans against the lamppost and watches her funeral, he is thinking over the situation with a natural revulsion of cynical wonder at his folly.

Now, as Dolly asks him, jerking her thumb back at the carriage, "Ain't yer comin' along?" Charlie shakes his head, and tells her:

TITLE: "Naw!... got something else to do."

With which he takes from his pocket the legal-looking paper Fancy gave him - explains it to Dolly - and thrust it back again. Dolly dabs at her tearful eyes with a wadded lace handkerchief, shrugs her shoulders, and turns away.

Scene 58.

EXT. BOWERY STREET: LONG SHOT AGAIN:

As the four men thrust the coffin into the hearse with the utmost callousness and scant tenderness. Two of the men mount to the driver's seat of the hearse - the other two the carriage. The hearse makes a short turn in the narrow street, and comes down past camera and out, followed by the carriage. As it comes abreast of Charley he straightens up and throws away his cigarette, and pulls off his cap in a half-awkward, half-heart-felt salute to the pitiful mother as she is carried past him. His eyes follow the pathetic cortege down the street after it is out of range of the camera, and we see the reawakening of the emotional crisis which made him give his promise. Then he hunches up his shoulders, buttons his coat, and turning on his heel starts back down the street with the step of a man going about his duty, as we FADE OUT ON HIM.

TITLE: LATER THAT EVENING ... AT EASY MONEY CHARLEY'S BACHELOR QUARTERS.

FADE IN ON –

Scene 59.

INT. CHARLEY'S ROOMS: FULL SHOT:

Supposedly in the vicinity of the Dead House, on the Bowery. It is the sort of a room suited to a bachelor of Charley's propensities and prosperity, and also of his limitations. It is clean, but bare, although comfortably furnished. On the wall are a few pictures of sporting interest, prize-fighters, race-horses and dogs. For these we may legitimately suppose to comprise the leisure interests of Easy Money Charley. Prominent in one place on the wall is a picture of Charley's poor little mutt -- the one we saw killed. Charley's sentimentality is evidenced by the little piece of black ribbon pinned across the top. In one corner is a narrow iron bed. There is a small table in the middle of the room, on which are some sporting papers, *Police Gazettes*, cheap magazines and a few books. Also a couple of boxes of cheap cigars, and a tray of pipes. A student lamp is on the table, and beside the table is an easy old leather arm-chair.

We open the scene with the entrance of the Widow McGee - a lovable, fat, bustling, middle aged Irish woman; neat as a pin, and with a motherly simplicity and joviality of disposition. She is carrying a tray. She sweeps aside the magazines and books, and sets up one end of the table with the cloth and dishes on the tray. When she has this just right, she lights the lamp - and then goes over to the mantle and looks at the clock ---

Scene 60.

INT. CHARLEY'S ROOM: CLOSE SHOT ON MANTEL AND CLOCK:

And on the Widow McGee, as she looks at the clock, which registers six-thirty - she shakes her head, as we introduce her with the title:

<u>TITLE</u>: THE WIDOW MCGEE... WHO GIVES CHARLEY A MOTHERLY CARE IN ADDITION TO ROOM AND BOARD..........

She shakes her head - then she hears his step, and turns, with a broad smile to greet him:

Scene 61.

INT. CHARLEY'S ROOM: CLOSE SHOT ON DOOR:

Instead of flying open as usual, the door is unlatched and opened slowly and softly, and as it opens, Charley is disclosed. He is carrying in his arms a sleeping child of three years, carrying her carefully and tenderly with her curly head pillowed against his shoulder.

Scene 62.

INT. CHARLEY'S ROOM: CLOSEUP ON MRS. MCGEE:

As her mouth draws into an "O-o-o" of amazement.

Scene 63.

INT. CHARLEY'S ROOM: FULL SHOT:

As Charley makes a gesture for silence, then comes down and nods toward the bed. Mrs. McGee, all in a fluster, understands, and precedes him to the bed. She flattens the pillows and prepares the covers to receive this strange little visitor. With infinite caution Charley places the child in its soft nest, and so careful is he, with Mrs. McGee's eager assistance, that the child does not awake.

Scene 64.

INT. CHARLEY'S ROOM: CLOSEUP ON HIM:

Mrs. McGee's skirts tipped into shot, and her hands, as she pulls the covers over the baby's legs. The child's little hand has closed over Charley's finger - an important piece of business to be achieved, if possible - the same finger we have seen the pet puppy wrestle with in the first sequence. And now the baby's grip is tight, even in her sleep. Charley looks down at it. Perhaps insert a closeup of it here. And the baby clutch holds him helpless; it has him by the heartstrings already. For a long moment he looks down at it, unwilling to break it. Then it is only with the utmost precaution and gentleness that he finally detaches the little fingers from his own, and draws away his hand. As he starts to get up...

Scene 65.

INT. CHARLEY'S ROOM: FULL SHOT:

As he draws Mrs. McGee down into f.g., and begins to assuage her almost bursting curiosity; he asks her, indicating the bed:

<u>TITLE</u>: "Can you take care of that kid for me?"

Mrs. McGee indicates eagerly that she can - that she would love to ---- but asks:

<u>TITLE</u>: "But, Mr. Charley… Who is she? Is she your own?

Charley shakes his head. Then says, with the quiet firmness of his decision:

<u>TITLE</u>: "But she's goin' to be -- from now on."

Mrs. McGee registers her emotional sympathy and pleasure at the prospect. Her Irish sentiment comes bubbling from her as she gazes at the sleeping child. She tells him:

<u>TITLE</u>: "Shure - the little darlin'… we'll keep her safe!"

Charley picks up his hat - and tells Mrs. McGee to look after the kid well. She stops him - indicates the dinner on his table in solicitous concern asks him if he isn't going to eat it. He shakes his head - and tells her curtly:

<u>TITLE</u>: "I got to work tonight… to make the coin for all this!"

He gets this over grimly - and then walks stiffly out, in spite of Mrs. McGee's flustered protests. Then as she sees he is really gone, and with a backward glance at the bed, softly closes the door, FADE OUT………

<u>TITLE</u>: THE DEAD HOUSE HAS HEARD THE NEWS…. AND IS FAIRLY

BUZZING WITH CONJECTURE AND WHISPERS..........

FADE IN ON **Scene 66.**

INT. THE DEAD HOUSE: FULL SHOT:

Dutch Dolly is seated at one of the tables -- and opposite her is Whitey. He pays the waiter for the drinks he sets down and we see from his manner that while still playing blind, he is pumping her with questions, and Dolly is telling him everything, rather important that she has so much to tell. At other tables heads are together, and conversation is rampant.

Scene 67.

INT. DEAD HOUSE: CLOSEUP ON ANOTHER TABLE:

At which are seated another group - two men and two women; talking together. One of the women is buzzing her gossip, and one of the men interrupts with a wise-guy crack out of the corner of his mouth, when the other woman grubs his arm - tells him "Cheese it, yuh damned fool" All look out - and register their embarrassment. This table should be near the door....

Scene 68.

INT. DEAD HOUSE: CLOSE DOOR ON CHARLEY: JUST INSIDE DOOR:

He has heard something that is burning him up. With a glitter in his eye - he comes down out of scene, his face hasty.

Scene 69.

INT. DEAD HOUSE: LONGER SHOT: TABLE IN F.G.:

As Charley comes down, the various groups of bums and derelicts in the place follow him with their eyes and the moment they are behind him fall to whispering busily among the selves. He stops challengingly in front of the table where the two couples have been talking. They sneer up at him in their typical wise-guy manner. He demands sharply:

TITLE: Well... what's on your minds? What's bitin' youse?"

They look up at him rather defiantly - but say nothing. Charley glares around the room then back at them with:

TITLE: "You seem to be a whole lot interested in me and my business... Spit it out- what's it all about?"

Before his menacing eye they lower their eyes and refuse his challenge. Charley with an angry sneer, nods as he looks them over with grim disgust, and turning and looking the others over, delivers himself of a comment which includes them all, including Whitey and everybody else in sight:

TITLE: "A fine bunch of bums.... Keep yer dirty thoughts and your dirty tongues of my business, d'ya hear."

He stops and glares around:

Scene 70.

INT. DEAD HOUSE: CLOSE SHOT ON WHITHEY'S TABLE:

Whitey is holding his pose of a blind man - but listening with a half sneer on his face. Dolly is frankly scared - guilty of having talked too much. Whitey is in the f.g., practically a closeup. It is important regarding Whitey that we are always aware of his secret power of sight, and when, as now, he is not talking with anyone, in closeup, we see him with one narrowed eye keenly observant, and full of nasty malice... ...

Scene 71.

INT. DEAD HOUSE: LONG SHOT: AS BEFORE:

Charley, talking to the room at large, continues:

TITLE: "The first guy who gets nosey with me... I'll smack him one in the beezer....

get me?"

Under his menacing frown, all pretend to be busy about other matters. None challenge his ability to do what he says he will. Charley stands with clenched fists for a second, hoping someone will call him. Then, as they ignore him, he hitches his trousers, and swaggers back toward the door to the Cripple Factory.

Scene 72.

INT. CRIPPLE FACTORY: MEDIUM SHOT:

Adolphe is alone, as Charley enters, still frowning. Adolphe greets him suavely, and Charley barely responds. Suddenly he turns angrily to Adolphe, who is amazed at his unusual grouch and a little curious - and with an angry thrust of his thumb back toward the outer room, asks:

TITLE: "All those moochers out there….they're talking about me!"

Adolphe shrugs plausibly, and replies:

TITLE: "What do you expect M'sieu Charley… Zey know all about your takin' Fancy's keed!"

Charley turns ugly again, as he grates, between his teeth: "Oh they do, do they?" Adolphe nods - and goes on:

TITLE: "And they think you've struck some graft… they don't think you'd have done it unless there were beer money in it!"

Charley sneers - that is what they would think - the grafters! He steps back to the door - and peeps outside: opens the door, just a crack.

Scene 73.

INT. DEAD HOUSE: THROUGH CRACK IN DOOR:

Showing action of busy talking and eager conversation - shooting past Charley's back as he looks. Now he closes the door, and turns - thinks hard.

Scene 74.

INT. CRIPPLE FACTORY: MEDIUM SHOT:

Adolphe enters shot, trying to appear busy about small tasks, but really with one eye on Charley, who suddenly wheels on him, and explodes:

<u>TITLE</u>: "I oughta known I couldn't bring her to this neighborhood... Those devils out there would always try to smear her name!"

He thinks hard, then come to a decision. Adolphe nods in agreement. Charley thinks hard for a moment, makes a short turn on the floor -- then arrives at a decision. Transfixing Adolphe with his forefinger, he warns Adolphe:

<u>TITLE</u>: "I'm going to make a clean break for her... If they ask about me, tell 'em the whole thing is off... that I sent the kid away to Fancy's relations!"

Adolphe promises. Then, with a last word of warning, Charley exits toward the alley door, and we

FADE QUICKLY.

FADE QUICKLY INTO

Scene 75.

INT. CHARLEY'S ROOM: FULL SHOT: NIGHT:

Mrs. McGee is sitting there beside the sleeping child in the dim light of the student lamp, when the door suddenly opens and Charley enters. Mrs. McGee, surprised, starts up. Charley motions for silence -- beckons her over to him. As she goes--

Scene 76.

INT. CHARLEY'S ROOM CLOSE SHOT ON HIM:

He is nervous, and worked up, as Mrs. McGee enters the scene. When she is close, he tells her with fierce directness:

TITLE: "We're clearin' outta this place right now -- and leavin' no address! Will you come with me and the kid?"

She looks at him, bewildered by the suddenness of it all. "Now? She asks him. He nods vehemently. He asks her::

TITLE: "There's nothin' or nobody to keep you, is there?"

Mrs. McGee shakes her head -- there isn't. And Charley tells her:

TITLE: "Then get your things packed and clear out of here...I'll send you word. Tomorrow where you can find us."

He starts out of scene toward the bed. Mrs. McGee grabs his arm -- and asks him - "Are you takin' her now?" Charley answers her tersely:

TITLE: "I'm getting' that kid outta this street this minute... before it ever finds or sees her.... I'm gonna find a place where we can bring her up decent -- you and me!"

Then, as he looks down at her troubled old face, Charley is tense with emotion as he asks her eagerly - for he needs her in his scheme of things!

TITLE: "Will you help me? ... Will you do what I say?"

Mrs. McGee looks over toward the bed -- mute assent. Charley exits scene:

Scene 77.

INT. CHARLEY'S ROOM: CLOSE SHOT ON BED:

The little girl is asleep, in her night-clothes, now, and Charley stands for a second, looking down at her rare beauty; his emotion in his face. Then, with the help of Mrs. McGee, who has followed him, with infinite care and tenderness, he picks her up, covers and all -- wraps them carefully around her, and without waking her up, he starts out. Mrs. McGee hurries ahead of him ----

Scene 78.

INT. CHARLEY'S ROOM: FULL SHOT:

As Mrs. McGee opens the door, and with a grim parting word Charley hurries out, while she remains staring after him through the open door, as we FADE OUT........

<u>TITLE</u>: THE THIRTEEN YEARS THAT FOLLOWED CHANGED INDIVIDUALS -- NATIONS - EVEN THE MAP OF THE WORLD ... BUT THROUGH THIRTEEN CENTURIES HUMAN NATURE HAS REMAINED THE SAME.......

FADE IN SLOWLY ON

Scene 79.

INT. THE CRIPPLE FACTORY: FULL SHOT:

Some few changes have been made in this set to indicate the passage of time. The place is dingier -- the props are rearranged on the walls, and are poorer and fewer. Some of the lockers are missing. The curtains of the alcove are worn almost to threads. But as the shot fades in we see Adolphe, now somewhat bent and gray, although still friendly and chipper and proud as ever of his art. He is receiving at the back door, a couple of boxes such as frocks are delivered in -- and a gaily striped hat box such as fashionable milliners use.

Scene 80.

INT. CRIPPLE FACTORY: CLOSE SHOT OF ADOLPHE:

Getting over the comedy effect of such deliveries on Adolphe. He is bewildered and somewhat put out with the size and number of them. Tipped into shot, near the door, is a chair, on which are piled other packages. Adolphe, registering that his eyes are not as good as they used to be, picks up one of them, and holds it close to read the name.

Scene 81.

INSERT CLOSE UP OF ELABORATE ADDRESS LABEL.

The name written in, is "CHARLES VANHERN, 212 The Bowery. (Back door)."

Scene 82.

INT. CRIPPLE FACTORY: FULL SHOT:

As Adolphe shakes his head -- the name means nothing to him. Then he takes them over and places them on the chair with the others. While he is thus engaged, Charley enters. He is in his begging outfit, and looks much the same as he did in our earlier sequences. Perhaps there is a touch of real gray at his temples, but it is a touch that, when he is dressed for home, makes him look more distinguished, rather than older. As he enters, he has thrown aside his beggar slouch and ambling gait, and is evidently in the happiest and cheeriest mood. He crosses quickly to the chair, and begins to inspect the packages, whistling to himself. Adolphe goes to him, and Charley slaps him briskly on the back. Adolphe indicates the things - "Those yours?" he asks. Charley returns ---

TITLE: "Sure they're mine .... didn't you see my name on 'em?"

Adolphe asks curiously - "But what are they?" Charley laughs -- and tells him:

TITLE: "Presents! For a birthday party! Can't you guess whose?"

A great light breaks upon Adolphe -- "Ah-ha" -- he cries and starts to speak a name: but Charley, with a quick gesture of warning, stops the exclamation behind his lips. He is suddenly sober as he warns Adolphe:

TITLE: "You're the only man in the world who knows, Adolphe... Don't ever breathe it around here!"

Adolphe solemnly promises, and as Charley, hurrying to his locker begins his usual evening change, remove his ragged coat, and then steps into the little dressing alcove, cut to ---

Scene 83.

INT. DEAD HOUSE: FULL SHOT:

Much the same atmosphere as before; But the character of the cafe has changed. We have brought the story to contemporary stages. Diamond Mike is still behind the bar, but he looks sadder and thinner. He no longer wields a bungstarter, for there are no bungs to start and no free lunch to protect. The signs on his bar now advertise such drinks as Sarsaparilla and Near Beer. The free lunch counter is gone, and in its place stands a big glass bowl, full of dry pretzels, against which leans a rudely lettered sign placed by some wag, reading "Volstead Free Lunch."

As the shot cuts in, Whitey enters. It is important to note the regular business for Whitey -- constantly in his character of a "blind man", habitually feeling his way with his cane, tapping before him. The tap-tap of the cane is always an indication of his approach. The time-lapse has not made many changes in our heavy. He is the same sinister and aggressive, bunched-up figure we have seen before. There is a touch of gray in his hair, too. And if anything, his snarl and sneer are a little more fixed -- a little more vindictive and envious than ever. He now goes over to the bar, for a word with Mike.

Scene 84.

INT. DEAD HOUSE: CLOSE SHOT ON BAR:

Getting over the changes in Mike and Whitey. Mike opens a bottle of near beer for Whitey, who tastes it, and makes a wry face. He looks at Mike, and the latter nods, as he tells him:

TITLE: "Not much like the old days, Whitey!"

Whitey agrees, with his usual snarl, and tells Mike, with his usual centering on his own troubles:

TITLE: "And a lot of easy money went out with the liquor ... there's a lot more charity in a guy when he has a couple of drinks aboard!"

Mike agrees with this, heartily. And as they go on talking:

Scene 85.

INT. CRIPPLE FACTORY: FULL SHOT:

Charlie is back at his locker -- almost ready for the street, while Adolphe, at his counter, is finishing counting out the change, and Charley's coat is hanging by him.

Scene 86.

INT. CRIPPLE FACTORY: CLOSE SHOT ON ADOLPHE:

Chair with Charley's packages back, as Adolphe counts out bills -- sweeps the pile of coins into his drawer, and with Charley's coat over his arm- the bills in one hand, he picks up the tin cup in the other hand, and starts back to the chair...

Scene 87.

INT. CRIPPLE FACTORY: CLOSE UP ON CHARLEY:

Close shot on Charley, as he is tying his shoe -- suddenly he stops -- pricks up his ears -- listens, with a quick sharp frown ---

Scene 88.

INT. DEAD HOUSE: JUST OUTSIDE DOOR: CLOSE UP ON FLOOR

And on Whitey's cane, as it crosses shot -- tap-tapping its staccato note of warning .... By this time it carries a distinct menace... both to Charley and to our audience.

Scene 89.

INT. CRIPPLE FACTORY: MEDIUM SHOT ON CHAIR:

As Charley, hurriedly pulling on his coat, comes quickly into shot -- tells Adolphe to hurry. Adolphe nods -- he, too has heard Whitey coming -- and straightens up the packages into a symmetrical pile. As he does so, he knocks the little tin cup, which he has placed on one of the packages, down into the piles. This prop should be small and very shallow tin cup, rusty, battered and dented, with little curved handle NOT JOINED AT THE BOTTOM. In other words the handle is merely a crook of tin to fit over the finger-hooked over - so that it might easily be caught and hang onto a piece of twine wrapped around the package. Then, as Adolphe counts out his money to Charley --

Scene 90.

INT. CRIPPLE FACTORY: MEDIUM SHOT ON DOOR TO DEAD HOUSE:

As it opens - Whitey enters, tap-taps his way down into a closeup - and stands there. At this range, we can see that his narrowed, uncovered eye, is taking it all in....

Scene 91.

INT. CRIPPLE FACTORY: CLOSE SHOT ON CHARLEY AND ADOLPHE:

Charlie has all the packages in his arms except the hat-box. Adolphe is about to hand him this, when, with his artistic soul he cannot repress the impulse to pry up the lid a little and peep inside. At sight of the thing he sees, he cannot refrain from an exclamation of French enthusiasm and admiration. But Charley warns him - his fingers at his lips - with a warning glance toward Whitey. Getting over that Charley still believes Whitey blind - and that if he can get out without a sound, Whitey will not know he is there. But Adolphe knows better - and so does the audience. And to impress it, we will go back to --

Scene 92.

INT. CRIPPLE FACTORY: CLOSEUP ON WHITEY:

And a grim and ill-boding smile of satisfaction at his own artistry that still fools one of his very associates.

Scene 93.

INT. CRIPPLE FACTORY: FULL SHOT:

As Adolphe quickly hooks the hat-box over Charley's finger, quickly opens the rear door and half-thrusts Charley out. The instant Charley is out - the door closed behind him, Whitey abandons all pretense of blindness, and crosses swiftly to Adolphe, who has turned busily to his make-up shelf. He asks sharp questions, pointing. Adolphe takes refuge in a pre-tense of entire ignorance, with many shrugs of his shoulders - turns his back on Whitey. The latter throws down his cane angrily - and snarls at Adolphe's uncompromising back, as we FADE OUT ON THEM....

TITLE: FOR MORE THAN A DECADE, MILES FROM THE STREET OF FORGOTTEN MEN, CHARLEY HAS FOUND WHAT "HOME" MEANS....

FADE IN ON **Scene 94.**

EXT. CHARLEY'S COTTAGE: LONG SHOT:

This is the home in which Easy Money Charley and Mrs. McGee have been bringing up Fancy Claire. It is a simple rustic cottage, supposedly located, we will say, somewhere on Long Island. It is an old-fashioned, one-storied bungalow, standing in its lawn little grounds, shrouded with trees and evergreens. Get a place with as much pictorial value as possible. It shows in a shot how well Charley has kept his trust.

As the shot fades in, a car drives up, handled by our lead, Philip Peyton - a handsome boy, about twenty-four years of age. He is the junior partner in his father's law firm. The Peyton estate may be supposed to be in the neighborhood, and we suggest a whole background of established friendship between the boy and the girl at once, as in the long shot, she runs down from the porch and down to the front gate to meet him.

Scene 95.

EXT. CHARLEY'S COTTAGE: CLOSE SHOT ON GATE:

As Fancy Claire enters shot - she is now a lovely young girl of sixteen or seventeen; simple, happy and innocent, but already a woman, with the charm and lure of a woman. She is tastefully dressed in what must be, naturally, one of her very best frocks. Her hands are outstretched, as we introduce her:

TITLE: Fancy Claire...

Philip enters shot, from camera - takes her hands eagerly.

Scene 96.

EXT. CHARLEY'S COTTAGE: CLOSE SHOT ON GATE: REVERSE:

To introduce Philip - getting over his boyish enthusiasm - it is love with Philip, definitely developed; on Fancy's shy and still unconscious. We should get some charming, old-fashioned love: business over the swinging gate, which should be built strong and heavy enough so that it will support both of them as they swing on it. Introduce Philip:

TITLE: PHILIP PEYTON, WHOSE ANCESTRAL GATES ARE JUST TEN MINUTES AWAY - BY HIS ROADSTER.

After the first eager words, Phillip takes from his pocket a small, paper-wrapped parcel and offers it. Fancy is surprised - asks him quickly - "For me?" pantomiming. Philip nods, smiling, as he tells her:

TITLE: "For your birthday."

Fancy, with charming by-play and eagerness, opens it - her lips purse into a round "0-o-o" of delight:

Scene 97.

INSERT CLOSEUP OF OPEN JEWEL BOX, containing a simple, but expensive little bracelet....

Scene 98.

EXT. CHARLEY'S COTTAGE: CLOSE SHOT ON GATE:

Fancy has stepped off the gate to open the box - as she exclaims in delight, Philip has opened it and entered. Now he stands close at her side - her elbows in his hands. Suddenly she has a qualm of doubt and modesty as it occurs to her that she does not know whether she dares to accept such a gift, and she indicates this plainly by pantomime. Philip laughingly reassures her, and as they turn toward the house...

Scene 99.

INT. CHARLEY'S COTTAGE: FULL SHOT:

We find a comfortable, low-ceiled, spacious living room. It has a Victorian quality of heavy old furniture, and the traditional appurtenances of prosperous propriety. At one side is a wide fire-place. Against the wall opposite is a piano with bench. Good pictures are on the wall. At one side is the door into the kitchen and Mrs. McGee's side of the house. At the other side, back, is a door to Fancy's room. Center - back - is a side archway behind which is Charley's own room. (This is suggested merely in order to give depth to the set.) As we open, the center table has been laid for supper - very tastefully, and with the idea of a special event. There is a glitter of silver and cut-glass, and bustling around the table, is the widow McGee, fatter and more cheerful than ever with the years, in spite of her whitening hair as she sets a little bunch of fresh garden flowers at each of three places. Now she hears the voices outside - goes quickly to the wide front window and looks out. At first there is a smile of responsive affection - then she sobers - becomes more thoughtful. The romance she foresees in her simple heart is one between Fancy and Charley himself. And now in view of evidence of a possible affair between Philip and Fancy, she is a little upset. She shakes her head a little - liking Philip, but stalwart in her loyalty to Charley and his interests. Then she quickly gathers up her skirts and goes rapidly to the kitchen door, where, with a look backwards, she vanishes, just as the young couple enter, still deep in their happy conversation. Fancy exclaims delightedly at the flowers on the table, shows it to Philip, demanding his admiration - and getting it. While we still move up to a closer shot on them:

Scene 100.

INT. CHARLEY'S COTTAGE: CLOSE SHOT ON THEM:

Fancy glances at a modest little wrist watch, and exclaims to Philip:

TITLE: "Almost time for Charley... Oh! -- I wish he'd come!"

At her words Philip smiles sympathetically - then he turns thoughtful - starts to speak and hesitates. Finally, with a manifest effort to be casual and unconcerned, he asks Fancy:

TITLE: "I don't think I've ever quite understood just what relation Mr. Vanhern is to you."

His manner is somewhat hesitant -- very respectful toward the girl, and toward the subject of his inquiry. But we can see that her answer is going to mean a great deal to him. Fancy, who has been rearranging one of the bunches of flowers, looks up quickly, as she replies:

TITLE: "None... He's just my guardian... and the dearest man in the world!"

Philip nods as he studies her earnest and lovely face. There is sympathy and response to her enthusiasm in his manner, but there is also a touch of lingering anxiety - because presently we shall have to definitely suggest his natural attitude of jealousy towards Charley. Fancy becomes animated again - and with a laughing word to Philip, runs out of scene toward the piano. Philip, with a tolerant and admiring smile, follows her ---

Scene 101.

INT. CHARLEY'S COTTAGE: CLOSE SHOT:

As Fancy sits down at the piano, and opening a piece of music, begins to play. As Philip comes up behind her - she looks up at him over her shoulder, playing - familiar with the music; her eyes shining - smiling - a picture that would precipitate a declaration from any normal youngster. She turns back to the music, while Philip leans closer - his cheek almost touching her hair as he, too, looks at the piece...

Scene 102.

INSERT CLOSE UP OF TITLE SHEET OF MUSIC - It is --- PETER PAN -- I LOVE YOU!

Scene 103.

INT. CHARLEY'S COTTAGE: CLOSEUP OF THEM:

As Philip suddenly sits down on the bench, Fancy is singing the first line of the chorus as he takes her hands from the keys, and sitting the reverse way on the bench, facing her, holding both bar hands close in his, he tells her earnestly...

TITLE: "And... Fancy Claire... I love YOU! Won't you marry me, dear... have a little home of your own?"

Fancy takes it as such a young girl would - her first proposal, but there is no ingénue simple; only a second's natural thrill and confusion - then she looks him straight in the eyes, and her smile sweet: thinks a second before she speaks - loath to hurt him. Philip waits with bated breath - the die is cast - and then she shakes her head:

TITLE: "No, Philip... I do like you... awfully... but I could never leave Gardy!"

Philip drops his head - his dejection at her decision manifest... Fancy looks at him - real tenderness in her eyes...

Scene 104.

INT. CHARLEY'S COTTAGE: FULL SHOT:

During the above scene, Mrs. McGee has reentered - her business being to complete the setting of the table. Her entrance comes just after Philip's proposal, but the innocence and simplicity of the young girl are not in any way disturbed by the presence of the old lady. We get the childlike sincerity of her nature in the way she is now able to refuse her first proposal, and at the same time include her old nurse in everything she does, because she turns at once to Mrs. McGee - and raising her voice in order to share the situation with her, she asks:

TITLE: We couldn't... could we, Nursey?" Mrs. McGee, although quite abreast of the situation, turns with affected surprise, and Fancy repeats the question:

TITLE: "I say ... we could never leave without our Gardy!"

At which Mrs. McGee, somewhat flustered by the child's utter frankness, gives hasty assent, and hurries back to the kitchen. Fancy turns to Philip - relents a good deal as she sees his painful disappointment. She reaches out and pats his hand - then suddenly jumps up and springs toward the door, just as Charley enters, briskly - happy and smiling, with his arms laden and pockets bulging with the surprises he has brought. At this moment we should get some feeling of the psychological changes which time has wrought in him.

This man, with his strange and semi-criminal background, has known many years of happiness in this little "hide-out". A tender and idyllic love has expanded his soul. And as he enters now, his face is lighted up - his whole bearing conveys the joy of service and affection. He looks like any prosperous and self-respecting head of a household returning after an honest day's work to his happy family. And it is so that he meets Fancy and receives her delighted endearments.

She springs to meet him, and exclaims ecstatically over her gifts, but first she clings about his neck and prints kisses of affection and gratitude on his cheek. He fends her off laughingly, with a touch of self-consciousness, for we must remember that these kisses mean much more to him than they would to a father, and in quite a different way.

Then he turns to Philip and greets him, man-fashion; they exchange a friendly clasp. It is evident that he knows all about Philip, and has frequently seen him there as a visitor. They chat while Fancy starts to open her presents. She naturally begins with the hat. When she opens the box, she finds a dainty and tasteful Easter bonnet. Naturally she greets it with delight, and nothing will do but she must try it on at once before the mantel mirror. It proves highly becoming, but as she turns to Charley, she has a sudden thought. She tells him, with lifted finger:

TITLE: "Before I take it - and before I thank you, you must promise me one thing."

Charley assures her "All right" - before he even knows what it is - smiling. And Fancy tells him:

TITLE: "You must walk out with me on Fifth Avenue next Sunday -- in your very best clothes."

During this scene Fancy has almost forgotten about Philip. He has been really neglected - and is feeling it------

Scene 105.

INT. CHARLEY'S COTTAGE: CLOSE SHOT ON PHILIP:

Getting over this thought very strongly. He has just learned that Charley is not related to Fancy -- he has just been refused, with the information that she would never leave "Gardy". Inevitably he cannot repress a pang of misgiving and poignant doubt as he witnesses the tender scene between Charley and Fancy. So much so that at last he can endure it no longer. We see his emotion and trouble. Now he braces himself - and tells them:

TITLE: "...And I'll meet you at 44th Street about five o' clock, in my car...….may I?" As he waits anxiously for her answer - at least he will get a little attention to this.....

Scene 106.

INT. CHARLEY'S COTTAGE: FULL SHOT AGAIN:

Both Fancy and Charley catch the little break in Philip's voice as he tries to do the conventional thing in the conventional way. Probably they both look at him for an instant, rather startled. With a lover's sensitiveness, Philip has felt him out of it during the preceding scene. But now, from the way in which Fancy turns to him, we can see how deeply and tenderly he occupies her thoughts -- and so does Charley! Fancy exclaims, indicating the third place at the table:

TITLE:

"But I thought you were going to stay!"

Philip carries it off, very politely making his excuse - that he has another engagement - or something of the kind, and in this manner he takes his leave. Fancy sees him to the door, reluctant to see him go -- perhaps more reluctant than she herself realizes. Charley watches them, as Philip bids her "Goodnight" and closes the door after himself. Fancy sees back to her other presents.

Scene 107.

EXT. CHARLEY'S COTTAGE: FRONT WALK AND GATE: CLOSE SHOT:

As Philip, pausing thoughtfully by the gate, looks back at the house. As he faces the camera, in a fairly close shot, we get a distinct flash of impatience and jealousy. Then he goes quickly through the gate - back to his car, standing at the curb, gets in, slamming the door after him, and starts out.

Scene 108.

INT. CHARLEY'S COTTAGE: FULL SHOT:

As Mrs. McGee triumphantly enters from the kitchen, carrying the birthday cake, which is as much a surprise to Charley as to Fancy. And we play here for all the human and affectionate touches we can get among these three people, to show how intimate and how happy has been their life together. After hugging Mrs. McGee gratefully, Fancy shows her her presents, littering the writing table at the side of the room, which are all opened. Then she turns to Charley, and asks, childlike –

<u>TITLE</u>: "Are there any more?"

Charley laughs, and pats the side pockets of his coat, and she rushes at him and begins to go through his pockets: While Mrs. McGee stands by, smiling at them.

Scene 109.

INT. CHARLEY'S COTTAGE: CLOSER SHOT ON THE THREE:

As she pulls out a couple of small packages. Then she "frisks him for a final inspection - and feels something else. With a little cry of delight, she reaches into the pocket - and exclaiming "Oh! There's another!" she reaches into the pocket, and then looks in astonishment at the tin begging cup. It means nothing to Fancy or Mrs. McGee - but to Charley, stunned for a moment by the shock of it, it is the emblem of his sordid secret, held in the hands of the innocent girl whom he loves better than his life - and who believes so in him. Then Fancy laughs out loud, and exclaims to him:

TITLE: "Why, Charley! What's this?... Did you bring this for me, too?"

Confused and ashamed, Charley almost snatches it away from her. To him it is a profanation even to see her touch the wretched object. He tells her, almost angrily:

TITLE: "It's nothing... just a cup I picked up at a drinking fountain somewhere - and forgot!"

He manages at last to conjure a grim smile, and she laughs at him for being an "absent minded old dear". But Charley loses no time in getting rid of the cup. He drops it in the waste-basket by the side table, already seven-eighths full of the papers from Fancy's presents. And at this juncture Mrs. McGee insists that they sit down. They move out of this close shot to the table - just tipped in. Mrs. McGee, in her cap and apron - starts back toward the kitchen.

Scene 110.

INT. CHARLEY'S COTTAGE: CLOSE SHOT ON TABLE.

As Charley seats Fancy: in front of her cake - then takes the place opposite. Our action now is Fancy's blowing out of the burning candles on her cake. As she talks and laughs - she stops - takes long breath. Charley, watching her mirrors in his face his adoration of her and his grimly suppressed emotion. Fancy blows with all her might - she puts out sixteen of the candles – but one still burns. This affords a dramatic hint of trouble to come. The child is really dismayed. With genuine apprehension in her eyes, she looks up at Charley, and exclaims:

TITLE: "Oh, Gardy... I missed one! That means bad luck... some trouble is hanging over me!"

Mrs. McGee has returned, with a tray bearing the soup plates: Irish - and Superstitious, as Fancy looks up at her for confirmation, the old lady's race shows her own doubt and disappointment. Charley looks at them both, and then himself completes our little allegory. Smilingly, casually, he reaches out, and with his fingers nips the little flame. And tells her:

TITLE: "You leave all your troubles to me... I'll take care of them! Just like that!"

And then, after a second's pause, he adds with a great pretense of sternness:

TITLE: "And now you, just sit there and eat your birthday supper."

The moment of suggested tension passes like a summer cloud. Fancy smiles, and then laughs, and as they begin to eat the soup which Mrs. McGee has served, and the old lady bustles back and forth, waiting on them, we FADE OUT.....

FADE IN QUICKLY ON: **Scene 111.**

INT. CHARLEY'S COTTAGE: FULL SHOT: NIGHT:

It is later in the evening, as is suggested by the fact that Charley is in his smoking jacket and slippers - the table in the center of the room is cleared and arranged for the evening, with centerpiece and bowl of flowers. Fancy is sitting on the arm of Charley's chair, fussing with his hair - twisting it into funny curls, and Charley is accepting her attentions smilingly.

Scene 112.

INT. CHARLEY'S COTTAGE: CLOSE SHOT ON THEM:

As Fancy straightens Charley's hair back again - she stifles a yawn - and Charley catches her at it, and tells her, laughing at her:

TITLE: "Go to bed - you sleepy head!"

Fancy laughs and assents - she kisses him affectionately, and gets up - suddenly remembers something. She steps back to the mantel and takes from it the box which Philip gave to her. Rather hesitantly she shows it to Charley, as she explains whence it came -- asking dutifully if he thinks it proper for her to accept it. Charley opens the box and looks at the bracelet - recognizes the value of it. He has become very grave again. We see he recognizes the significance of this boy and girl affair. But finally, he tells her, in pantomime, if possible, that he sees no reason why she should not accept the gift if she wishes to. Fancy, greatly relieved, thanks him - takes it back; and lingeringly closes the box. Then she kisses him again - and flits out toward her own room. Charley, left alone, does not have to conceal his sadness and his troubled soul is revealed to us in his expression. His eyes are fixed on the floor, just out of shot, and suddenly there is the most delicate transition - a shadow of loathing and repugnance darkens his sad expression - as he sees:

Scene 113.

INT. CHARLEY'S COTTAGE: CLOSEUP ON WASTE-BASKET:

And the tin cup, lying on top of the papers: Hold long enough, to register its significance.

Scene 114.

INT. CHARLEY'S COTTAGE: CLOSE SHOT ON CHARLEY:

As with a gesture of shame and anger - he reaches out with his foot and thrusts the basket away from his sight - turns his head away. He gets up and exits the close shot into --

Scene 115.

INT. CHARLEY'S COTTAGE: MEDIUM SHOT ON DESK TABLE:

As Charley sits down and opens the center drawer -- takes out three worn bankbooks -- looks at them!

Scene 116.

INSERT CLOSEUP ON THREE BANKBOOKS: One is marked HOME SAVINGS BANK -- A SECOND NATIONAL BANK - and the third SECURITY TRUST COMPANY.

Each of them, on the cover, under the name of the bank, carries his name and address: "Charles Vanhern, 123 Lavender Road."

Scene 117.

INT. CHARLEY'S COTTAGE: FULL SHOT:

Charley inspecting the entries in the bankbooks, broodingly, as Mrs. McGee enters from the kitchen, minus her cap and apron, and patting down her dress -- giving the impression that her work is over for the night. As she starts to fuss around with the center table -- fixing the flowers, and so on, Charley's eyes fall on her -- he calls her over to him, and begins to question her.

Scene 118.

INT. CHARLEY'S COTTAGE: CLOSE SHOT ON THEM:

Charley asks her:

TITLE: "What do you know about this young fellow Peyton? He's been here a good deal lately, hasn't he?"

Mrs. McGee nods. Charley goes on:

TITLE: "He's been seeing a good deal of Fancy, hasn't he?"

Again Mrs. McGee nods assent. From her manner Charley sees she knows more than she is telling. He leans forward toward her in commanding, yet friendly manner -- the manner of a man who is accustomed to run things in his own house, and to expect an answer when he wants it. After a second's keen scrutiny of Mrs. McGee, be asks her, almost sharply:

TITLE: "Well -- what about it? How far has this affair gone?"

The good Widow McGee, flustered but loyal - finds the time ripe to tell what she knows. She begins confidentially, and in the manner of the privileged servant. Pointing to the piano bench, she tells Charley:

TITLE: "True as you're sittin' there... Master Philip proposed to her this very same evenin'!"

She pauses for a second, to give point to her next statement:

TITLE: "And -- shure …. She rayfus-ed him!"

She gets this over as a piece of good news. But Charley sits, tense and troubled. He asks her, puzzled a bit, for he is sure Fancy cares for Philip: "Are you sure?" Mrs. McGee nods impressively: tells him: "I heard it wid me own ears, sor!" Charley demands insistently -- almost to himself:

TITLE: "But why did she refuse him, I wonder?"

Mrs. McGee looks down at him - and dramatizes herself a bit as she puts both arms akimbo, her lips compressed. We may suppose that the coming revelation is one which her loyal soul has long suspected, and which she has been yearning to tell Charley -- and now he has practically told her to do so:

TITLE: "I'll tell you why, sor… It's because she said she'd never leave you!"

Charley stares up at her, transfixed:

TITLE: "It's because she thinks she loves you -- and she does…. the dear innocent child!"

The words are like a knife to Charley's heart. Mrs. McGee, Irish to the core -- loving romance and a part in it, goes on in a flood of words! "Sure -- love is all alike to her", she tells him. What does she know of it yet….. She thinks there is no other man in this world but only yourself, sor!" Charley starts up with outstretched and trembling hand, as if to stop her -- as if to shut out the suggestion these words bring to his mind. Mrs. McGee goes on, wheedlingly:

TITLE: "Ah! …. but you must have seen that yerself, sor….. you must have guessed -- - as I did - long ago!"

To this revelation Charley reacts with the utmost emotion. He springs to his feet: exclaims -- "No -- no" You must be wrong -- she couldn't think of me that way!" Mrs. McGee becomes a little indignant. There is something militant almost, in her defense of him against himself, as she tells him quickly:

TITLE: "There's no one could make her happier than yerself, sor"

But Charley turns on her fiercely: He tells her:

TITLE: "This Peyton boy is good, clean... he's honest.... he's worthy! Who am I that I should stand in the way of him!"

But Mrs. McGee doesn't get him -- and she doesn't like his self-depreciation. She tells him:

TITLE: "She love you, too, sor... It's sure I am that as long as you are near Fancy she'll niver think twice of any other man!"

Charley gets this, as we go to ---

Scene 119.

INT. CHARLEY'S COTTAGE: CLOSEUP ON HIM:

His soul is on the rack -- he is torn; tempted. Actually there is no obvious bar to his doing exactly what Mrs. McGee suggests. He has come to love Fancy as a lover. He knows that she could easily so love him. Should he take this great boon -- should he regard it as his rightful reward? But now -- as he stands propped up by the table, his eyes once more on the floor -- he sees again!

Scene 120.

INSERT CLOSEUP ONCE MORE OF BASKET --

Shooting down on it this time -- and the tin cup, with all its ugly significance.

Scene 121.

INT. CHARLEY'S COTTAGE: CLOSEUP ON HIM:

As he stares at the emblem of his shame. He realizes in a vivid flash of understanding that for him -- a common street beggar, to pluck that flower of innocence and purity, would be a dastardly and hideous act. Bracing himself against the table, he cries out, from a breaking heart:

TITLE: "Then -- By God -- I must not be near her any longer!"

Scene 122.

INT. CHARLEY'S COTTAGE: CLOSEUP ON MRS. McGEE:

She is staring at him -- open mouthed -- sure he is crazy; she does not understand, nor realize what underlies his terrific emotion:

Scene 123.

INT. CHARLEY'S COTTAGE: MEDIUM SHOT:

As Charley relaxes a little -- he tells her:

TITLE: "Leave me alone now... I must think this out by myself!"

Charley waves the old lady away with a gesture so stern and so tragic that she backs away from him in awed obedience - and as Charley's chin falls on his breast,

FADE OUT ON HIM.

TITLE: EASTER SUNDAY .... ON FIFTH AVENUE.

FADE IN ON

Scene 124,
Scene 124-A-B-C, ad lib

EXT. FIFTH AVENUE: THE FASHION PARADE:

Fading in on the first long shot, and using actual shots, ad lib, of the Fashion Parade.

Scene 125.

EXT. FIFTH AVENUE: SIDEWALK:

A traveling shot -- trucking the camera ahead of Charley and Fancy, as they walk down the Avenue. She has her new clothes and her wonderful new Easter bonnet, and is in the seventh heaven of delight as she walks beside her beloved Charley, her hand in the crook of his elbow. While Charley has done himself proud -- and is dressed in the most precise fashionable attire -- perfectly tailored--- light trousers, cutaway coat; patent leathers, cane, gloves and silk hat. He looks like any member of the "400", with Fancy tripping golightedly beside him, full of innocent animation and happiness, to which Charley responds. Suddenly Fancy stops -- checking Charley with her hand -- he looks at her quickly, to find her looking out of scene, her face suddenly full of tragic pity. She points out of scene and tells Charley, tremulously.....

TITLE: "Oh, Charley -- see that poor man! .... how' pitiful!"

Charley looks -- and his face hardens into a stone mask, as he sees:

Scene 126.

EXT. FIFTH AVENUE CORNER: CLOSE SHOT ON WHITEY:

With his patch over his eye -- his other eye turned up until only the White Shows -- leaning against the wall in a position of helpless dejection, wearing a battered sign slung around his neck -- "I AM BLIND"; his cup offered for the charity of the passerby.

Scene 127.

EXT. FIFTH AVENUE: SIDEWALK: CLOSE SHOT CHARLEY AND FANCY:

Charley has gotten an ugly shock. His first impulse is to lead the girl away from this reminder of his own evil profession -- away from a danger which he has always half-suspected. But the girl is looking at his set expression with surprise: Now she exclaims:

TITLE: "Do give him something, Charley!"

So Charley has no choice. It is a highly ironic and dramatic situation. He has to stop, fumble in his pocket and find a coin. He finds a coin -- and without a glance at

Fancy, steps out of the scene: Fancy looks after him ----

Scene 128.

INT. FIFTH AVENUE CORNER: CLOSE SHOT ON WHITEY:

As Charley steps into the scene and drops the coin in the cup. As he does so, he looks down, instinctively searching the face of the beggar with keen hostility -- to see if the other has any intimation of the situation. But Whitey's face is absolutely blank -- his one eye turned up sightlessly in his head. At the clink of the coin he whines his usual formula of thanks. Relieved, Charley turns quickly to rejoin Fancy.

Scene 129.

EXT. FIFTH AVENUE: SIDEWALK:

As he rejoins Fancy and she again takes his arm -- they start out...

Scene 130.

EXT. FIFTH AVENUE: CORNER: CLOSEUP ON WHITEY:

As Whitey's one eye is in use -- narrowed -- he looks after Charley, in a malignant rage. He has recognized Charley, and suspected the girl. All his venom is aroused by the episode -- he curses at them between his teeth, as he watches.

Scene 131.

EXT. FIFTH AVENUE AND CROSS STREET: MEDIUM LONG SHOT:

Showing Philip waiting in his car, as Fancy and Charley enter scene from camera. Fancy spies the car at about the same second that Philip sees her. And Fancy half pulls Charley across the street -- and to the car.....

Scene 132.

EXT. FIFTH AVENUE AND CROSS STREET: CLOSE SHOT ON CAR:

As Philip greets Fancy effusively, and Charley with some restraint. He opens the door for them, and Charley puts Fancy in beside Philip. At the latter's invitation to join them, Charley shakes his head -- turns to Fancy and tells her:

TITLE: "My outing is over... I must go to the office and work."

Fancy is frankly disappointed - "You mean you have to work today -- on Easter Sunday?" she exclaims. Charley nods -- tells her to have a good time. Naturally Philip is not displeased at this. He wastes no time in arguing with Charley, but telling him goodbye, he starts the car away. Then Charley starts down the side-street.

Scene 133.

EXT. FIFTH AVENUE CORNER: CLOSE SHOT ON WHITEY:

Watching all this. A casual passerby stops --- drops two copper cents into the cup while Whitey is busy watching -- At the clink of the coins, Whitey glances down into the cup -- sees the coppers -- then looks up at his benefactor with a glare and a curse which takes him completely out of character and sends the unfortunate charitable person reeling back in amazement and anger, as Whitey, with all pretense of blindness thrown aside, swiftly leaves his place and follows Charley in the manner of a pursuer, and we FADE OUT ON the charitable person staring after him, speechless with anger.

FADE OUT ....

FADE IN ON

Scene 134.

INT. THE CRIPPLE FACTORY: FULL SHOT:

Charley is almost finished with changing into his beggar outfit. Adolphe, with a little faceline brush in one hand - a pigment pot in the other is waiting for him by the little curtained alcove. Charley's arm is already strapped to his side-- his good clothes are all in the locker except the coat which is banging carelessly over the opened door of his locker. As Charley and Adolphe step inside the little alcove;

Scene 135.

INT. CRIPPLE FACTORY: CLOSE SHOT ON ALCOVE:

As Adolphe steps close to Charley and begins to deepen one of the artificial lines on his face with the point of the brush --

Scene 136.

INT. CRIPPLE FACTORY: FULL SHOT:

The door opens -- Whitey comes in -- his manner furtive; manifestly taking every precaution against being heard. He comes down -- listens to the sound of voices from the alcove: He is standing close by Charley's locker.

Scene 137.

INT. CRIPPLE FACTORY: CLOSE SHOT INTO ALCOVE:

As Adolphe finishes, and surveys his work with the satisfaction of the true artist. He is chattering to Charley-- and now says:

TITLE: "It's a shame -- how hard you work yourself? Why don't you take some rest from business-- sometime?"

Charley answers him grimly ----

TITLE: "Business ain't what it used to be .... and besides, I gotta make all the money I can!"

Adolphe has a flash of comprehension -- he nods --

TITLE: "You mean for her... for the keed!"

Charley checks him with a quick gesture of warning -- that is something never to be talked about. But Adolphe is in a moment of uplift and Gallic emotion, as he tells Charley:

TITLE: "T'ink of it ... that little keed you take care of all dese years .... Portland Fancy's ... little... keed!"

Charley repeats his gesture of warning -- and this time shuts off Adolphe's flow of talk. Adolphe now turns Charley's head under the light -- inspects the make-up minutely.....

Scene 138.

INT. CRIPPLE FACTORY: CLOSE SHOT ON WHITEY:

He has a flash of a brilliant idea as he notes the coat. Hurriedly he frisks it- and in an inside pocket he finds the three bankbooks, bound together with an elastic. He scans ---

Scene 139.

INSERT CLOSEUP ON BANKBOOKS -- with the name on the top one.

Scene 140.

INT. CRIPPLE FACTORY: CLOSEUP ON WHITEY:

As he notes the name - and address -- and grins evilly. Then he opens the books -- as he sees the entries in the deposits columns, his face snarls back into envy and hatred. Suddenly he glances out of scene - hastily snaps the rubber band around the books -- is busy fumbling them as we cut to ---

Scene 141.

INT. CRIPPLE FACTOHY: CLOSE SHOT ON ARCH TO ALCOVE:

Charley is standing there, watching. We do not know how much he has seen -- but we do know that he has discovered at last that Whitey can see! His eyes are narrowed -- his face twisted with suspicion -- hate -- loathing of this crawling thing he is watching.... With slow and cat-like tread he starts out of scene. Over his shoulder Adolphe, his face scared, has been staring -- now he, too emerges, frightened at the denouement....

Scene 142.

INT. CRIPPLE FACTORY: FULL SHOT:

Whitey has managed to fumble the books back into the pocket, and now, frightened, and defiant, he scuttles away across the floor, tapping busily with his stick, and trying in vain to re-establish his character as a blind man. Charley

Scene 143

implacable as fate, moves slowly after him. As Whitey reaches the wall, he props himself up against it, and turns at bay......

Scene 144.

INT. CRIPPLE FACTORY: CLOSE SHOT ON WHITEY:

As he calls out, quaveringly:

TITLE: "That you, Charley? .... I thought I heard you in there?"

The next second Charley cones into scene-- Whitey, always an artist- still trying to carry out his deception, fumbles down for the chair, finds it, and lowers himself into it with his usual business of helplessness and apparent pathos. Meanwhile he keeps on talking, while Charley stands looking down at him contemptuously:

TITLE: "A fine day on the Avenue.. they tell me... I didn't do so good, though!"

Charley looks down -- Whitey stops talking. There is something in Charley's grim silence that makes him squirm. Then Charley speaks, with a rasp in his voice.....

TITLE: "Right you are, Whitey.... you've had a very bad day!"

And now Charley grabs him. Remember that Charley throughout this and subsequent action, has only one hand. The other is under his coat, strapped, and the fake arm in the sleeve. As he grabs Whitey by the throat, he leans down, and grates:

TITLE: "You liar... you dog!"

Whitey, finally aware that his secret is discovered, suddenly leaps up, tears himself loose, at the same time grabbing the chair and spinning it in front of him as a defense. Charley follows him right up -- Whitey half raises the chair. Charlie tells him:

TITLE: "You snake... you saw me on the Avenue today!!"

Whitey's lips draw back over his teeth like a dog at bay, in a snarl. All his hatred and malignance surge up in him. He does not step back as he snarls at Charley:

TITLE: "Yes! I saw you! You and that girl you bem keepin' all these years! Portland Fancy's kid!"

Charley is tense- poised to spring- but Whitey, bigger-- alert-- knowing that one of Charley's arms is strapped down; he is half helpless, snarls and sneers- goes on!

TITLE: "A great little scheme:... Well - I don't blame you -- I like 'em young myself"

At this Charley takes him. Whitey makes an effort to use the chair, but it is wrested from him and hurled into a corner and the fight is on ---

Scene 145.

INT. CRIPLE FACTORY: FULL SHOT:

The fight- ad lib. Charley is simply intent on crushing and obliterating his enemy. Whitey is fighting furiously - a cornered rat. Meanwhile Adolphe is jumping around with wild Gallic excitability. Finally, as the fight rages, he runs out of the back door. The fighters go to the floor.

Scene 146.

INT. CRIPLE FACTORY: CLOSE SHOT ON FIGHT:

On the floor.... Charley finally has Whitey between his legs-- and with his one hand, has him by the throat. Suddenly Whitey throws up both hands, as in an ecstasy of terror - and puts them across his eyes, with an abject cry, as Charley, letting go his throat, pulls back his clenched fist to drive it home:

TITLE: "My God --- don't hit me... my eyes! My eyes!

Charley halts the blow -- looks at him keenly suspecting another trick -- Finally Whitey takes his hands from his eyes. With his one uncovered eye he blinks up -- and gives a great cry of relief:

TITLE: "Thank God! For a minute I thought I'd gone blind like the doctors said I would some day.... but I can see! ...... I can see!"

Charley is looking down at him -- he has desisted with his innate decency-- also with more or less contempt for the other's abject quitting -- he now starts to climb up...

Scene 147.

INT. CRIPPLE FACTORY: FULL SHOT

As Officer Quinn arrives, via the back door, with the terrified Adolphe, and going over, he jerks Charley to his feet, and helps Whitey to his. Then he stands between them, looking from one to the other with quizzical humor. Whitey continues to whine and rub his eyes--blinks them, as Officer Quinn explodes with--

TITLE: "A blind man fightin' a cripple! That takes the cake!"

At which Adolphe, dancing almost in his excitement, and now animated by keen partisanship for Charlie, pointing accusingly at Whitey, screams:

TITLE: "He ain't blind... he ain't blind at all!"

To which Whitey, now partly recovered from his panic, and with a resumption of his snarl, indicates Charlie, and retorts----

TITLE: "No more than he's a cripple!" The situation strikes Quinn as the height of sardonic and ironic humor - which it is. He grins, then turns sternly on both adversaries, and delivers the moral lesson:

TITLE: "Thin more shame to yez both... ye're a pair of fakes…yez oughta stick together and be friends!"

Back, as he surveys them both sternly -- then takes the part of aggressive peacemaker, as he commands:

TITLE: "Come on, now…let's see yez shake hands - or I'll run yez both int!"

There is no resisting the power of the law. The two men sidle toward each other and touch hands. Quinn nods with satisfaction - then with his club, he pushes Whitey back toward the swinging door, through it and out. Before departing, however, he turns and looks Charlie over with an ironic and philosophic eye.

Scene 148.

INT. CRIPPLE FACTORY: CLOSEUP ON QUINN

By the door, getting over the contempt behind his slowly delivered and impressive thrust straight to the shrinking and guilty soul of Easy Money Charley.

TITLE: "A fine sort of a game for a man like you…..You got brains, and ye've got yer health!"

He gets this off and it goes into Charley like a barb…..

Scene 149.

INT. CRIPPLE FACTORY: CLOSE SHOT ON CHARLEY:

Adolphe tipped in - watches Charley, who fairly quails before Quinn's contempt and words……he averts his head.

Scene 150.

INT. CRIPPLE FACTORY: CLOSEUP ON QUINN AGAIN:

He is not through - he delivers himself of this:

<u>TITLE</u>: "Ye sh'd take shame to yerself... wid yer fakin' and cheatin'!... Have ye no manhood left in ye?"

And with a final scathing and lancinating look of contempt, he turns on his heel and follows Whitey through the door.

Scene 151.

INT. CRIPPLE FACTORY: CLOSE SHOT ON CHARLEY AND ADOLPHE:

This is a whale of a scene for Charley. It is the end of his leeching career. We see the reaction upon Charley. With all the emotional impacts he has had to stand in the last few weeks, he is now left a hateful and loathsome spectacle in his own sight.... his tortured eyes finally come up slowly--then distend with an almost inhuman hate as he sees---

Scene 152.

INT. CRIPPLE FACTORY; MEDIUM SHOT ON MIRROR:

A full-length mirror against the wall by Adolphe's shelf, reflecting Charlie and Adolphe---

Scene 153.

INT. CRIPPLE FACTORY: MEDIUM SHOT CHARLEY AND ADOLPHE

From another angle, Charley and Adolphe in f.g. as Charley's face twists hideously with hate and loathing. He breaks, and in a paroxysm of almost insane rage, he picks up a chair as though it were a feather, and with superhuman strength flings it through the mirror. And as Adolphe shrinks back in renewed terror, Charley, with a frantic gesture, tears at the sleeve and the hateful artificial arm, and screams at the terrorized Adolphe:

TITLE: "Take it off, damn it!... Do you hear me...take it off, I tell you!"

Adolphe, frightened out of his wits, comes timidly to him - starts to help the now thoroughly frantic Charley, who screams at him, over and over again.

TITLE: "I'm through, by God... D'ye hear! I'm through with this damned trade!"

And as Adolphe, bewildered and frightened, tries to help him as he struggles to rid himself of the loathsome garments of his abandoned profession, FADE OUT ON THEM.

TITLE: THE FOLLOWING DAY PHILIP PEYTON HAS AN UNEXPECTED CALLER....AT HIS OFFICE.............

FADE IN ON

Scene 154.

INT. PHILIP'S OFFICE: FULL SHOT:

As the shot fades in a clerk is just telling Philip who is calling on him, and Philip registers strongly his amazement, as he tells the clerk to show him all, by all means. He rises to his feet, as the clerk beckons to someone outside, and Charley enters. Charley is somewhat awkward and self-conscious--perhaps also with a little touch of defiance in Philip's presence, with all of its significance to him. Philip welcomes him with the utmost respect and warmth. As Charley approaches the desk, his only defense is his acquired hard-boiled exterior--one with which Philip is as yet unfamiliar. To Philip's natural question, he tells him curtly that he has come to see him on business. Somewhat taken aback, Philip motions him to chair, and as he sits down-----

Scene 155.

INT. PHILIP'S OFFICE: CLOSE SHOT ON THEM:

As Philip waits politely for Charley to begin. The tempo here is slow. Charley is gathering himself together for the biggest thing he has ever done... He seems to pull himself together - leans forward - and begins his story with:

TITLE: "To begin – I've got to go back thirteen years-------

And then, as he goes on talking, FADE OUT SLOWLY ON THEM.....Philip, as this shot fades out, is listening merely with polite interest and some curiosity. FADE OUT.

FADE SLOWLY IN ON

Scene 156.

INT. PHILIP'S OFFICE: CLOSE SHOT ON THEM:

The same shot - but with a marked difference in their attitudes. Philip is now leaning forward, his eyes riveted to Charley, his expression full of amazement, almost incredulity. There is no need for slopping over here. Charley is finishing in his deliberate, hard-boiled manner - just as he started. And now he concludes, with a gesture which plainly says - "And that's the story!" Philip continues to look at him, and now his face shows conviction - and more than a trace of pity. He sits back a little - then asks Charley point-blank:

TITLE: "Why have you told me this?" Charley regards him man-fashion - face to face. And replies in turn with a question:

TITLE: "You love her?"

Charley pauses. Philip answers in the same key - "Yes!" Charley leans forward a little, regards the boy with fierce intentness, as he asks:

TITLE: "It does not make any difference that she is the child of Portland Fancy - the unfortunate woman who turned to me for help so many years ago."

Philip meets the test. He compresses his lips, and doggedly and definitely shakes his head. Then Charley gets up and puts his final question:

TITLE: "And it will never make any difference to you who her parents were?"

And again Philip is there. He indicates that so big is his love for Fancy that nothing else in the world matters. Charley at last is satisfied. He looks at the younger man for a moment with tribute, approval, and envy in his eyes. The boy has registered 100% with him. And actually, in his soul, it is in this moment that he hands over the girl he loves to the keeping of the man who has qualified to be her husband and to give her happiness. Then he tells Philip:

TITLE: "I'm making you my executor -- and her guardian."

And while Philip stares at him in amazement, he takes from his pocket the three handbooks - a bundle of bonds - and some other papers, including the old paper given him by Portland Fancy. Philip starts to ask him -- "You mean---" Charley interrupts with:

TITLE: "I mean nothing beyond that... I'm going on a long trip... a very long trip, and I'm asking you, as a lawyer, to take charge of my affairs until I come back!"

Philip stares at him - then comes back with a perfectly natural question:

TITLE: "But why... why is it necessary for you to do this?"

Charley regards him in silence for a moment. Then he decides. For the first time in his life, he is going to reveal his real secret to a living soul. Then he asks or makes a statement that is apparently irrelevant:

TITLE: "You lunch every day at the University Club."

Philip, puzzled, nods. Charley tells him - "Watch." And, picking up a little ash-receiver from the desk, he exits shot, leaving Philip staring after him.

Scene 157.

INT. PHILIP'S OFFICE: CLOSESUP ON WALL:

Charley enters, and turning, backs up against the wall, as we first discovered him backed up against the entrance to the club on Fifth Avenue. With a jerk, he pulls his arm out of one coat-sleeve, and pulls the coat around, with the empty sleeve. Then he crouches suddenly into his accustomed begging position, crouched together - holding out the ash-receiver as he is accustomed to hold the little tin cup. He looks up, and in the same expression - the whine and intonation with which he used to beg - he asks Philip!

TITLE: "Have you never seen me before?" He holds the pose - looking up at Philip.

Scene 158.

INT. PHILIP'S OFFICE: CLOSE SHOT ON HIM:

Staring out of scene at Charley with a startled gaze, in which incredulity is being relieved by recognition. Suddenly he gets it. He starts up from his chair with pointed finger -- and cries out--

TITLE: "The beggar... at the club door... 'Easy Money Charley'!"

Charley enters the scene, straightening his coat - he replaces the ashtray on the desk, smiles and nods. And tells Philip:

TITLE: "Right.... Everybody knows Easy Money Charley!"

And then, while realization and understanding dawn upon Philip, Charley stands regarding him with a recovery of ironic poise. He tells Philip- "That's why!" And with a curt goodbye - exits scene toward the door. Charley, still half dazed, looks after him - then with a cry, springs after him.

Scene 159.

INT. PHILIP'S OFFICE: CLOSE SHOT ON DOOR:

As Philip's cry halts Charley, with his hand on the knob. He turns back, as Philip hurries into the scene. The younger man looks Charley in the eye. The appreciation of the unprecedented love and sacrifice of this street beggar has come home to him. Finally impulsively, he thrusts out his hand, man-fashion, in a way to offer his admiration and his heartfelt tribute. Charley looks at the youngster - down at his proffered hand - starts to take it, then pulls back his hand, and shakes his head. He tells Philip, in his own hard-boiled manner:

TITLE: "No... You wouldn't want to remember....

He breaks off without finishing, abruptly, and shoulders through the door, closing it behind him. Philip stands for a second, unmindful of his hand, still outstretched. Then as he drops it, staring after Charley helplessly, FADE OUT ON HIM.

TITLE: DEPARTURE

FADE IN ON **Scene 160.**

INT. CHARLEY'S COTTAGE: FULL SHOT:

Opening in the midst of his preparations for departure. A trunk is being carried out by two men - Mrs. McGee holding open the door, while two big bags stand, all packed, and handbag on a chair, still open. Fancy is sitting on the arm of the chair, obviously has been putting in the last little things, but now she is dabbing at her eyes with a handkerchief - and crying quietly to herself. We may assume that he has already announced to the bewildered household, Mrs. McGee and Fancy, that he has been called a way on business, - abroad.

At this juncture Charley himself enters from his own room, through the arch, carrying his hat and stick, overcoat on his arm. He is doing his best to appear business-like and off-hand, as if this were the most ordinary event. He comes down - and asks briskly: "Is everything ready... I'll have to hurry." Then he notices Fancy, and goes over to her.

Scene 161.

INT. CHARLEY'S COTTAGE: CLOSE SHOT ON THEM:

Fancy's eyes are swollen with weeping, and she dabs at them, with her handkerchief, as she looks up, in her dismay, and tells him - half-choking.

TITLE: "Gardy - I think this is too cruel of you!... to go away like this and leave us - on scarcely a day's notice!"

As Charley looks down at her, he has to hold himself strongly, tightly, in check. But he managed with an effort to appear smiling and casual. He tells her plausibly:

<u>TITLE</u>: I couldn't help it, my dear... it was very sudden, and I had just time to catch the steamer."

Fancy reaches up her arm to him, and Charley leans over; she clings to him, and with her face to the camera, she lets herself go into unrestrained sobbing!

Scene 162.

INT. CHARLEY'S COTTAGE: CLOSEUP ON HIM:

Reverse shot; as with Fancy's face buried in his shoulder - and his own away from Mrs. McGee, we get a big study of him. Remember, this man about to part voluntarily with the great love of his life, with the one thing he desires. And he has to do it with a smile - off-hand - easily, so that there will be no suspicion of the permanency of his departure. So that this shot is the loophole through which we can portray the agony of soul through which he is passing. It is the face of a man who is committing soul-suicide - the face of a man with a breaking heart. And he permits himself this second of letting go, as he feels against his shoulder the face he wants to stay and live to kiss - feels the shaken body, racked with sobs, of the women he loves better than life itself.

Then, suddenly, he realizes this can't go on - with iron will he straightens the grief-distorted features - manages a smile, which at first is ghastly. Then his will power softens it to a more natural mien. Then, and only then, he gently begins to release himself.

INT. CHARLEY'S COTTAGE: MEDIUM SHOT:

As Charley tenderly releases Fancy's clinging arms from about his neck. He looks into her loving eyes for a last instant, and draws her to him in one last, lingering embrace. Then, with a final effort, he pulls himself back pulls himself back into his part, and tells her, almost choking:

<u>TITLE</u>: "It's all right!... The cab is waiting... I must go! Don't cry!"

The strain is becoming more than he can bear. He starts out blindly - and Fancy follows him. Mrs. McGee, flustered and bustling, runs across, snaps the open bag closed - and run after him. At the door a man takes the two suit-cases, and Mrs. McGee forces the hand-bag into his hand. Just once more he turns back to Fancy - there is a last short, clinging embrace - then he turns, and almost dashes out.

Scene 164.

EXT. CHARLEY'S COTTAGE: WALK AND GATE:

The taxicab waiting, as Charley almost runs out and down the path to the cab - as he start to get in.

Scene 165.

INT. CHARLEY'S COTTAGE: MEDIUM SHOT AT DOOR:

Fancy starts to run out, sobbing. But Mrs. McGee closes it and bars her way - telling her---

TITLE: "Don't make it any harder for him, dearie…. Shure --- he sufferin' enough!"

Fancy gets the force of this, and nods pitifully that she wants to be brave, but the impulse is too strong for her - she runs to the window - throws it up, and sobbing, waves out…

Scene 166.

EXT. CHARLEY'S COTTAGE: CLOSE SHOT ON TAXI:

Charley, looking out of the window - still forces his smile - and waves back, as the cab starts out of shot:

Scene 167.

INT. TAXICAB: CLOSEUP ON CHARLEY:

As he waves - then leans back in the cab - and here, in the privacy of the taxi, we see the lonely and desolate man half-collapse. He seems to fairly wilt and shrink, as he buries his grief racked face in his hands - and we FADE OUT ON HIM.

TITLE: SOME FOUR MONTHS LATER PHILIP PEYTON RECEIVED A SHOCK... BUT ONE FOR WHICH HE WAS MORE THAN HALF PREPARED..........

Scene 168.

INT. PHILIP'S OFFICE: CLOSE SHOT ON HIM:

He is reading a letter, and his face betrays its serious import, even before we see it:

Scene 169.

INSERT CLOSEUP ON LETTER - on letterhead of a steamship company - THE AUSTRALIASIA STEAMSHIP COMPANY, dated from Sidney, Australia, and reading:

Mr. Philip Peyton,
60 Wall Street,
New York, N.Y.

Dear Sir:

This is to inform you that a passenger on my vessel, the "MELBOURNE", of this line, Mr. Charles Vanhern, was swept overboard during a storm on the 15th inst., in the Australian Bight. On examining the effects of the said Charles Vanhern, the enclosed was found addressed to you. Am forwarding the baggage of this passenger, whose loss was regrettable but apparently unavoidable. The body has not been recovered.

I remain, your obdt. servant.
Capt. E.R. SMITH.

Scene 170.

INT. PHILIP'S OFFICE: CLOSE SHOT ON HIM:

As he lays down this letter, and from the envelope before him he takes another - addressed to him. This he tears open, and we see another letter, this time in the handwriting of Charley himself.

Scene 171.

INSERT CLOSEUP OF CHARLEY'S LETTER:

Mr. Philip Peyton, Esq.,
60 Wall Street,
New York, N. Y.

Dear Sir:
In the event of my death, I hereby appoint you sole executor of my estate. I devise and bequeath all my property, without reservation, to my ward, Miss Fancy Claire.
CHARLES VANHERN.

Scene 172.

INT. PHILIP'S OFFICE: CLOSE SHOT ON HIM:

He lays this down on the other letter, and then takes from the envelope the third enclosure - a newspaper clipping:

INSERT CLOSEUP OF NEWSPAPER CLIPPING:

MARITIME NEWS.

The Australiasian Line steamer, the Melbourne, Capt. E. R. Smith, arrived in port yesterday, from New York. Capt. Smith reported the disappearance of a passenger, Mr. Charles Vanhern of New York, three days ago. Mr. Vanhern disappeared and was supposedly washed overboard during severe storm. Owing to darkness and heavy weather there were no witness of the tragedy and the disappearance of Mr. Vanhern was not discovered until the next day. Capt. Smith reported the matter to the port authorities and turned over to them all effects of the unfortunate passenger.

Scene 174.

INT. PHILIP'S OFFICE: CLOSE SHOT ON HIM:

As the impact of these communications makes its effects felt on Philip. He realizes that the painful duty now confronting him is to carry this news to the girl he loves. And as he stares down at the document, his face troubled and thoughtful, we FADE OUT SLOWLY.

FADE SLOWLY IN ON **Scene 175.**

INT. CHARLEY'S COTTAGE: MEDIUM SHOT:

We pick up the sad scene of Philip's announcement, in the midst of the action, avoiding his entrance and unnecessary titles of explanation. Philip, full of love and pity toward Fancy, has already broken the news to her and Mrs. McGee. He is showing them the documents. Both women are overwhelmed with grief. Fancy turns to Mrs. McGee, and looks at her piteously for a second - then buries her face in the older woman's shoulder - and sobs. Mrs. McGee, herself crying - looks significantly at Philip - then down at Fancy. Philip gets her once, and coming down to her, dropping on one knee, he gently disengages her arms from around Mrs. McGee's neck - turns her toward him. Fancy looks at him - her lips trembling in her effort to hold back the sobs. Philip, without saying anything, gently pets her hand, and finally, Fancy tells him simply and naturally:

TITLE: "What should I do without you, Philip... one friend we can count on!"

And in his heart felt response, Philip dedicates himself to that service, as we FADE OUT ON THE SCENE.

TITLE: MONTHS OF DEVOTION AND SERVICE FINALLY BROUGHT THEIR REWARD......

Scene 176.

EXT. GARDEN PARTY: LONG SHOT:

A garden party on the grounds of a luxurious suburban home. The setting and effects are of the most elaborate description. Costumes, lanterns among the trees, arbors and summerhouses about the grounds. A raised dance floor in the middle of the garden - all is life and merriment, with dancing and laughing, splendidly dressed couples dressing the set. Among these are Philip and Fancy.

Scene 177.

EXT. GARDEN PARTY: CLOSE SHOT ON GROUP:

Laughing and talking, as Philip pulls Fanny to one side, and whispers to her. She laughs and agrees, and without excusing themselves to the others who haven't noticed - they hurry out ...

Scene 178.

EXT. GARDEN PARTY: CLOSE SHOT ON RUSTIC BENCH: GARDEN WALL:

This wall is about six or seven feet high, with a broad copping. Get a pretty light effect, through heavy shrubbery - the party back through trees and shrubbery, as Philip brings Fancy in and sits her down... as he begins to talk to her—

<u>TITLE</u>: WHILE MONTHS OF HUNTING AND SPYING ALSO BRING THEIRS:

Scene 179.

EXT. GARDEN PARTY: CLOSEUP TOP OF WALL:

Overgrown with vines, as the vines slowly part, and either by the moonlight, or the reflected flicker from the lanterns, we get a glimpse of the evil face of Whitey. Stealthily he pokes his head through - and watches the couple below, leering.

Scene 180.

EXT. GARDEN PARTY: CLOSE SHOT ON PHILIP AND FANCY:

He has her hands now - and is pleading his cause - he has proposed and is begging her for her answer. And she gives it to him. She sways toward him a little, and Philip takes her in his arms and holds her close for a second before he looks, down - she puts up her lips for his kiss.

Scene 181.

EXT. GROUNDS: OUTSIDE OF WALL: CLOSE SHOT:

As a pair of feet drop cautiously into the shot, and a second later Whitey drops into the shot from the wall. He stands a second, chuckling to himself in evil triumph - then as he turns and scurries out of shot --- ----

Scene 182.

EXT. GARDEN PARTY: CLOSE SHOT ON PHILIP AND FANCY:

They have started apart - are listening in some alarm. Then Philip laughs - reassures her - and as he again takes her in his arms - FADE OUT ON THEM .....

TITLE: THE ENGAGEMENT WAS A SURPRISE TO SOCIETY....AND RECEIVED SOME ATTENTION IN QUITE A DIFFERENT QUARTER...

FADE IN ON **Scene 183.**

INT. DEAD HOUSE: FULL SHOT:

Getting over the usual atmosphere of the place, already well established - and then cut to ---

Scene 184.

INT. DEAD HOUSE: CHOSE SHOT ON TABLE:

At which are seated Whitey, and a florid, flashy woman of the bird-of-prey type - evidently his favorite Doxie; in low-voiced consultation with this woman under cover of the smoke and movement and chatter all around them, Whitey has put aside his pretense of blindness. He has a newspaper spread out before him on the table. Pointing to a certain column, and item, chuckling and grinning over it, he tells his companion to read it. As she leans against his shudder to read it, we will also take look:

Scene 185.

INSERT CLOSEUP ON NEWSPAPER ITEM:

Main Head: SOCIETY ENGAGEMENT ANNOUNCED.

PHILIP PEYTON, SCION OF OLD KNICKERBOCKER FAMILY, TO MARRY LONG ISLAND HEIRESS.

"Among the spring engagements comes the interesting news that Philip Peyton, brilliant and well-known young lawyer, and member of one of New York's oldest families, is to wedded on April 20th at the Little Church Around the Corner, to Miss Fancy Claire, of Long Island. Society is stirred because young Peyton, one of the catches for whom fond mothers have angled ever since his graduation from Yale, has succumbed to the charms of a young lady scarcely known in the inner circles of Park Lane and its devotees."

Scene 186.

INT. DEAD HOUSE: CLOSE SHOT ON WHITEY'S TABLE:

TITLE: "That means Palm Beach for you and me, sweetie.... a sort of graft for life.... we're tapping into a family worth ten millions!"

He lets this sink in, as the woman's eyes widen, and she shares his avaricious excitement without actually understanding what it is all about. Whitey goes on boasting:

TITLE: "I gotta twist on these people that's goin' to be worth a fortune!"

He does not tell-her how he intends to accomplish this graft. But she believes him, as he squints his triumphantly sinister eye upon her. He chortles again:

TITLE: "And that sap - Easy Money Charley - he thought he'd fixed a bank account for life – all to himself!"

Evil laughter shakes him as he considers the beautiful graft onto which he has stumbled: But across the newspaper and the brightly lighted table, a shadow moves - the form of a man. Now it is still. Whitey sees it - then he looks up back of him with a snarl.

PAN THE CAMERA just enough to move the woman out, and there stands Easy Money Charley. He is in rough sailor garb this time; with the cap of a sea-farer tilted over one eye. Transfixed, Whitey stares at him as though at a ghost. Charley does not move. He has gotten the whole situation - has heard the last title. And Whitey gets the fatal news from his narrowed, vicious gaze - the threat in it. The two look into each others' eye.

Scene 187.

INT. DEAD HOUSE: FULL SHOT:

Every eye in the house is on table - back, where drama is taking place and a group in the f.g. are whispering eagerly - one of them is evidently a stranger, and another - more familiar, tells him disgustedly ----

TITLE: "It's Easy Money Charley himself... come back again!"

The other nods as though he had heard of this famous pan-handler - they watch ---

INT. DEAD HOUSE: CLOSE SHOT CHARLEY AND WHITEY:

Charley speaks - deliberately - venomously:

TITLE: "I heard what you said... and I know what you meant to do - you snake ...... you dirty rat!"

Whitey is breathing hard with hatred and defiance, tinged with terror. He now yells at Charley:

TITLE: "Yeah?... I'm wise! .... that brat- and the money she's marryin' ..... it's my graft now- not yours .... understand?"

Charley, tensed for the fight he knows is coming, takes another cat-like step toward Whitey. He speaks with the same cold, deadly precision:

TITLE: "You'll never touch that graft, Whitey!"

Whitey springs to his feet - and as he did once before, he swings his chair between him and Charley. Now he almost shrieks:

TITLE: "NO?.... And who's going to stop me?"

Again Charley replies - again with the cold preciseness and rasp in his voice:

TITLE: "I'll stop you! I'll stop you - because I'm going to kill you - now!"

And he springs. This time Whitey, prepared, swings the chair fairly over his head. Charley is staggered, but comes back and leaps forward into a clinch. As the two men reel out of the close shot --

Scene 188.

INT. DEAD HOUSE: MEDIUM SHOT END OF BAR NEAR DOOR:

As Diamond Mike - knowing this is a fight to the death, vaults the bar and instead of interfering - he swings the heavy door of the cafe to - and bars it - then turns to watch. This action will impress the audience with the fact that Mike knows there's no use interfering here - the lock is lethal - to the death.

INT. DEAD HOUSE: AD LIB SHOTS OF FIGHT:

This is a fight - the battle of a cornered and desperate rat against a man who is fighting for what he has virtually given up his life for - the happiness of the only creature in the world he loves. There are no rules - no quarter is asked, expected or given. Close shots should show eye gouging - hair clutches - everything foul and rotten- as far as can be gotten by the censors.

INTERJECT THIS FIGHT WITH THE FOLLOWING:

Scene 190.

INT. DEAD HOUSE: CLOSE SHOT ON WHITEY'S WOMAN:

A raging partisan, screaming filthy advice and encouragement to Whitey: She grabs a bottle from the table and it is slapped from her hand by someone else...

Scene 191, and 191-A, B, and C.

EXT. DEAD HOUSE: CLOSE SHOTS ON DOOR:

Officer Quinn hammering on the door. In the last shot he throws his weight against it repeatedly - and it crashes in....

Scene 192.

INT. DEAD HOUSE: CLOSE SHOT ON CLINCH: FINAL SHOT OF FIGHT:

As Charley knocks Whitey clear out of shot:

Scene 193.

INT. DEAD HOUSE: CLOSE SHOT BY WALL:

As Whitey falls into shot. He picks himself up - and deliberately rushes the wall - hits it in a terrific shock - and goes down again. Charley in from camera- prepared to finish him - crowd close in - as Whitey gets up - weaving on his feet - his face twisted with terror. He stands a second - then gives a terrible scream of terror - grabs his eyes with both hands, as he screams into the camera:

<u>TITLE</u>: "Oh, my God...it's come...it's come.. I'm done!"

Charley, with a sneer; closes in to finish him -- Whitey drops to the floor and grovels in abject terror. Charley looks down at him ---

Scene 194.

INT. DEAD HOUSE: CLOSEUP ON WHITEY:

On the floor. He is pushing up one red eyelid - then the other - he blinks. This is bound to be repulsive - and it MUST be repulsive, - the most terrible punishment that can fall on men has really befallen Whitey this time. And he finally calls it out in a horrible, frightened croak....

<u>TITLE</u>: "I'm blind! I'm blind! I'm really blind!"

He continues to push open his eyes - try to see:

(It is at this point that Quinn finally crashes the door and enters:)

Scene 195.

INT. DEAD HOUSE: MEDIUM SHOT:

As some of the other habitues of the place laugh sarcastically. One of them, in f.g., beside Charley - yells down at Whitey, groveling, on the floor:

<u>TITLE</u>: "Arrr.... A helluva way to quit!"

But there is no doubting the sincerity of the unfortunate Whitey. He is whimpering, quivering hulk, as Charley, still suspicious and wary, bends and looks at him, and Officer Quinn pushes his way through the crowd. He looks at the two assailants, and then growls:

<u>TITLE</u>: "You two bums at it again?"

Then he sees the piteous, hopeless whimpering of Whitey. Quinn stoops beside him. Charley stands looking down at them.

Scene 196.

INT. DEAD HOUSE: CLOSEUP ON QUINN AND WHITEY:

Whitey is whimpering over and over again "I'm blind....blind" Quinn growls at him:

TITLE: "Blind? What d'ye mean... ain't ye been fakin' that all your life?"

Whitey gropes for Quinn - finds him - pulls on his coat - and sobs, abjectly --

TITLE: "But it's true... this time it's come true, like the doctors always said it would... Oh, God -- have mercy on me!"

Even Quinn's natural skepticism is moved by this. Propping Whitey up against his knee, he lights a match and passes it before the other's eyes. And it is apparent as they look close. The wretched beggar has told the truth at last. He is really blind! Quinn looks up, and says:

TITLE: "That's what the priest 'ud call a judgment, I guess."

He gets this over grimly, as he releases Whitey and starts up out of the closeup.

Scene 197.

INT. DEAD HOUSE: MEDIUM SHOT:

The tempo now drops. Quinn, straightening up, looks at Charley. The latter, torn and disheveled from the fight, is looking down at Whitey - the tiger gone - his face even reflecting a growing pity -- a repeated emphasis that anything really helpless has always appealed to his better side. Quinn, stooping, lifts Whitey to his feet, and holds him up -- although the other is sagging -- all self-control gone. He states the result.

TITLE: "This man's stone blind.... has he anyone to look out for him? If he hasn't I've got to take him to the Island hospital....."

As Quinn gets this over-- Whitey, in sudden access of terror begins groping -- calling out --

Scene 198.

INT. DEAD HOUSE: CLOSEUP ON WHITEY:

As he stares and gropes -- and whines abjectly --

TITLE: "Don't leave me, Charley... for God's sake.... don't let 'em send me to the Island!"

He continues to cry out and beg -- a pitiable and horrible sight.

Scene 199.

INT. DEAD HOUSE: MEDIUM SHOT ON GROUP:

Charley in group – Whitey continuing action of close-up, as Quinn looks at Charley. And Charley, with no more than a momentary hesitation, tells Quinn roughly, with more than an assumption of his old tough, hard-boiled manner ---

TITLE: "Forget that Island stuff... leave him to me... I'll look after him!"

While the crowd, Adolphe in the foreground, stare at him in amazement, he steps forward -- asserting his true nobility of character, as he undertakes the responsibility of nursing his deadliest enemy for the rest of his life. And as he takes Whitey's elbow, and supporting him, leads him out, between the parting crowd -- toward the door -- FADE OUT.

TITLE: JUNE WEDDING.....

FADE IN ON

Scene 200.

EXT. LITTLE CHURCH AROUND THE CORNER: FULL SHOT:

It is spring - and the church is set for a wedding. An awning is spread to the curb - a carpet under the awning- a curious crowd of onlookers are gathered outside to see the bridal party as it issues. Cars in droves are lined on both sides of the street. Run long enough to get over the significance of it all--

Scene 201.

INT. LITTLE CHURCH AROUND THE CORNER: MEDIUM SHOT ON ALTAR:

If you use this particular church, reproduce the first few pews and the altar. Philip and Fancy are standing before the clergyman. It is a small wedding -- only a maid of honor and best man. The pews in camera angles are filled with a fashionable crowd of Philips relatives and friends. Everything is conventional, but as pictorial as possible.... The ceremony is on -- and as the couple kneel for the final prayer -- cut to ---

Scene 202.

EXT. SIDE STREET: SIDEWALK:

Just a flash of two somber, sordid and pathetic figures. One, is Whitey, and as he and his companion come down to the camera, we see Whitey, shambling--- helpless, except for the patient figure who guides him. Around his neck is the old sign, only now it reads, "I AM BLIND!" With the "AM" underlined heavily. He carries a little bundle of pencils. As they come down and pass the camera, his guide is recognized as Charley. He is holding Whitey by the wrist, guiding him. His clothing is worn - shabby, back in his beggar role; abject, decrepit, apparently, acting his part as of old.

Scene 203.

EXT. MADISON AVE. CORNER:

As the couple come around, Charley guiding Whitey. They come down past camera.

Scene 204.

INT. LITTLE CHURCH AROUND THE CORNER: FULL SHOT:

Or medium shot, if economy of setting is desired: As the couple start back up the aisle toward the door, and the guests close in behind them - Fancy is clinging to the arm of her husband, a lovely bride in her moment of exquisite happiness -- Philip looking down at her proudly as they pass the camera---

Scene 205.

EXT. SIDEWALK: CHURCH AROUND THE CORNER:

Tipping the curious crowd and the awning and church entrance, as Charley leads Whitey in -- he gets him settled in his regular begging attitude--- then Charley - turns back and watches the Church. Whitey is abject - passive - offers no objection-- and as Charley watches ----

Scene 206.

EXT. LITTLE CHURCH AROUND THE CORNER:

As the happy pair emerge from the church - down the walk -- through the aisle of curious on-lookers-- toward the curb:

Scene 207.

EXT. CHURCH AROUND THE CORNER: CLOSE SHOT ON CHARLEY:

Our last big scene with him: In his rag-tags he stands, and his eyes follow the slow progress of the couple from the gate to the curb. His face is twisting with emotion -- with a curious mingling of broken heart and pride. HE did it--and he's glad of it -- and yet he is dying on his feet. As he watches:

Scene 208.

EXT. LITTLE CHURCH AROUND THE CORNER: CURB:

As the couple, closely pressed by their friends, foremost among whom is ---

Scene 209.

EXT. CHURCH - CLOSEUP ON MRS. MCGEE:

Dabbing at her eyes with a handkerchief in one hand, and throwing a handful of rice with the other...

Scene 210.

EXT. CHURCH: CURB: MEDIUM SHOT ON PIERCE-ARROW OR ROLLS:

As the couple duck into it -- and it starts out with a jerk ---

Scene 211.

EXT. CHURCH: CLOSEUP ON CHARLEY –

Watching his eyes still follow the car -- he turns out of shot.

Scene 212.

EXT. CHURCH: CLOSE SHOT ON WHITEY:

As Charley re-enters the scene. Whitey feels his nearness-- he gropes-- and Charley, looking down, takes him by the hand. Whitey looks up -- and asks him:

TITLE: "What is it --- what are you lookin' at, Charley."

CHARLEY looks down at him -- and tells him shortly:

TITLE: "Nothin'!"

BACK, as he helps Whitey up -- they start out.

The Scenario

An early studio ad, linking the magazine story to the film. *Motion Picture News*, May 16, 1925

MAKING THE FILM

Articles began to appear in the press about *The Street of Forgotten Men* only a few weeks after Turner's story was published in *Liberty* magazine. A mid-March mention in Kelcey Allen's "Amusements" column in *Women's Wear (Daily)*, for example, stated, "Three new productions are in preparation, and work on them is expected to start soon.... George Kibbe Turner's story, *The Street of Forgotten Men*, will be Herbert Brenon's next production. Mary Brian is the only player chosen so far." (3-20-1925) Less than two weeks later, a piece in the New York *Daily News*, headlined "*Forgotten Men* Roles Assigned," noted "Percy Marmont, Neil Hamilton and Mary Brian will have the leading roles in *The Street of Forgotten Men*, which Herbert Brenon will direct at the Long Island studios. Which makes this department exceedingly happy that Percy is coming in from the coast...." (4-1-1925) This brief piece not only suggests its author had a soft spot for the film's star, it reveals at least a few other key decisions regarding the production had been made by the end of March.

In early April, Allen's "Amusements" column in *Women's Wear (Daily)* ran another bit on the film. This time it noted, "Paul Schofield, well known film scenarist, has just signed a contract under which his entire time for one year will be devoted to preparing scripts for Paramount.... Schofield's first task under his new contract will be the adaption of George Kibbe Turner's story, *The Street of the Forgotten Men*." (4-2-1925)

By mid-April, most of the cast had been chosen, as bits in newspapers and magazines reported the signing of various actors and actresses. Some were actors or crew with which Brenon had worked in the past. In early May, with filming well under way, *Billboard* magazine gave a near complete summary of where things stood. "Working under the direction of Herbert Brenon, who is making *The Street of Forgotten Men* at the Paramount Long Island Studios, are: Percy Marmont, Mary Brian, Neil

Hamilton, Riley Hatch, Josephine Deffry, Dorothy Walters, John Harrington and Juliet Brenon, daughter of the late Algernon Brenon, music critic of *The Telegraph* and niece of Director Brenon. The cast also includes Lassie, canine movie star." (5-9-1925) Not mentioned by *Billboard* was one of film's uncredited players, Louise Brooks, who had only recently been given a screen test and assigned a small role. Beating *Billboard* to the punch, the screen notes column in the New York *Herald Tribune* gave the aspiring actress a shout-out, writing a week earlier, "Louise Brooks, one of the Ziegfeld beauties from *Louis the 14th*, will have a part in Herbert Brenon's production of *The Street of Forgotten Men*." (5-2-1925)

This on set production still corresponds to the first scene in the film, an establishing shot depicting the Bowery in the past. The man wearing a hat and holding a megaphone in the lower middle of the frame is likely the film's director, Herbert Brenon. The woman to his right, with her back to the camera and wearing a boldly striped skirt and a feathered hat, is standing next to an apple cart; as the film opens, she completes her purchase and then strolls down the lively street. *Author collection*

According to various accounts, work on *The Street of Forgotten Men* began on April 6th. The film was shot, by and large, at Paramount's Astoria Studios on Long Island. (The somewhat new studio complex, located at 35th Street in the Astoria neighborhood in Queens, was constructed for Famous Players-Lasky between 1920 and 1921.) Location shooting for the film was done elsewhere on Long Island (including in the neighborhood known as Little Neck Hills, and on the Nicholas F. Brady estate – known as Inisfada), as well as on the streets of Manhattan, notably on various stretches of Fifth Avenue, and at the landmark Little Church Around the Corner on East 29th.

A relaxed cast and crew are seen in this (early morning?) production still taken on the Nicholas F. Brady estate at Roslyn, Long Island. (The Gold Coast estate was the scene of the dance near the end of the film.) Herbert Brenon, wearing a hat, is seated in a chair whose extension holds a bottle of milk and boxed food. Neil Hamilton, seated to the right on the camera stand, raises a cup. *From the Core Collection Production files and the Paramount Pictures photographs of the Margaret Herrick Library, Academy of Motion Picture Arts and Sciences*

Screen captures of two of the film's location shoots: (Left) Traffic and crowds on Fifth Avenue in NYC. (Right) Extras and curious onlookers during the wedding scene outside the Little Church Around the Corner. *Courtesy of San Francisco Silent Film Festival*

In mid-April, with filming well underway, Martin Dickstein of the *Brooklyn Daily Eagle* paid a visit to the set of *The Street of Forgotten Men*. His account, "Slow Motion," is the first to discuss the making of the film. "Your correspondent broke away from the toils of chronicling views of the celluloid drama long enough one day last week to browse among the Cooper-Hewitts and electric cables which look like treacherous reptiles among the cameras and countless sets over at the Famous Players-Lasky studio in Astoria. He saw pictures in the making – four of them, to be exact – and, talking the subject over with each of the four directors, was informed that here, in embryo, was a quartet of films than which there have never been any more worthy of being hailed as epics. Their claims, I think, are not without good foundation…."

Dickstein visited with D.W. Griffith on the set of *Poppy* before turning his attention to Brenon's latest effort. Both directors, Dickstein suggests, were demanding. "For *The Street of Forgotten Men* an interior of a department store of the late '90s has been built on the big stage in Astoria. There, in the silverware department, Herbert Brenon was painstakingly instructing one of the players on the art of transferring a bundle of teaspoons from the showcase to the top of her muff. The 'N.G.' sign was brought out here more frequently than it was on Mr. Griffith's set. But Herbert Brenon is patient. He is also punctilious, as many players who have worked with him attest…." (4-19-1925)

A few days later, a syndicated piece suggested the department store sequence had been among the first shot. The piece, titled "Herbert Brenon's New Paramount Filmplay Started in New York," reported on the signing of cast members, referenced the department store scene, and noted: "The players were quaintly dressed in the fashions of the day, the most conspicuous being lavishly plumed hats; long, dust-gathering skirts, and the wasp waistlines of the ladies." (4-22-1925, Los Angeles *Illustrated Daily News*) An attention to detail didn't end with how the actors looked in period clothing. It even extended to how they smelled. *Billboard* reported "...while interviewing Percy Marmont during the filming of the picture *The Street of Forgotten Men*, we had detected a particularly pungent perfume worn by some questionable ladies of the Bowery." *Billboard* asked H. M. K. Smith, head of the Astoria Studio costume department, about the scent. "'Oh,' he replied, 'that was a bit of realism. The streets, types and clothes were all true to the Bowery; so why not the perfume? It contributed quite a kick to the characterizations'." (9-4-1926)

The department store scene, in which Portland Fancy (Juliet Brenon) is shown stealing a silver spoon, is depicted on one of the film's eight lobby cards. Along with the shoplifting scene, two other scenes likely shot early-on include those which show the consequences of her desperate act, including Fancy's appearance before a judge, and eventual incarceration. Each were likely included in the lost second reel of the film.

The rare scene still shown at the top of the next page was published in *Motion Picture News* on May 16, while the film was still in production. It depicts Portland Fancy as she surrenders her child and is jailed. Surrounding her are two men, presumably detectives or jailers, and a female probation officer or matron. This dramatic still is notable for its rarity – and likely comes from the lost second reel.

The department store arrest. *Credit: George Eastman Museum*

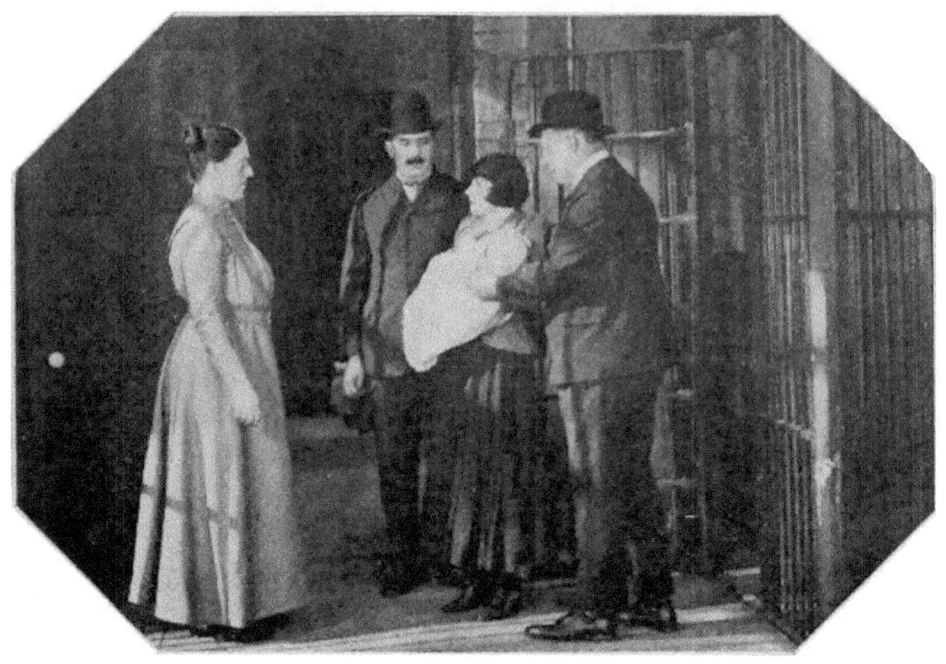

Four other stills from the film were also published in the May 16 issue of *Motion Picture News*. Each depict early scenes from the film, including the time Easy Money Charlie (Percy Marmont) spoke with Portland Fancy and promised to take care of her child, Charlie's subsequent return to his boarding house, and the introduction of the child to the housekeeper (Dorothy Walters). Accompanying the stills was a short article stating work on the film was well advanced.

With the critical acclaim and commercial success heaped on *Peter Pan* (1924), Brenon and his films came under increased attention. Magazine profiles of the director took note of his attention to detail, as well as his rigorous methods.

Harriet Underhill, film critic for the New York *Herald Tribune*, was among those who paid an early visit to the Astoria studio. In "Herbert Brenon Proves a Versatile Director," the journalist profiled the director as much as the film-in-progress. Underhill wrote, "Herbert Brenon speaks French, Italian and German – we heard him – and he has infinite patience – we saw him. He is doing *The Street of Forgotten Men* over at the Long Island studio, and the people who are playing the small parts – there are no extras in this picture – all seem to have been born on foreign shores. Hence, Mr. Brenon's involuntary display of versatility. We are so intensely interested in what was going on on the stage that we sat in an easy chair marked 'Mr. Marmont' all day and watched Mr. Brenon direct."

Underhill continued, "… after watching those scenes in the beggar's rendezvous, we decided that one man can lead a horse to water, but one man can't make ten horses drink simultaneously. The set was small and crowded – an exact copy of the real rendezvous which once was the backroom of a saloon on Park Row in the old days. There was Easy Money Charlie – Mr. Marmont himself; there was Blind Ben, Harry the Hop, Dumb Dan, Adolf the face artist, Bertram the Barber, Legless Lew and a lot of others. Mr. Brenon rehearsed them singly. They counted and each did his stuff to one, two, three, four, beautifully. But in the ensembles it was not so good. 'Venez vos ici – approchez!' he would shout to Harry the Hop. 'No, non; sei tu' to Bertram the Barber and 'Das ist gut' to Dumb Dan. It was just like the tower of Babel. It didn't seem as though anyone could ever get order out of that chaos."

The Irish-born Brenon, having previously worked in Europe, may well have known a smattering of other languages. But whatever his linguistic facility, and whatever patience he may have sometimes shown, the famed director still came across as exacting. Underhill finished her piece suggesting as much, "Mr. Brenon changed their entrances, he changed their exits, he changed their numbers, he changed his mind. And when you see that scene in the beggar rendezvous please take a good look at it and realize what it meant for him to film it. Of course, there is another way of looking at it. A stage production will be in rehearsal as many weeks as the screen drama will be in hours and never let anyone tell you that just because it is a silent drama that the actors do not have to learn lines. They do." (4-26-1925)

Another scene shot in April was the sequence depicting large crowds leaving church; this scene, according to various press reports, was shot on Easter Sunday, which took place on April 12, 1925. *Exhibitors Herald* ran a bit which mentioned the location shoot, as did *Moving Picture World*. The latter wrote, "The new Herbert Brenon production got underway on Easter Sunday, when many shots of the famous Easter parade on 5th Ave, including the crowds at several of the big churches on the thoroughfare, were made. These scenes in which some of the principal characters appear, form an important part of the story." (5-9-1925)

Herbert Brenon tells Percy Marmont how to become a successful beggar. First you get your license; then you set up in business on a busy street corner. Marmont has the leading role in "The Street of Forgotten Men," an unusual story of the underworld

Photoplay magazine, July 1925

An anonymous article in the *New York Times* titled "Sunday Morning Beggar" also reported on a location shoot, which may or may not have been the same Easter shoot.

"It appears that one Sunday morning when he should have been at church or playing golf, Herbert Brenon was at work directing scenes for his current effort, *The Street of Forgotten Men*, in which there are a number of players who impersonate fake beggars. John Harrington was clad as one of the beggars of the story, with the sign hanging around his neck reading: 'I am blind.' When Harrington was sitting in one of the automobiles, in the front seat of which was a chauffeur, three persons in 10 minutes walked over and gave him alms, the contributions amounting to 27 cents. Afterward when Harrington was doing his bit before the camera an elderly well-dressed woman walked toward him and dropped a coin into his cup. When one of his assistants tried to intercept her, the lady glared at the interferers, apparently believing that they were a hard hearted lot. By this time the director insisted that no further money should be received. Nevertheless, Mr. Harrington received two more contributions." (5-17-1925)

> Fifteen minutes work resulted in a total of 95 cents. "The Street Of Forgotten Men" is already a box-office success.

Hartford Courant clipping, May 17, 1925

Along with reporting on a location shoot, the *New York Times* also visited the set of *The Street of Forgotten Men*, where its reporter observed one of the early scenes being filmed. The anonymous article, titled "From a Camera Platform in the Astoria Studio," detailed the lengths to which Brenon attempted to paint a colorful, realistic portrait of Bowery life. "At the Paramount Astoria Studio, one day last week, Herbert Brenon was discovered directing scenes for *The Street of Forgotten Men*, translated to the screen from the story by George Kibbe Turner. One of the settings for this picture depicts the inside of an old squalid bar room, with frowzy females attired in long skirts and big hats and men of the sea fraternizing with pickpockets and fake cripples. In the rear of this dive is supposed to be a room which is termed 'The Cripple Factory,' and according to the story the beggars were want to go to this room to receive suggestions and an outfit for which they were thought to be best qualified.

Some wanted to pose as blind men and they received instruction. Others elected to become legless men who trundled themselves along in a truck which concealed their real nether limbs. Then there were the deaf and dumb and those without arms."

The reporter remarked on the realistic nature of the set. "One could not help but be interested in the detail of this setting, as even the costumes looked real. Percy Marmont who scored his first success in this country as Mark Sabre in *If Winter Comes*, has the leading role in this film. He is cast as a one-armed man. His real left arm was strapped to his side, while a fake arm was attached to his shoulder, and even in the glare of the lights there was something very real in the presence of this portrayal of an impostor."

The *New York Times* noted that the bar and the adjoining Cripple Factory were supposed to have existed twenty years earlier, "In the narrative the beggars, who have been whining and begging from good folks all day, congregate in the saloon, first to pay a percentage of the day's gains to the inventor of their fake condition, and also to quench their thirst with large schooners of beer. It is supposed to be the one place where they could safely go and rid themselves of their cripple signs…. There was the fat woman who danced with the agile crook, and the downcast heroine who sat staring in melancholy fashion at the table on which were several half-filled glasses of beer. The bartender was busy going from the bar to the different tables, and running through the tables was Mr. Brenon's police dog."

The *New York Times* article continued, describing Brenon's working methods while offering a more nuanced picture of the director, who comes off as less patient and more punctilious than others had depicted him. The article notes, "Mr. Brenon, perched on a platform with the camera, overlooked the scene and then peremptorily gave the order for action. Following this came the whistle for the players to go ahead up to Mr. Marmont's entrance.

'Come on, boys,' urged Mr. Brenon, 'we've got a lot to do. Where's Dan? Never mind we'll get along without him. Music!'

Old-time tunes came from the piano and violins as the players went through the antics demanded of them. Mr. Brenon being quick to notice when one of the actors was too slow. The first 'take' was not quite satisfactory, and Mr. Brenon scolded one or two players. The barroom had to look like a real production of such an interior, and therefore it had to be filled with smoke. Part of this effect was obtained by having the players puff quickly on their cigarettes, cigars and pipes. One 'extra' at the end of the saloon could not understand why he should smoke when the camera is not being turned, and the quick-witted woman snatched away his cigarette and puffed seven or eight times and made as much smoke as she could in the time.

'I'll take it,' observed Mr. Brenon, putting out his own cigar.

Just before the camera men began winding again, Mr. Brenon found a girl who was out of place.

'Move up a bit there, dear,' he said. Then to the fat woman – who must have been fully 220 pounds – he shouted: will you sit there, dear, please?"

At the back of the saloon was a sign which read, 'Biggest in the city, 5 cents.'

When that scene was taken Mr. Marmont appeared ready with his realistic looking crippled arm.

'Would you mind, Herbert, if I wore these shoes? The others hurt me. I'll change them if you like'."

Just as an omnipotent god controls all things, an omnipotent director controls every aspect of his production. "Mr. Brenon looked at Mr. Marmont's rather neat footwear and concluded that it would not matter for that scene, and Mr. Marmont, who held a pair of Chaplinesque shoes in his hand, cast them to one side. The cameras were still again, and more smoke was needed.

'Puff up, puff up, puff up!' instructed Mr. Brenon, impatiently. The small orchestra reeled off 'The Sidewalks of New York' and a deaf and dumb fake beggar staggered up to the bar.

As the camera began grinding again Mr. Brenon frowned peevishly. 'There's a lack of spirit about this scene,' he shouted. 'Not enough spirit.' Then in French to the bartender who chanced to be a French actor, he said 'Vous etes trop tard avec le mendicant la bas. Arrivez plus vivement.' In his haste Mr. Brenon used 'vite.'

The director gazed over the throng, and again he urged everybody to smoke up. Then he reminded one player that he had to appear a little drunk.

'You see,' Mr. Brenon explained to a visitor, 'Marmont is a cripple, licensed by the city to sell pencils.'

'Flop in the chair panting,' observed Mr. Brenon to the fat woman...."

"Finally Mr. Brenon obtained the effects that satisfied him and he moved the players over to another setting which depicted a street, an old horse car and various features of life in that squalid district of New York a score of years ago. There was the girl in the check dress and the flaming red hat, the man who is proud of his pearl derby and pink and yellow necktie and the sailor who rolled like a ship in a storm.

Mr. Brenon said he was very enthusiastic about *The Street of Forgotten Men*, the story of which he finds inspiring. Nous verrons." (5-3-1925) Expressing a bit of doubt, these last words translate as "We will see."

This production still is dated on the reverse May 21, 1925, suggesting the day this photo may have been taken. The snipe on the reverse reads "Herbert Brenon, Percy Marmont, Riley Hatch and John Harrington looking over the fake arm of the 'King of Beggars' in Brenon's new production, *The Street of Forgotten Men*." *Author collection*

Along with the *New York Times*, the New York *Herald Tribune* also took an interest in *The Street of Forgotten Men*. During the course of the film's production and prior to its debut, the newspaper ran three feature stories on the film. As already noted, the first, by Harriet Underhill, was published on April 26 and titled "Herbert Brenon Proves a Versatile Director." It highlighted the director's personality and working methods. The second, an anonymous piece published on May 17, was titled "Herbert Brenon had the best of advice." It references the film, though largely features a lunchtime interview with the director which focused on the advice given Brenon at the beginning of his career from the likes of Joseph Jefferson and Ada Rehan. (Percy Marmont was also present during the interview, and is also quoted.) The third piece, an anonymous article published on June 21, was titled "Brenon proves his interest in realism". It was subtitled, "Blow on the jaw nearly destroys theories of the Paramount director." Like other commentary from the time, this third piece emphasized the realism in which *The Street of Forgotten Men* was steeped.

The June 21 piece began, "Herbert Brenon is a firm believer in realism. His belief isn't quite as firm as it was a day or two ago, but it is still pretty well set.

It was Percy Marmont's fist that nearly jarred his ideas and his teeth loose and left the large bruise on his jaw. It happened this way. In an old-time Bowery saloon constructed on the Paramount Long Island Studio stage a fight took place, between Easy Money Charlie and Whitey.... In fact, it was a riot that wrecked the place.

The scene was being made for *The Street of Forgotten Men*. Percy Marmont was playing the role of Easy Money Charlie and John Harrington was Whitey. Marmont entered the saloon from the back room and discovered Harrington examining his bankbooks. Marmont drove at Harrington, as per the script, grabbed him by the throat and forced him against the wall.

'Terrible,' shouted director Brenon. 'No realism, too artificial. Choke him!'

'They did it over. Marmont grabbed Harrington's neck. His tongue came out, his eyes bulged.

'Camera,' Mr. Brenon ordered. 'Great! The facial expression is wonderful.'

They milled about. The scene was soon over. Harrington staggered forward, reached for a glass of water and slumped into a chair. Mr. Brenon fanned him for a moment and began acting out the remainder of the fight with Marmont while

Harrington rested.

Three times they struggled across the sawdust covered floor of the saloon, with Mr. Brenon impersonating Harrington's role. Each time Mr. Brenon seized the stool and tried to crash it over Marmont's head, but he dodged. The force of the falling chair was to make the holder stagger against the lunch counter and Marmont was to finish the fight with the blow on the chin. When Mr. Brenon was watching for this blow he could ease the force of it by tipping his head back. The last time, however, he turned his head toward Harrington to see if he was getting all the details of the action.

The movement was so sudden that Marmont couldn't stop. There was a dull thud; Mr. Brenon's knees sagged. He fell backward into the sawdust.

'Great!' commented Harrington, without rising from his stool. 'The facial expression was wonderful.'

Mr. Brenon rubbed his chin, tried to get his collar into place, and looked reproachfully at Marmont. Then he staggered across the saloon, thew his arms across the bar and shouted: 'I am blind!'

Some of the extras ran to the rescue. He pushed them back angrily and motioned to Harrington to do the same thing.

The scene was repeated. Harrington took the bang on the chin, plunged across the bar and smashed a mustard glass. Blood began to spurt from his hand. The prop man rushed in with liquid courtplaster; Mr. Brenon offered the use of his handkerchief.

'This realism is a great thing,' commented Harington, as they stopped the flow of blood.

'It is,' agreed the director; 'my jaw is out of joint.'

'Huh!' interjected Marmont. 'My knuckles are skinned'." (6-21-1925)

Even with the assistance of the make-up artist, Percy Marmont's preparation for his role in "The Street of Forgotten Men" (Paramount) is a lengthy process.

Motion Picture News, June 20, 1925

This third *Herald Tribune* article pre-dates the release of the film by a month. Interestingly, the anecdote at the heart of the story, likely true or somewhat true, proved colorful enough to be repeated nearly word-for-word as "Fight Scene in *The Street of Forgotten Men* a Bear For Realism—Never Before Equaled in Motion Pictures" in the Paramount Press Sheet.

The scene just before the fight between Bridgeport White-Eye, seated right looking at a newspaper on a table, and Easy Money Charlie, who is off screen. White-Eye's companion, played by Louise Brooks, also sits at the table. *Credit: From the Core Collection Production files and the Paramount Pictures photographs of the Margaret Herrick Library, Academy of Motion Picture Arts and Sciences*

Because of his attention to detail and involvement in most every aspect of a film, Brenon gained a reputation as a demanding director, someone who ruled over his sets and pushed his actors and crew. In a 1925 profile, *Film Daily* described Brenon as a studio "Svengali," suggesting he was somehow able to manipulate others. While on-set reports from *The Street of Forgotten Men* intimate as much, they never go so far as to state Brenon was harsh, or that those working under the director resented his behavior.

However, all may not have been as depicted in the press at the time. In 1979, film historians Richard and Diane Kozarski interviewed Louise Brooks regarding her work at the Astoria studio. The Kozarskis noted that Brenon's handling of actors favorably impressed the 18-year-old, then a newcomer to film. However, when Brooks saw a sandbag crash to the stage a few feet from where the director was standing, she suspected relations with the crew might not have been entirely positive.

In late April, 1925 *Variety* reported that Brooks, "one of the most popular members of *Louie the 14th*" (a Ziegfeld production) had "mysteriously disappeared from the cast of this musical comedy several days ago and her absence has been traced to the scouting agents of a moving picture company with studios on Long Island." (4-25-1925) It was around then that Brooks was given a screen test. By the first week of May, various publications including the New York *Herald Tribune* and New York *Evening Post* reported Brooks had been cast in *The Street of Forgotten Men*.

Brooks' screen test, held on a set at the Astoria studio, was overseen by director Allan Dwan. It went well, with the result being Brooks was assigned a bit part as a moll, a companion to Bridgeport White-Eye (John Harrington). John Russell's notes describe her character as a "trull" or "doxie" with whom Whitey "plays the scene over the newspaper. Let her appear actually heavy: a hard-boney, sneering little rip of a woman, with a face like flint — frankly predatory, so that we hate her at sight."

Sometime following her screen test, and with the film already in production, Brooks was introduced to Brenon. On May 16, she and the director attended the Kentucky Derby in Louisville, Kentucky. A few days later, on May 20 according to some sources, Brooks' brief scene was shot. The newcomer appears in only one scene near the end of the film in which there is a brawl in the saloon. Brooks is on screen for a couple of minutes, and though she vamps and acts somewhat melodramatically and dashes across screen like a dancer — she makes an impression.

Throughout her career, Brooks reportedly didn't bother to see herself act on screen. The one exception may have been her brief appearance in *The Street of Forgotten Men*. In a 1928 interview with *Pour Vous* regarding *Die Büchse der Pandora*, Brooks told the French magazine that she had not seen the German film, as it was a principle for her "not to go see herself on the screen. 'I did,' she said confidently, 'during my first film. I won't do it again, though I can't say why. Seeing myself gives me an uncomfortable feeling'." (12-6-1928) Later in life, Brooks said little about her debut, except to acknowledge her role in the film. In *Lulu in Hollywood*, she dryly commented, "In May, at Famous Players-Lasky's studio, in New York, under Herbert Brenon's direction, I had played with no enthusiasm a bit part in *Street of Forgotten Men*."

Besides Brooks, another showgirl given a bit part in *The Street of Forgotten Men* was Elizabeth Meehan. She would go on to a distinguished career as a screenwriter, and

At the end of the fight between Easy Money Charlie, standing middle, and Bridgeport White-Eye, kneeling helplessly before him. Louise Brooks peers over Charlie's shoulder, as Riley Hatch, the saloon keep, looks on. *Credit: From the Core Collection Production files and the Paramount Pictures photographs of the Margaret Herrick Library, Academy of Motion Picture Arts and Sciences*

would work with Brenon on a number of his subsequent films.

According to a 1929 profile of Meehan in *Smart Set* magazine, she was one of a number of Ziegfeld dancers who picked up extra income by working as an extra in films. "One day a friend suggested that they go out to the Paramount Studio on Long Island and get themselves a little extra work in the movies. Ziegfeld girls were much in demand and got as much as fifteen dollars a day for posturing gracefully in the background of films.... Paramount, at that time, was doing a picture called *The Street of Forgotten Men* and Miss Meehan had a bit. She had to walk across the set, be accosted by a beggar and recognize in him a long lost friend. It didn't work out at all. Twice she tried it and twice a sharp voice barked at her from the sidelines." That sharp voice was Brenon, who gave Meehan a "hot two-minute address on the general subject of acting and her own efforts in particular. Finally she managed her mite successfully." (2-1929)

Despite her inexperience, it is probable Meehan's bit — which likely came in the missing second reel — was retained in the film. A year later, according to the *Smart Set* profile, the struggling actress turned aspiring screenwriter encountered Brenon again. He recalled her poor performance in *The Street of Forgotten Men*, but still encouraged her interest in writing. In the years that followed, Meehan would go on to script a dozen Brenon films.

Another who had a bit part in *The Street of Forgotten Men* was Whitney Bolton. A journalist by profession, Bolton dabbled in film — at first in front of the camera as a bit player, and later behind the scenes as a screenwriter and wordsmith.

In a 1958 remembrance of Brenon, who had then recently died, Bolton recounted one of his three screen roles. "And the next Monday morning, at 8 o'clock, I was at Astoria, Long Island, ready to act, no matter what. The picture, *The Street of Forgotten Men*, was an item about the Bowery, its professional beggars and fake cripples. The star was a Briton named Percy Marmont, I showed up hair-cutted, shaved and in the best suit I could get at Brooks Brothers, a new pair of Frank Brothers shoes, a knit tie, with a neat pearl pin in it, and a supply of bewilderment.

Herbert Brenon, the man I am talking about and at that time one-third of the Great Three: Griffith, DeMille, and Brenon, took one look and turned pale. His Irish face betrayed his concern.

'My dear young man,' he said. 'Your clothes are impeccable, your mustache is waxed and you have shaved to the skin. You look like a junior member of the Union League Club. I had you down to play a besotted young bum in a sordid Bowery saloon. You were to share a table with two young ladies playing unfortunate girls in a distressing profession. You won't do at all this way.'

I played it the Scott Fitzgerald way: cool, detached, casual.

'That's all right. Mr. Brenon,' I said. 'I wouldn't have been much help to you, anyway.'

'But you are going to be,' he said. 'I insist.'

He clapped his hands and people came running. He told a wardrobe man to get me a torn, soiled, bedraggled suit, dying shoes, a ragged cap. He told a makeup man to give me a three-day stubble of beard and to put some dirt on my face. He had the hair-man do things with scissors that gave me a look of not knowing even how to spell the word comb. I became, in 15 minutes, a bum, a filthy, furtive, no good bum. I also became an actor for five days at $25 a day. It was a princely income." (6-30-1958)

Bolton ended his syndicated piece noting that he and Marmont became friends, while Brenon, although always pleasant when they encountered one another, never asked him to act again. In another syndicated column, from almost ten years later, Bolton told the story of how his acting career came to an end. "I played not just a bum – I was a bum's bum, a museum piece of abject economic failure. Mr. Marmont used to take delight in watching my slovenly, tattered, stained form slouch along the set – a downtown New York Street – and say with utter London charm: 'You'll never be an actor, old boy, but you do look like a loathsome, smelly, contemptible derelict. That's something, at least'." (5-31-1967)

Billboard magazine was on hand for the filming of a scene which featured another uncredited actor. Its article, which largely focusses on Percy Marmont, captured the moment when the star and a bit player – the canine actor known as Lassie, performed together in a scene which some found heart wrenching, and others found disturbing. "He was mourning over the inert form of a trained dog, which was obediently simulating death, stiffening inch by inch in the arms of Mr. Marmont at the command of his master, who stood in the offing." (5-9-1925)

In fact, Lassie's death scene (from the lost second reel) was played so effectively that some were convinced she must have been killed, or at least, cruelly beaten. Dog lovers, women's groups, and Societies for the Prevention of Cruelty to Animals complained, with the result being newspapers syndicated an article featuring a signed affidavit from Lassie's handler, Emery Bronte, stating the canine actor had not been harmed.

According to one such article, "The scenario of *The Street of Forgotten Men* called for a dog to be killed by having a heavy barrel roll over it. Lassie, the fine actor dog of Emery Bronte, of New York, was selected. Lassie appeared 'in person' before the camera as the barrel started to roll, but when the barrel reached what seemed to be the prostate body of Lassie a dummy dog was substituted and the 'dead dog' picked up after the barrel had passed over it . . . so that Lassie received not a scratch." (9-19-1925, *Detroit Free Press*) Similar articles also recounted Lassie's death scene and the apparent realism with which it was staged.

(Bellow) Whitey holds Charlie's dog during a pivotal scene from the missing second reel in which the animal is killed. *Author collection*

(Above) An intertitle describes the canine character as "the one love of Charlie's life – the one welcome that touched his heart." (Below) A mourning photo of the dog is displayed in Easy Money Charlie's room. *Courtesy of San Francisco Silent Film Festival*

Hunter's Point Undertaker Drives Hearse As 'Philadelphia Kitty' Is Buried—On Astoria Movie Lot

They buried "Philadelphia Kitty" the other day and one more link with the Bowery of the old days was severed as Undertaker Joe Trudden of Hunter's Point drove the black hearse down the narrow street. For Kitty was one of the old-timers.

Down at Nigger Mike's it was Kitty who started the fun, dancing among the tables—and maybe on them—playing jokes on the "saps" who were out for a big night, always gay, always full of life and joy, no matter what terror or sorrow had that day entered her heart from the whispering shadows of that sinister street which she called home. She's gone now and Undertaker Trudden and his two coach drivers—that's all the street could afford—drove slowly several times around the block.

Midnight usually found Kitty at "The Slide" or "The Sylvan Den" with some over-convivial companions, and when the gaslights of the deserted streets were blurred with the coming of the pallid daylight, her voice could be heard in some even lower dive where the pitiful wrecks of men and women tried to dull too bitter memories.

"The Street of Forgotten Men" they called the street. They came there, furtive, hunted by the police or haunted by dreams and in the kennels of the tenements they buried themselves by day, and at night crept along the shadows to eke out a living from a sort of crookedness or to drown their troubles in the forced hilarity at one of the saloons or dance halls.

"Easy Money" Charlie was one of them, a man of curiously mixed character who had come from nobody knew where, and was stopping here weary and beaten before taking the last step-to the river. On the other hand, "Bridgeport Whitey," was a typical product of the slums, a burly, spineless coward.

The two beggars made their headquarters in the rear room of a notorious saloon. Here Adolphe, a expatriated Frenchman of doubtful antecedents, ran a "cripple factory" in which he cleverly disfigured healthy men until they had all the appearance of pitiful objects of charity. Easy Money Charlie was the cleverest of them all, the best known panhandler of his time. Some cynical denizen of the Bowery once dubbed him the "King of the Beggars", and by this title he was known until the day when he disappeared under mysterious circumstances. Bridgeport Whitey was his rival, and the hatred between them knew no bounds. A young girl was thrown into this maelstrom of petty passions. Perhaps she would have grown up to be another Philadelphia Kitty, had it not been for Charlie who saved her from that fate before he disappeared and who saved her again from Whitey when he suddenly disappeared.

Herbert Brenon has made a photoplay woven around these characters at the Astoria studio with Percy Marmont as Charlie, John Harrington as Whitey and Mary Brian as the girl. Undertaker Trudden, his hearse, coaches and drivers were hired for several days for the funeral scenes. "The Street of Forgotten Men" makes the old Bowery live again.

Other reportage from the time also described the film and its making. Some of it was little more than studio hype, anecdotal bits meant to draw attention to aspects of the film. One such piece, a paragraph that ran in the *Brooklyn Daily Star*, reported how "there was a strong emotional scene in which pretty Juliet Brenon faints in the arms of Percy Marmont. It was found necessary for the players to hold this position while the cameras were moved forward for a closeup. 'Can you hold that pose for a minute Percy?' asked Director Brenon. 'What do you mean, a minute?' Marmont demanded." (7-3-1925) A longer piece, full of local color, appeared the same day in the *Brooklyn Daily Star* under the title "Hunter's Point Undertaker Drives Hearse As 'Philadelphia Kitty' Is Buried—On Astoria Movie Lot." The piece describes a significant scene in the film, Portland Fancy's funeral, though inexplicably it changes character names. Portland Fancy becomes Philadelphia Kitty, while the saloon keep, Diamond Mike, is referred to as Nigger Mike, and Bridgeport White-Eye is called Bridgeport Whitey. (7-3-1925)

The Street of Forgotten Men: From Story to Screen and Beyond

Two examples of Hal Rosson's cinematography, for which at least some of the success of the film should be credited.

(Left) The romantic young couple, played by Mary Brian and Neil Hamilton, beautifully lit and standing in near silhouette.

(Below) Observing them is a leering Bridgeport White-Eye, played by John Harrington, on the grounds of the estate. His head echoes the shape of the garden greenery. *Courtesy of San Francisco Silent Film Festival*

Two more examples of Hal Rosson's outstanding camera work.

(Right) One frame from a series of dynamic tracking shots, better termed "trucking shots," showing crowds leaving church. These mobile shots were reportedly obtained by mounting a disguised camera on a flat-bed truck which drove down a busy Fifth Avenue.

(Below) An overhead view of the much-praised fight scene near the end of the film. *Courtesy of San Francisco Silent Film Festival*

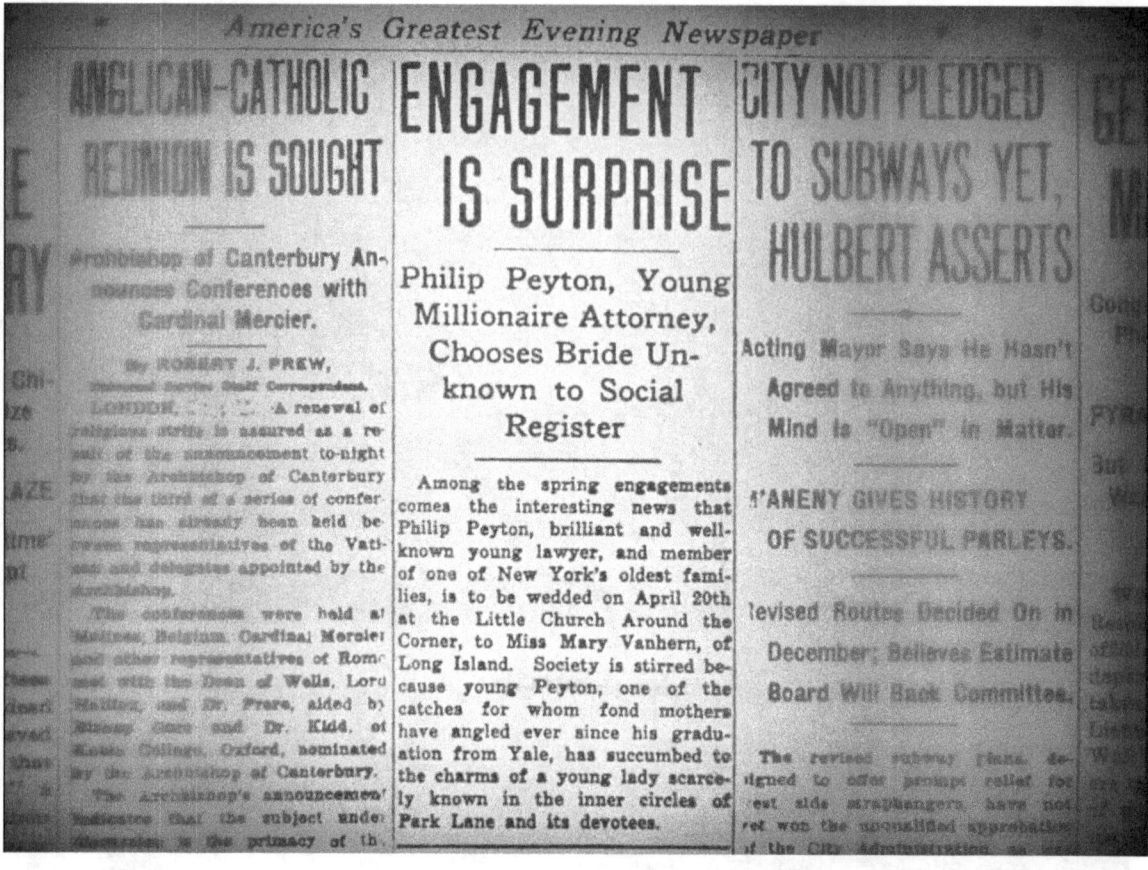

(Above) The "scene over the newspaper" which precedes the fight between Bridgeport White-Eye and Easy Money Charlie was staged using two different, though identifiable editions. The image above depicts a doctored copy of the *New York Evening Journal.* Notably, the stories which flank the film's prop article are actual news reports published during the third week of May, 1925 – a bit of detail which helps date when the scene may have been shot.

The article to the left concerns a religious conference in England. The piece to the right concerns a proposed subway line, about which then acting mayor George Murray Hulbert said the city was not yet committed. The prop article, "Engagement is Surprise," notes Philip Peyton and Mary Vanhern were to be married on April 20 at the Little Church Around the Corner.

(Above) Bridgeport White-Eye and his moll discuss the wedding announcement and the graft they hope to realize. However, the actual newspaper on the table is not the page seen above, but the page shown on the following page.

132

Though the "scene over the newspaper" was called for in John Russell's adaption notes, the bravura staging of this shot – dark shadows set over the light frame of a newspaper, must surely be credited to cinematographer Hal Rosson.

The image above depicts an actual newspaper, another issue of the *New York Evening Journal*, a Hearst newspaper. The page over which the looming shadow hovers likely dates from the second week of May, 1925 – a detail which also helps narrow down when the scene was filmed. The page shown here containing the headline "Killing Love by Suspicion" also features a Nell Brinkley cartoon titled "Could Such Things Be" (dated May 5, though likely published about a week later), and the popular advice column "Dear Beatrice Fairfax" (the name of the first newspaper advice column published in the United States). Along with the wedding date in the prop article, the fact that actual newspapers were used lends a degree of verisimilitude. Each of these four images come from the film and are *Courtesy of San Francisco Silent Film Festival*

According to press reports, work on *The Street of Forgotten Men* was completed during the week of June 6. Sometime between then and the film's debut on July 19 at least two, and perhaps as many as four advance screenings of the film took place. A syndicated newspaper article from late June stated, "A print of Herbert Brenon's latest production, *The Street of Forgotten Men*, was shown recently to a group of movie executives at the Paramount Long Island studio, and it is said it created a sensation. Not since *The Miracle Man*, according to these experts, has a motion picture revealed such pathos, artistic realism and tender love." (6-28-1925, *Philadelphia Inquirer*)

Another advance screening is referenced on the cover of *Exhibitors Trade Review*. The cover depicts a letter from Studio Manager Edwin C. King, dated July 8, which states, "Get all set to shoot the works on Herbert Brenon's new production, *The Street of Forgotten Men*! We saw a finished print today and the picture is positively a dramatic sensation. Another *Miracle Man*. It has the hard-boileds here clutching their chairs and crying like kids – and loving it!" (7-25-1925)

As was just about every film from the time, *The Street of Forgotten Men* was "Passed by the National Board of Review," suggesting a third advance screening. (A legend, stating the film was passed, appears at the beginning of the film.) Begun in 1909 as the New York Board of Motion Picture Censorship, the group evolved over time, changing its name and expanding its reach and responsibilities a number of times. Eventually opposed to censorship, the group instead published reviews, recommended movies, and engaged in the education of the movie going public. The board's stamp of approval opened the door to exhibiting a film just about anywhere.

However, in New York State, where *The Street of Forgotten Men* was to debut, the film also needed to be passed by another group, the New York Motion Picture Commission. Prior to its July 19 premiere, Famous Players-Lasky submitted the film to the state commission. This group, similar to others set up in cities and states around the United States, was charged with reviewing films shown to the public. The New York Motion Picture Commission was, in effect, a statewide censorship board.

A "Report of Examiner" and corresponding letter from the Deputy Commissioner, both dated July 14, requested two cuts be made to the film. In reel 1, the studio was asked to "Eliminate scene of Salvation Army episode." In Reel 3, "Eliminate underlined word in sub-title 'How could I, when I swore it on the crucifix?'"

Making the Film

A letter promoting *The Street of Forgotten Men* was featured on the cover of the July 25, 1925 issue of *Exhibitors Trade Review*, a leading industry journal. The note states that a finished print of the film was seen on July 8.

According to the letter, the reason for the two requested eliminations were that they were "sacrilegious". The Motion Picture Commission then requested, "If you will make the above eliminations in all prints to be exhibited in New York State and will write us a letter, advising us that the same have been made, using the form of letter required by this office, it will not be necessary to return the same for rescreening." That request indicates a fourth advance screening.

Two days later, Glendon Allvine of Famous Players-Lasky responded to Mr. Donnelly of the Motion Picture Commission. Allvine's July 16 letter stated, "In an effort to save time we showed you an unfinished print at the same time that another print of *The Street of Forgotten Men* was being revised at our studio. It was the opinion of the people at the studio that the scene to which objection was made by your Commission in reel 1, did not belong in the picture and it is missing from all of the prints to be shown throughout the United States." Allvine's letter continued, "In regard to the subtitle in Reel 3, it is the opinion of most people, including some Catholics, that the scene and the references to the crucifix are seriously and reverently done and we would ask that your objection to the word be waived." The letter then went on ask that a letter be returned cancelling the Commission's July 14 letter.

On July 17, the Commission's deputy director wrote a letter acknowledging Paramount had cut the Salvation Army scene in Reel 1, and, without additional explanation, the commission waived its objection to the use of the word crucifix in Reel 3. Additionally, the group further stated its letter of July 14 had been cancelled, and *The Street of Forgotten Men* was free to be shown in New York state. It was just in time for the film's July 19 premiere.

In all likelihood, that first license (dated July 16) was affixed, in the form of a seal, to the print of the film shown at its debut at the Rivoli theater in New York City. However, more exhibition prints would be required, and with them, additional licenses, as the film would soon come to play in Brooklyn and Buffalo and Syracuse and Albany and Rochester and elsewhere around the Empire State. Famous Players requested, and received at a cost of $2.00 per reel for the seven-reel film, additional seals on July 18 (for nine duplicate prints), July 21 (five duplicates), July 24 (two duplicates), August 12 (two duplicates), and August 18 (four duplicates). A few weeks later, on September 11, Famous Players received a sub-seal, or replacement seal, for

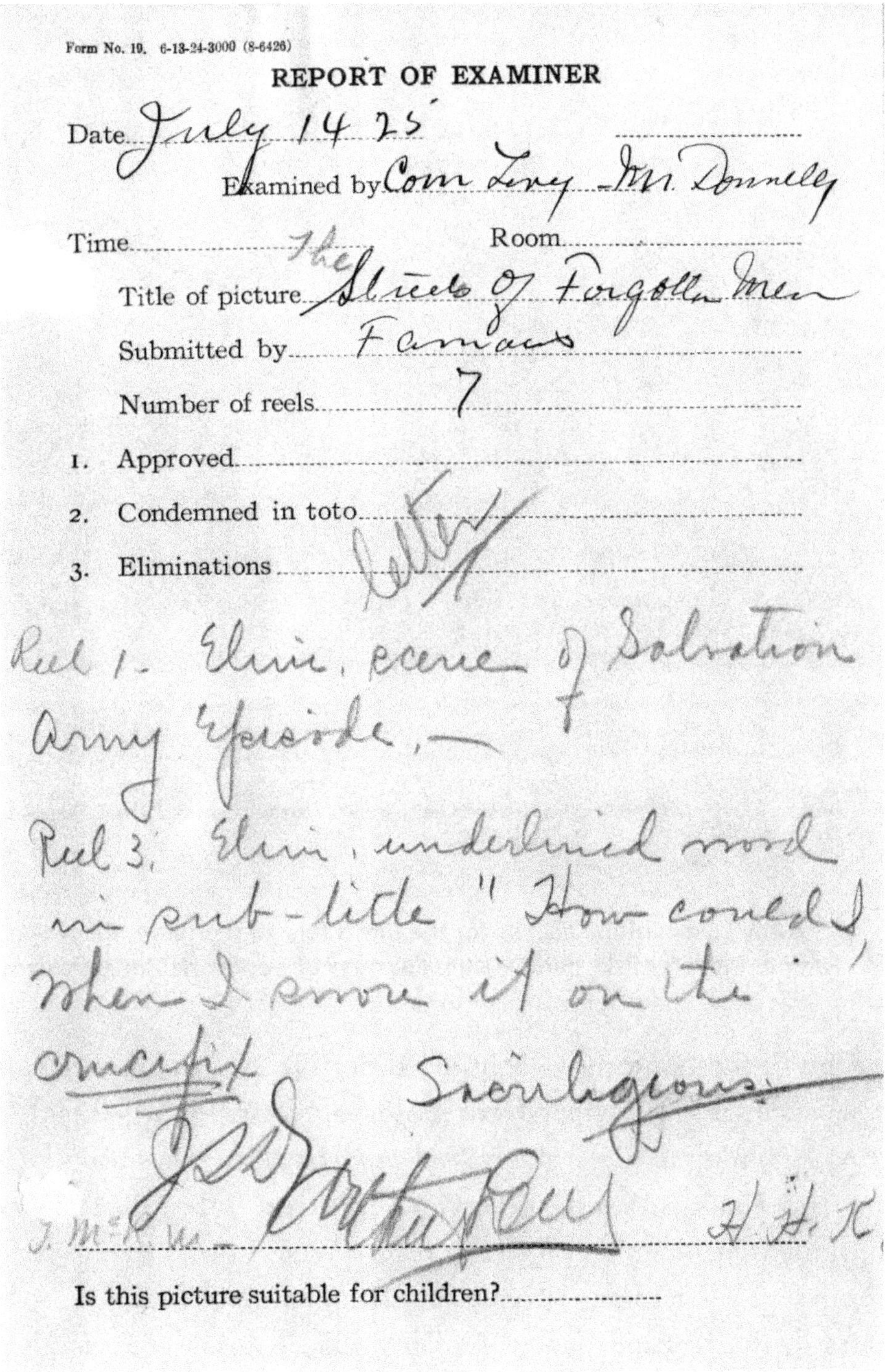

Form No. 19. 6-13-24-3000 (8-6426)

REPORT OF EXAMINER

Date July 14 25

Examined by Cora Levy - Mr. Donnelly

Time .... Room ....

Title of picture The Streets of Forgotten Men

Submitted by Famous

Number of reels 7

1. Approved
2. Condemned in toto
3. Eliminations

Reel 1. Elim. scene of Salvation Army episode, —

Reel 3. Elim. underlined word in sub-title "How could I, when I swore it on the crucifix" Sacrilegious.

J. McK. m.   H.H.K.

Is this picture suitable for children? ....

The New York Motion Picture Commission report calling for cuts to the film.
Courtesy of New York State Archives

The July 16 exhibition license for the film's July 19 premiere, for which Famous Players-Lasky paid $21.00. *Courtesy of New York State Archives*

a duplicate print of the film originally licensed on July 24, but subsequently lost.

In general, state or city censorship records are difficult to obtain. To date, few other records pertaining to *The Street of Forgotten Men* have been found. One exception comes from the Kansas Board of Review, who on July 30, 1925 called for the elimination of an intertitle in reel 6 which read, "Well, I don't blame you none – I like 'em young myself." The line, spoken by Bridgeport White-Eye to Easy Money Charlie, refers to the teenage Fancy Vanhern. The Kansas records also caution that the film contains smoking, though no action was recommended on that point.

In April, 1926, *The Street of Forgotten Men* was mentioned during a hearing of the Congressional Committee on Education, which was reviewing two bills, H.R. 4094 and H.R. 6233, which sought to create a body to be known as the Federal Motion Picture Commission. The function of this governmental agency would be to review the suitability of films shown to the public. Some of those who testified spoke on the "evil" effect some motion pictures had on movie goers, especially the young. The testimony also addressed the motivations of some movie makers, who, it was suggested, wanted to make "bad pictures" as there was profit to be made in doing so.

Canon Chase, a reform minded Episcopal pastor based in Brooklyn, had long been calling on the American government to clean up the movies and prevent the "debauching of the American mind." During his testimony, Chase stated, "Some producers claim that they cannot get enough good pictures. Others say that as long as some people want vile films they have a business right to produce them." Chase was asked to list "pictures that pay." He then listed more than two dozen films of merit that also proved profitable. Not surprisingly, *The Ten Commandments* was named first; it was followed by *Charlie's Aunt*, with *The Freshman* and other films tied at third, *The Hunchback of Notre Dame* and others tied at fourth, and *The Street of Forgotten Men* tied at fifth, along with *Peter Pan*, *The Unholy Three*, and others.

Amended to the Congressional testimony was a "selected list of better films . . . worthy of patronage." A catalogue of 572 selected pictures were named, these pictures having been screened by various community groups, some of whom were tied to two review publications of the time, *Film Progress* and *Exceptional Photoplays*. Included among the 572 films was *The Street of Forgotten Men*; the Brenon film was marked with an asterisk, having being judged "Especially interesting or well done but not necessarily exceptional." Despite the film's unsavory realism and unexceptional standing, it had been deemed safe for general viewing.

> *Street of Forgotten Men, The, Fam. Pl., 7, Percy Mormont. A fraudulent cripple adopts a baby and when she grows up sacrifices himself that she may marry well without having the stain of her foster-father's profession revealed; unusual scenes of the cripple factory. (Liberty Magazine story by George Kibbe Turner.) F. 11.7.

A clipping from a catalogue of 572 selected pictures. The film was recommended for "Fam." or family. Notably, the name of the film's popular star, Percy Marmont, is misspelled.

The Street of Forgotten Men: From Story to Screen and Beyond

The cover page of the Paramount Press Sheet for *The Street of Forgotten Men*.
Courtesy of Library of Congress

THE PRESS SHEET

A "press sheet," "press book," or "campaign book" are some of the names for the promotional flyer, pamphlet, or booklet issued by motion picture studio's beginning in the 1910s. Such publications – which could range from one to a few dozen pages – vary in form and content. Intended for the press as well as exhibitors (namely movie theaters), these ephemeral publications contained all manner of information about a film, including its story and stars, as well as editorial, promotional, and advertising content which give background to a film and its production.

As boldly stated under the banner of the Press Sheet for *The Street of Forgotten Men*, its "PURPOSE" was "To Help You Sell the Picture to the Public." This eight-page publication contained pieces about the film and its making, about the director and cast, and a synopsis of the film story. Along with articles, there are also suggested reviews which newspapers were free to use or adapt. In fact, many small-town newspapers utilized such material without attribution.

The Press Sheet also contained clip art, generic advertisements, and images of the film's poster, lobby cards, herald, coming attraction slide, and window displays. These promotional pieces, as well as photographs and newspaper advertisements, could be obtained from the regional studio exchange for a small fee.

As a publicity document, this and any press sheet should be viewed with a wary eye, as some of its anecdotes and articles may be little more than the invention of studio publicists. Did Brenon and Marmont once exchange blows while rehearsing a scene? And did Marmont really attempt to rent an automobile with humorous results? We may never know if either of these incidents, later reported as factual in newspapers across the country, were real – or mere ballyhoo.

Nevertheless, the value of this or any press sheet lay not so much in what it may tell about a film and its making – but in how the studio *wished* the public to think about the film itself. That is the press sheet's greatest value. In the case of *The Street of Forgotten Men*, some of the Press Sheet pieces stress the film's bold realism, while others suggest a hazy nostalgia for the time and place in which the film takes place. Similarly, other pieces reveal an ambivalence in how to describe the relationship between Marmont's character, Easy Money Charlie, and Mary Brian's character, Fancy Vanhern. In one piece, it's stated that Charlie has fallen in love with Fancy. In another, it's stated Fancy had fallen for Charlie. But what was the nature of this "love"? To a notable degree, the Press Sheet (and the scenario) are at odds with the film itself; in the former, there are suggestions of an unrealized romance. However, in the latter, the affection Charlie feels for Fancy is depicted, largely without complication, as that of a Father for his (adopted) daughter.

Though hundreds or even thousands of copies of the Press Sheet were printed, today it is rather scarce. The copy pictured here comes from the Library of Congress "Motion Picture Copyright Descriptions Collection, 1912-1977," where it had been submitted along with a print of the film (later returned) and other publicity materials for the purpose of enabling descriptive cataloging for motion picture photoplays registered with the United States Copyright Office. Despite the fact this particular Press Sheet remained with the Library of Congress and was later microfilmed, it shows its age in the creases, tears and chips of its brittle paper.

What follows are a number of the most telling pieces from Press Sheet. Each has been faithfully transcribed, though omitted from most are the last few sentences which repeat the names of the director and actors involved in the production.

These pieces reflect their time, and some may find their language or attitudes old-fashioned, disquieting, or offensive. Now nearly a hundred years old, these pieces also contain a number of unusual words and terms, such as "emanced" (referring to an emancipated woman) and "leg o'mutton sleeves" (referring to old-fashioned shirt sleeves). A number of such terms are included in a petite glossary at the end of this book. Along with unusual usages, as well as the names of actual historic locales (Bleeker Street, McGurk's Suicide Hall), individuals (O. Henry), and "tinpan" songs ("East Side, West Side"), these pieces form a cultural lens through which to view the film.

Cinderella and a Beggar Who Lost Himself for Love

If there is ever to be another *Miracle Man*, this is it! *The Street of Forgotten Men*, produced by Herbert Brenon, who made *Peter Pan*, from George Kibbe Turner's *Liberty* Magazine Story, deals with the class of people who are half crooks, half objects of pity, and their strange life, never before revealed.

Percy Marmont, Neil Hamilton and Mary Brian (*The Little French Girl*) are featured in the principal roles of production which was adapted for the screen by Paul Schofield.

The million readers of *Liberty* hailed the story as a masterpiece. After reading the synopsis below you can readily see its marvelous possibilities for the screen and can rest assured that Paramount has realized them to the limit.

The Street of Forgotten Men, a romance of the underworld – the strange story of a Bowery Cinderella and a beggar who lost himself for love – is an even stronger story than the Meighan-Tucker classic.

Short Synopsis

The Street of Forgotten Men is a short street running off the Bowery. Diamond Mike's Saloon is the best known dive in it for it is there all the professional beggars of the city gather. And it is in a backroom of the saloon – the Cripple Factory, they call it – that Adolf the Disguiser turns Husky men and women into fake beggars who take in hundreds of dollars a day by working on the sympathies of the crowd.

The best known faker of his time is Easy Money Charlie (played by Percy Marmont) who is called the "King of the Beggars." His chief rival is White-Eye who fakes blindness not only to the public but even to his fellow-fakes

Portland Fancy, one of the women hangers-on in Diamond Mike's, is dying, and she sends for Charlie. She tells him she has a little girl, four years old, that she is in an orphan asylum and she begs Charlie to take her out and bring her up away from the street and give her a decent chance in life. At first this King of the Beggars is appalled with the idea of bringing up a girl but the woman is dying and he can't refuse.

So he got himself a housekeeper and a little bungalow away from the city and he got the kid and started trying it out. Year after year he took care of her, keeping her off the streets and never letting her know who she was. For thirteen years he went on with this double life between his new home and the Street of Forgotten Men and he learned so to love the little girl that he dreaded the time when she would grow up. And when it came and a fine fellow, an ambitious young lawyer, (played by Neil Hamilton) asked her to marry him, the girl refused because, as the housekeeper later confided to Charlie, she was secretly in love with him.

To save the girl (played by Mary Brian) Charlie, because he knows he is unworthy of her, decides to go out of her life. But before he goes, he visits the young lawyer and tells him all, tells him the kind of life he has led, tells him he is not even fit to shake hands with Phillip and that he has decided it is best for him to go out of the girl's life altogether. So he takes a long sea voyage and Phillip is not greatly amazed when he receives a letter telling him that Charlie was swept overboard during a storm. A little later when Philip again proposed to the girl she accepts him.

In the meantime White-Eye, Charlie's arch enemy, had learned about the girl, had threatened to tell her everything once even before Charlie decided to go out of her life, but the King of the Beggars had given him a sound thrashing. Now when he reads of her engagement in the newspaper, he

Ad or Program Catchlines

Has the underworld a heart? See "The Street of Forgotten Men."

The director of "Peter Pan" has produced another masterpiece.

Is there romance in the lives of New York's professional beggars?

The strange story of a Bowery Cinderella and the beggar who lost himself for love.

A drama of great human heart thrills sweeping on to a stupendous climax.

determines to become a blackmailer and extort money from her to keep her secret. Charlie returns to the street having suspected White-Eye's intent. They argue and a terrible fight ensues in which White-Eye actually goes blind. When White-Eye, coward that he is, pleads for mercy, Charlie realizing that White-Eye can do the girl no harm, pities him and promises to help him. The last shot shows the girl coming from the church in her bridal crown, with White-Eye and Charlie hidden in the crowd on the sidewalk – the one who gave her up that she might be saved from the Street of Forgotten Men, the other who would have dragged her down had not fate taken a hand. And the girl – she never knew there were such men, nor the place where they fought over her.

Paramount Picture Underworld Romance
The Street of Forgotten Men **Herbert-Brenon-Paramount Production**

The Bowery in the 90s!

Talk about your covered wagons and your mining camps — they had nothing on this picturesque district when it was at the height of its fame.

Naturally, as colorful a place as this has been a fertile field for writers and playwrights. Many of the old thrillers of the stage, such as the perennial favorite *A Night in Chinatown*, were laid in the blood-and-thunder atmosphere of this picturesque corner of New York. The sentimental and sugary novels of the Laura Jean Libby, Bertha M. Clay and Horatio Alger school made liberal use of the Bowery as a setting for their highly moral plots. With the gradual change of literary tastes, established authors of our own time have also recognized the possibilities of the district as a setting for sincere and less hysterical writing. O. Henry found in it material for some of his inevitable stories, and George Kibbe Turner has recently given an unusual glimpse of one of the most interesting and little known phases of life in his story, appropriately titled, *The Street of Forgotten Men*.

"Different" Story

This deals with a class of petty criminals who practiced begging as a profession. In a dingy room in the rear of one of the most noted dives, a crafty Frenchman conducted a "cripple factory" in which the pan handlers were cleverly made up to appear sick and old and woe-begone and were fitted with artificial limbs and other apparatus which gave them the appearance of crippled men and women. So convincing and appealing were they that it was nothing unusual for them to "earn" a hundred dollars or more apiece each day from sympathetic citizens in the more respectable parts of the city.

As is the usual thing with gangs of criminals of every kind, the begging profession had its leader, or "king." This character is portrayed by Percy Marmont and the Paramount screen version of the story, produced by Herbert Brenon, who made *Peter Pan* and *The Little French Girl*.

Recreates "Old Days"

An unusual combination of circumstances makes him the guardian of a child of the streets who is looked upon by his "subjects" as a legitimate recruit for their profession. But while the story of the "king's" sacrifice of his throne to save the girl is gripping and appealing, the re-creation of the old Bowery days and scenes is equally interesting, both to the "old timers" who remember the brown derbies and leg-o' mutton sleeves of those times and to the younger generation to whom the Bowery is just an old-fashioned song and not a reality.

Three-column Newspaper Advertisement 3A

Street of Forgotten Men Bowery Romance
Herbert Brenon – Paramount Picture Feature at Rialto Theater

The Bowery and the late 90s!

That was the heyday of romance and sentiment, of simplicity and unsophistication, all of which was reflected in the songs of the period. "Little Annie Rooney," "East Side, West Side," "The Belle of Avenue A" – what memories these simple melodies bring back to the men and women of today who were just stepping into mature years when the Bowery was the country's center of romantic interest!

The romance, however, was mostly in the imaginations of those who didn't know the district from first hand experience. The wise men in those days found the Bowery a mighty fine place to stay away from, and the stranger who ventured into its sinister confines counted himself lucky to get out again with a whole skin. Many an innocent and unsuspecting sightseer could vouch for the truth of the experience is related in that familiar song, "The Bowery."

Probably there was no tougher place in the world than this congested area in the 90s and the early years of the present century. Here was a hotbed of crime, political corruption and violence of every kind. Here plots were hatched and plans laid for atrocities that make the blood run cold in remembrance of them. "Billy" McGlory's saloon on Hester Street was one of the most notorious of the many gathering places for the night-blooming gentry of the district, and other dives such as The Glass Barrel, The Silvan Divan, The Slide and "The" Allen's on Bleeker Street contributed to the outward gaiety and the inner maliciousness of the old Bowery.

When the hordes of foreign born swept into the country in the latter half of the nineteenth century, the "East Side" became the nation's melting pot, and the Bowery was its center. Gangsters, criminals and degenerates from all over the world congregated within its boundaries, and the district took on a sinister malevolent aspect which made it a by-word among honest and law abiding citizens. The Bowery by 1890 had become truly "the street of forgotten men," where the wrecks of life and the dregs of manhood took refuge in obscurity. Existing like the lowest of animals, they wrung from the world a living by every kind of violence, from petty thievery to capital crime. The story is described as an underworld romance – the strange tale of a Bowery Cinderella and a beggar who lost himself for love.

Another One for Crossword Puzzle Addicts

What's a four letter word meaning a beggar, crippled or otherwise, who solicits your aid at subways entrances and on the streets?

The answer is – fake!

John D. Godfrey, mendicant officer for the Brooklyn Bureau of Charity, says there isn't a deserving beggar at large today. Herbert Brenon who produced *The Street of Forgotten Men* at the Paramount Long Island studios, called in Mr. Godfrey to assist in creating the proper authentic atmosphere for the "cripple factory" which the "King of the Beggars" uses as his headquarters when off duty.

"Twenty years ago, the period in which the story is laid, these 'cripple factories' did a rushing business," says Mr. Godfrey. "Many of their devices for fooling the public were very ingenious. The practice still persists to some extent, and it is often difficult to spot the fake cripple."

"But while these fakes can be detected when they are arrested and examined at the station house, the hardest one to catch has always been the deaf-and-dumb faker. Many of them learn the sign language, and up to a few years ago there wasn't much that we could do about it. But nowadays we give them the other test. When a deaf-and-dumb beggar is arrested, and we are reasonably sure that he is a fake, we take them to a hospital and have a doctor administer ether until the beggar is unconscious. Then he is allowed to come out from the anesthetic – and if he can talk, he always does talk, in large quantities. Today when such a faker is locked up, the mere threat of this test will make him throw up the sponge."

George Kibbe Turner has laid the scene of this story, *The Street of Forgotten Men*, in the haunts of the pan handlers who used to take in hundreds of dollars a day apiece. The unusual life and customs of these people are used as the background of an appealing story of love and self-sacrifice.

"Cripple Factory" Screen's Strangest Scene in *Street of Forgotten Men*

One industry of New York City which you won't find listed in the census reports of 20 years ago was the making of cripples. In the early years of this century there were several so-called cripple factories known to the police where day and night shifts of professional beggars were fitted with fake bandages, artificial arms and legs, false high heeled shoes and other trick paraphernalia for the luring of sympathetic coins into battered tin cups.

Herbert Brenon shows one of these cripple factories in operation in his new production, *The Street of Forgotten Men*. Every detail is authentic, for the set was built and furnished under the supervision of John D. Godfrey, who for over 20 years has been mendicant officer of the Brooklyn Bureau of Charity and who assisted Mr. Brenon in technical and research work on this story.

Here are shown beggars being made up under the expert hand of Adolphe, a little Frenchman who was famous in his day for his artistic transformations. Piles of artificial limbs, canes and crutches give atmosphere to the place, as do the mugs, or pictures, of famous beggars which adorn the dingy walls. There are signs reading "I Am Blind" and "Please Help a Cripple" which add a note of sardonic humor, especially when these "blind" and "crippled" men are seen stowing away their street clothes in lockers while they don their begging costumes. The "monikers" which are scrawled on these lockers are interesting in themselves: Bridgeport White-Eye, Easy Money Charlie, London Tip, Ed the Flop, Chicago Stick and others, even including Handsome Harry and Diamond Dick.

There is just as much faking done today as there ever was, according to Mr. Godfrey, who recently took Herbert Brenon on a tour of investigation through the hearts of the professional beggars in greater New York; but it is pretty crude today compared to the "artistry" of twenty years ago. There are no known cripple factories now in operation, the beggars working nowadays on the "lone wolf" principal instead of in organized gangs as they used to. However, thousands of dollars a day are extracted from too sympathetic people by beggars who find it far easier to reap rich pickings in this way than to earn an honest living. "It is nothing uncommon," says Mr. Godfrey, "for a beggar to collect five hundred dollars or more in a single day."

The Street of Forgotten Men centers around the "king of the beggars" and tells an interesting story of a double personality assumed by him because of a young girl who has been entrusted to his care. Percy Marmont has in this role a character part which suits him better than anything in which he has been seen in some time, and Mary Brian, *The Little French Girl* and the adorable Wendy of *Peter Pan*, is the girl. Neil Hamilton completes the trio of players featured in the principal roles of the production, which is adapted for the screen by Paul Schofield from the *Liberty* magazine story by George Kibbe Turner.

The Street of Forgotten Men Is an Absorbingly Interesting Tale of "Inside" Life of the Old Bowery

The Bowery of today is a calm and placid place compared to the famous street as it was a quarter of a century ago. Most of the "dives" have been turned into ice cream parlors or carefully stage-managed showplaces for tourists. The criminals and degenerates who used to make it a by-word among respectable people have given way to shiftless wrecks whose nerve is great enough only for the filching of an unwary pocketbook.

But in one respect things are much the same. In the old days, the denizens of the Bowery, whose lives form the interesting background of *The Street of Forgotten Men*, a new Herbert Brenon production for Paramount, used various terms to designate people and things with which they came into most frequent contact. This argot, or slang, was not only picturesque and typical of the crooks and professional panhandlers who used it, but also was of practical value to them, for it was a kind of code which prevented the stranger (who was usually the victim) from understanding the trend of the conversation. The guileless tourist, for instance, who was wont to come to the Bowery in search of a thrill which he could afterwards relate – with embellishments! – to the home folks in Hicksville, wasn't likely to suspect that the amusing Bowery tough had anything sinister in mind when he spoke to a confederate about a "super" or a "leather." Only when it was all over did he realize that they were discussing the watch and wallet which flitted from his pockets soon afterward!

This code of slang phrases has come down to the present day pretty much unchanged. A pickpocket is still a "dip," and a safe-breaker a "peterman." Everyone knows that a "mark" is a sucker and that a banknote is a "wrapper." Now, as in the old days, a precious stone is a "prop," a gold watch chain is a "red slang," a sneak thief is a "heelman."

George Kibbe Turner, in his story on which *The Street of Forgotten Men* is based, has given an absorbingly interesting picture of the "inside" life of the Bowery in the old days. Many phases of it, such as the operations of the "cripple factory" and activities of the professional beggars and the panhandlers, will come under the head of "absolutely new" to most people. It will be especially startling to those good folks who have been giving generously to beggars to learn that these mendicants, both of yesterday and today, are fakes who deliberately prey on sympathetic passers-by. John D. Godfrey, who had had over twenty years' experience with beggars, and who assisted Herbert Brenon in the production of this picture, says that in all his dealings with mendicants he has yet to find a single deserving case.

Beggar in *Street of Forgotten Men* Looked So Pathetic That Passers-by Insisted on Giving Alms

New York may have a reputation for being a cold, heartless city, but it has its generous moments – moments of curious, unreasoning generosity.

Recently Herbert Brenon, Percy Marmont, Mary Brian and John Harrington were driven down Fifth Avenue in an inexpensive automobile. Following them was a light truck in which a camera was concealed, for they didn't want to draw a crowd. The car and truck parked on the west side of the avenue diagonally opposite St. Patrick's Cathedral. Services were still in progress.

Mr. Brenon, Mr. Marmont and Miss Brian were dressed naturally, like the other Sunday morning strollers, and attracted practically no attention as they rehearsed a scene near the cathedral. Mr. Harrington, however, was attired like a beggar. His hat looked as though it had been run over by a few trucks. The suit wouldn't have brought twenty cents in a Salvation Army store. He had a sign hanging on his neck: "I am blind."

But – and here's the part Brenon can't explain – Harrington was sitting in the seat of an automobile. A chauffeur was on the front seat. In spite of this sympathetic persons dropped coins into Harrington's cup. In less than 10 minutes he received three contributions totaling twenty-seven cents.

In the meantime the camera truck had been moved to the other side of the avenue and Harrington was stationed on the corner near the cathedral. Mr. Marmont and Miss Brian were to walk down the avenue and drop a coin or two in Harrington's tin cup and proceed.

Harrington had hardly taken his place when an elderly well dressed woman walked toward him and dropped a coin. One of Director Brenon's assistants tried to intercept her. She looked at him coldly, made a cutting remark about heartless detectives and proceeded.

By this time Mr. Brenon was insistent that no further money should be received. He ordered his aides to prevent contributions, as he didn't want to appear to have taken advantage of anyone's generous impulses. The scene was hurried, but before Mr. Marmont and Miss Brian could get near Harrington two more women had tried to put money in his cup.

Brenon's assistant held his arm out to prevent one of the contributions. He received a sharp reprimand from the stranger. He explained the scene was for motion picture and the woman exclaimed:

"Isn't that too bad he looks so pathetic!"

By this time Harrington was becoming embarrassed and Director Brenon was afraid a crowd would gather if a beggar refused any further alms, so the scene was completed with passersby dropping coins at will. In the few moments that this took, sixty-eight cents was collected, making a total of ninety-five.

When Mr. Brenon started filming *The Street of Forgotten Men* for Paramount he called for advice from some city officials and was told most beggars were fakers and that most of them also made large sums daily. This apparently proves these statements, Mr. Brenon points out, because the whole episode lasted less than 15 minutes at an hour in the morning when the pedestrians were few in number.

Street of Forgotten Men, Kibbe Turner Story, New Paramount Film

Do you remember the days when a big glass of beer cost five cents and a free lunch went with it? And do you remember the German bands that used to play in the good old summer-time? Then surely, you remembered the Bowery, the famous playground of New York City in the late nineties.

Those were the days of brown derbies and leg o'mutton sleeves. Those are the days of McGurk's "Suicide Hall," The People's Theater, The Atlantic Gardens, Steve Brodie's Place, Tony Pastors, The "Glass Barrel," and "The Silvan Divan." Perhaps there were some things you've never even heard of. For instance, there was Diamond Dick's "Dead House." It was located in the rear of a saloon on the Bowery.

The late 90s was the time when New York cops used to stroll in pairs, never alone. Some parts of the street were considered quite dangerous and the immediate vicinity of the "Dead House" was no exception to this rule.

Herbert Brenon has brought it all back to the screen in *The Street of Forgotten Men*. It is the nearest thing to the famous *Miracle Man* that has ever been made.

"Easy Money" Charlie was one of "The Forgotten Men" who met in Diamond Dick's "Dead House." Here the gang disguised themselves as cripples and went out on the streets to beg for alms. These scenes give one a remarkable sense of realism, so well is the period portrayed.

A dying woman entrusts him with her child. He promises to bring it up as his own. Then begins for Charlie what is virtually a dual life. He is two persons at the same time. In his apartment with the girl and a housekeeper he is a prosperous businessman, but by day he is still Easy Money, the "crippled" beggar.

As the years pass, the child grows up ignorant of what her guardian really is. She becomes a beautiful girl and he, reluctant to admit as much, falls in love with her. But she, with her higher education, loves the young millionaire. The picture holds one's interest every minute of its stay on the screen.

Before it comes to a close, the tangled strings are all straightened and everyone is happy. Contrary to the usual order of movie plots, Charlie does not marry the girl.

There's a surprising twist at the climax.

Mary Brian Married—for First Time on the Screen

Mary Brian's gone and done it!

Got married, that is. But the wedding was not of the "till

PUTTING IT OVER RIGHT

As this is a story from the ever-growing LIBERTY MAGAZINE, build a false front to the lobby, of beaver board, containing entrance and exit. Paint this front as the front cover of an issue of LIBERTY, bearing the announcement, "A Paramount Picture," in the center, for an illustration, a cut-out from one of the posters. Or adapt the same idea for a large sign to stand in the center of the entrance to lobby.

Snipe arrows of cardboard all over town, all pointing in direction of theatre reading:— TO THE STREET OF FORGOTTEN MEN. Put these up before announcing the picture and benefit by their teaser value.

Advance teaser ads for newspapers:—
Have YOU walked THE STREET OF FORGOTTEN MEN?
Where is THE STREET OF FORGOTTEN MEN?
Who lives on THE STREET OF FORGOTTEN MEN?
Is——St. THE STREET OF FORGOTTEN MEN?
Tie-ups with savings banks using the slogan:—SAVE your DOLLARS now so you will never tread THE STREET OF FORGOTTEN MEN. Use newspaper tie-up ads, windows, circulars, and possibly the issuance of special $1 bank checks to be used for the opening of new accounts. Many banks have done this—talk it over with them!

Advertise as—A romance of the underworld—the strange story of a Bowery Cinderella and a beggar who lost himself for love.

How about a card for your grocers, butchers, etc. — "Have you FORGOTTEN anything, madame? Don't forget to see 'The Street of Forgotten Men' at the ...."

Employment agencies: "Let us find a job for you. Get off THE STREET OF FORGOTTEN MEN."

Tie-up with the Salvation Army for a collection of wearing apparel, etc., to go to unfortunates on "the street of forgotten men."

Get a street map of New York, and instead of The Bowery, letter in, preferably white on black, The Street of Forgotten Men.

Run a series of teaser ads, each one headed The Street of Forgotten Men and featuring a man once prominent and now little remembered.

Get a picture of a prominent street in your town the way it looked fifty years ago and label it The Street of Forgotten Men, with a sub-head telling what street it really is. This will arouse much local interest and curiosity.

death do us part" variety, as the bridegroom in the case, Neil Hamilton, already has a charming wife.

But a first wedding, even if solemnized for screen purposes only, is an exciting and thrilling event to be prepared for with all due ceremony.

As the search for wedding finery progressed in New York's best shops, Mary Brian found herself the central figure in many humorous and awkward misunderstandings on the part of unduly sympathetic sales people, who are perhaps too eager to help in the selection of an outfit for the young bride-to-be. One envious spinster of uncertain age was overheard in the remark: "Something ought be done about these child marriages. It's an outrage, to permit such a youngster to marry!"

Percy Marmont in Best Role In *Street of Forgotten Men*

MARY BRIAN IN THE PARAMOUNT PICTURE "THE STREET OF FORGOTTEN MEN"
Production Mat 1PB

Percy Marmont gives one of the greatest character portrayals of his career in the role of "Easy Money" Charlie in *The Street of Forgotten Man*, which is Herbert Brenon's newest production for Paramount. This story deals with a petty panhandler who adopts a little girl and brings her up in the ignorance of his profession, only to see the one fine thing in his life threatened with ruin through the evil plotting of one of his fellow crooks.

George Kibbe Turner, who wrote the story for *Liberty* Magazine has created an unusual and exceptionally interesting character in Easy Money Charlie. Most of the dramatic action of the story is laid in a dive bar near the Bowery to which the flock of hopeless, battered wrecks whom life has forgotten – a novel background against which Charlie and the girl stand out appealingly.

In such a role, Percy Marmont is in his element. Here he is seen as a beaten, hopeless wanderer, forced by the circumstances into a life of petty crookedness which almost buries the idealism which he had hope to use in bettering the world in general. Then with dramatic suddenness, he becomes the guardian of a small girl. To bring her up like a lady, he is forced to remain in the surroundings he despises and to keep her in ignorance of his profession. When she reaches womanhood, he falls in love with her; but this, too, he is forced to conceal and, by shamming death, he leaves her free to marry young man in her own sphere of life.

Here's a Laugh!

When Percy Marmont was engaged to play the leading role in Herbert Brenon's *The Street of Forgotten Men* at the Paramount Long Island Studio, he sent a letter and check from Hollywood to an automobile agent in New York so that he would have a car during his stay there. On his arrival, he called on the concern and said he was ready to drive away.

"Good grief!" gasped the agent, collapsing in his chair. We thought you wanted the car in California, and we shipped it a week ago. But cheer up," he added hopefully, "we'll try to catch it, and you ought to get it back in not more than three weeks."

That's fine, said Marmont. They'll give me about two whole days of driving before I leave again for the Coast!"

Here's One on the Men, Girls!

The emancipation of woman seems to be an established and recognized fact. In fact, they have emanced in some directions to a point where men are being crowded to the wall. This is illustrated during the filming of Herbert Brenon's new production *The Street of Forgotten Men*. The scene was a tough bar room on the Bowery in the 90s, filled with men and women none of whom would have won a prize either at a beauty show or a peace conference. To get the proper atmosphere, before the camera started grinding Mr. Brenon ordered them to smoke up as hard as they could for a few minutes. The men puffed away at the pipes and cigarettes, all except one

"Hey, you at the piano! the director shouted; go ahead and smoke! Take six big puffs!"

The sallow youth at the tinpan piano took a few puffs that wouldn't have equaled the efforts of a boy with his first cigarette.

"For the love of Pete! exclaimed the irate Mr. Brenon. "Try again. No – wait! Let that woman do it!"

The woman, a mere slip of a girl, lighted a cigarette and took a half dozen mouthfuls that completely enshrouded her corner of the set. Having achieved the wished for "atmosphere," the director gave the word to the cameraman while the crowd laughed and the studio orchestra struck up "It Was Not Like that in the Olden Days!"

> *Don't keep the pictures you run a secret. There's cash in the flash of peppy Paramount paper!*

PARAMOUNT EXPLOITEERS

HERE are the trained showmen assigned each Paramount exchange exclusively for the purpose of helping you put your pictures over. Get in touch with your exploiteer:

Name	Address	City
ANSLEY, SEYMOUR	1610 Davenport St.	Omaha, Neb.
BALSLY, LEE D.	265 South Front Street	Memphis, Tenn.
BIRCH, AL G.	1625 Court Place	Denver, Colo.
CALLAHAN, JOHN	134 Meadow St.	New Haven, Conn.
CORCORAN, EDWARD F.	119 Seventh St.	Milwaukee, Wis.
CUNNINGHAM, EARL	110-112 W. 18th St.	Kansas City, Mo.
DANZIGER, WILLIAM	Pioneer & Broadway	Cincinnati, O.
DUNHAM, CURTIS	300 S. Jefferson St.	Dallas, Tex.
EAGLES, HARRY C.	2017 Third Avenue	Seattle, Wash.
FRANKLIN, KENTON	514 West Grand Ave.	Oklahoma City, Okla.
GAMBRILL, GEORGE	3721 Washington Blvd.	St. Louis, Mo.
GEYER, ERNEST	51 Luckie St.	Atlanta, Ga.
HAAS, J. A.	444 Glisan St.	Portland, Ore.
HELLMAN, JACK	1100 First Avenue N.	Minneapolis, Minn.
KANTNER, OSCAR	201 Golden Gate Ave.	San Francisco, Cal.
MALONE, TED	211 South Mint Street	Charlotte, N. C.
McCONVILLE, JOHN P.	8 Shawmut St.	Boston, Mass. (and Portland, Me.)
MENDELSSOHN, WILLIAM	1563 East 21st St.	Cleveland, O.
McINERNEY, JOHN E.	206 Victoria St.	Toronto, Can.
MOON, RUSSELL B.	1327 S. Wabash Ave.	Chicago, Ill.
PICKERING, HAROLD W.	133 E 2nd South St.	Salt Lake City, Utah
PUTNAM, LUTHER L.	501 Soledad Street	San Antonio, Tex.
RENAUD, KENNETH	2949 Cass Avenue	Detroit, Mich.
ROBSON, WILLIAM N.	1018 Forbes St.	Pittsburgh, Pa.
SWIFT, HARRY	924 S. Olive St.	Los Angeles, Cal.
WALL, EDWARD J.	1101 N. Capitol Ave.	Washington, D. C.
WATERSTREET, IRVIN A.	116 W. Michigan St.	Indianapolis, Ind.
WIEST, JAMES M.	110 North Lee St.	Jacksonville, Fla.
WILLIAMS, GEORGE E.	254 Franklin St.	Buffalo, N. Y.
WRIGHT, WILLIAM H.	251 N. 5th St.	Columbus, Ohio
ZELTNER, IRWIN	62 N. State St.	Wilkes Barre, Pa.

"Paramount Exploiters" notes the locations around the United States of the studio exchanges from which exhibitors could obtain publicity and display materials.

Advertising Price List

NOTE:—Owing to duty, additional transportation charges, etc., the prices quoted below do not apply to Canada. Get Canadian Price List from your Exchange.

FOR OUTDOOR ADVERTISING—POSTERS

One Sheet (1A and 1B)	$ .15
Three Sheet (3A and 3B)	.45
Six Sheet (6A)	.75
Twenty-four Sheet (24A)	2.40
3' x 10' Banner	2.00

PHOTOS FOR YOUR LOBBY

22 x 28 (Colored)	.40
11 x 14 Set of Eight (Colored)	.60

FOR NEWSPAPER ADS—ADVERTISING CUTS

One Column	.35
Two Column	.65
Supplementary (two column)	.25

MATS, ADVERTISING, PRODUCTION, ETC.

One Column	.05
Two Column	.10
Two Column Supplementary	.10
Three Column	.15
Four Column (Adv. Only)	.25

FOR GENERAL EXPLOITATION

GILT-EDGED FRAMES (Size 17 x 43 in.)	1.50
Insert Cards (14 x 36 in. to fit above)	.25
22 x 28 Gilt Frames	1.50
Combination Lobby Frames	2.00
Cardboard Frames for Stills	.15
Herald, per thousand	5.00
Window Card	.07
Announcement Slide	.15
Publicity Photos	.10

Trailers—National Screen Service
  126 W. 46th St., New York City
  845 So. Wabash Ave., Chicago, Ill.
  917 So. Olive St., Los Angeles, Cal.

PRESS BOOKS AND MUSIC CUES ARE GRATIS.

The film's title card, which suggests the film is a romance

Juliet Brenon in the shoplifting scene, an usual choice for a lobby card

Actors Percy Marmont and Josephine Deffry

Actors Percy Marmont and Juliet Brenon

Unknown extras flank Percy Marmont and bit player Whitney Bolton

Officer Quinn stands between Whitey and Charlie, as Adolphe looks dejected

Actors Percy Marmont and Mary Brian

Actors Dorothy Walters, Mary Brian, and Neil Hamilton

"The Sidewalks of New York" sheet music, circa 1921. *Courtesy of New York Public Library*

ENTR'ACTE:
A MUSICAL INTERLUDE

Silent movies were never silent, neither in their making, nor in their exhibition. In fact, the films of the silent era inhabited a world of sound both off screen and on.

During the Teens and Twenties, it was common practice to have a musician or group of musicians on hand during the making of a film. This was done to help set the mood, and to provide a musical atmosphere in which the actors might better draw upon their emotions. As reports from the time note, that was the case during the making of *The Street of Forgotten Men*. One *New York Times* article, "From a Camera Platform in the Astoria Studio," made note of music on the set of the film, stating "Old-time tunes came from the piano and violins as the players went through the antics demanded of them." Further on in the article, the *Times* reporter mentioned two songs in particular, "The small orchestra reeled off 'The Sidewalks of New York'…. The next tune from the orchestra was 'The Bowery,' the Bowery. They say such things and they do such things – on the bowery!" (5-3-1925) Along with the *New York Times*, the studio Press Sheet also made mention of another song played on the set, "It Was Not Like that in the Olden Days".

The songs mentioned by the *New York Times* would have been familiar to much of the film's cast and crew, as well as to many movie goers. "The Sidewalks of New York," with lyrics which "tripped the light fantastic" into its familiar lilting refrain, "east side, west side, all around the town," dates to 1894 – around the time the opening scenes of *The Street of Forgotten Men* are set. Once described as "New York's Theme Song," it was already something of a nostalgic piece during the Roaring Twenties. In fact, the song was so evocative of a time and place – namely the "good old days," that Al Smith, the four-time Governor of New York, made it an official campaign song during his 1928 run for President. The other song mentioned in the *New York Times* article, "The Bowery," dates from 1891. It comes from a long-running Broadway play, *A Trip to Chinatown*. The song's refrain, slightly misquoted in the *New York Times* article, suggests the Bowery was a shadowy, even sordid place. "The Bow'ry, the Bow'ry! / They say such things, / And they do strange things / On the Bow'ry! The Bow'ry! / I'll never go there anymore!" Like "The Sidewalks of New York," "The Bowery" was popular; its sheet music reportedly sold a million copies.

Children dance around the man on the left who is entertaining the street with a wheeled, barrel piano. *Courtesy of SilentHollywood.com*

In setting its own scene, the Paramount Press Sheet also turned nostalgic, and similarly made mention of songs evocative of the Bowery of the past: "That was the heyday of romance and sentiment, of simplicity and unsophistication, all of which was reflected in the songs of the period. 'Little Annie Rooney,' 'East Side, West Side,' 'The Belle of Avenue A' – what memories these simple melodies bring back to the men and women of today who were just stepping into mature years when the Bowery was the country's center of romantic interest!" This bit of puffery was run in newspapers across the country, as was another similar bit drawn from the film's Press Sheet, to which the Queens (N.Y.) *Daily Star* added mention of the "old Bowery in the days when German bands played 'In the Good Old Summer Time'." (9-4-1925)

Along with music played during the making of the film, music is depicted in the film itself. Early on in the story, these depictions include children dancing in the street around a man playing a barrel piano, a group of (Salvation Army?) street musicians, and during the first scene inside the Dead House, the saloon pianist; later in the film, Fancy (Mary Brian) is shown playing the piano, and at a garden party, couples are shown dancing (with the source of music off screen). Each of these depictions of music can be considered visual cues meant to trigger the memories of moviegoers.

In one early scene set inside Diamond Mike's, the saloon pianist is shown entertaining the regulars. Another man, wearing a suit and a bowler, sits alongside and observes the goings-on, which includes a jovial, dancing couple. Placed on the piano are four pieces of sheet music, most of which can be identified. These sheets help dress the set, but more importantly, they cue the viewer who notices them to the music of a specific era. The sheets are Alice Lloyd's "Never Introduce Your Bloke to Your Lady Friend," another unidentified piece on which Alice Lloyd's name is prominent, a third sheet, "Why Don't You Write When You Don't Need Money" – a hit for both Bob Roberts and Gus Edwards, and a fourth sheet which is obscured.

Alice Lloyd (1873-1949) was a British-born music hall artist who achieved her greatest acclaim in the United States, where she headlined in Vaudeville between 1907 and 1921. At the time, sheet music sales rivaled and even surpassed sales of recordings. "Never Introduce Your Bloke to Your Lady Friend" was an early hit for Lloyd, as were other suggestively titled songs like "Stockings on the Line," "Who Are You Looking At?" and "The Tourist and the Maid." (Another song associated with the artist and issued on sheet music was "Little Church Around the Corner," from 1913.) Notably, Alice Lloyd's sister, Marie Lloyd (1870-1922) was a superstar in her native England. She was once described by poet T.S. Eliot as "the greatest music-hall artist of her time in England: she was also the most popular." On either side of the Atlantic, the names of both Lloyd sisters would have certainly evoked a time and place – the first decades of the 20th century – and perhaps even brought a remembered song to mind. Their placement in the film seems intentional.

In another scene in *The Street of Forgotten Men*, Mary Brian's character is shown playing the piano at home. The camera cuts from the actress to the sheet music set before her, which is shown to be "Peter Pan (I Love You)" – the theme song from the Brenon film which Brian starred in the year before. (This camera shot is explicitly called for in the scenario.) Though an odd, self-referential moment, few seemingly noticed or made mention of it. One publication that did was the *New York Times*, which took exception, noting how Mary Brian's role in *Peter Pan* was "unnecessarily stressed." (7-21-1925) Was it just this one brief visual cue which irritated the *Times*? Or was it the title card, in which Brian's character describes her guardian in terms which recall Peter Pan, "he knows how to play–he'll never grow old." Or was it the *Peter Pan* theme, whose playing is called for in the cue sheet?

Though largely missing from the surviving film, four street musicians are seen performing in this rare still. *Credit: From the Core Collection Production files and the Paramount Pictures photographs of the Margaret Herrick Library, Academy of Motion Picture Arts and Sciences*

(Top) The saloon pianist and his sheet music. *Courtesy of the San Francisco Silent Film Festival*
(Bottom) Fancy Vanhern at the piano. *Courtesy of New York Public Library*

During the silent era, films were seldom shown silently. According to Richard Koszarski's seminal 1990 book, *An Evening's Entertainment*, a survey conducted in 1922 revealed approximately 46% of respondents used a theater organ to accompany films, about 25% used a piano, and some 29% used small orchestras or musical ensembles (typically two to five players). But what did they play?

Generally speaking, there were three kinds of film scores during the silent era: an improvised score, a composed score, and a compiled score. Except for blockbuster films which sometimes had an original composed score, most films were accompanied by a combination of a compiled / improvised score.

Experienced instrumentalists, such as an organist or pianist, might improvise on their own, or, they might play from a thematic music cue sheet available from the studio. A cue sheet, which typically ran two or four pages, would list the title and author of a musical passage or song, when to play it, and how long to play it. Often, additional notes were given for tempo, sound effects, and so on, so that every important passage in the film would be given an appropriate musical setting.

A thematic music cue sheet was issued to accompany *The Street of Forgotten Men*. It was compiled by James C. Bradford. (Bradford was one of the most prolific compilers of the time; he was employed by the Cameo Thematic Music Co., the dominant firm supplying the various studios with cue sheets in the 1920s.) Like other scores of the time, it was a combination of both popular songs and classical or orchestral music.

The Thematic Music Cue Sheet for *The Street of Forgotten Men* calls for the film to begin with "The Sidewalks of New York," suggesting a time and place while setting a nostalgic mood. It continues with the similarly familiar number, "The Bowery," and includes among other pieces "New York by Electric Light," "The Mansion of Aching Hearts," "The Jolly Minstrel," and "That's an Irish Lullaby" (played during the scene when Charlie puts Portland Fancy's baby to bed); there is also a tune made popular by Isham Jones, "I'll See You in My Dreams," as well as a concluding number at the film's end, Irving Berlin's wistful "All Alone." Weaving in and out of this medley of popular and nostalgic songs are bits and pieces of classical and orchestral music, namely cues from J.S. Zamecnik and Ernö Rapée – two noted film score composers of the time, as well as compositions by Tchaikovsky, Grieg, and others, including Mendelssohn's popular "Wedding March," near the film's end. Altogether, these popular and classical cues provide for a rich musical atmosphere.

The sketch of an alternative score, written by Wesley Ray Burroughs, was printed in *The Diapason*, a Chicago-based publication devoted to the organ. (Its masthead described itself as both the "Official Journal of the National Association of Organists" and the "Official Paper of the Organ Builders' Association of America.") *The Diapason* served the interests of various communities, and carried news for and about professional and amateur musicians alike.

Burroughs was a well-known theater organist whose residencies included prominent venues in Philadelphia, Detroit, New York City, and Rochester, New York. A contributor to *The Diapason*, he penned a column, "With the Moving Picture Organist." One of his 1925 columns noted, "It seems to us that the late feature films are much better than formerly, and to illustrate the great variety of music which the picture organists must have in his library and especially certain numbers that are usable many times we select six of the last 20 played."
(12-1-1925)

One of the six titles Burroughs highlights is Brenon's then recent release, for which the columnist-musician sketched an alternative score. "*The Street of Forgotten Men* features Percy Marmont's best role, that of a Bowery crook. 'Sidewalks of New York,' 'The Bowery,' 'Streets of New York' (Red Mill), by Herbert, and 'Old Chestnuts Waltz' were used in the first reel. The second – light dramatic and pathetic – continues into the third until the fade out of the mother's death. On the title 'At Charley's Rooms' Kate Vannah's song 'Sleepy Baby' was used. A direct queue in the fourth reel calls for 'Peter Pan.' The fourth is bright and neutral – quiet until the title, 'Easter Sunday.' Here 'Adestes Fideles' for the church scene is especially good. Then follows Fauchey's 'Prologue,' Andino's 'Dramatic Tension,' Rapée's 'Appassionato' and Fauchey's 'Meditation.' At the title, in sixth reel, 'Be a Brave Girl,' use Raynard's 'Legend of a Rose.' A wedding march followed by Berlin's 'All Alone' ends the picture." (12-1-1925) Though similar to Paramount's score, Burroughs' suggestions amount to a worthwhile alternative.

169

Thematic Music Cue Sheet issued by Paramount. *Credit: George Eastman Museum*

Entr'acte: A Musical Interlude

171

Besides the feature film and its musical accompaniment, another draw for just about any theater was its pre-film entertainment, usually a combination of stage show and/or film shorts which ran prior to the main attraction. Typically, such live entertainment could include local musicians, the theatre organist, a touring performer, novelty acts, or Vaudeville.

The Street of Forgotten Men premiered at the Rivoli theater in New York City on July 19, 1925 – with Ben Bernie and His Orchestra as the opening "act". Bernie was a popular bandleader whose signature expression, "yowsah, yowsah, yowsah," became a national catchphrase. He was also a radio personality and recording artist who had appeared in a 1925 DeForest Phonofilm sound short, *Ben Bernie and All the Lads*. [It can be seen on YouTube.] His orchestra would go on to record a handful of popular songs. Among them was "Sweet Georgia Brown," which Bernie co-wrote and which hit #1 in July 1925, just as the orchestra was appearing at the Rivoli.

In scheduling Bernie's 11-man group (which, at the time, included noted saxophonist Jack Pettis and a teenage Oscar Levant on piano), the Rivoli was daring to offer something different from what most theaters offered – namely "hot jazz." Typically, theaters might offer light orchestral music, an organist, or novelty numbers – though nothing that might compete with the theater's main attraction, the feature film. At a time when jazz, especially up-tempo jazz, was considered suspect in some quarters, Rivoli ads assured patrons "Everybody Likes the New Jazz Policy."

Bernie proved popular. *Variety* described the group's musical offerings – which included a musical sketch titled "Montmartre" (after the bohemian neighborhood in Paris) as a "wow" which went over "tremendously." (7-22-1925) Besides Bernie, there was also a film short – a Grantland Rice Sportlight titled *Why Kids Leave Home*, which *Variety* also said carried "considerable kick" – as well as a novelty program of old-fashioned "Songs that You Have Sung" performed by the house organist. Also part of the pre-film entertainment was an 11-minute-long pictorial featuring brief films from International, Pathé, Fox, and Kinograms. An additional program titled "Evolution" was shown on Wednesday mornings. Its presentation coincided with the just concluded Scopes Monkey trial.

Musical Courier, a national trade journal which also reviewed the Rivoli program, agreed with *Variety*, noting the large crowds that turned out to hear Bernie and enjoy the theater's recently installed air-conditioning. "The picture, *The Street of Forgotten Men*, was fairly entertaining, and at least held interest. The audiences are getting what they want ... and then, of course, the Rivoli is the ideal spot for hot days and that's another big drawing card." (7-30-1925)

Most of the New York City press also liked Bernie, with the New York *Evening Journal* noting, "The remaining half of the Rivoli's program really is deserving of more praise than we can give it in the little space at our disposal. Ben Bernie and his gang have crammed into their allotted half hour more good music, exceptional dancing, clever comedy and pretty effects then you can ordinarily find in an entire bill of so-called big time vaudeville." (7-23-1925)

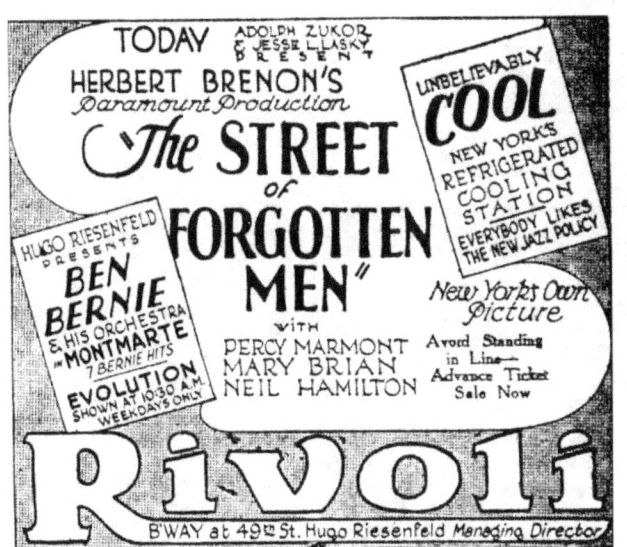

(Left) A New York City newspaper advertisement for the first showing of *The Street of Forgotten Men*. Along with the film, the ad also promotes the theater's recently installed and "unbelievably cool" air conditioning, as well as the appearance of popular band leader Ben Bernie, who provided some of the pre-film entertainment. Under the direction of Hugo Riesenfeld, the Rivoli also presented a Wednesday morning only showing of "Evolution," a news short about the recently concluded Scopes Monkey Trial. New York, New York – July 1925

One aspect of the Rivoli offerings which came in for criticism was the house organist, Harold Ramsbottom. Besides his nostalgic, pre-film organ melody of old songs, Ramsbottom also accompanied *The Street of Forgotten Men*, likely improvising off the cue sheet provided by Paramount. Harriet Underhill of the New York *Herald Tribune* thought his Wurlitzer playing merely "nice." But Dorothy Herzog of the *Daily Mirror* did not. Herzog lashed out at the musician, writing "The organist plays throughout the picture. He plays fearfully loud, which becomes both tiresome and nerve-wracking." Ramsbottom's loud accompaniment, however, did not take away from the critic's appreciation of the Rivoli's main attraction, the film on the screen.

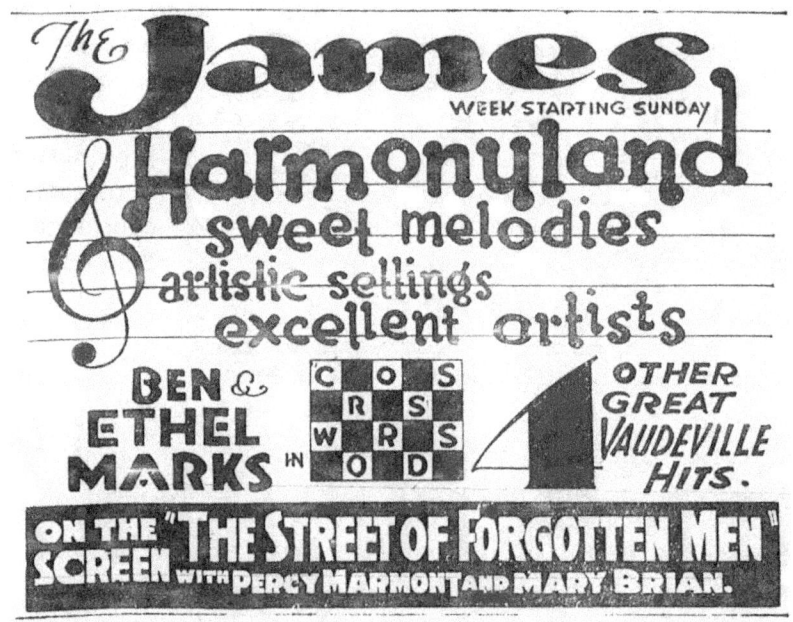

Besides Ben Bernie, other famous recording artists who appeared in conjunction with showings of *The Street of Forgotten Men* include Ted Weems, Henry Halstead, and Paul Ash, as well as regional acts like Ted Rose, Milo's Minstrels, and others. Various Vaudeville acts also opened for the film, and once, a Charleston lesson was given. (Top) *The Miracle Man* of 1925 meets the jazz minstrels of 1926. Chicago, Illinois – July 1925 (Bottom) Ben & Ethel Marks were a song and dance act who toured the country with "Crosswords," a humorous novelty act. Columbus, Ohio – August 1925

Appearing as an added feature at this Ohio screening was the House of David Band, composed of followers of the Christian Israelite faith. This long-haired musical group was part of a nearby religious community based in Michigan whose members refrained from sex, haircuts, shaving, and eating meat. Despite such strictures, these "Shave-less Sheiks of Syncopation" were said by the *Toledo Times* to "play unusually well and inject plenty of comedy into their program of syncopated numbers." Toledo, Ohio – March, 1926

Paramount's one sheet poster for the film.

A FILM HISTORY

Nineteen twenty-five was an especially good year for film. Among the still remembered works which dominated both the box office and critic's attention were epics such as *Ben-Hur* and *The Big Parade,* comedies like *The Gold Rush* and *The Freshman,* westerns including *The Pony Express* and *Riders of the Purple Sage,* and memorable dramas such as *The Merry Widow* and *The Phantom of the Opera.* That year also saw the release of still other significant works starring the likes of Clara Bow (*The Plastic Age*), Colleen Moore (*Sally*), Buster Keaton (*Go West*), Douglas Fairbanks (*Don Q, Son of Zorro*), and Rudolph Valentino (*The Eagle*), among others.

The Street of Forgotten Men didn't reach the heights of *The Big Parade* or *The Gold Rush* or some of the other just mentioned films – but it did garner its fair share of commercial success and critical accolades. *Exhibitor's Trade Review,* one of the leading industry publications, stated the film was tied for fifth (along with 18 others) among the year's biggest money makers, rendering it a kind-of top 40 hit. Among the other notable works with which it tied were Lon Chaney's *The Unholy Three* and Mary Pickford's *Little Annie Rooney,* as well as *Tracked in the Snow Country,* starring Rin Tin Tin. The film also tied with a few earlier releases still in circulation and still doing brisk business, including Brenon's *Peter Pan,* which was released in 1924. (Remarkably, according to that same piece in *Exhibitor's Trade Review,* the second biggest money maker of 1925 was Cecil B. DeMille's *The Ten Commandments,* which had been released two years earlier, in 1923.)

The commercial success enjoyed by *The Street of Forgotten Men* was matched by a similar degree of critical acclaim. The National Board of Review named the film one of the 40 best pictures of 1925 – a list which included many of the year's most notable releases; it was also named one of the year's ten best films by a handful of newspapers including the *Houston Chronicle, San Francisco Call & Post, Tacoma Daily Ledger, Tacoma Times,* and Topeka *Daily Capital.* As well, the *Pittsburgh Gazette Times* named it the very best film of the year, while the *Rochester Herald*, in upstate New York, gave it an honorable mention.

The film was also praised by some of the national and regional publications which gave coverage to the movies. Among them was *Liberty* magazine, which first published George Kibbe Turner's story; the magazine described *The Street of Forgotten Men* – a little uncharacteristically – as an "enjoyable film" which provided "a pleasant hour or two of screen entertainment." (9-12-1925) *TIME* magazine also gave the film a brief review, noting "Percy Marmont gives an especially good performance, the detail is excellent, the entertainment fair." (7-27-1925) *Judge*, another newsstand publication, thought it "good drama" and "to a certain extant a de-hokumized *Miracle Man*," (8-15-1925) in referring to the sensational Thomas Meighan - Lon Chaney film, the second highest grossing movie of 1919. In subsequent issues, *Judge's* Carroll Carroll declared *The Street of Forgotten Men* "better than *The Miracle Man*," as well as an "intelligent expose of professional begging."

One other publication, a newcomer to American newsstands, issued a considered though mostly negative review. *The New Yorker*, which debuted in early 1925, thought the movie more melodrama than heartfelt realism. Under the initials T.S., Theodore Shane wrote, "There is a depth of imagination to *The Street of Forgotten Men*. It is a story with vast possibilities in dramatic irony and character portrayal, but these have only been developed partially and are almost snowed under by truck sentimentality, movie theatricality, poor juveniles and inconsistent, punchless story detail. Had the cruelty of the blind man's nature been more fully intensified and the queerness of Mr. Marmont been more completely studied, the picture might have been great." Somewhat curiously, *The New Yorker* concluded its review by stating, "If only a Russian had written it!" and then adding, "As it is, it is well worth a trial visit." (8-1-1925)

A few special interest publications also took notice of the film. Both the *Catholic Telegraph* (from Cincinnati, Ohio) and *Catholic Advance* (from Wichita, Kansas) printed Charles A. McMahon's syndicated review, issued via the National Catholic Welfare Conference wire service; in it, McMahon declared *The Street of Forgotten Men* an "effective, interesting and entertaining melodrama," adding "Herbert Brenon has constructed an interesting and decidedly out-of-the-ordinary picture." (9-12-25) *Child Welfare Magazine* also recommended the film to its readers, as did *Common Ground* (a

Massachusetts teachers' magazine), *American Agriculturist*, and other publications. The latter ran an editorial bit supplied by the National Committee for Better Films which described the movie as a "picture dealing with fraudulent cripples," suggesting only those high school age and up see it.

The *Photoplay* review, from October 1925.

The many trade journals and fan magazines devoted to film also reviewed the production, giving it mostly positive press. Some praised its sense of realism – which was considered striking for the time. Most also highlighted its direction, its staging, or acting. What critics couldn't agree on was Brenon's use of melodrama – which a few thought too liberally applied; as well, the film's atypical ending was either praised or disliked. Those publications which expressed reservations regarding one or another aspect of the film still singled out the performances given by Percy Marmont and John Harrington, and to a lesser degree, others in the cast, including Juliet Brenon.

Whatever they said, whether pro or con, these reviews reflected the values of their time – including various aesthetic and moral values and attitudes, especially toward the poor, homeless and down-and-out. Notably, no publication dismissed the possibility that otherwise fit men and women dressed as "cripples" in order to fool the public. And, no publication thought the film too harsh or unforgiving toward the indigent. Was *The Street of Forgotten Men* a blow for realism in an age dominated by melodrama and romance? Many seemed to think so.

The most striking review the film received was given by *Movie Magazine*. Its anonymous critic wrote, "Seldom does a picture achieve artistry and still remain sordid and uncanny. *The Street of Forgotten Men* is one that rises to heights even though it deals with beggars, slums and other things associated with this atmosphere. It is quite novel and enjoyable even though the sordid moments come often. The hero, if he may be so-called, is 'Easy Money Charlie'…. Mary Brian and Percy Marmont are superb." (10-1925)

Alma Talley struck a similar tone in *Movie Weekly*. She wrote "*The Street of Forgotten Men*, is a film of real artistic merit, but it is sordid. Its atmosphere is largely of the slums, and has to do with fake beggars and kindred unpleasant things. But the story is extremely novel, and well worth seeing, if you don't mind a few morbid moments…. Percy Marmont is ideal as the beggar hero, who loves the heroine too much to let her marry him. The role calls for pathos and it doesn't call in vain, with Mr. Marmont playing it! Mary Brian is sweet as the orphan girl, and Neil Hamilton plays her aristocratic lover. Juliet Brenon (the director's niece) does outstanding work as 'Portland Fancy'." (8-22-1925)

Aside from the film's sordid & morbid atmosphere, *Film Mercury* made special note of the acting. It compared *The Street of Forgotten Men* to another Paramount production. "The work of Percy Marmont in this picture can be termed 'great.' A triumph of characterization. Mary Brian makes another step nearer her goal. The two of them cop the picture," wrote critic F.W.F. "The finest thing that can be said about this picture is that it's ending is consistent with its body. Marmont does not try to glorify 'Easy Money Charlie.' He infuses realism into his role. The audience reaction to Easy Money Charlie is a mingling of disgust, pity and affection. John Harrington as Bridgeport White-Eye does sterling work and should lose no time in capitalizing on his effective role in this film.... Brenon's directorial treatment is commendable. There are some parts of the picture that smack of old-time melodrama, but these parts form a small minority. Chalk this up as Marmont's best work; another step for Brian, and an audience picture that will please the majority of critics. This is, in general, akin to Paramount's *The City That Never Sleeps*, but much better. A money getter beyond a doubt." (9-18-1925)

Film Daily gave the film a near rave review, applauding its acting and noting the film's novel atmosphere and "*Miracle Man* flavor." Its review also singled out the film's ending. Its anonymous critic wrote, "Percy Marmont as a fake cripple beggar adds a choice one to the select list of outstanding character-creations of the screen. Can't recall a more sympathetic part ever filmed. Mary Brian again proves as she did in *Peter Pan* and *The Little French Girl* that she is one of the most winsome of players. Neil Hamilton as her suitor displays his usual charming manner. John Harrington excellent. Not a happy ending but a powerful punch. Higher grade audiences will welcome this as something worthwhile and the underworld atmosphere and unusual love story give this picture all around appeal. Herbert Brenon shows himself a master of atmosphere." (8-2-1925)

The Street of Forgotten Men—Drama

WHEN you have a story of the Bowery in its halcyon days of yesterday, you can depend that it will be tinted with a mellow glow. Here is George Kibbe Turner's yarn of two Bowery derelicts. We have had plenty of such tales on the silversheet, but none has contained more genuine heart touches and local color than this production, directed by Herbert Brenon. You will sympathize with Portland Fancy, a wreck of womanhood, who, as death approaches, begs Easy Money Charlie to take care of her little four-year old child, an inmate of an orphan asylum. And Charlie makes good. Percy Marmont is a fine choice to humanize such a rôle and Juliet Brenon, making her screen debut, portrays Portland Fancy with fine naturalness. Mary Brian, Neil Hamilton and John Harrington contribute effective performances.—*Paramount*.

Motion Picture magazine, November, 1925

Other magazine reviews were similarly positive, though brief. (As was typical at the time, few reviews were of any substantial length, and usually ran just a paragraph or two.) Among these "capsule reviews" was the piece printed in *Photoplay*, whose critic, M.B., described the film as "gripping and entertaining." (10-1925) *Screenland* said the film struck a "distinctive note." (8-1925) *Film Progress* thought the picture "ably directed." (Midsummer 1925) *Exhibitor's Trade Review* stated, "This recent opus of Herbert Brenon's is not a great picture, but it is a mighty good one. Realism is its keynote, and the director has even declined to toss in the sop of a happy ending." (8-8-1925) *Motion Picture* magazine (see prior page) stated "We've had plenty of such tales on the silver sheet, but none contain more genuine heart touches and local color than this production." (11-1925)

C.S. Sewell, writing in *Moving Picture World*, provided one of the more interesting critiques. "Paramount is offering a decidedly out-of-the-ordinary picture in the Herbert Brenon production *The Street of Forgotten Men*. Director Brenon has injected a lot of colorful atmosphere with a variety of underworld types and the women in the quaint costumes of the period…. audiences will find the backroom of this saloon of unusual interest." Sewell continued, "Considerable drama is developed in the unfolding of this story and especially forceful and logical is the ending where this beggar returns in his rags and secretly watches the girl's wedding. There are a number of other good touches throughout, including a fight between the fake cripple and a fake blind man who is the villain…. Exceedingly melodramatic but effective. Another excellent scene that has strong emotional force is the death of the kid's mother."

Sewell's thoughtful review then shifts from Brenon's staging to its cast. "There was good concentration of interest in this picture, for although there are a large number of characters, only four of them are of any importance. Rivaling the fine work of Percy Marmont is that of John Harrington in the particularly exacting role of crook who throughout almost the entire picture feigns blindness, showing only the whites and a bit of the iris of his eyes, and even standing the test of a lighted match in front of his face without blinking. Mary Brian is charming as the young girl and Neil Hamilton makes a good appearance opposite her but has very little to do. This story is decidedly impressive, out-of-the-ordinary and interesting and we believe that it will be quite generally liked." (8-1-1925)

One rather unusual assessment of the film appeared in *Exhibitors Herald*, which gave the film not one, but two reviews which it termed "unchecked reports." Each of these short write-ups were written independently of one another. One is by Douglas Hodges, a regular contributor to the trade journal. The other is by Martin J. Quigley, the journal's well-known editor and publisher. (*Exhibitors Herald* doesn't reveal who wrote which piece.) Nevertheless, each were exceedingly positive; the first piece declares the film "forceful throughout and impressive," while the second states the film "so vitally and so boldly told that it is shocking." (8-15-1925)

TWO UNCHECKED REPORTS ON "STREET OF FORGOTTEN MEN"

DOUGLAS HODGES saw "The Street of Forgotten Men" at McVickers early last week. I saw it later. We did not discuss it. We never discuss pictures until we've written about them. I have his report of the picture, but I have not read it. I shall read it first when this page is in type.

One of the following reports is by Mr. Hodges. The other is by yours truly. It is not necessary or important that you know which is which. Here they are:

First Report

"The Street of Forgotten Men" is not a pleasant picture. Its unpleasantness is its chief characteristic. It is graphic in detail and ensemble, forceful throughout and impressive. It has a logical ending instead of the kind customarily forced upon otherwise good stories in this country.

The story is of a bogus cripple who devotes his life to rearing as a lady the daughter of a street woman. Percy Marmont is the upright grafter and had "If Winter Comes" not established him permanently among the great, his work in this picture would do so. As matters stand, this role seems to me to lift him at least one notch higher.

Mary Brian is the girl whose rearing and subsequent protection by the fraudulent beggar provides the motivating impulse of the drama. She continues too sugar-y sweet for general purposes but in this instance the contrast makes it alright. She is much better in the earlier footage, enacting the dying street woman with real power.

John Harrington, supposedly blind foe of Marmont, is great in the heavy assignment. His is a terrible job done beautifully. Neil Hamilton is the young suitor, doing well enough with the slight chance the role gives him.

The scene is New York, mainly the Bowery, before and since the war, which does not figure in the story. It is admirably sustained. Save for one or two awkward time hurdles and a dragged-in reference to "Peter Pan," the direction is better than the usual Herbert Brenon routine.

Second Report

The picture called "The Street of Forgotten Men" is so vitally and so boldly told that it is shocking to even a sophisticated theatregoer. Which means it is well told.

All of "The Street of Forgotten Men" that you want to see is there. Not a precious foot was wasted in the cutting. It is the kind of picture that becomes a part of you, thrusting an impression upon you that is unforgettable. That street of shabby pawnshops with their black alpaca coats on display—that street filled with the forgotten derelicts of a tough embittered world —and then the profession of beggars who patrol the streets of the well-to-do. The beggars who are viewed with pity by millionaires who contribute a quarter and by working people who contribute a dollar limp their way through the crowds, their faces distorted, their backs bearing humps and their legs swinging pegs. The beggars after a successful day of begging $100 or so return to "The Death House" and shake of their humps, shake off their peg legs and straighten their faces to count their coin like the business men they are.

The hero of this pitiful tale is one of these business men.

Mary Brian comes into the story late to do the best acting she has done since "Peter Pan." She has the ability of making a throaty something well up in her audience. . . . if she just wouldn't run across the room. Remember, Mary, you're not a nymph.

The rest of the glory of the picture, and there is much of it, goes to Percy Marmont whose characterizations are drawn with hair line accuracy. That modest, unboastful Marmont, it appears, is a man appreciated wholesomely by everyone.

Two "unchecked reports" on the film were published in *Exhibitors Herald* on August 15, 1925.

Another unusual review came from P.S. Harrison, of *Harrison's Reports*. The opinionated, independent reviewer found it difficult to accept the film's moral ambiguity, something only touched-on by others. Harrison writes, "This picture has good points, but it also has some bad ones. The good points are: the hero's self sacrifice – he keeps his promise to a dead woman (a crook), which promise he had made at her death bed, to rear her orphan daughter (heroine), thus preventing her from following her mother's example; the hero's struggle to keep the heroine's antecedents a secret so that she may not be made unhappy; and his courage in revealing his crooked career to the young man (hero) who loved the young heroine. All these acts stir the spectator's emotions."

Harrison's telling review, which struggled to come-to-terms with Easy Money Charlie as an anti-hero of sorts, wore its moral discomfort on its sleeve. "The bad points are, rather the bad point is, the fact that the hero is a thief – he is a professional beggar, transforming himself into a cripple, and playing upon the sympathy of the public. It's difficult for one to sympathize with the crook, even though he is shown to have a white streak in him; less so because of the fact that he does not reform when the spectator thinks he ought to – after he had taken the orphan baby from the orphan asylum, and had made-up his mind to give her as good a rearing as plentiful money can give a girl. His failure to reform at that time, in fact, displeases the spectator; one does not wish to see a charitable heart paired with a perverted mind. The atmosphere is sordid almost all the way through." Harrison concludes, "No fault can be found with Mr. Brenon's directorial work. It is probable that the picture will satisfy over-sentimental people, but it is doubtful if it will appeal to the cultured classes." (7-25-1925)

Very few films receive uniform praise or uniform condemnation. There always seems to be a mix of praise and criticism. Another qualified review – one of the least flattering from any national publication, came from *Variety*. Its critic, named Fred, found fault not with the film's moral ambiguity, but with what might be termed aesthetic ambiguity, especially the film's ending. Fred wrote, "To those who read the George Kibbe Turner story in the *Satevepost* the picturization of *The Street of Forgotten Men* is going to come along as a disappointment more or less. It was a corking story. One cannot say as much for the picture. However, it will average up with the usual run of program attractions that Famous is turning out, but it won't be the box office knockout expected…. The trouble would seem to be in the film adaption. It does not follow the story in the principal theme and detracts from the punch and unfortunately does not place victory into the hands of the hero who has won the audience's sympathy. In direction Herbert Brenon has done exceedingly well, even though he slurred over a few points early in the picture where 'planting' was most necessary.

Because of the fact that he did not plant his character sufficiently well with his audience was another reason that the story was weakened."

Despite reservations and confusion over which magazine published the story – *Liberty* magazine not the *Satevepost* (*Saturday Evening Post*) – Fred found other aspects of the film he liked. "New York of today and of the pre-prohibition period are the scenes in which the story is laid…. The early Bowery days tingling with atmospheric touches, the scenes in the bar-room and the later date conversion of the bar to a quick lunch counter which also dispenses booze, are all very well done and carry conviction. Here Brenon has done some of his best work and he has handled a couple of fight scenes decidedly well. Percy Marmont is doing probably his best work, and both Mary Brian and Juliet Brenon in the roles of daughter and mother, respectively, standout. John Harrington as the heavy scores, where Riley Hatch as the barkeep, looks the part to perfection. *The Street of Forgotten Men* won't stand the crowds on their heads, but it will do to play in the bigger houses as well as the smaller ones." (7-22-1925)

One other review from the time is also worth noting. It appeared in *Cine-Mundial*, the Spanish-language version of *Moving Picture World*, a New York-based film journal whose title translates into English as *Cinema World*. (Though related to *Moving Picture World*, the content found in *Cine-Mundial* often differed from its parent publication.)

The *Cine-Mundial* write-up of *La Calle de los Olvidados* is attributed to Ariza, who, like others, appreciated the unusualness of the production. Ariza noted "In an effort to find themes that go off the beaten path, Paramount came up with this one…. in any case, better new and well-intentioned than known and… hackneyed."

Ariza also praised Brenon's staging, especially the criminal's lair, adding "the dramatic adventures – or better said, melodramatic – of a group of false cripples, constitute the plot of the production. The actors are especially good." (10-1925)

LA CALLE DE LOS OLVIDADOS
(The Street of Forgotten Men)
"Paramount" — 1800 metros

Intérpretes: Percy Marmont, Mary Brian, Neil Hamilton, John Harrington, Juliet Brennon, Josephine Deffry, A. Bargato, Riley Hatch y Dorothy Walters.
Dirección de Herbert Brenon.

En el afán de buscar temas que se salgan del camino trillado, Paramount dió con éste. Ojalá que el esfuerzo persista, aunque no en igual sentido, ya que también entre lo extraordinario puede haber lacras. Pero, de todos modos, más vale nuevo y bien intencionado que sabido y… sobado. La Calle de los Olvidados está en Nueva York, naturalmente, y presta refugio a las heces del vicio. La sola exposición fotográfica de aquella guarida de gentes de mal vivir es un homenaje al sentido estético del director. Las aventuras dramáticas — o mejor dicho, melodramáticas — de un grupo de falsos tullidos, constituyen la trama de la producción. Los intérpretes, singularmente felices. — **Ariza**.

(Above) The Rivoli theater at the time air-conditioning was first installed. The film on the marquee is Herbert Brenon's *The Little French Girl*, starring Mary Brian, Alice Joyce and Esther Ralston.

(Left) In the 1920s, New York City had a number of non-English language newspapers. Shown here is a German language ad for one of the first showings of *The Street of Forgotten Men*. Paired with the Rivoli ad is an ad for the theater's sister venue, the Rialto. Adjoining ads show some of the live entertainment with which motion picture theaters had to compete. New York, New York – July 1925

The summer months could be a challenging time to release a film. In the mid-1920s, relatively few theaters were air-conditioned, and with warmer seasonal weather, many were thought stuffy and uncomfortable. Movie attendance was expected to fall off, and usually did. In fact, in many parts of the United States, moviegoers who went to see a picture during the summer often brought their own fan.

The Street of Forgotten Men was released in the summer of 1925. The film debuted at the Rivoli theater in New York City on Sunday, July 19, before opening elsewhere around the country in the weeks that followed. The very first public showing of the film was a Sunday afternoon matinee.

The 2,000-plus seat Rivoli was considered a prestige venue, a "movie palace," and one of the grandest theaters on the East Coast. Over the years, many notable Famous Players-Lasky and Paramount productions opened or played there. Some six weeks prior to the debut of *The Street of Forgotten Men*, Willis Carrier completed the installation of his much-vaunted air-cooling system at the Rivoli. The installation, one of the first in any theater in New York, would be an important test for Paramount, so much so, studio head Adolph Zukor came from California to experience the new system firsthand. The occasion was the debut an earlier Brenon release, *The Little French Girl*.

As the curtain lifted on the hit Brenon film, Carrier's system kicked-in. Slowly, cool air filled the large space, and moviegoers began to put down their fans. Carrier's system worked, and worked well. From then on, the Rivoli, aware of the advantage it held over the city's other theaters, promoted itself as "New York's Refrigerated Cooling Station."

In the 1920s, New York City was home to a more than two dozen newspapers. And not surprisingly, a number of local critics took an almost proprietary interest in *The Street of Forgotten Men*, a movie which was set and made in the city, and which featured a handful of local actors likely familiar to critics and those who went to the theater. One newspaper encouraged every New Yorker to see the film. While another billed the movie as "New York's Own Picture." In fact, the film's Rivoli debut received more than a dozen local reviews, as well as other write-ups in other newspapers located in the metropolis' five boroughs. The majority of reviews were positive – even glowing, though a few were tempered, and one critical. Connie Miles, film critic for the *New York Evening World*, was one who described *The Street of Forgotten Men* favorably. Miles thought the movie ". . . one of those too rare offerings that have everything to be desired in a film production," adding, "As might be expected from the direction of Herbert Brenon, this Paramount picture has action from start to finish, moves gracefully over the course of an unusual love theme and reaches heights of dramatic values that might not have been except for such a capable cast." (7-21-1925) Katherine Zimmerman, of the *New York Telegram*, echoed her colleague's assessment. Zimmerman described the film as "an excellent motion picture," noting "It has humanity, sentiment, drama, atmosphere and love. And it has Percy Marmont in the best bit of acting he has done yet." (7-21-1925) In a review titled "Remarkable Photoplay," Dorothy Herzog of the *Daily Mirror* declared, "Every now and then, a picture that is different comes to the silver sheet. Such a picture plays the Rivoli this week." (7-21-1925) Mildred Spain of the *Daily News* took a more nuanced approach, describing the film as "Altogether a nourishing movie meal, but not for the children." (7-21-1925) Similarly, Donald Burney of the *New York Review* (one of the few male critics on the scene) thought the film an "entertaining and dramatically effective picture," adding, "it should prove a winning attraction." (7-25-1925)

The *Brooklyn Daily Eagle* also offered praise. The paper's critic, Martin B. Dickstein, declared, "This is a film which misses by inches being Herbert Brenon's proudest accomplishment.... There are to be had in the Rivoli film more than one glimpse of ingenious direction. There is much evidence, as well, of capable acting." (7-22-1925) A few days before, the *Brooklyn Daily Times* made a point of noting the picture "deals with the professional beggars who haunted the Bowery some years ago." (7-19-1925)

The *Brooklyn Daily Eagle* gave the film a second review in August, when it opened at Loew's Metropolitan. The review, one of the best it would receive, is notable for its frank description of the film's major characters. An anonymous reviewer wrote, "One of the current fads in filmdom is picturing the quaintness and glamour of the New York of the good old days. The production of *Little Old New York* two years ago seems to have started the thing and of late New York has been depicted in many stages of its development in various productions, many of which have been of considerable merit. Among these may be listed *The Street of Forgotten Men*." (8-12-1925)

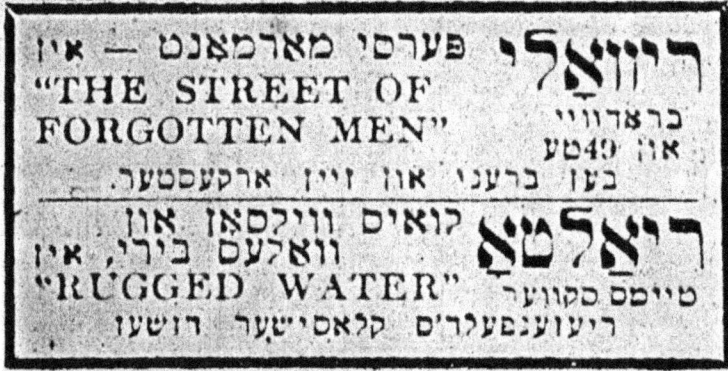

Three newspaper ads from New York City's non-English language press. The fact that the film was advertised in the ethnic press suggests Rivoli management felt the film would find an audience with those whose first language was not English.

(Top) An ad from *Uj Előre*, a Hungarian-language paper, where *The Street of Forgotten Men* is titled *Az Elfelejtett Emberek Utcája*.

(Middle) A bilingual ad for the Rivoli and Rialto theaters from the Jewish *Forward*, also known as *Forverts*. The text above the title notes the film stars Percy Marmont. Text below the title notes the appearance of bandleader Ben Bernie.

(Bottom) An ad from the German-language *New Yorker Volkszeitung* (one of the city's three German-language papers), where the film is alternately titled *Die Strasse vergessener Menschen*.

Notably, both the Hungarian and German titles translate into English as the slightly different *The Street of Forgotten People*. New York, New York – July 1925

"*The Street of Forgotten Men* carries us back to the late 90s, when horse cars moved up the Bowery under the shadow of the 'L' and men and women derelicts quaffed 'the biggest in the city' in cars which masked the rat holes of mendicants and criminals. One of the most successful of the underworld characters is Easy Money Charlie, who, by posing as a pitiful armless man, often extracts $150 a day from a charitable public. Easy Money Charlie has no one in the world but his dog, and when that loyal animal is slain he is prevailed upon to adopt a child of a dying slum mother. With his abundant means he raises the child in a fashionable Long Island suburb in the ignorance of her lowly origin. He falls in love with the growing girl, but, convinced that he is unfit to touch her because of his parasitical career, he leaves her to a suitor of good family and loses himself in 'the street of forgotten men'."

The Brooklyn review continued. "All of this has been very capably picturized by Herbert Brenon, but a large share of the credit must go to the convincing acting of Percy Marmont and the difficult role of Easy Money Charlie. Mr. Marmont is one of the finest portrayers of sensitive natures at the command of the casting directors. John Harrington, in the part of a bogus blind man, whose greatest fear is of really becoming blind, likewise gives a colorful and convincing performance. Mary Brian and Neil Hamilton are also in the cast, but have little to do. Due largely to the efforts of Mr. Brenon and of Mr. Marmont, the picture has an authentic flavor which will appeal to lovers of the picturesque old days." (8-12-1925)

A number of NYC reviews also emphasized the film's local color. In "Old Bowery Days Pictured at Rivoli," the anonymous critic of the *New York American*, who "heartily enjoyed" the film, thought it "Almost as fascinating as its setting, partly because of its setting." (7-20-1925) Likewise, the *New York Evening Journal* stated "this unusual and extremely pleasing film" contained "some excellent scenes of the Bowery of two decades ago." (7-23-1925) Connie Miles of the *New York Evening World* began her piece by stating, "The glamour of the old Bowery has been revived through the medium of the motion picture screen. It comes back via the Rivoli theater this week in the film *The Street of Forgotten Men*, comes back vividly in several phases of its interesting past." (7-21-1925)

If Miles was nearly nostalgic, then Mildred Spain of the *Daily News* was almost rhapsodic. She thought the film entertaining and teaming with color, stating "*The Street of Forgotten Men* dips into the dark pools of life. It shows you the beggars of life – apologies to Jim Tully – and in showing them it shows them up. They aren't beggars, they're professional men whose art calls for more acting than a first performance on Broadway." (7-21-1925) The *New York Post* held a similar, though more prosaic, opinion. The paper headlined its review "More of the Bowery's Chicanery Comes to Light," and suggested the film playing at the Rivoli "might be carelessly mistaken for anti-beggar propaganda." (7-21-1925)

Even more than the film or its setting, its cast came in for praise. Most was heaped on the film's star. "Percy Marmont, in a vivid characterization, ads new laurels to his fine career," wrote Dorothy Herzog in the *Daily Mirror*. (7-21-1925) Connie Miles of the *New York Evening World* likewise stated, "Percy Marmont is such a capable actor that he seems never to be miscast…. Marmont scores one hundred percent in Pantomimic achievement." (7-21-1925) Two others singled out for special praise time and again were John Harrington and Juliet Brenon. The New York *Review*, *Daily Mirror*, and *New York Herald Tribune* praised each for their excellent work.

One of the film's most favorable reviews was published in the New York *Morning Telegraph*. Its article, titled "Herbert Brenon Contributes Absorbing Film at Rivoli," was penned by Dorothy Day, a one-time bohemian journalist and later social activist who, in more recent years, has become a candidate for sainthood in the Catholic Church. Day begins her review by setting the scene. "The feature film at the Rivoli this week *The Street of Forgotten Men*, is an absorbing story, done by cast the people who really know how to act and directed in a skillful manner by Herbert Brenon. It is one of those 'miracle men' themes, showing the trade of a group of charlatans who play on the sympathy of people in order to make a living. The opening scene shows the Bowery and the old days when women had hips and men did not need hip flasks, for beer was served in brimming glasses, and the horse cars, like a very plebeian bug of nursery rhyme, had no wings at all, but they got there just the same. In back of a saloon – you know, those things with swinging doors they used to have on corners – the beggars congregate. They are a healthy group of men, but by skillful makeup are made into cripples and blind men…."

Day's review shifts to a critique of the actors, including a sympathetic appreciation of the otherwise unsavory characters they portray. "Percy Marmont as Charlie gives a beautiful performance. A newcomer to the screen, Juliet Brenon, plays the part of the unfortunate girl who dies, gives promise of becoming a screen luminary of strong emotional character. Her brief performance in this picture is appealing and full of heart throbs. We ought to hear big things from her soon."

Day continued, "Two excellent performances are given by Josephine Deffry and John Harrington, both members of David Belasco's *The Dove*. Miss Deffry, resplendent in lace shirt waist and billowy skirt of the early part of the century, is simply grand as Dutch Dolly, a 'lady' of the underworld. Mr. Harrington, as the blind beggar, is an actor of real ability and, if he could be spared from the speaking stage, would undoubtedly find an important place for himself among the first rank of motion picture actors – artists would be a better word. His performance is forceful, convincing and horribly fine. He actually makes you shudder…. Mary Brian and Neil Hamilton are good as the young lovers and the rest of the cast live up to the standards set forth by the principal players."

Day concludes her review by stating, "Mr. Brenon has done some interesting things in the directorial line and achieves some splendid effects. All in all *The Street of Forgotten Men* makes for an absorbing and entertaining session." (7-20-1925)

A few of the other local critics, however, were less impressed with the production. After giving high marks to the entertainment which preceded the film, Underhill of the *New York Herald Tribune* opined, "Then comes the feature, *The Street of Forgotten Men*. This was rather disappointing, and we can't say just why. Percy Marmont as Easy Money Charlie couldn't have been better, and the scenes on the Bowery were very well done. The old cafe where, almost in the twinkling of an eye, strong, upright men become lame, halt and blind, was interesting, too. In fact, the screened prologue was full of promise. But…" Underhill added, "this promissory note was not redeemed." (7-20-1925)

The critic for the New York *World*, writing under the initials W.R., also professed a vague dissatisfaction. "We could not summon any fierce enthusiasm over this melancholy matter. It does not bother much with the subtleties of sorrow nor cry its heart out quietly. It sighs for sympathy in bulk." (7-20-1925)

The Moviegoer, the anonymous by-line for a critic writing in the *New York Sun*, similarly thought the photoplay "picturesque and interesting," but oddly added, "to me it seemed somewhat undramatic." Though Brenon's direction was praised by most New York critics, The Moviegoer took exception. In fact, the critic for the *Sun* expressed considerable disappointment. "There are striking moments at the Rivoli in *The Street of Forgotten Men*, which is the latest effort of Herbert Brenon, movie producer of *Peter Pan*, and his crew. Mr. Brenon here attempts to recreate the picturesque, suds-soaked Bowery of long ago, and at various points he pictures for us telling, vivid incidents in the lives of the professional beggars who sauntered from its lower depths into the sunnier near golden lead stretches of the city. But despite these high points and despite the authentic atmosphere with which *The Street of Forgotten Men* is laden, it must be said that the photoplay is only moderately successful."

The Moviegoer continued, "When *Peter Pan* appeared over the movie horizon shedding fairy dust in tinkling with fantastic overtones, I thought that Mr. Brenon must be one of the few directors with the Olympian touch. His cinema version of *The Little French Girl*, which was laden with taste but rather lacking in talent, shook that theory to an appreciable degree, and now *The Street of Forgotten Men* shakes it still further. It is too bad."

"Brenon was here furnished with a new story by George Kibbe Turner, which appeared under the same title in the incessant weekly rival of the *Satevepost* known as *Liberty*. *The Street of Forgotten Men* is, of course, the magazine and movie name for the Bowery, but the author was principally concerned with the weird establishment on the street — a saloon in the dim, shadowy backroom of which healthy denizens of the slums were turned by artificial means into cripples, blind men and other grotesques of nature, therefrom to wind their crooked ways into such neighborhoods of the city as would shower coins in their sham, false alms cups. Now for Mr. Brenon's atmospheric and picturesque rebuilding of the old Bowery I have nothing but praise, and I must also voice my admiration for his directorial touches in vivifying the scenes of this cripple factory, this inverted clinic. But with the illusion of reality achieved as far as backgrounds are concerned, it is all the more pity that the story paraded in front does not keep up with that illusion."

The Moviegoer's criticism of the film continued. "I think that Mr. Brenon has only been partially successful in making his characters live, and that, you must admit, is rather fatal in a 'plotty' movie of this kind. The affair is reminiscent of a story by

Leroy Scott, dubbed, if I remember, *The City that Never Sleeps*, which was rather tellingly picturized by James Cruze, who, no matter how improbable the plot, so animates the figures that incongruities are rather lost sight of. Unfortunately Herbert Brenon is not a Cruze."

The Moviegoer's pointed complaints softened a little. "I have been a carping critic in this instance inasmuch as Mr. Brenon comes so close to being one of the first rate directors that his deficiency stand out like babies first teeth. In *The Little French Girl* he was hampered by a scenario that called for long lapses in time and for too many situations, here he is similarly hampered. But it was his job to bring the photo play to life – no matter how the scenario was built – and I think that he has just missed doing so. Perhaps he will triumph again with Barrie's *A Kiss for Cinderella*, which is to be released sometime during the coming year. I sincerely hope he will." (7-20-1925)

Harriet Underhill's review in the *New York Herald Tribune* and The Moviegoer's review in the *New York Sun* come-off as opaque rumblings of discontent. Not so with the *New York Times*, which was far more exacting in its critique. The anonymous critic who penned the piece may or may not have been Mordaunt Hall, the first regularly assigned motion picture critic for the paper who worked for the *Times* between 1924 and 1934. However, Hall's writing style, which was described in his *Times* obituary as "chatty, irreverent, and not particularly analytical," seems at odds with this particular piece. Unlike other critics, Hall was said not to be interested in analyzing cinematographic technique. Yet, this review is full of such analysis.

The *Times* review, titled, "The Bowery and Afterward," begins "This picture just misses being a notable one, but it will never be accorded the highest rank, although a great many people are going to like it. Unfortunately it is not a case of there being one or two week spots, which could be ignored in favor of the whole impression, but of there being continual infinitesimal blemishes…. What appears to be wrong is the lack of imaginative elasticity in the directing, that is to say, elasticity enough to take in all the detail of the production."

Despite admitting that in many respects the directing was excellent, the review continued its critical assessment. "In the first place, one recognizes there was a difficult story to put over. Its principal figure is a fake beggar who is made-up daily with others in a Bowery mendicant factory. He is induced to take the baby girl of a dying woman of the streets and care for her. He sets up a suburban establishment in Long Island, where she lives for years in ignorance of the fact that her guardian every day goes into the city and makes the money they live on by donning the rags of a crippled beggar."

"That is a situation which strains the credulity, and this is a play in which they cannot afford that because it is produced in the key of a realistic story from life. The story could have been altered to do away with that strain on the credulity without losing its essentials; indeed, one could see how its appeal might have been heightened."

The *New York Times* review continues, "Granting the story as it is, however, the director might have given a more discreet handling to make its treatment more individual. For one thing, for instance, he has failed to get out of the old movie stereotype of having a crowd around almost every time anything happens. When Easy Money Charlie's dog is killed, the denizens of the dive must all come out and crowd the doorway to witness his emotion. There must be nearly a dozen mendicants being made-up to give an unreal chorus effect. Every time Easy Money Charlie (Percy Marmont) enters the saloon he must get the traditional hail from everybody present and wave his hand in answer like the newest heavyweight champion. These are small points, but they are representative of others making up an aggregate of indiscretion that prevents the production being notable for a fresh and vigorous treatment."

Such detailed analysis of cinematic technique – surprising for a newspaper at the time – abates, and the *Times* reviewer concludes by putting forth some favorable aspects to the production. "There is much to interest audiences in the picture, however, all these things aside. No one can say it is not unusual and colorful. Percy Marmont is one of the few men who could make a part like this smack of reality. If there is any actor of the screen who excels him in conveying a sense of spiritual values, that actor's name does not come to mind. Without the sensitive intelligence he brings to bear on the role it is hard to imagine it conveying conviction at all. Mary Brian, who Mr. Brenon brought out as Wendy in *Peter Pan*, a fact which is unnecessarily stressed in this piece, plays the ward Easy Money Charlie brings up in innocent affluence. She's an excellent type for the role. Neil Hamilton is fresh and pleasing. A very good piece of character acting is done by John Harrington as

Bridgeport White Eye, enemy and at the end companion of Easy Money Charlie. Juliet Brenon makes a pathetic figure of the mother who confides her baby to the care of Easy Money Charlie. A. Bargato, Riley Hatch and Dorothy Walters are excellent in small parts." (7-21-1925)

Witnesses to emotion, and a pivotal scene in the film – the death of Charlie's beloved dog. *Credit: George Eastman Museum*

With all the attention (pro and con) paid to the film in the New York press, *The Street of Forgotten Men* proved to be a BIG hit. Originally scheduled to play just one week, the film was held over and played a second. It also outperformed the competition, which included a new Norma Shearer film, *A Slave of Fashion*, and the popular Rin Tin Tin vehicle, *Tracked in the Snow Country*. In fact, the Brenon film took in more than $60,000 in admissions during its two-week run – a remarkable amount considering Rivoli tickets were then priced at 50, 85 and 99 cents. *Variety* observed "Ben Bernie and this feature surprised" before breaking down the numbers for the second week. "Figured after first week's big box office return business due for drop and it would be off possibly to the extent of $3,500 or $4,000 dollars. Instead, house got $30,410.70. [Only] $400 less than business of previous week." (7-29-1925)

In the years following its 1925 release, *The Street of Forgotten Men* was shown in all manner of venues. These venues included grand movie palaces and modest, second run and small-town theaters, as well as churches, school gymnasiums, converted opera houses, town halls, and local Y.M.C.A.s. The film was nearly always shown to make a profit, although on at least a couple of occasions it was shown as a fundraiser to benefit a local cause.

One of the most unusual screenings of the film took place under the auspices of the United States Navy. Just after its debut, but just before its official release date, *Our Navy* reported that *The Street of Forgotten Men* and other new releases had been "secured by the Bureau of Navigation for exhibition in the near future on Naval ships and at Naval stations." (8-1-1925)

Whether or not *The Street of Forgotten Men* was actually shown at sea, or instead on land at a naval hall, is not known. Also not certain is what American sailors might have thought of the film about a group of strange land lubbers.

NEW MOVIES

The following are the latest moving picture releases secured by the Bureau of Navigation for exhibition in the near future on Naval ships and at Naval stations:

"After Business Hours," Hammerstein-Tellegen; "Steele of the Royal Mounted," Bert Lytell; "The Kiss Barrier," Edmond Lowe; "The Sporting Chance," Tellegen-Phillips; "The White Outlaw," Jack Hoxie; "Smooth As Satin," Evelyn Brent; "How Baxter Butted In," M. Moore-Devore; "The Denial," Claire Windsor; "The Ten Commandments," LaRocque-Naldi; "Night Life of New York," Torrence-Gish-LaRocque; "In the Name of Love," Cortez-Nissen; "The Lucky Devil," Richard Dix; "Rugged Water," Lois Wilson-Baxter; "Beggar On Horseback," Ralston-Nissen; "The Street of Forgotten Men," Marmont-Hamilton; "The Texas Trail," Harry Carey; "Siege," Valli-O'Brien.

During the summer of 1925 the Rivoli experienced a $100,000 increase in business over the prior year, according to reports from the time. What's notable is that a substantial part of the theater's summer boom – more than $60,000 – was taken in during the two-week run of *The Street of Forgotten Men*. Some of that increase was due to the overlapping appearance of the popular musical act, Ben Bernie, as well as to newly installed air conditioning – though the Capitol, another NYC theater with a new air-plant, failed to see a rise in its summer revenue.

Within a week of its July debut, *The Street of Forgotten Men* opened in a handful of other major markets including Pittsburgh, Cleveland, Chicago, and Bridgeport, Connecticut – followed by Philadelphia and San Francisco. As the film's national roll-out continued, and as prints shipped out from one of the 30 Paramount exchanges located around the country, *The Street of Forgotten Men* came to play in most cities and towns across the United States and Canada. By the end of 1926, there were few North American markets that hadn't shown the film at least once. In fact, the film continued to play here and there well into 1927 and even 1928. In an era before home video and streaming – when the only way to see a movie was in person – popular or well-regarded films continued to show as long as there was interest. *The Street of Forgotten Men*'s two-week run at the Rivoli marked not only its debut, and also the start of the film's long, four-year exhibition history.

In the 1920s, Chicago was the second largest city in the United States. And like New York, then and still America's largest city, it was home to a number of newspapers. In fact, there were six daily newspapers serving Chicago, as well as a number of ethnic, college, and suburban papers. Most all of them either reported on films playing in the area, advertised their showing, or both. These publications, together with the many theaters which showed movies (either new or second-run), contributed to the city's rich movie culture.

Chicago was one of the first cities outside New York to show *The Street of Forgotten Men*. The movie debuted at McVickers theater on Monday, July 28, 1925. The accompanying stage act, led by popular band leader and "hyperkinetic" recording artist Paul Ash, had been in residence at McVickers for four months when the Brenon film opened. Like Ben Bernie, Ash had considerable drawing power. Ads from the time, which promoted Ash more than the feature film, boasted a "Two-Hour Show in 60 minutes! 45 Dancers, Singers, Jokers. Ash's Gang at His Best."

Actors John Harrington and Percy Marmont. *Author collection*

The lighthearted nature of Ash's act contrasted with the sometimes-downbeat tone of *The Street of Forgotten Men*, a contrast noted by Genevieve Harris in the *Chicago Evening Post*. "As a more serious contribution to a program for the most part hilarious comes the feature picture, *The Street of Forgotten Men*, at McVickers this week. The note of pathos, of tragedy, which is struck in the title, continues to sound throughout the production, even at the finish which, while conventionally happy, is more fitting and less saccharine than most picture conclusions." Harris also noted, "An unusually good role falls to the lot of Percy Marmont in this production. Marmont has been in danger of being swamped in the mire of sentiment ever since his success as the long-suffering hero of *If Winter Comes*. He has appeared thereafter always as the persecuted weakling with a heart of gold. Imagine him for a change therefore, as a crook, a fakir! Of course he never appears to be a very wicked individual. Somehow he isn't temperamentally suited to portray cruelty or deep-eyed evil. But as Easy Money Charlie, who twists his body into strange shapes so that he may beg money as a cripple, he gives a good impersonation of a clever cadger, a sneaking sort of thief...." In conclusion, Harris stated, "*The Street of Forgotten Men* is set forth smoothly and effectively. It is an entertaining picture to watch and is sufficiently out of the ordinary to be very interesting." (7-28-1925)

Mae Tinée (the pseudonym of Frances Peck which evokes the word "matinee") was the well-known film critic of the *Chicago Tribune*. However, another critic at the famed paper, Roberta Nangle, was assigned to review *The Street of Forgotten Men*. In "You'll Like This Tale of Bowery Underworld," Nangle noted, "*The Street of Forgotten Men* was made from George Kibbe Turner's story of the same name, which appeared in *Liberty* magazine a few months ago. It is a startling tale of Bowery life, of the soiled, tawdry ladies and broken men of the underworld.... The first scenes are back in the Gibson girl days, long before Volstead was thought of, and when begging was a more flourishing profession than it is now. Percy Marmont was an ideal choice for the difficult leading role, and his work, as usual, is quiet, clean cut and convincing. Mary Brian is a sweet peaches and cream heroine, and Neil Hamilton is likable as the nice boy who marries her...." In conclusion, Nagle wrote, "Direction and photography are splendid, making the movie decidedly worth seeing." (7-28-1925)

Polly Wood (a pseudonym sound-alike for Hollywood?) of the *Chicago Herald and Examiner* also praised *The Street of Forgotten Men*, though she expressed reservations about the film's ending. "Percy Marmont gives an excellent performance and Herbert Brenon has, save for an anticlimax, made a good movie in *The Street of Forgotten Men*. Here is a reversion to the slums of New York, with an almost technical expose of the tricks of beggars. And it is expertly good entertainment, to say nothing of education[al], save for the final ten minutes of the story." Wood thought well of the overall film, but expressed reservations about the ending. "Mr. Brenon's direction is safe and sane, without an emotional slopping over of tears and chest heaves. He could have made a better drama by leaving off the postscript climax. But we fans demand the overflowing measure of emotion, if not the perfect plot construction. Marmont is splendid as Charlie and he is surrounded by many interesting types. I fear for the financial security of beggars, however, after this expose of their manufactured ills is generally released." (7-28-1925)

Chicago's lone male film critic at the time, Eugene Stinson, observed in the *Chicago Daily Journal*, "Thanks to the movies, the Chicago banker and baker and candlestick maker can sit in his loop or neighborhood theater and travel many a place he might never have gone before the cinema was perfected. One of the newest haunts provided the movie fan is a trip to a beggarland. Anyone who sees *The Street of Forgotten Men* at McVickers this week may do as he pleases about believing everything he is told is true. But he will learn a great deal, at any rate, of what someone else believes is the truth about the world of mendicants and cripples. It is a well-known theory that most of the beggars we feed so pitying on our street corners are better off, financially, then many a person who drops a penny into the outstretched cup. This may or may not be so. A lot of people believe it is. In *The Street of Forgotten Men*, a whole colony of imitation cripples beg on the streets of New York. Their art is to make themselves up into the semblance of maimed and disabled human beings. Their income is gained from those who drop pennies into their misleading hands...."

Despite his skepticism about the film's portrayal of begging, Stinson approved of the production and its actors. "Percy Marmont is striking as the uneasy, but prosperous beggar. In many of his recent pictures he has taken himself very importantly indeed. In *The Street of Forgotten Men* he is considerably given over to grief, but at all times he is an intelligent and restrained actor who is able to hold the chief attention in a strong and serious film. Mary Brian, Neil Hamilton and many others help make the picture interesting." (7-29-1925)

From 1920 to 1928, the acclaimed poet Carl Sandburg reviewed movies for the *Chicago Daily News*. He wrote about most of the films which passed through town. On Saturday, August 1, he turned his eye on *The Street of Forgotten Men*. Sandburg's review is not particularly revealing, nor poetic, but it does end with a sly compliment paid to the musical act which preceded the feature film. The future two-time Pulitzer Prize winner wrote, in part, "The blind men with their cups and the cripples with their stumps at the street corners will not like to hear about *The Street of Forgotten Men*.

Beggars stand to lose millions of dollars. For the picture seems to take us behind the scenes and show us how street beggars live and work and fake.... A fight between a beggar who can see though wearing the sign 'I am blind,' and a supposedly crippled beggar is the high spot of the picture.... Herbert Brenon directed this Paramount picture, which is showing at McVickers Theater, where it may be the photoplay or it may be the West Coast demon, Paul Ash, who is responsible for audiences filling all seats to the top row of the top balcony." (8-1-1925) Sandburg's ambivalence was an echo of another review the film received in the Hearst-owned *Chicago American*, which declared, "The picture without being in any way notable is fairly good entertainment." (7-28-1925)

In the months that followed, *The Street of Forgotten Men* returned to Chicago (as it did to other large metropolitan areas), where it played the neighborhood and second run houses – sometimes in two or three locations at the same time – during the months of August, September and October. Those return engagements kept a spotlight on the movie. In the Windy City, the film and its lead actor, Percy Marmont, were also mentioned in two letters to the editor printed in the *Chicago Tribune*. In a note addressed to Mae Tinée, a correspondent named J.M. wrote, "Glad to see some of the old pictures being shown again. *Broken Blossoms*, *The Miracle Man*, and others. They surely are worth seeing.... Any picture or play with a good moral is worthwhile. *Chickie* not so good. *The Ten Commandments* best ever, worth seeing many times. *The Street of Forgotten Men* should be seen by everybody once." (10-11-1925)

Another letter addressed to Tinée, this one from a correspondent with the initials H.P.C., enthused about Marmont. "I missed your review of *The Street of Forgotten Men*, but I hope it was a good one for I maintain that Percy Marmont is the greatest actor on the screen. He never 'hogs' the camera or poses, but as a gray haired star he could make Lewis Stone look to his laurels. Wasn't he handsome in that scene in Neil Hamilton's office – and can't he wear an overcoat better than Jack Holt? I have never forgotten *The Light that Failed* and *If Winter Comes*, and I would again like to see both of them again. Percy doesn't belong in any of the accepted types for he has individuality. Really, I can't think of all the nice things I'd like to say about him. But I believe everyone who has seen him will acknowledge his greatness, even if his pictures are not the ordinarily popular type...." To this gushing note, Tinée responded with a brief

"Editor's note" which read, in its entirety, "Rabid!" (10-25-1925)

What follows is a representative selection of advertisements for *The Street of Forgotten Men* as published in newspapers around the United States. This sampling exhibits a variety of layouts and designs, and shows how some exhibitors adapted Paramount's Press Sheet and promotional materials, while others created pieces more individualized and better suited to the needs of their community and venue. Except for one, all of the pieces shown here date from 1925.

A characteristic newspaper ad. Washington D.C. – August 1925

As the adjoining advertisements show, *The Street of Forgotten Men* opened in two different theaters at the same time in Pittsburgh, Pennsylvania. The primary showing took place at Loew's Aldine, a 1,700-seat downtown venue which opened in 1913 as the Victoria. Prior to the film, the Aldine Concert Orchestra (the house band) performed a medley titled "Old Time New York." Also performing on stage was Ted Weems and his band. (A Pennsylvania native, Weems achieved long lasting stardom, performing at the inaugural ball of President Warren Harding in 1921, and in 1936, giving singer Perry Como his first national exposure.) The smaller Cameraphone, also known as the East Liberty Cameraphone, was a neighborhood house which dates to 1908 (other sources state 1913). It seated 900, and was one of five Cameraphone theaters opened that same year. Pittsburgh, Pennsylvania – July 1925.

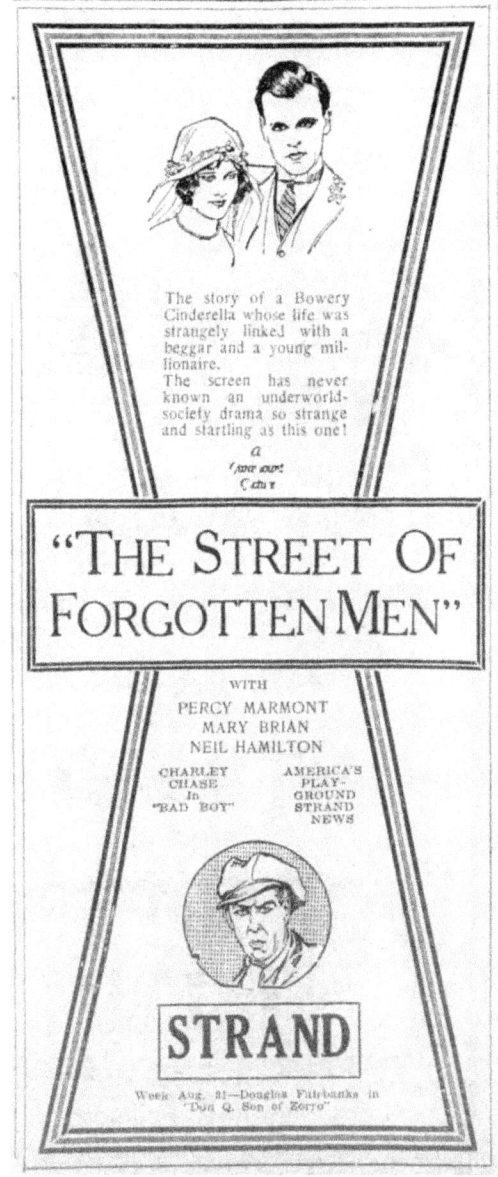

Many newspaper advertisements looked similar, as they were based on the same set of promotional materials supplied by Paramount. These two ads prove the exception. (Left) The Strand theater used photographs instead of line drawings to promote the "Positive Sensation" which kicked-off the local Greater Movie Season. And unusually so, the ad claimed "You will grip your seats – you will cry like a kid." Seattle, Washington – August 1925 (Right) This unique ad was singled out in *Motion Picture News* for making "clever use of stock cuts and rule borders." Despite an attractive ad and a positive review from local critic & future *Weird Tales* contributor Pettersen Marzoni, many moviegoers' attention was instead focused on Violet and Daisy Hilton, Siamese Twins from San Antonio, Texas who performed ahead of *Riders of the Purple Sage* at Loew's Temple. Birmingham, Alabama – August 1925.

(Left) In Cleveland, the film was shown simultaneously in three theaters as part of Paramount's nationwide Greater Movie Season campaign. Cleveland, Ohio – August 1925

(Above) Unusually so, this ad carried the provocative catchphrase, "I'm the Worst Faker in the United States." Minneapolis, Minnesota – August 1925

In Kansas City, *The Street of Forgotten Men* was shown as part of the Greater Movie Season, a promotion which aimed to get more people to go to the movies. (The Greater Movie Season took place in different cities across the United States at different times of the year, though usually in the fall to coincide with the rush of new releases.) According to trade journal reports, business was above average during the film's weeklong run, pulling in $14,000 in admissions at the 1980-seat Newman. Kansas City, Missouri – August 1925

"A Night at Coffee Dan's" – a "joyous jollification" of "Los Angeles' most unique café," was a heavily promoted stage show featuring local celebrities and talent. Despite this added attraction, the film did only average business after having received middling reviews. Los Angeles, California – August 1925

(Top) The 1,7000-seat Stanton regularly featured multi-week runs of films, with new releases playing two or more weeks. According to *Variety*, *The Street of Forgotten Men* "won excellent notices" but did "nothing unusual in the line of business." As a matter of record, the film played two weeks and took in $14,500. Philadelphia, Pennsylvania – August 1925 (Bottom) At the "Home of the Superplays." Cincinnati, Ohio – September 1925

Two different, visually striking advertisements. (Left) Promoting "A drama you must not miss." San Antonio, Texas – August 1925 (Right) In less populated towns where fewer went to the movies, shorter, three-day run were the norm. Here, the film shows Sunday through Tuesday. As an added attraction, footage of the California saengerfest (state singing festival) was also shown. Stockton, California – September 1925

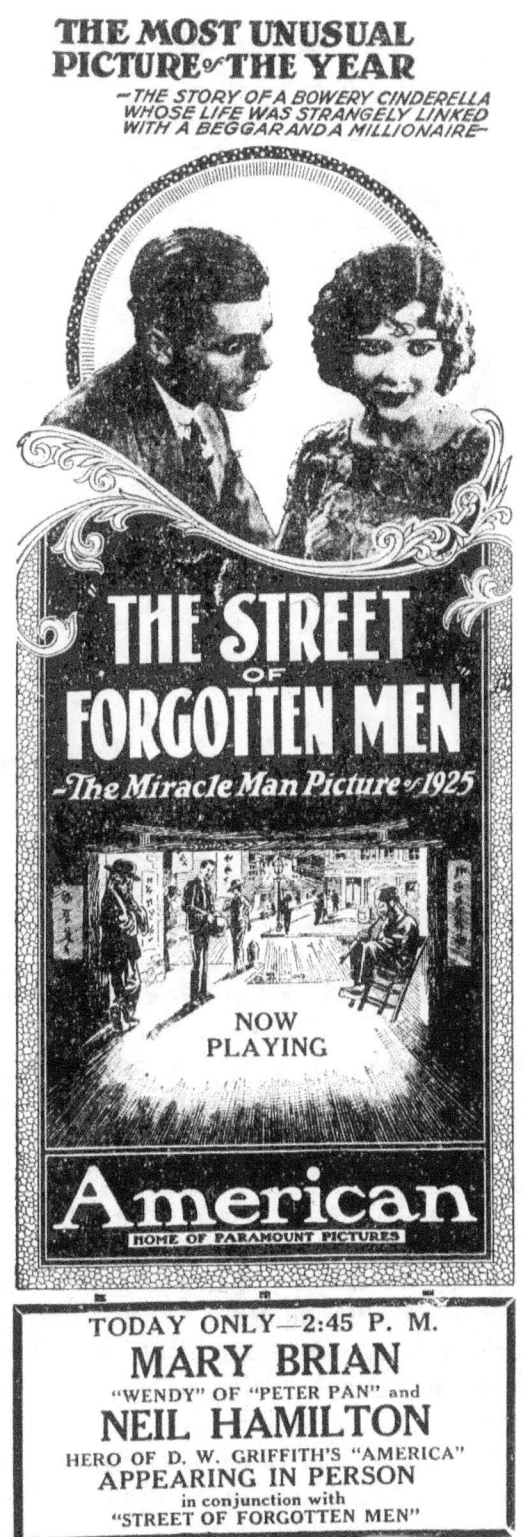

As part of the Greater Movie Season, the American theater in Oakland, California kicked-off the 8th Annual Paramount Week with a special screening of *The Street of Forgotten Men*. On Saturday, September 5, stars Mary Brian and Neil Hamilton made an in-person appearance at a matinee showing of the film, at which many turned out. (The two were in San Francisco, with a handful of other Paramount stars, on a promotional tour. The day before, Brian and Hamilton along with Wallace Beery, Noah Beery, Billie Dove, Warner Baxter and others appeared in-person at the Imperial theater, where *The Pony Express* had made its world premiere.)

The Street of Forgotten Men proved especially popular. American ads five days later claimed the film was "Taking Oakland by Storm" and enjoying "capacity business." Oakland, California – September 1925

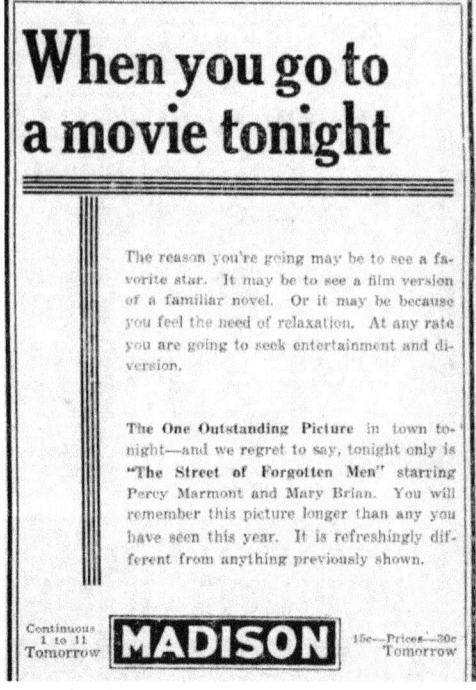

Some different approaches to advertising: (Above) This eye-catching newspaper ad relies on evocative visuals (an image in silhouette) to attract readers attention. Nashville, Tennessee – September 1925 (Top right) Except for a few design elements – namely vertical and horizontal lines – this advertisement relies only on text to relay its message, "The one outstanding picture in town tonight…. It is refreshingly different from anything previously shown." Madison, Wisconsin – September 1925 (Bottom right) A combination of approaches, with a distinct font working as the visual element. The paper in which this advertisement appeared, the local *Fort Worth Star-Telegram,* described the film as a "crook picture that burns into the memory." Fort Worth, Texas – September 1925

(Left) An ad with a spare, minimal look. Charlotte, North Carolina – Sept. 1925

(Right) An ad with a WARNING! which notes "If you haven't seen *The Street of Forgotten Men* you will be very sorry…". Helena, Montana – September 1925

(Bottom) In addition to the "Attraction Extraordinary," an ad with a busy, maximal look. Pomona, California – September 1925

This newspaper advertisement also employs evocative visuals (an image in silhouette) to attract viewers, while adding something unique to the scene in the form of a blind bearded beggar. Notably, the advertisement also announces that at next Tuesday's show (featuring *The Phantom of the Opera*), election returns would be announced from the stage "by special wire." Why stay home and listen to the radio? News Brunswick, New Jersey – October 1925

(Left) This chatty newspaper ad contains a personal appeal from the management which notes it has been more than a year since they wholeheartedly recommended a picture – "Dear folks… cast everything else aside and see this one picture." Lancaster, Pennsylvania – October 15, 1925

(Right) It hard to know what to make of "Leonard School Notes." Normally, this article might be taken as a piece about goings-on at a small-town school. But every few paragraphs the newspaper interjected the title *The Street of Forgotten Men*, which is announced as showing on November 20. But where? The New Janus theater, the local "Home of High Class Pictures," was set to play an Evelyn Brent picture, *The Broadway Lady*, on that day – which leaves the school auditorium, the local opera house, or the local Star theater as possible venues. The latter two showed films, but only advertised (in a traditional manner) irregularly. Shelbyville, Missouri – November 17, 1926

(Below) One in a short series of local teaser ads. Marion, Ohio – October 1925

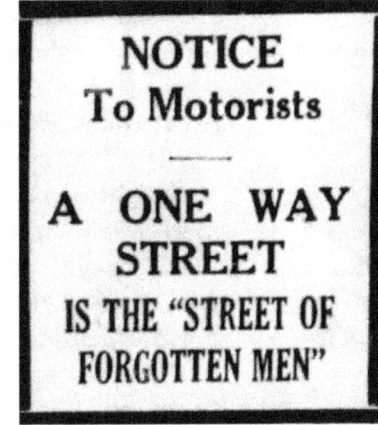

Moving multiple prints of multiple films around the country, usually by rail, could be complicated. Shown here are two examples (among others) of ads stating the previously announced film might not be shown. Coincidentally, both advertisements date from the same day.

(Above) The two-day run of *The Street of Forgotten Men* was extended one day when management of the Empress theater learned *The Gold Rush*, starring Charlie Chaplin, wouldn't arrive in time, having been mis-shipped from St. Louis. Owensboro, Kentucky – December 2, 1925

(Left) The NOTICE---! at the bottom of the Rialto ad reads, "A telegram was received at a late hour last night saying that *The Street of Forgotten Men* might not arrive in time for showing Wednesday. If it fails to come we will hold over *That Royle Girl*." The film did not show up, and the D.W. Griffith film starring Carol Dempster & W.C. Fields played again. Missoula, Montana – December 2, 1925

Three unusual newspaper ads. (Top left) It wasn't uncommon for small town newspapers to feature advertisements, including movie ads, on the front page. Medina, New York – September 30, 1925. (Top right) An unusual pairing of *The Street of Forgotten Men* with "Stereoscopik Luna-cy," one of the first 3D films. Queens, New York – January 1926 (Bottom right) The Three Bees Candy Shop presumably sponsored a contest in which the winner, namely one Amelia Smith, received a free ticket to see *The Street of Forgotten Men* at the local Crescent theater. Ithaca, New York – November 1925

By and large, most newspaper critics in New York and Chicago and elsewhere praised the film. Critics who took exception to particular aspects of the production where in the minority. However, that wasn't the case in Los Angeles, where the local press seemed not to take to *The Street of Forgotten Men*. Was the film too New York, or not enough Hollywood?

Writing in the Los Angeles *Illustrated Daily News*, H. B. K. Willis stated, "*The Street of Forgotten Men* at the Metropolitan is Herbert Brenon at his usual. It is not a great picture like *Peter Pan*, but is good program entertainment." (8-31-1925) Jimmy Starr expressed similar disappointment, opining in the *Los Angeles Record*, "Herbert Brenon brought Barrie's *Peter Pan* to the screen, displaying much skill. He has brought Turner's yarn to the silver sheet with ability." (8-31-1925) Starr's juxtaposition of "much skill" and [mere] "ability" makes his point, though obliquely. Other reviews in the *Los Angeles Evening Express* and *Los Angeles Herald* were likewise non-committal, almost tepid. Herbert Boyd, writing in the *Los Angeles Examiner*, almost gave the film something of a compliment when he stated, "Herbert Brenon has striven for realism but not morbidness. His interpretation throughout is sincere even to avoiding a sugar-coated ending." (8-31-1925)

The Street of Forgotten Men received one its poorest reviews in the *Los Angeles Times*; its anonymous critic wrote, "Were it not for Percy Marmont, *The Street of Forgotten Men* might well be forgotten. But in the inimitable Marmont manner, he has again managed to dominate, apparently without effort, a quite inadequate vehicle. And, standing as the one player immeasurably ahead of the other principles, he is also contrived to make temporarily real the unreal…. There is a desperate effort in this production, directed for Paramount by Herbert Brenon, to give the impression of the drabbest of drab sides of life. At times, to his everlasting credit, the illusion is strong, but the overstressing, inescapable in view of the plot, is fatal."

Such "drab" realism led the anonymous *Times* critic to also find fault with the acting of Mary Brian and Neil Hamilton, which the critic suggested was dull. However, favor was shown to others in the cast. "[T]he character work, in addition to the artistry of Marmont – who is a great enough actor to give conviction even to the maudlin ending, where the man who has sacrificed for love makes some time worn remarks on the eternal scheme of things – is excellent. As the 'blind' beggar, John

Harrington is appallingly real, while Dorothy Walters, as the faithful old housekeeper is the final word in comfortable motherliness. Juliet Brenon and Josephine Deffry, ladies of the demi-monde, also merit commendation."

The anonymous *Times* critic ended their review by highlighting the work of an uncredited, bit player in the film. It was the only publication to do so. "And there was a little rowdy, obviously attached to the 'blind' man, who did some vital work during her few short scenes. She was not listed." (8-31-1925) That uncredited bit player was Louise Brooks, who received her one and only notice for her role in *The Street of Forgotten Men*. As such, it was her first film review.

Louise Brooks, standing left, in her sole scene in the film. *Author collection*

The first decades of the 20th century are sometimes thought of as a "heroic age" in American journalism. Magazines and newspapers were then a robust industry, and

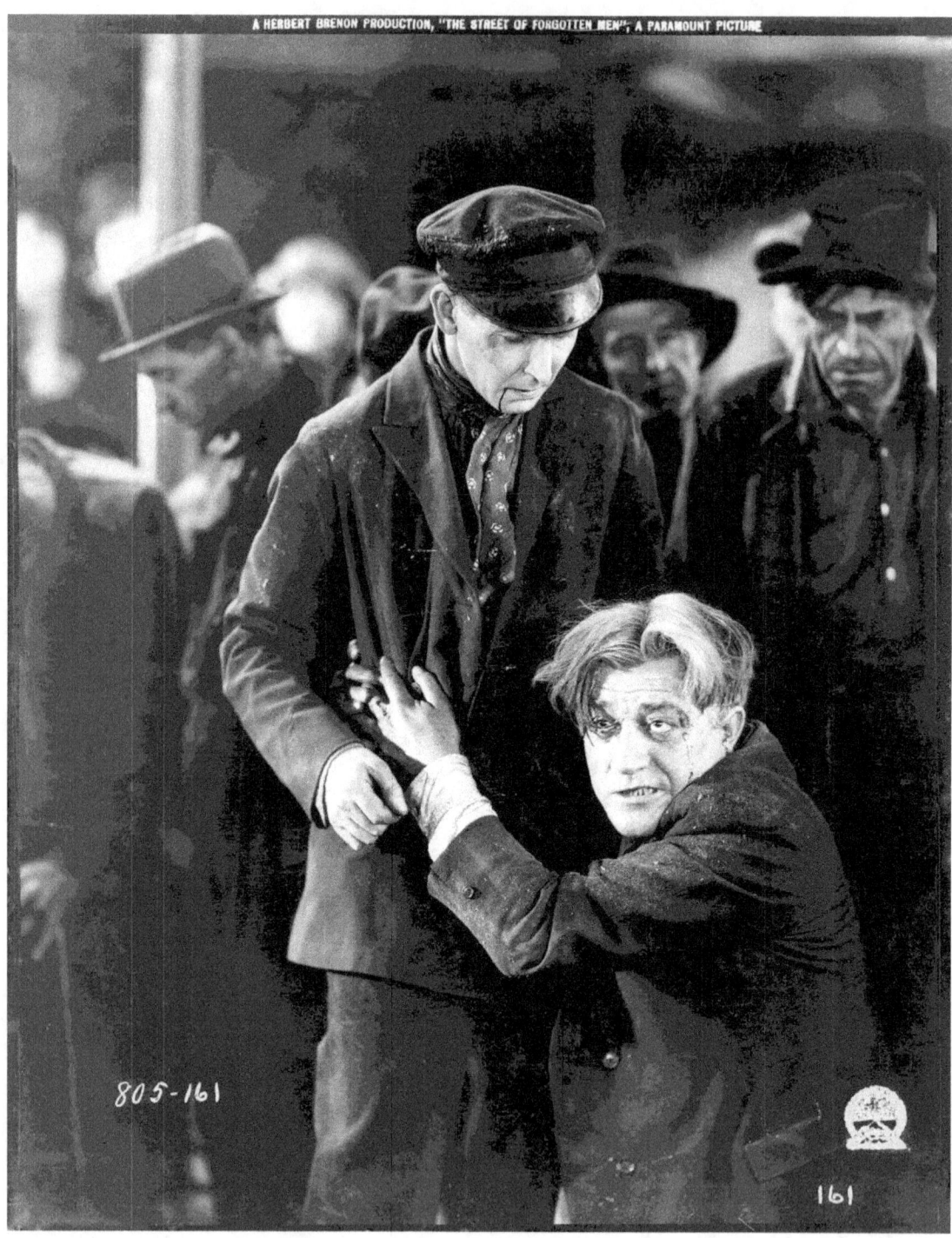

The adversarial relationship between the characters played by Percy Marmont and John Harrington dominates the film. In every regard, they are the real stars of *The Street of Forgotten Men*. Courtesy of *SilentHollywood.com*

their standing and broad market penetration made them a force hard to ignore in shaping public opinion on just about anything, including the movies. In fact, in the 1920s, most cities and towns could boast at least two newspapers, one issued in the morning, and the other in the afternoon. This held true for even the smallest municipalities, like Cherryvale, Kansas, for example, which maintained two newspapers despite a population of less than five thousand. Larger American cities, like Detroit or San Francisco, had three, four, or more daily papers. And that's not counting the various ethnic, political, religious, college, or suburban papers – some of which carried movie ads or theater listings, and some of which gave occasional editorial coverage to new films. All were part of the mix in forming public opinion and filling theater seats.

Significantly, newspapers in larger metropolitan areas like Boston, Buffalo, or Baltimore had their own critics and offered original reporting which reflected the interests of the reviewer and/or the values of their community. Today, these reviews still make for interesting reading. It is also worth noting that local newspaper coverage, whether from larger cities or smaller towns, sometimes reported on more than the film on the screen; such "local color" might include a connection to the film (a hometown actor or nearby shooting locale), audience reaction, a stage performance if there was one, other related happenings like a promotion or give-away, and even the weather, should it have affected turn-out. All of this additional information, some of it no doubt extraneous, helps paint a more detailed and at times vivid picture of the movie going experience in the silent era.

[In contrast, the coverage found in many small-town newspapers is of less significance. Owing to the lack of advance screenings and the short duration of many small-town runs, and to the fact most small-town papers were without a dedicated movie critic, the mostly anonymous "reviews" found in small-town papers amount to little more than cut-and-paste articles adapted from studio Press Sheet or out-of-town notices.]

All told, there were many original pieces of movie criticism found in American newspapers. Some could be surprisingly insightful. One that stands out is by a *Washington Herald* reviewer writing under the initials H.S.H. In a piece titled "*Street of Forgotten Men* An Out-of-Ordinary Drama," the Washington D.C. critic cried out for greater realism in films. The piece begins, "When the cinema shall faithfully portray life as it is lived in this particular mundane sphere, then, and only then, shall it be said it has reached the status of an art. The truest art is that which comes closest to the core of life, not that which attempts to escape it."

The piece continued, "It is noteworthy that the cinema is driving toward this end. Such films as *The Street of Forgotten Men*, the Herbert Brenon production now at the Palace Theater, are undoubtably a step in the right direction. For years this reviewer has longed for a picture which would at least in a measure spurn the conventional and untruthful happy ending. In *The Street of Forgotten Men* the director has tossed a crumb to those who feel that they must have the fade-out in copybook style and has cut a nice fresh loaf of hard pumpernickel for that section of the populace which demands the truth, no matter how it hurts."

"Percy Marmont, chief actor in this production, which deals with the life of professional beggars, displays that same degree of intelligence which is characterized his previous cinema appearances. Marmont, and such others like him as the motion picture industry can boast, furnishes the screen with an element of truth and sincerity and genuine ability of which it stands in vital need."

"*The Street of Forgotten Men* has for its dominant interest the filthy Bowery of the 90s. It shows with an acceptable degree of realism how the professional mendicant acquired his false bodily afflictions and the jealousies among the clan of vagrants. The first part of the picture is excellent; the denouement equally so. That portion in which the heart interest is allowed full sway is only saved from absolute frothiness by this splendid work of Marmont." H.S.H., the *Washington Herald* reviewer, concluded, "*The Street of Forgotten Men* fits in well with the greater movie season idea. If that which this film promises is carried out, the cinema has a real future in the realm of mentally stimulating realism. For this reviewer, Marmont and portions of such films as the Palace is showing this week serve as a stimulus to enthusiasm for the motion pictures." (9-17-1925)

Another critic who praised the film's realism was W. Ward Marsh of the *Cleveland Plain Dealer*. Marsh was a leading midwestern critic whose reviews often received the kind of attention given the New York and Los Angeles critics. Over the course of his half-century long career, Marsh reviewed some 23,000 films and befriended directors and actors alike. He wrote well, could turn a phrase, and was often insightful.

Marsh gave the film one of its first newspaper reviews outside NYC. He began his review with a straightforward statement, "Here is a quality melodrama approximating the worth of the *Miracle Man*, and of somewhat the same theme, though the religious flavor is wholly absent." Marsh then sets the scene, the Bowery "when 'leg o' muttons,' waistlines and 'V's' were quite the rage," and notes as well, "it discloses the secrets of the 'begging business' pretty thoroughly and most interestingly." The Cleveland critic then declared, "In fact, it is an unusually well told story, with Percy Marmont giving as fine a performance as I've seen him give."

Marsh highlighted the film's realism by highlighting its unusual ending. "The ending shows that Paramount is beginning to do the 'real' as opposed to the 'movie' endings. Whether we would like to have the sacrificing 'Easy Money Charlie' marry the girl just for the story's sake doesn't matter. In real life we would find such [an] ending quite distasteful, and when life is given as finely on the screen as it is in this picture, there's no reason why this silly ending should find its way to the screen. The true ending is what many of us have been crying for – and here it is. The film is most highly recommended." (7-27-1925)

A number of newspaper critics compared Percy Marmont to Lon Chaney, noting the latter's ability to contort his body in depicting a character – something Marmont did in *The Street of Forgotten Men*. Marsh, however, finished his remarkable piece by instead comparing another of the film's actors to Chaney: "John Harrington as a kind of villain, playing the role of a fake blind man, is a character player of much promise. Faking his blindness…. Harrington gives a performance which is startingly Lonchaneyesque."

Another appreciation of Brenon's realism was given by *Washington Times* reviewer, J.R., who stated "Brenon's genius dominates this picture…. he pilots the story away from the shoals of hokum." (8-17-1925) Charles J. Richardson, writing in the *Detroit Times*, likewise noted, "Mr. Brenon's direction is realistic. He handles his material in his usual debt manner, making the most of the material provided right to the surprise ending which made Sunday's audiences gasp at its novelty and effectiveness." (9-7-1925)

"It may not be what the audience would consider a happy ending," wrote Nie, the critic with a single (pseudo-)name who wrote for the *St. Louis Post-Dispatch*. (9-7-1925) Across town, the film's down-beat tenor left another critic feeling uncomfortable. Frances V. Feldkamp wrote in the *St. Louis Globe-Democrat*, "The Street of Forgotten Men. That's what the Bowery was called, and this is the first time that an entire film has been devoted to the showing of one section of life there. This was the quarter in which cripples, blind men and other wrecks of humanity were 'made-up' from able bodied men, who capitalized on their transformed appearance to prey on the sympathies of New Yorkers. It is real. It is Life with a capital, with some humor; some pathos, some comedy and some tragedy. But it is drab, there is no getting away from that. It all depends on how the beggar affects one in real life. Personally, it is depressing." (9-7-1925)

Echoing a sentiment found in its rival *Santa Barbara Daily News*, the anonymous piece in the *Santa Barbara Morning Press* put its praise another way. "When it comes to dramas of the underworld, the moving picture industry, unfortunately, generally lacks settings and local color. But every once in a while an inspired director happens to combine a particularly good cast and the correct environment. Such a one is *The Street of Forgotten Men*, a feature attraction that opened to a packed house." (9-1-1925)

When the movie played in Atlanta, *Weekly Film Review*, a regional trade journal, declared, "Paramount has given us another *Miracle Man* in this story of powerful heart appeal and drama. *The Street of Forgotten Men*, playing the Howard this week, is out of the usual mold, has that breadth of the rickety-slums of the late 90s – that excites the imagination and gives romance with a twist in it. Percy Marmont's role in this picture is one that will stand out above all else he has created, and one that you will remember after the picture is gone." Dorothy Evans of the *Sacramento Union* added an exclamation point to such critical applause when she noted the film's "theme goes deeper than the average motion picture." (8-10-1925)

The film's "powerful heart appeal" moved audiences not only in Atlanta, but elsewhere around the United States including Tacoma, Washington. The *Tacoma News Tribune* noted, "Perhaps the most touching scene comes when Charley adopts the child and stands with his landlady looking down at the sleepy baby who refused to loosen her hold on one of Charley's fingers. It held the packed house of Saturday night with its undeniable beauty and not a few men were heard to clear their throats huskily." (9-6-1925).

Elsewhere, A. F. Gillaspey of the *San Francisco Bulletin*, summed-up the feelings of many critics when they noted "For fine dramatic detail, for unusualness, for giving us a glimpse into a world we never see and into the other sides of characters we simply pass in pity on the streets, *The Street of Forgotten Men* is a photoplay revelation." (8-10-1925)

Two newspaper ads from the film's triumph in San Francisco, where it played as part of the local Greater Movie Season and drew large crowds and was highly praised. In his *San Francisco Examiner* review, "Bowery Film Wins Audience," future novelist Idwal Jones praised the movie's realism, calling it a film about a "tough epoch" that was "fascinating to look at." (8-10-1925) Nearly a century later, in 2022, the surviving film was restored and shown at the city's historic Castro Theater.

Additional Press from Around the United States

anonymous. "Drama of Underworld of Stirring Quality." *Philadelphia Record*, August 4, 1925.
— "At last we have a stirring drama of the underworld…. The outstanding figure in the cast is that of 'Easy Money Charlie,' a part played by Percy Marmont with consummate skill."

anonymous. "Offerings at Local Theaters." *Washington Post*, August 17, 1925.
— "*The Street of Forgotten Men* is not likely to be forgotten soon itself. The story told by this picture is one of the most amazing ever unfolded. It is the kind of story that haunts you long afterward."

Taffe, Agnes. "Strand." *Minneapolis Star Daily*, August 24, 1925.
— "A rather startling picture is on at the Strand theater for the week beginning today…. an unusual picture as to subject matter and one ably directed by Herbert Brenon, who has not missed a single opportunity for presentation of real dramatic situations. Percy Marmont is the star of this picture and in it he does the best thing to date in his screen career, playing admirably with Mary Brian and Neil Hamilton."

anonymous. "At the Movies this Week." *San Antonio Express*, August 24, 1925.
— "*The Street of Forgotten Men* is no 'honey-dripping' screen romance, yet this realistic and gripping story of the New York underworld has a love story far more life-like than the average, and introduces a set of characters and a theme entirely away from the usual kind."

Marzoni, Pettersen. "Picture Reviews." *Birmingham News*, August 25, 1925.
— "There are a lot of big moments in the film…."

C., S. L. "Metropolitan Has Notable Picture." *Baltimore Daily Post*, August 26, 1925.
— "There's no use mincing words about it. Nobody'll ever forget *The Street of Forgotten Men*, being shown at the Metropolitan this week. Some press agent says '*The Miracle Man* of 1925' can best describe the film, yet we think darn site more of the current picture, to say the least."

D., Q. E. "For Film Fans." *Baltimore Evening Sun*, August 26, 1925.
— "The ending is perfect. Percy Marmont is quite fine as Charley – probably the best thing he's done…. Herbert Brenon's direction is all that it should be."

O., F. P. "James." *Columbus Citizen*, August 31, 1925.
— "Marmont does some good work in a Jekyll-Hyde character."

Ellarcotte, Roy. "Reel Players." *Detroit Free Press*, September 7, 1925.
— "Percy Marmont shoulders a regulation Lon Chaney role with fair success."

K., K. T. "Asbestos." *New Orleans Times-Picayune*, September 25, 1925.
— "It is principally distinguished by the sterling performance by Percy Marmont, all of whose performances have been excellent. On this occasion his ability is framed in a picturesque and

grotesque setting and a good story. Marmont, has a role much like that of Lon Chaney in *The Miracle Man* and makes as much of it as the artist could have."

D., H. E. "At the Theatre." *Honolulu Advertiser*. September 29, 1925.
— "One of the best titles in many moons. Also one of the best underworld film plays I have ever seen. As a rule, 'underworld' stories are lurid – and often objectionable. *The Street of Forgotten Men* is colorful, but not lurid. A human vein runs through it – pathos, heartbeats, tears – and now and then some happy moments. It is also a strange story, dealing with strange people, and told in a strange sort of way…. Herbert Brenon has molded his material into a picture that stamps him as an interpreter of human moods. He has brought out the contrasts in excellent style, avoiding the melodramatic as much as possible. However, there is some humor in it, because the story takes one back to the days of twenty years ago – and you know what women's hats looked like then. If you don't remember them – or never saw them – take a look-see at the movie at the Princess this week."

anonymous. "*Forgotten Men* Pleases in Return Showing." *Evening Journal*, December 4, 1925.
— "At the Majestic yesterday, a remarkable picture had a return showing here in Wilmington. The film is *The Street of Forgotten Men*, a drama that has attracted world-wide attention and when first shown here several months ago at the Arcadia Theatre was viewed by audiences of increasing size."

* * *

"The Street of Forgotten Men"—F. P.-L.—Granada, San Francisco
(Week ending Aug. 15)
BULLETIN—* * * Marmont always wanted to do something different. In "The Street of Forgotten Men" he is given his opportunity and as if realizing this he seems to throw all his reserve energies into this play. He gives it everything he has. The result is a truly splendid dramatic picture.
* * *
CALL AND POST—* * * Here is a picture which, to our mind, is an even greater piece of work than "The Unholy Three," with Percy Marmont actually outdoing Lon Chaney in the matter of character and makeup and the screen story itself eclipsing its forerunner ni both conviction and fascination. * * *
CHRONICLE—* * * Brenon has the faculty of throwing a glamor over any theme he touches, and even in dealing with the criminally mendicant, the fakers who prey on the charitably inclined, he has put beauty and a certain amount of romance into his story. * * *
EXAMINER—* * * Marmont can make any picture pleasing, and does well in this unaccustomed role. The extreme of realism abounds in scenes wherein the fakers transform themselves into cripples and go out to impose upon the charitable. * * *

The Street of Forgotten Men went over big in San Francisco, California. According to *Variety*, the film "came in hitting on all six." Its success was aided by a robust promotional campaign and by the many glowing reviews the film received in the local press.

(Left) *Film Daily*, the prominent trade journal, regularly featured a round-up of reviews from major cities. Pictured here is their round-up for *The Street of Forgotten Men*, which played for a week at the Granada theater in San Francisco. (8-27-1925)

San Francisco, the City by the Bay, was home to a handful of newspapers in the 1920s. Not included in the *Film Daily* round-up is a review which ran in the *San Francisco News*. It also praised the film, describing the Herbert Brenon picture as "an underworld drama, stark and naked in its picturing of the beggars and fakers who prey on the public." (8-10-1925)

Newspaper and magazine critics weren't the only individuals who voiced their opinion about new films. So did exhibitors. In the mid-1920s, two trade publications, *Exhibitors Herald* and *Moving Picture World*, published reports from the field in which theater owners and managers submitted brief accounts regarding how a film played in their venue. These reports, which typically ran just a sentence or two or three, might detail audience turn-out or audience reaction, and sometimes, they might note how the weather affected attendance, which day of the week the film played best, or how much a venue might charge for admission. The majority of contributors were independent theater owners who operated 200 to 500-seat houses in towns of just a few thousand. These weren't reports from big cities like San Francisco or Chicago, but small places like Glasgow, Montana and Hollywood, Kansas.

In *Exhibitors Herald*, the column in which these reports were printed was called "What the Picture Did For Me," while the column in *Moving Picture World* was called "Straight From the Shoulder Reports." As "Verdicts on Films" in the "unvarnished language" of exhibitors, and as "Exhibition Information Direct from the Box-Office to You," each stressed immediacy and authenticity. Small town exhibitors, somewhat removed from the flow of information about motion pictures, relied on these reports in choosing pictures to show to their patrons. As such, these mini-reports offer a distinct perspective on individual films from a little documented segment of the movie-going public.

(Despite the addition of an extra reel), regular contributor George Marlow of the Washington theatre in Atoka, Oklahoma penned what can be termed a typical report in the December 19, 1925 issue of *Exhibitors Herald*.

> **THE STREET OF FORGOTTEN MEN:** Percy Marmont—An excellent picture; price right; pleased 90 per cent. Made some money. But in and step on the advertising. Eight reels.—George Marlow, Washington theatre, Atoka, Okla.—Small town patronage.

Similar typical reports came from the Grand Theater in Pierre, South Dakota, "A fine drama. Lots of favorable comment as people left the theater" (*MPW*, 10-17-

1925) and Reel Joy in King City, California, "This was a very good picture. Pleased my crowd which was not a very large one." (*EH*, 11-14-1925) Other reports added more nuance. The "Y" theatre in Nazareth, Pennsylvania noted the film was "Not very good for a Saturday night, as it is a sad picture" (*EH*, 4-3-1926), while the S.T. theatre in Parker, South Dakota, stated "Good picture of a more serious trend. Pleased large Sunday business." (*EH*, 12-12-1925) Elsewhere, the Star theatre in Montevideo, Minnesota described the film as an "Underworld story that satisfied. It's different and can be bought to leave a profit." (*EH*, 1-9-1926)

The 250-seat Liberty Theater in Leonard, Texas (then a farming town of 1380) nearly raved. "Another *Miracle Man*. Bear down on this one and get the money. It will stand a little increase in price. You will get a picture like this about every three years. Buy it. Tone, OK. Sunday and special, yes. Appeal, 90%." (*MPW*, 3-20-26) Also raving was the 250-seat Grantsville Theatre in Grantsville, West Virginia, which proclaimed *The Street of Forgotten Men* "A real picture; had many comments on this one. Paramount is there with the goods. The small exhibitor can well afford to stay with them on this…. Fine tone, appeal, 95%. Yes for Sunday." (*MPW*, 10-2-1926)

Some of these mini-reports went beyond best practices or issues of commerce and almost ventured into critical commentary. The Regent Theatre in Bogota, New Jersey thought the film "a crackerjack picture." (*EH*, 11-14-1925) However, the Palace theatre in Newark, Arkansas thought it "A little too long," though "patrons made several favorable comments." (*EH*, 12-26-1925) The Cozy theatre in Fayette, Iowa thought it "A very good picture although many were disappointed in the way the picture ended." (*EH*, 3-27-1926)

The Char-Bell theatre in Rochester, Indiana stated *The Street of Forgotten Men* was a "Very good picture. Well acted and teaches a splendid moral. Picture full of pathos in good drama, but doesn't become monotonous at any time." (*EH*, 11-28-1925) Similarly, the Paramount theatre in Wyoming, Illinois said the film was "A great deal better than the average run of pictures. Mary Brian proves to be a very clever little star. Percy Marmont does some real acting in this picture. Play it. You can't go wrong." (*EH*, 3-27-1926)

In a few instances, exhibitors reported the film's rough-and-tumble, big city backdrop did not appeal to their small-town audience. The American theatre in

Wautonan, Wisconsin noted, "This is a good underworld story, but my patrons do not seem to take to that kind of stories, so they didn't enthuse, and it didn't draw, either." (*EH*, 2-27-1926) Similarly, the Columbia theatre in Columbia City, Indiana stated, "Fair first night; poor the next. Famous Players may consider this entertainment but my clientele did not, we having several walkouts. The picture is too depressing, the Bowery drinking scenes in this dry state don't add to the value of the production and I do not believe that people come to the theater to have the dregs of humanity paraded before them, with all the misery and poverty there is in evidence in this picture. Further, Marmont may be good on the speaking stage but he is a heck of a long way from having any drag with the moviegoers. The consensus of opinion of those whom I asked how they liked it next day said it was as close to zero as they cared to sit through, that if it had not been that I recommended it rather highly they would not have been attracted to it. There is where I made a mistake. I laid it too heavy in my newspaper ad." (*EH*, 11-21-1925)

Another extended bit of commentary came from the Rex theater in Salmon, Idaho, who said, "Sometimes I wonder if Paramount knows a good play when they make it. They seem to boost the lemons and forget the really good ones. I think perhaps they boost the big stars and do not realize that the play is the essential thing (of course with good acting). Here is a wonderful production that has been forgotten by Paramount. The acting is perfect. Marmont's characterization of the fake blind beggar is simply great. Herbert Brenon's detail work in depicting the faker factory scenes is of very high order. Mary Brian is very fine in this, the rest of the cast excellent. If you haven't played this but have it bought, play it up big as a wonderful picture, on the par with *Miracle Man*. The ending is sad, as the old man gives up his ward (whom he has raised from a baby, taken from the slums) to a younger man and in so doing keeps society from the knowledge of the girl's lowly and questionable birth. It did not draw, but I could have made it draw if I had played it up as a big play with my high class patrons." (*EH*, 9-25-1926) [Harrington, not Marmont, played the fake blind beggar.]

One last solitary exhibitor report appeared as late as 1927. It was run in another publication altogether, *Movie Age*, a regional trade journal based in Omaha, Nebraska. On its "Box Office Reports" page, an unnamed exhibitor from the Parish Hall in Conception, Missouri described *The Street of Forgotten Men* as, simply, "A sad, but very fine picture." (10-1-1927)

How one small-town exhibitor went about selecting films was the subject of an article published in the weekly *Fallon County Times*, from Baker, Montana. The article, "Film Representative in Baker," detailed the circumstances around which Mr. Lake, owner of the local Lake Theater, chose films for the upcoming year.

In 1925, Baker was a small town (population 1100) located in the American west. It is 225 miles from Billings, and was named after a railroad construction engineer. It was also the hometown of Irene [Lentz], the onetime actress turned mononymous fashion and costume designer.

The article in the *Fallon County Times* noted that Joe English, a representative of the Paramount Picture Corporation, had recently spent two days at the Lake Theatre "negotiating for the present big releases" and "future outstanding pictures" released by the studio. The article noted, "It is quite a task for an exhibitor to choose pictures which will please his patrons, and in a small town it is especially hard because the theatre going crowd is always the same. Through his Paramount contract Mr. Lake will receive the biggest pictures of 1926 within a month or two after their completion." (Such a claim was likely not true.)

The Lake Theater planned an ambitious schedule. The article stated, "Fifty per cent of these pictures are in the making but are already contracted for…. The dates for the showing of these pictures have already been set in the contract. *The Ten Commandments* is booked for February 21 and 22."

Also selected by the Lake was *The Street of Forgotten Men*, as well as other Paramount offerings including three other Brenon films, *Peter Pan*, *The Song and Dance Man*, and *Dancing Mothers*, two films starring W.C. Fields, *That Royal Girl* and *It's the Old Army Game*, and a handful of comedies such as Harold Lloyd's *For Heaven's Sake*, and *Behind the Front*, featuring Wallace Beery and Raymond Hatton. There were also a couple of films with Western settings, *Pony Express* and *The Vanishing American*. And unusually so, two documentary films, Robert J. Flaherty's *Moana* and the Merian C. Cooper and Ernest Schoedsack production, *Grass*. The article also noted Lake had contracted with First National, "taking their entire output for 1926. Every play date for the next eight months is now filled."

Optimistically, the article ended by stating, "The manager of the Lake Theatre is anticipating a big business during the coming year and has contracted for considerable space in the *Fallon County Times*, so with every issue of this paper you will find the Lake Theatre program in the upper right hand corner of the back page." (12-25-1925)

In the January, 1926 issue of the trade journal, *Transactions of the Society of Motion Picture Engineers*, Eric T. Clarke published an article titled "An Exhibitor's Problems in 1925." Clarke, the Director of the Eastman Theatre in Rochester, New York focused his piece on the same issue raised by the Rex theater and other exhibitors – namely, how to select appropriate films that draw an audience. Clarke's 16-page piece was, in fact, the text of an earlier talk given before the S.M.P.E., to which was added the transcript of the discussion which followed Clarke's address. Notably, *The Street of Forgotten Men*, and its merits as a film, were mentioned in Clarke's article, as were some of the other films in circulation in 1925.

Clarke noted the Eastman Theatre needed to draw at least one-eighth of the local population every week if it "did not wish to lose money." But what to show, and to what segments of the population should a film appeal? Clarke discussed various selection strategies centering on the film's star, director, or producer, as well as what kind of story the film contained. Stories with strong sex appeal were frowned upon. Clarke stated, "It is a discriminating audience that distinctly prefers real quality to tawdry allurements. The most successful features are never morally questionable." Also considered were the venue and its adornments, promotion and advertising, the pre-film music and entertainment, and even the length and projection speed of a film. All were factors in making a selection. Summing up, Clarke thought the "problem in program making, expressed commercially, is the desire to get the people to come to the theatre in the expectation of seeing a good show rather than to decide according to the attractiveness of the feature picture alone. Until we succeed in this endeavor, we shall be subject to the wide fluctuation in drawing power of the feature pictures."

In the floor discussion that followed, an attendee named Dr. Hickman (representing Rochester's Regent theater) stated, "I gathered in listening to Mr. Clarke's paper that to fill the largest theatre in any town one has to appeal to a very large percentage, and therefore it is essential that the program shall have a popular flavor, the roping in of the high-brows becoming a matter of secondary importance. If that is so, one must assume that it is impossible to give the best program in the largest theatre in any town; it must be given by the house of second importance. Mr. Clarke has based his argument on the behavior of Rochester and taken the Eastman Theatre as an example. It has the opportunity of the best of everything, but always one hears the expression: 'There is a magnificent film at the Regent this week, but the family prefer the Eastman building.' During the last few weeks we have had three or four films of outstanding importance: Harold Lloyd in *The Freshman*, *The Beggar on Horseback*, and *The Street of Forgotten Men*. The last is a magnificent film; it was the less superior Harold Lloyd picture, which received the advertisement and drew the people."

Later in the piece, Clarke responded to various points raised by other exhibitors. "With regard to *The Street of Forgotten Men*: The exhibitor, after all is in business, and ... [with the] Eastman Theatre I don't have to show any profit, I have no endowment, and I must run the Theatre so that it will attract the largest audience. You can measure the success of a picture only by the size of the audience. I thought *The Street of Forgotten Men* was one of the best pictures of the kind I had ever seen, but it is one on which unfortunately we could only expect a limited audience. I am not trying to arrange that the Eastman have all the good pictures and the Regent the poor ones; I am trying to arrange them to get the best audience for the picture. This picture could have been presented at the Eastman, but I think it would have fallen below the average. At the same time we are not strictly commercial. We had *The Beggar on Horseback* – a picture five years ahead of the public taste. The Eastman owed it to the industry to present that picture with a big orchestra, but we died with it. I might sum up the point by saying that Mr. Eastman did not build the theatre with the idea of duplicating the type of performance given elsewhere."

The following year, in the January, 1927 issue of *Transactions of the Society of Motion Picture Engineers*, Clarke authored a follow-up piece, "An Exhibitor's Problems in

1926." Clarke admitted he was still confronted with the problem of selecting films. "Screening features is lazy work, but an awful lot hangs by it. When I started it, I was advised by an old-time picture man to beware of second thoughts in deciding on pictures. It is the first impression which is important in trying to gauge what the public will like. I have found this very sound advice."

Later in his 1927 piece, Clarke mentioned *The Street of Forgotten Men*. "In the discussion following my paper last year, I was asked why certain pictures of outstanding importance were not shown at the Eastman. Two pictures were under question – *The Last Laugh* and *The Street of Forgotten Men*. I explained that we had not shown either as we thought that only limited audiences would appreciate them. I added that we had shown *The Beggar on Horseback*, because we felt we owed it to the industry to sponsor such an unusual picture which, as I said, was five years ahead of the public taste. This picture, coming at the height of the season, held the low record for the year. I have changed my mind. I know now that I was wrong in letting the Eastman take sides with Art against the Public. It was not our business to show a picture which the big public did not care to see."

Percy Marmont and unknown extras in *The Street of Forgotten Men*.
Courtesy of SilentHollywood.com

Whatever drew the public's interest, movies were a primary form of entertainment in the 1920s; every week, millions of Americans went to what was once known as the "picture-show." Some went to keep up with new releases, while others went to take in old favorites. With such demand, it's not surprising *The Street of Forgotten Men* remained in circulation for four years, a long but not unusual amount of time during the silent era. Many, if not most screenings took place in 1925 and 1926. The film continued to play, although less frequently, well into 1927; included among that year's screenings was a February showing at the "thoroughly heated" Atkins Theater in Yuba City, California in which the film was paired with a stage play called *The Waifs of New York*.

One of the first showings of *The Street of Forgotten Men* in 1928 – its fourth year in circulation, took place on January 6 at the cleverly named Fotosho theater in Miami, Florida. This showing, like most of the others that year, was held at a second-run house and lasted only one day – though all day. The film was shown continuously between 10:30 am and 11:00 pm., without set start times in between. At the Fotosho, patrons could come and go as they wished, taking in the end of the film, and then the beginning.

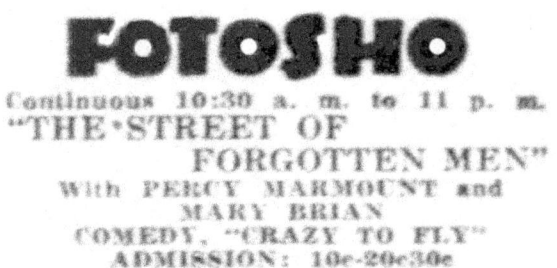

The following month, on February 27, the film was shown for two days at the Kent in Philadelphia; the film was originally scheduled to be shown just one day, but according to the *Philadelphia Inquirer*, it was held over due to greater than expected interest. Despite it then being an older release, the newspaper gave the film an editorial shout out – one of its very last such notices, describing it as a "decidedly worth-while picture." The actors, the newspaper also noted, gave "gripping interest to the leading roles." (2-28-1928)

A few months later, *The Street of Forgotten Men* was shown at the Avalon in Bellingham, Washington. On Friday nights, the Avalon played double bills which included a recent feature along with a "Revival Picture." On April 20, 1928, *The Street of Forgotten Men* – promoted as a "picture you'll always remember," served as the revival film, the underside of a double bill with *Wolf Fangs* (1927), a Fox Film made on nearby Mt. Baker which starred Caryl Lincoln and Thunder the Dog.

That April, *The Street of Forgotten Men* was also shown as a benefit in a non-theatrical setting. This unique event took place in Hastings-on-Hudson, New York – near the Riverview Manor home of author George Kibbe Turner. On April 20, the film was screened in the village school auditorium as "benefit entertainment" to raise funds for uniforms for the local high school band. This otherwise minor affair received a bit of local buzz. The *Hastings News* ran a banner ad along the bottom of its April 20 front page, while the *Yonkers Statesman* and *Yonkers Herald* each ran articles ahead of the event. According to the *Hastings News*, the fundraiser proved to be a "big success". The *Yonkers Statesman* reported 400 attended the benefit, noting "Eight reels of the story written by Mr. Turner were enjoyed by those present..... Miss Margaret Williams, a student of New Platz Normal School ... played the piano during the entire performance." (4-21-1928)

(Left) An announcement ad runs across the bottom of the front page of the April 20, 1928 issue of the *Hastings News***. (Right) The ad for the college town Rialto theater. Champaign, Illinois – July 1928**

Two screenings of *The Street of Forgotten Men* took place in July of 1928. On July 18, the film was shown at the Rialto Theater in Champaign, Illinois. This 850-seat, college town theater was a prominent revival house which promoted its second-run features as "Re-shown by Request."

A few days later, *The Street of Forgotten Men* enjoyed what is thought to be its last two day run, this time at the Lyric in Billings, Montana, where on July 20 and 21 it played continuously with a Larry Semon comedy. After four years in circulation, the film still carried its original tag-line, "The screen has never known an underworld-society drama so strange and startling as this one!"

Three weeks later, the last documented screening of the film in the United States took place at the Dumont Theater in Hackensack, New Jersey, where it showed for one-day on August 15, 1928. After that, *The Street of Forgotten Men* disappeared from American screens, but not from view….

Percy Marmont and Juliet Brenon in a contemplative scene from the film's now missing second reel. Marmont holds what is likely the Bible. *Author collection*

A LEGACY

Herbert Brenon's 1925 film shares a distinction few other movies can claim, namely, its title became a catchphrase. And what's more, that catchphrase shaped the way Americans thought about the down-and-out for decades to come. As commentators have remarked, the phrase "street of forgotten men" is not only evocative, it is also memorable – and despite its air of despair, it is also somewhat poetic. This singular phrase entered into use around the time of the film's release – not only as another name for the Bowery in New York, but broadly as short-hand for those parts of any town where the poor and unfortunate congregate.

Although the phrase "street of forgotten men" originated with George Kibbe Turner's magazine story, the term made-up of its last two words has a longer history. While inextricably linked, the phrase "street of forgotten men" (referring to a place) and the term "forgotten man" or "forgotten men" (referring to individuals or groups) have distinct histories which inform one another and overlap in time.

Decades before the release of the 1925 film, the term "forgotten man" was used to refer to an individual who falls on hard times and into socio-economic obscurity. One of its earliest uses was in 1876 in an essay by the sociologist and Yale professor William Graham Sumner. He further developed the theme of the "forgotten man" in a series of articles published in *Harper's Weekly* in 1883. After Sumner's death, his writings were published in a book titled *The Forgotten Man, and other Essays* (1918).

In the years following the end of first World War, the two-word term turns-up time and again in editorials on the nature of poverty. One editorial, which appeared in the Raleigh (N.C.) *News and Observer*, asked "Who is the Forgotten Man? And can the State prosper unless it takes steps to see that he is held in practical remembrance and given a better chance in life?" (9-25-1921) Another editorial, likewise titled "The Forgotten Man," appeared in the *Wall Street Journal*. It begins by noting Sumner's writings had, by that time, taken their place "among the classic American contributions to political economy." (9-5-1922)

The term "forgotten man" gained renewed currency during the Great Depression when President Franklin Roosevelt used it in a 1932 radio address to refer to poor Americans who required New Deal help. In the 1945 supplement to his classic book, *The American Language*, H. L. Mencken described the use of the term during the New Deal as a "novelty" and "curious perversion."

Slowly, the meaning of the term shifted as it worked its way into popular culture, supplanting Sumner's original socio-economic concept. In the film *I Am a Fugitive from a Chain Gang* (1932), for example, an unjustly-treated prisoner named James Allen (played by Paul Muni) disappears – and in so many words, the film asks, "What has become of James Allen? – Is he too, just another forgotten man?" In *Gold Diggers of 1933* (1933), which includes scenes of mass unemployment, Joan Blondell sings "Remember My Forgotten Man" in one memorable sequence. And in *My Man Godfrey* (1936), a wealthy Bostonian played by William Powell is mistaken for a tramp when a frivolous socialite, played by Carole Lombard, is sent on a scavenger hunt for a "forgotten man."

The title-phrase *The Street of Forgotten Men* began its journey into the American language and culture just before the film's debut. Although the movie premiered at the Rivoli on July 19, 1925 – that may not have been the first time the public got a look, or perhaps a sneak-peak, at the memorably titled work. A few weeks prior to its debut, Brenon's film was the focus of an event at the Chelsea Methodist Episcopal Church in New York City. Newspaper descriptions of this June 28 event vary. According to a piece published in the *New York Herald Tribune*, "Scenes from the new picture, *The Street of Forgotten Men*, will be shown at the night service to-morrow." (6-27-1925) The next day, the *New York Times* ran a piece which stated, "Herbert Brenon, a director of motion pictures with the Paramount Picture Corporation, will describe a new picture, *The Street of Forgotten Men*, this evening at the 'Happy Sunday Evening' service." (6-28-1925)

The Church that hosted the event was headed by the Reverend Dr. Christian F. Reisner, a well-known preacher sometimes described in the press as "colorful." Reisner was an exponent of so-called new methods, and believed in showmanship when it came to preaching. After the first World War, he penned a syndicated article which stated religion should take pointers from the theater, suggesting the ablest sermons may be staged behind the footlights. He also authored books with titles like *The Church as a Social Center* and *Church Publicity: the modern way to compel them to come in*. A few weeks prior to the June 28 event, Reisner was the subject of considerable press attention when he proposed building a skyscraper dedicated to Christianity to be known as the Broadway temple.

Given the subject of *The Street of Forgotten Men*, the June 28 event may have served as a lure to secure donations toward Reisner's ambitious plans – which, notably, featured housing and services for the poor. There is little else known about the event except for a bit of reportage which appeared in a syndicated newspaper column called "Cheerful Churches by a Layman." What is certain is that the June event helped introduce the film and its evocative title to the world. The column read, "Moving picture directors rarely get into a church pulpit, but one of them who achieved this seeming impossibility availed himself of the 'Happy Sunday Evening' service in a metropolitan church to give those present a pleasant description of a new picture *The Street of Forgotten Men*. To even matters up the movie-man was followed up by the pastor of the church who spoke briefly on 'Motion Picture dangers.' At the conclusion of this joint appearance of the apostles of religion and riot the audience stood in front of the church and participated in a community 'sing.' Accounts all agree that it was an evening well spent in behalf of the spirit of religion and helpful to the community." (7-11-1925, Jackson, MS *Clarion-Ledger*)

A few months later, the film was the focus of similar event which occurred at the Lewis Avenue Congregational Church in nearby Brooklyn. On October 18, the Rev. Allison Ray Heaps gave a "sermon lecture on *The Street of Forgotten Men*." (Brenon is not known to have attended this event.) A brief article in the *Brooklyn Daily Eagle* stated, "Lantern slides from the motion picture will be used to illustrate this story of the old Bowery life." (10-17-1925) *The Chat*, another Brooklyn paper, also carried a piece on the Lewis Avenue sermon-lecture. In it, the local paper gave a description of the film which suggests what churches thought the moral behind Brenon's production: "Sunday, evening 8 p.m., *The Street of Forgotten Men*. This is the story of a man living in the old Bowery of New York City who by a combination of the virtue of self-sacrifice and the spirit of unselfishness was able to rise into newness of life, realize an ideal, and render a service to his fellow men. Percy Marmont impersonates the 'forgotten man.' The slides are from the motion picture production." (10-17-1925) Notably, this event, which incorporated a slide show of unknown origin, took place during a week in which the film was showing in Brooklyn at four second run theaters, the Peerless, Ablemarie, Farragut, and Eden Movies.

The content and theme of the event at the Lewis Avenue Congregational Church was seemingly repeated a few weeks later at a different venue. On November 7, Universalist pastor Thomas Edward Potterton, D.D. gave an illustrated lecture on *The Street of Forgotten Men* at the Church of Our Father. (The two churches sometimes shared sermons and slide shows; on November 14, for example, each presented a "colored lantern slide" retelling of the moralistic Channing Pollock play, *The Enemy*.)

Brooklyn, New York – October 1925

Religious interest in *The Street of Forgotten Men* was not confined to New York or Brooklyn. Nor was it restricted to sermons illustrated with lantern slides. In fact, religious interest extended to the West Coast, and sometimes featured either a straight-forward talk or even a screening of the film itself.

According to a short write-up in the *Los Angeles Times*, a local pastor, Dr. G. A. Briegleb, was scheduled to deliver an evening sermon on "The Gold Rush and the Street of Forgotten Men" at the Westlake Presbyterian Church in Los Angeles. Like Reverend Reisner of New York, Briegleb was a proponent of employing new methods in spreading the good word. He also spoke on somewhat off-beat topics which hinged on the premise "what would Jesus do" (today's W.W.J.D.), as in what would Jesus do if he was on the local city council, or owned a newspaper. The talk set to take place ahead of Briegleb's October 10, 1925 sermon tied to "The Gold Rush and the Street of Forgotten Men" was titled "What Would Jesus Do if After Marriage He Discovered That He Was Wedded to the Wrong Woman?"

A year later, another preacher and another church made use of the film. The *Los Angeles Times* reported "The motion picture *The Street of Forgotten Men*, and an address by Dr. James Lash will feature [at] the services tomorrow evening at the Hollywood Congregational Church. Salvador Baguez will be the soloist." (10-2-1926)

> **HOLLYWOOD CONGREGATIONAL CHURCH**
> James Hamilton Lash, D.D., Minister. Hollywood Blvd. at Sycamore Avenue.
> 11 A.M. Communion Meditation: "Life's Covenants"
> 7:30 P.M. Picture: "The Street of Forgotten Men"
> Address, Dr. Lash.
> 9:30 A.M., Church School.   6:15 P.M., Young People's Groups

Los Angeles, California – October 1926

Another screening of *The Street of Forgotten Men* within the confines of a church took place in New Britain, Connecticut. The film itself had shown in this Connecticut town in October, 1925 at the local Palace theater. Some six months later, it returned to New Britain when it was shown on a Sunday evening at the city's historic South Church, then a Congregational denomination. A newspaper advertisement for this April 25, 1926 event billed the film as "A Picture of Unusual Human Interest."

> **CONGREGATIONAL | CONGREGATIONAL**
> **MOTION PICTURES**
> **Central Congregational Church**
> ELLIS STREET AND CARNEGIE WAY
> WITHERSPOON DODGE, D.D., MINISTER
> 11:00—Sermon, "Winning One's Soul."
> 8:00—Motion Picture, "The Street of Forgotten Men."

Atlanta, Georgia – April 1928

Another screening of *The Street of Forgotten Men* also took place within the confines of a church – in 1928, nearly three years after the film's debut. The Central

Congregational Church in Atlanta, Georgia, whose services were headed by Witherspoon Dodge and described as "cheerful and refreshing," occasionally showed films on Sunday evenings under the banner "Religious Movies" or "Free Motion Pictures." In 1928, the same year the Atlanta church screened *The Street of Forgotten Men*, it also screened popular movies such as the Milton Stills - Doris Kenyon feature *Men of Steel* (1926), Reginald Deny's *Fast and Furious* (1927), Raoul Walsh's *The Wanderer* (1925), and Merian C. Cooper & Ernest B. Schoedsack's *Chang* (1927).

On April 29, 1928 Atlanta's Central Congregational Church screened *The Street of Forgotten Men*, believing its theme of self-sacrifice an uplifting one – or perhaps, the church simply hoped to draw new congregants by providing what it thought was wholesome entertainment. Besides marking the last documented screening of the film in a church, it was also one of the very last documented screenings of the film anywhere in the United States.

As most churches did not promote or advertise their religious services, it is difficult to know just how many other houses of worship either screened the film, or made use of the related illustrated sermon. Fortunately, those that did created a paper trail. It is known, for example, that *The Street of Forgotten Men* was the subject of Dr. J.R. Macartney's Sunday morning sermon at the First Presbyterian church in Waterloo, Iowa on May 15, 1927. Likewise, the North Congregational Church in Portsmouth, New Hampshire presented the film story, "illustrated by stereopticon," on April 22, 1928, preceded by an organ recital. *The Street of Forgotten Men* was also the subject of an evening sermon at St. Paul's Evangelical Lutheran Church in Camden, New Jersey on September 16, 1928. And on April 28, 1929, a stereopticon lecture of *The Street of Forgotten Men* was given at the Congregational Church in Burlington, Vermont.

In some communities, local newspapers published the text of sermons given at area churches. On October 28, 1929 the Rev. Walter Krumwiede gave a sermon at the Grace Lutheran Church in Rochester, New York which referenced the film catchphrase, stating "Yet we know that there stretches through life a terrible highway called *The Street of Forgotten Men*, where countless numbers of defeated and enslaved men and women go, with weakness in their bodies, darkness in their mind, and terror in their soul."

One of the last two known uses of the film-title within an institutional context occurred on January 24, 1934 when the Rev. C. H. Bloom, an evangelical, spoke on the subject of "The Street of Forgotten Men" at the Church of Christ in Sayre, Pennsylvania. His sermon received a short write-up in the local paper. As did the September 12, 1936 copyrighted talk on "The Street of Forgotten Men" given by the Rev. Dr. Samuel W. Purvis, a methodist preacher in Philadelphia, Pennsylvania.

After that, use of the catchphrase (or at least a paper-trail of its use) shifted from the pulpit to other forms of religious literature, including articles in Christian magazines and newsletters. Many of these latter uses – which occurred in publications like the *Christian Advocate* (1936), *Christian Herald* (1946), *Moody Monthly* (1951), *Together* (1957), and *American Jewish Times-Outlook* (1963), referenced the down-and-out. In 1956, a brief note in *The Mennonite* regarding the Butterfield Church in Butterfield, Minnesota took the catchphrase a bit further, noting "A film entitled *The Street*, was presented by our Christian Endeavor Society Sunday evening, Nov. 13. The film showed how the street of forgotten men became a highway to heaven." (1-10-1956)

When Dorothy Day died in 1980, *Commonweal* called her "the most significant, interesting and influential person in the history of American Catholicism." Among other things, she helped establish the Catholic Worker's Movement, which sought to combine aid for the poor with nonviolent action. In 2015, during an address before the United States Congress, Pope Francis included her among four exemplary Americans who built a better future. Today, she is a candidate for sainthood.

Before her conversion to Catholicism, Day was a bohemian writer and sometime journalist. Among her early writings was a 1925 newspaper review of *The Street of Forgotten Men* published in the New York *Morning Telegraph*. Day thought favorably of the film, and its evocative title seems to have made an impression.

In later years, Day was a regular contributor to *The Catholic Worker*, a publication which she co-founded in 1933. In 1937, Day penned a piece titled "Feeding the Forgotten" in which she used the 1925 film title in describing conditions during the Depression. "Every morning still hundreds of men, sometimes two hundred and sometimes as many as five hundred, come to us to be fed. They are the lame, the halt, the blind. Some are unemployed, and some are unemployable. From all over, men drift into New York for work or for food … New York will always have her street of forgotten men…." (8-1937)

Another of Day's articles which recalled the film title was "And There Remained Only the Very Poor," which was written for the July-August 1940 issue of *The Catholic Worker*. The piece begins with news from France during the early days of the second World War. "Those were the words contained in a news account of the evacuation of Paris. But they apply to New York in the summer. The poor cannot get away. There is always a residue of the destitute which remains in the city like mud in a drained pond. You see them in the parks, you see them lying on the sidewalk in broad daylight along the Bowery, that street of forgotten men."

> **THE RESCUE SOCIETY, INC.**
> 5 Doyers Street   New York 13, N. Y.
> 51 Steps from The Bowery
> Gospel service every night since 1893
> "The Old Shack on the Street of Forgotten Men"—*Tom Noonan*
> Shelter, food, clothing, medical care, and jobs for the needy.—Never closed!
> Howard Wade Kimsey, Superintendent

Tom Noonan was a well-regarded ex-con known as the "Bishop of Chinatown" whose death in 1935 drew throngs of admirers. Fifteen years later, his use of the catchphrase was quoted in this advertisement for a Christian mission in the Bowery. *Sunday School Times* – **July 1950**

Sermons, religious literature, stereopticon slide-shows, and screenings in churches all helped spread the word, so to speak – not only of a Christian message drawn from the film, but in keeping the catchphrase in use – though a use eventually divorced from any association with the 1925 film.

Besides a moral lesson found in *The Street of Forgotten Men*, other non-religious groups found an inspirational message. "A Weekly Meditation" was the title of a regular opinion piece in the *Daily Argus-Leader*, a newspaper published in Sioux Falls, South Dakota. The paper's October 24, 1925 column was titled "The Street of Forgotten Men." The piece begins by noting the film had recently shown locally, adding "in choosing it for our theme we do not intend to speak of the production itself, splendidly filmed as it is. Nor shall we speak of the matchlessly interpreted roles

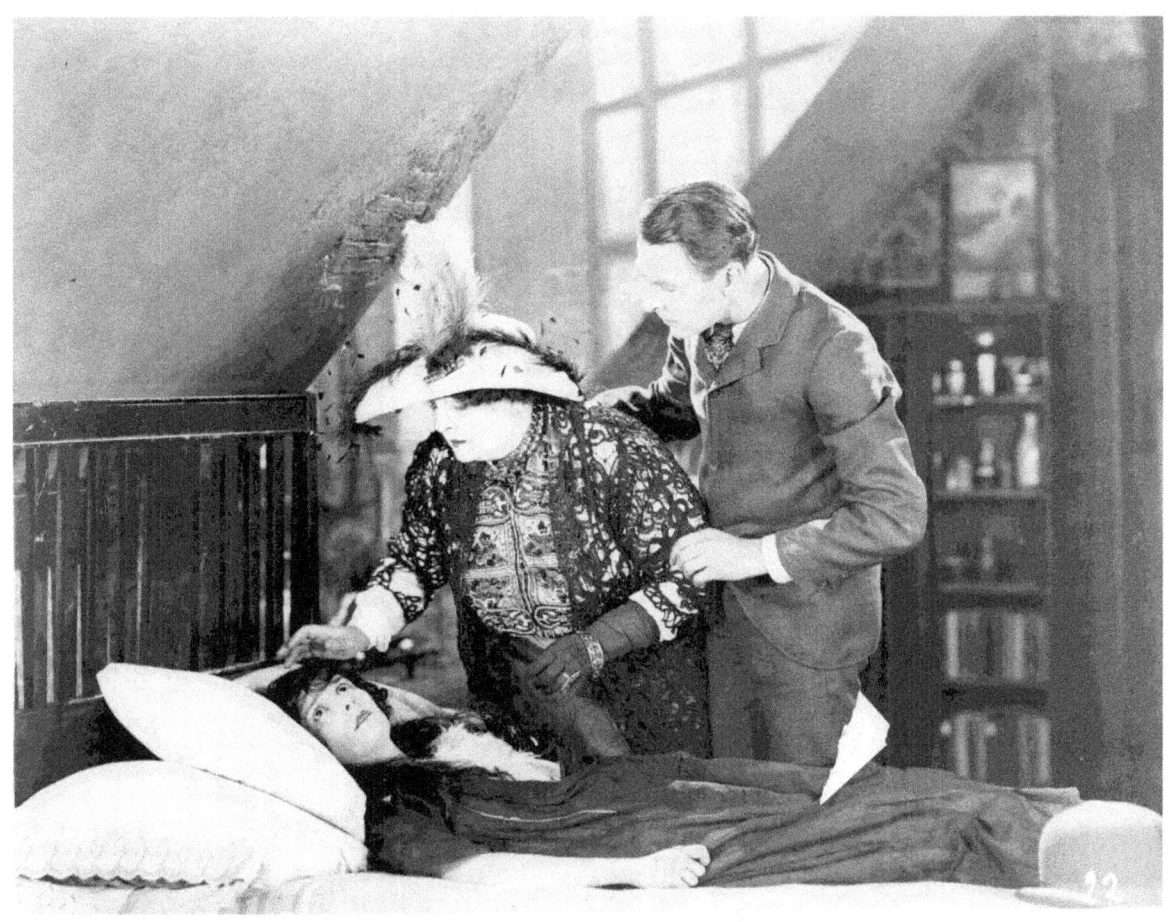

The death of Portland Fancy, played by Juliet Brenon. *Author collection*

of the stars in that unusual screen drama…" before summarizing the film over a number of sentences in what amounts to a long introductory paragraph.

The anonymous author of "A Weekly Meditation" – presumably someone on the staff, then notes, "Leaving out the crooks and other undesirables who have to live and hide, literally, on the Street of Forgotten Men as long as the police is on their trail, we can find many men and women who, in another sense, had lived or still live on that street." The remainder of this long, rambling column is a kind-of riff on the metaphor of a street inhabited by individuals no longer remembered, everyone from the famed Australian opera singer Nellie Melba to child actors Baby Peggy and Wesley Barry to

The Street of Forgotten Men: From Story to Screen and Beyond

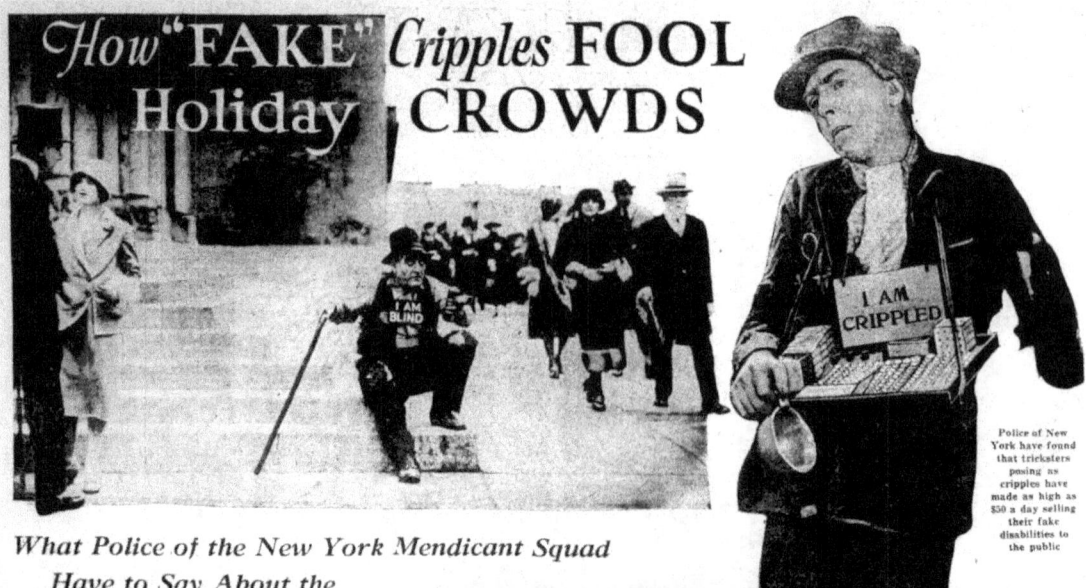

This syndicated newspaper feature, which made use of four images from the film, appeared in newspapers around the United States in December of 1926.

baseball stars Christy Mathewson and Walter Johnson. As much as it is a meditation on the nature of fading fame, the *Daily Argus-Leader* column stands as yet another early example of how the film and its title was used apart from a cinematic context. The *Daily Argus-Leader* column still seemed to resonate, even decades later. Despite the fact that *The Street of Forgotten Men* had been released a quarter of a century earlier, "A Weekly Meditation" was reprinted verbatim in the October 28, 1951 issue of the South Dakota paper.

At the heart of *The Street of Forgotten Men* (both the film and the short story on which it was based) is the gloom of poverty and various dramatic incidents in the lives of characters caught in a cycle of desperation. At the time of its release, Brenon's film was considered realistic. No one doubted its basic premise, that some street beggars and panhandlers were faking disability. One syndicated newspaper article from the time, headlined "Picture Commended," contained a statement from John C. Faries, who was identified as the director of the Institute of Crippled and Disabled Men in New York City. "I congratulate you most heartily," wrote Faries "upon your production *The Street of Forgotten Men* featuring Percy Marmont. During my eight years of experience in the service of the worthy disabled men – the man who wants to earn an honest living – I have been constantly distressed at the way in which the public is being fleeced by fake crippled beggars. In my opinion this film tells the truth in a startling manner." (11-8-1925, *Buffalo Express*) Other iterations of this same piece, one under the title "Film Tells Truth of Beggars Methods," appeared in newspapers elsewhere around the country.

The following month, another more widely circulated feature article appeared in newspapers. It was titled "How 'FAKE' Cripples FOOL Holiday Crowds." The anonymous piece was reportedly based on a "visit to the Mendicant Squad at police headquarters in New York City." The article notes there are licensed peddlers, "bona fide blind men and cripples who hobble around and tap pavements with their canes," as well as other "beggars who are actually disabled." The article then details a third group, the "kings of rascality. They are the fakers, the malingerers, the sly and sneaky, lazy and dishonest panhandlers who gouge the gullible public through sheer and unadulterated duplicity and chicanery." (12-19-1926, *Philadelphia Public Ledger*)

This widely syndicated newspaper feature from 1928 continued to evoke the film.

Illustrating the piece were four images from the Brenon film, including a still captioned, "Interior view of a 'cripple factory' constructed for the motion-picture film, *The Street of Forgotten Men*, and said to be an exact duplicate of a place in New York where beggars go to be made up and 'crippled' for begging purposes." That article, which conflated the film with real conditions, was followed in 1928 by another widely syndicated exposé titled "Begging – A $100,000,000 A Year American Industry." This later piece also featured two illustrations from the film.

Between the appearance of these two feature articles were similar pieces which not only mentioned or alluded to the film, but lent further credence to *The Street of Forgotten Men* as an accurate portrayal of fake-beggars. One article, which appeared in the *New York Times* and was titled "Speakeasy Equips Beggars as Cripple," suggested the film had inspired actual criminal behavior, though it confused actors Percy Marmont and Lon Chaney. After reporting on the arraignment of an individual arrested for begging, the article reported "The police are investigating the speakeasy. It was recalled that several months ago a motion picture, *The Street of Forgotten Men* .... showed just such an establishment for equipping 'cripples' as that described by Williams, and the police thought the movie idea might have been put to practical use." (6-15-1926) Another article from the time, a syndicated piece titled "Synthetic Cripples Turned Out To Beg On New York Sts." began, "They're turning out cripples in wholesale lots these days in the Bowery, New York city's street of forgotten men...." (8-9-1926, *El Paso Herald*)

SPEAKEASY EQUIPS BEGGAR AS CRIPPLE

"One-Armed Soldier" Reveals Scheme When Detectives Find an Arm Under Bandages.

HIS FRIENDS TRY IT, TOO

One Went Out From the Bowery as a Hunchback, Culprit Tells Court—Gets Six Months.

While panhandlers who impersonate the disabled have long been a fact of life, their exposure in the early years of the 20th century can be traced back, at least in part, to the efforts of John D. Godfrey, a mendicant officer in Brooklyn who also served as a technical advisor on *The Street of Forgotten Men*. As far back as 1903, articles in Brooklyn and New York newspapers (some of which were syndicated nationally) reported on Godfrey's activities to "clear the streets." He also lectured to "large crowds" on "fakers and frauds" and the tricks employed by various "imposters."

Mendicant officer John D. Godfrey shows Herbert Brenon an apparatus used by "fake beggars" on the set of *The Street of Forgotten Men*. Credit: *Museum of the Moving Image*

A Legacy

While other cities and towns like Detroit, El Paso, Memphis, San Francisco and even little Marysville, California were each said to have their street of forgotten men, it was Chicago which most often claimed its own. In the decades that followed the release of the Brenon film, numerous articles appeared referencing one of two thoroughfares in the Windy City. Madison Street drew the most comparisons, though on a few occasions, adjoining Clark Street was also mentioned.

One syndicated newspaper article from 1927, "Writer Mingles with Misfits," described how Theodore Dreiser, the author of *Sister Carrie, An American Tragedy* and other novels, was seen wandering around Madison Street. "For the past fortnight, it is said, a tall, slightly stoop-shouldered visitor with a serious face and inquiring eyes, has been seen in the vicinity of the café, which is headquarters for the lowest of the low of that 'street of forgotten men,' hoboes and adventurers. The tall stranger is Theodore Dreiser, prince of American fictionists." (10-4-1927, *Springfield Leader and Press*) Over the years, there followed a number of other pieces linking Madison with the street of forgotten men. A decade later, John Vande Water published *The Street of Forgotten Men* (c. 1937) a memoir detailing his missionary work on Madison and elsewhere in Chicago. And three decades later, an article in *TIME* magazine noted, "Death comes routinely in the dingy warren of Chicago's Madison Street, 'the street of forgotten men'." (7-29-1966)

When it was released in 1929, one reviewer described Harvey Warren Zorbaugh's *The Gold Coast and the Slum: A Sociological Study of Chicago's Near North Side* as a book not only about Chicago, but "a book about every other American city." In familiar language, Zorbaugh placed the evocative street not on Madison, but elsewhere in the city. "Clark Street might well be called 'the street of forgotten men.' There are several old hotels and rooming-houses in its vicinity which are populated largely by the physically handicapped beggar – especially the blind beggar – and by those who through simulation and 'make-up' are able to ply the same trade. The old Revere House, for one, has a considerable coterie of blind 'professionals'."

Since the release of the 1925 film, the terms "the Bowery" and "street of forgotten men" came to be used interchangeably. A syndicated article on the area quoted an Irish policeman walking his beat. "There's no glamour, no cabarets, nothing to really attract people to this street of forgotten men they've heard about. The merchants are talking about changing the street's name to something else, but it's been the Bowery for a long time. I don't think they'd get away with that." (10-23-1942, A.R. *Hope Star*)

They didn't. In 1947, a proposal was put forth to change the name of the Bowery, in order to dissociate it from its unsavory past. There was also a plan to clean-up the historic neighborhood. Despite its intentions, the proposal drew considerable resistance. One letter to the editor in the *New York Times* put it this way, "… whether it is to be called Fourth Avenue South or any other name, it must cease to earn the title of 'The Street of Forgotten Men'." (12-10-1947)

The 1947 proposal also brought forth a flurry of articles which made use of the catchphrase, while spurring renewed use in other contexts. The phrase even made its way into comics. That year, the "street of forgotten men" turned up in the speech bubble of a popular, wryly fantastic newspaper strip, *Tiny Tim*, by the Chicago artist Stanley Link. In 1947, it also became the setting for an adventure featuring the popular superhero, Captain Marvel – a 9-page story titled "Captain Marvel and the Street of Forgotten Men". And yet another usage followed in 1949 in DC Comics' *Mr. District Attorney* #7 – it contained a similarly themed 8-page story titled "The Street of Forgotten Men". In familiar language, and in visuals penciled by Howard Purcell and inked by Charles Paris, this second comic told of criminals who preyed on the "derelict victims that flocked" to the street of forgotten men.

Two cells from the April 6, 1947 Sunday comic strip "Tiny Tim," by Stanley Link.

A Legacy

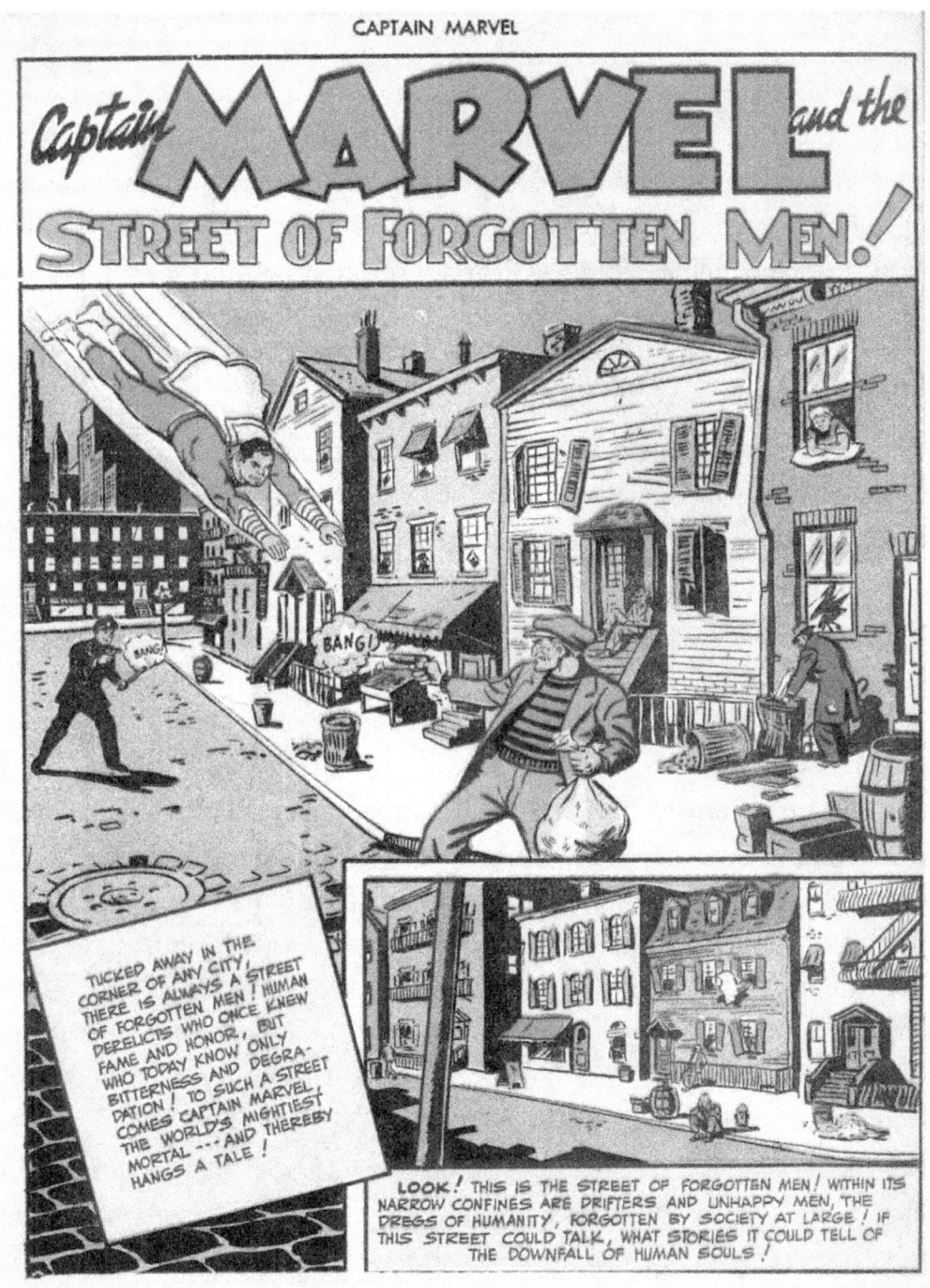

"Captain Marvel and the Street of Forgotten Men" appeared along with two other stories in the November 1947 issue of *Captain Marvel Adventures* (#78), from Fawcett Publications. This gripping comic with an unusual setting was co-authored by the noted Chicago sci-fi writer Otto Binder, who like others, saw the street as home to men who "know only bitterness and degradation."

As a catchphrase, as another name for New York's Bowery, or as a euphemism for the less desirable parts of town, "street of forgotten men" remained in use for decades – in fact, well into the 1980s. The phrase (by this time long disassociated from the film) turns up just about everywhere, not only in sermons, editorials, and unrelated newspaper and magazine articles, but also in a secular context in popular fiction, poetry, memoirs, travel guides, and the aforementioned comics.

Early on, the catchphrase even served as the punchline to a humorous anecdote. One bit ran in the "Campus Scout" column of the *Daily Illini*, the student newspaper at the University of Illinois in Champaign. The anecdote went this way, "I say, Iago, a minute while I expound on a subject of vital importance to this campus. Did you ever stop to think about Sorority Row? On Monday, Tuesday, Wednesday, Thursday, Friday, Saturday and Sunday there comes a different sidekick for each girl? Truly, is it not a Street of Forgotten Men?" (1-12-1926)

Early on, *Hollywood Filmograph* also made use of the phrase without referencing the film. The movie journal quipped, "Carmen Lombardo's song entitled 'Why Did You?," published by M. Witmark & Sons, was recently recorded for Columbia by Guy Lombardo, Carmen's brother. And now all the song-writers along the 'Street of Forgotten Men' are seriously thinking of having their pedigrees probed in hopes of discovering a long-lost brother, preferably one who is a recording artist." (7-13-1929)

Another early use of the catchphrase can be found in the sports pages of the *Mid-west Free Press*, which reported, "They are going to make an effort to sign Jack Sharkey off the street of forgotten men with Mickey Walker, the middleweight champion who fights anything but middleweights." (2-3-1931) The following year, *Popular Mechanics* noted, "On New York's Bowery, the famous 'Street of Forgotten Men', an automatic hotel has been opened." (10-1932)

As an indication of its widespread use, the phrase "street of forgotten" also shows-up in articles in both mainstream and specialty publications like *Financial World* (1925), *Smart Set* (1926), *The Century* (1928), *Irish Advocate* (1932), *Newsweek* (1933), *LIFE* (1942), *Christian Science Monitor* (1943), *The New Yorker* (1946), *American Mercury* (1954), *Caribbean Quarterly* (1955), and *American Jewish Times-Outlook* (1962).

In 1952, Herbert Asbury, the famed author of *The Gangs of New York*, penned a travel piece about New York for *Holiday* magazine, writing, "On the way to

Chinatown from mid-town New York, the sight-seeing bus turned into the Bowery, and the guide said: 'We are now entering what I have nicknamed the 'Street of Forgotten Men,' the home of the famous Bowery bum. It's late in the day, but if you'll look close you may see a bum sleeping off last night's drunk on the sidewalk. If you spot one call out, so we can all see'." (10-1952)

In 1956, folklorist and scholar B.A. Botkin published his classic study, *New York City Folklore: Legends, Tall Tales, Anecdotes, Stories, Sagas, Heroes and Characters, Customs, Traditions, and Sayings* – and in passing referenced the Bowery as "The Street of Forgotten Men." The following year, *Copp's Guide to New York City* warned tourists "... the street of forgotten men – not advisable to go there at night unless by cab to and from." Similar use of the term, as another name for the Bowery neighborhood, continued for decades. Erwin A. Single's *The Gold Lay on the Streets*, a 1987 portrait of ethnic New York City, utilized the phrase twice, including once when it noted, "Before the Bowery lost its glamor and became the 'Street of Forgotten Men,' it had acquired a different kind of fame as the rendezvous of the city's gangsters and other undesirable elements."

This anonymous poem was published in *Seth Parker Fireside Poems*, a 1933 collection of folksy poems originally broadcast by Seth Parker (Phillips H. Lord), a popular radio personality and the host of the long running program, *Jonesport Neighbors*. Parker was quite famous in his day, and in 1932 he starred in a motion picture produced by RKO Radio Pictures which was based on another of his books. In that film, *Way Back Home*, he starred opposite Bette Davis.

A note accompanying the poem reads, "This poem was handed to Mr. Lord during his Monday night broadcast from his 'Bowery Den' (the old 'Tunnel Saloon' on the Bowery) by one of the men in the bread-line. It was written in pencil on an old scrap of paper. When questioned as to why he had written this poem, the author's only reply was, 'My tribute to Phil Lord for what he is doing for us boys down here'."

THE STREET OF FORGOTTEN MEN
(Anonymous)

The bread-lines form at the close of day—
Ragged men of the gay White Way,
Hungry men—you can hear their sighs,
But all you can see is their staring eyes—
Eyes that mirror the beaten souls
Of those who have failed to reach their goals,
Eyes that gleam with a desperate hope,
Eyes that even through darkness grope;
Eyes that had once seen the light of a home
And little ones vanished in sorrow's gloam;
Eyes that during the War in France
Faced the foe with an eagle glance;
Eyes of sailors with cheeks still tanned,
Home from sea—out of luck on land;
Helpless eyes of the weak and frail,
And bitter eyes of the ones who fail;
Eager eyes that seek only a job,
Shifty eyes that seek only to rob;
Staring eyes of the hopelessly maimed;
Downcast eyes of those ashamed;
Ragged men of all walks of life,
Humble men in the bread-line strife;
Who knows but his own may go this way?
The bread-lines form at the close of day.

The first use of the phrase "street of forgotten men" in literature (apart from Turner's story) likely occurred in William Edge's *The Main Stem: The Adventures of Slim and Blondey*. Edge's novel, about two hobo philosophers and their adventures tramping across the United States, was published by the progressive Vanguard Press in 1927. The "main stem" in the title refers to any local main street, though within the context of this book and the hobo life it describes, it was the place where transients congregated. Like the famed hobo author Jim Tully, Edge was an itinerant laborer turn writer who lived a hard scrabble life. Edge likely felt Turner's story, and the film made from it, romanticized or sentimental. In his novel, Edge referred to one main stem as "That street of forgotten men, as I believe some mushy novelist calls it."

A not dissimilar book from the time, "Written out of twenty or more years of criminal life, most of them spent behind prison walls," is *Philosophy of the Dusk*, by Kain O'Dare. This 1929 memoir placed the main stem elsewhere. "The wreck that drifted out of the flotsam of San Francisco's street of forgotten men found refuge in a dark hallway," wrote O'Dare, who one reviewer likened to O. Henry.

Much of Dot Allan's work focused on class and gender in Glasgow during the early 20th century. *Hunger March*, which the noted Scottish writer published in 1934, employed the catchphrase twice, "'Look, look, look!' the nasal voices, the grinding wheels, the clanging overhead railway insisted. 'This is the street of forgotten men. Here abide the down-and-out, here amid the decaying garbage of the city'." A few paragraphs later, the phrase is used again, "In that street of forgotten men, the torrid midsummer heat was invoking the torments of hell."

The famed American novelist John O'Hara was the author of such bestselling works as *BUtterfield 8*, *Ten North Frederick*, and *Pal Joey*, each of which were made into successful films. O'Hara was famous for a frank realism which dared reveal what went on behind closed doors. Significantly, he is also known for having helped shape the *New Yorker* style of short fiction.

It is not known when O'Hara might have seen *The Street of Forgotten Men*, but it likely was in Pottsville, Pennsylvania, where O'Hara worked as a journalist in the early to mid-1920s. (O'Hara wrote for the *Pottsville Journal*, whose archive from the time is lost.) The film played big in Pottsville, showing three times in 1925. The other local newspaper, the *Pottsville Republican*, stated "It would be useless to make any attempt to describe the merits of this production. One of our patrons who saw this picture while at Atlantic City, recently informed us that it was a regular 'whiz' and he has been waiting to see it again." (10-7-1925) The next day, the same paper stated, "This is not just an ordinary picture, it is one of the biggest things the Paramount Company has ever done." (10-8-1925)

Early on, O'Hara reviewed films for *Newsweek*. In 1941, he reviewed *Major Barbara*, the movie (based on the George Bernard Shaw play) about a young, idealistic woman who works for the Salvation Army. O'Hara didn't care for the film, noting "Technically the picture is of the genre of 'the street of forgotten men.' It seems to have been directed with a whisk broom instead of a whip." (5-26-1941) More than twenty years later, O'Hara published *The Hat on the Bed*, a 1963 collection of stories. In one story, "Yucca Knolls," O'Hara again evoked the Brenon film. A character states, "'I go there every so often,' he continued. 'I almost expect to see Percy Marmont turn up there some day. You know. The Street of Forgotten Men. They don't know who I am or anything about me except what I tell them, and I've told them some beauts. No worse than some they've told me'." Evidently, the film, or at least its memorable title, made an impression on the noted writer.

Other fiction also made use of the catchphrase. One contemporary work which did so is *Headlong*, a 1981 novel by Emlyn Williams. The acclaimed Welsh writer and dramatist was also an actor who made a name for himself in roles in a number of notable early films, including *Major Barbara* in 1941. In *Headlong*, which is set in the 1930s, a character states "I told him the whole thing… the street of forgotten men. The vivid old face listened and nodded, nodded and listened."

As with literature, the phrase "street of forgotten men" left its mark in the visual arts, as well as cinema. Among the many visual artists who depicted the economic suffering of the 1930s, at least one made use of the familiar catchphrase. Eli (or Elias) Jacobi was an Ukrainian-born printmaker and illustrator who came to live in the Bowery in New York. Today, he is best remembered for his work for the Federal Arts Project of the Works Progress Administration. In the last half of the 1930s, he created a memorable series of linoleum cuts titled "The Street of Forgotten Men." These strident, yet lyrical works depict groups of men, a street scene, a bar, a church gathering, etc.… In 1939, prints from series were shown at the Print Club of

Philadelphia and Art Institute of Chicago, while others were collected by the Museum of Modern Art and Metropolitan Museum of Art in New York. Additionally, five of Jacobi's emblematic Bowery prints were published in the Federal Writer's Project *WPA Guide to New York* (1939), as visual representations of the neighborhood.

Little about the 1927 exploitation film, *Street of Forgotten Women,* can be traced back to *The Street of Forgotten Men* – except for its obvious indebtedness to the title of the earlier film. *Street of Forgotten Women* is a dreadful production about a rich girl who decides on a career on the stage, and fails. She is then reduced to dancing in her underwear in a saloon, before turning to prostitution.

After that, two obscure documentary shorts were issued which carried the title *Street of Forgotten Men*. One film, a Nu-Art Picture issued by Walter Futter circa 1930, was shot by hiding a camera in a truck. An intertitle to this silent travelogue describes individuals on the street as "sidewalk scavengers." Other unemployed men are shown waiting for sandwiches in the St. Marks Place breadline of Mr. Zero, who the film notes, "deserves his name, for he is the last hope of the street of forgotten men." (This short can be viewed online on YouTube.) Another documentary film with the title *Street of Forgotten Men* dates to 1935. This three-minute sound short is described as a newsreel showing life on the streets of the Bowery. It was shown as recently as June 24, 1990 at the San Francisco Cinematheque as part of a program titled "Forgotten People."

Sometime in the late 1950s, a short film titled *The Cross Roads* was released by the Pacific Garden Mission, a prominent homeless shelter in Chicago, Illinois. This 18-minute, 103 frame filmstrip (with full color and sound) is described in advertisements as featuring "Actual scenes from the street of forgotten men and women." (Show here is an advertisement dating from 1960.)

In 1985, Nika Cavat made a 10-minute video titled *The Street of Forgotten Men*. Shot on location in the Bowery – where Cavat then lived, it tells the story of three men who found themselves alone and without shelter in New York City. At the time, the future poet was a graduate student studying film at Columbia University. For one class, Cavat was asked to make a short fiction film, but instead shot a non-fiction short about the homeless men who were her neighbors. According to a 2023 email from Cavat, "this project almost got me kicked out of film school because I was supposed to be making a short fiction film, not a documentary." It wasn't until her directing teacher screened the dailies in class that she received any positive feedback. After looking at almost two hours of student work, and then screening Cavat's submission, her directing teacher declared, "Now that's film making." The teacher turned out to be Milos Forman, who went on to praise her work for what the aspiring filmmaker described as "several long minutes." Later, Cavat's film was shown as part of a benefit program called "Homeless at Home" in November of 1985.

"THE STREET OF FORGOTTEN MEN"

The phrase "street of forgotten men" began to fade from use around the end of the 20th century, but not before one writer tried to fix its origin. Jerome B. Agel was the prolific author of 60 books, some collaborations with celebrated thinkers like Marshall McLuhan, Carl Sagan, and Isaac Asimov. In two of his books, *Beyond Trivia* (1985), and *Cleopatra's Nose: The Twinkie Defense, and 1500 Other Verbal Shortcuts in Popular Parlance* (1990), Agel included an entry on the Bowery. In *Beyond Trivia*, and in somewhat familiar language, Agel placed the catchphrase in context, "It became New York's 'Street of Forgotten Men' because the neighborhood had the cheapest beer in the city. One could put down five-cents-a-glass whiskeys until one passed out. Half of the cheap lodging houses were there…. In the 1870s, 105 Bowery was noted as a resort for some of the toughest characters abroad: 'There, the blind man recovered his sight, the cripple laid aside his crutches and straightened his twisted leg, the one-armed man released the arm that had been bound tightly to his body all the day, the boiler explosion victim removed his bandages'."

The June 12, 1927 issue of *Le Film Complet*, a French story magazine.

L'ECOLE DES MENDIANTS

The afterlife of *The Street of Forgotten Men* continued in another usual way…. During the silent and early sound era, a handful of European publishers issued soft-cover, magazine-like booklets featuring fictionalizations of current films. Similar to American movie story magazines, these illustrated fictionalizations (in the form of a short story or novella) were, typically, a loose rewrite of a film story. Each differed in varying degrees from its original source material.

In France, *The Street of Forgotten Men* was turned into just such a story titled "L'Ecole des Mendiants" (which translates into English as "The School for Beggars"). Authored by Yves Miroël, "L'Ecole des Mendiants" was issued in June of 1927 (around the time the film was released in France) by *Le Film Complet* as part of its series of Roman Cinè, or cinema novels. This long running story magazine was distributed throughout France and other countries where French was spoken (namely Belgium, Luxembourg, and Switzerland); notably, as well, subscriptions to the publication were offered in Austria, Czechoslovakia, Denmark, Estonia, Finland, Germany, Italy, The Netherlands, Norway, Portugal, Sweden and elsewhere.

"L'Ecole des Mendiants" (which is the film title of *The Street of Forgotten Men* in France) is a descriptive retelling of key scenes from the film. Along with the story, this 16-page publication contains a number of stills, two of which stand out. One is the cover image of Bridgeport White-Eye holding Easy Money Charlie's dog; it comes from a pivotal scene in the film which is now lost. Also notable is the second from last image in the publication. It depicts another pivotal scene, the fight between Whitey and Charlie. This still includes a somewhat obscured Louise Brooks, an unknown actress who played an uncredited role as Whitey's companion. As such, it represents a rare published depiction of the young actress in what was her first screen appearance.

LE FILM COMPLET

L'École des Mendiants

Roman-Ciné par Yves MIROËL. — *Film Paramount.*

DISTRIBUTION :

Charles Vanhern	PERCY MARMONT.
Marysette	MARY BRIAN.
Philippe	NEIL HAMILTON.

I

Situé dans le plus misérable faubourg de New-York, le Bar Ramon, sorte de bouge infect fréquenté par la basse pègre, était le lieu de réunion favori, le « club » des principaux mendiants de la cité.

Ramon, le tenancier de cet établissement, louche individu que n'étouffaient pas les scrupules, avait installé dans son arrière-boutique un véritable atelier de camouflage, qu'il avait mis à la disposition d'une bande d'individus qui, pour se procurer des ressources au prix du moindre effort, ne trouvaient rien de mieux que d'exciter la commisération publique. Moyennant un honnête pourcentage sur leurs recettes, ils pouvaient trouver là les accessoires les plus variés, propres à transformer, du moins en apparence, un homme parfaitement valide en un lamentable estropié.

Sur les murs crasseux étaient accrochés des béquilles, des jambes de bois, des moignons de bras, et dans un coin, traînaient deux ou trois de ces petits chariots, qui sont l'accessoire indispensable des culs-de-jatte. Au milieu de ce décor hideux, trônait, toujours très affairé, « le père Tom », un vieux barbier que les habitués du lieu appelaient pompeusement l'« artiste », parce qu'il n'avait pas son pareil pour opérer un savant maquillage. Ses clients appréciaient à leur juste valeur sa science et son habileté ; aussi, en récompense de ses appréciables services, ne lésinaient-ils pas sur les pourboires.

Parmi cette corporation de faux éclopés, de véritables exploiteurs de la charitable naïveté de leur prochain, il en était un qui paraissait à première vue infiniment moins vil, moins dégradé que les autres. C'était un homme de trente-cinq ans environ, au physique agréable, au regard plein de franchise, qui, de son vrai nom, s'appelait Charles Vanhern, mais que l'on ne connaissait que sous le sobriquet de « Charley le manchot ». C'était le fils d'un aventurier qui avait roulé sa bosse un peu dans tous les pays du monde à la recherche d'une occasion de faire fortune sans se donner aucune peine et qui n'était parvenu qu'à mourir misérablement à l'étranger en laissant pour tout héritage à son unique enfant, dont il ne s'était d'ailleurs jamais guère occupé, que son irrésistible penchant pour la paresse. Affligé d'une pareille hérédité et livré à lui-même, Charles Vanhern courait de gros risques de rester dans l'avenir le dévoyé qu'il était aujourd'hui.

Le triste métier qu'il avait choisi lui avait cependant réussi à merveille ; il y gagnait non pas seulement de quoi suffire très largement à sa subsistance, mais encore assez pour réaliser de notables économies et pour faire d'avantageux placements dans une banque où l'on ignorait naturellement tout de sa double personnalité.

La chance dont il était favorisé n'était pas sans lui créer nombre d'envieux ; les camarades auxquels la fortune réservait moins de sourires le jalousaient, et il en était même un, William Baxter, qui, sans rien en montrer, poussait cette jalousie jusqu'à la haine. Moins intéressant encore si possible que ses congénères, il se faisait passer vis-à-vis d'eux pour être réellement aveugle alors qu'il n'était atteint que d'une très forte myopie, et il était parvenu à leur cacher entièrement son jeu. Très habile simulateur, il avait été baptisé par eux. « l'homme aux yeux blancs » et il profitait de ce qu'autour de lui l'on croyait réellement à sa cécité, non seulement pour exploiter habilement la pitié de ses propres camarades, mais encore pour surprendre habilement certains de leurs secrets. Il n'avait d'ailleurs aucune raison particulière d'en vouloir à ce point au « manchot » qui ne lui avait jamais causé le moindre tort. Bien au contraire, celui-ci avait toujours fait preuve vis-à-vis de lui d'excellents instincts de camaraderie, et s'était montré prêt à lui rendre service toutes les fois que l'occasion s'en présentait. En dépit, en effet, de son existence uniquement basée sur les duperies et le mensonge, Charley possédait une âme tendre et se montrait toujours prêt à compatir aux malheurs de son prochain. Jamais on ne faisait en vain appel à sa générosité.

N'ayant aucun grief direct à faire valoir contre lui, le faux aveugle ne pouvait ouvertement lui chercher noise, et il eût d'ailleurs été, en tout état de cause, beaucoup trop poltron pour cela. Mais, par derrière, il s'en prenait lâchement à un petit épagneul dont Charley ne se séparait jamais, répétant, à qui voulait l'entendre, que c'était sa seule affection, son seul ami sur terre. Baxter, chaque fois qu'il était sûr de n'être pas vu, ne manquait pas de décocher à la pauvre bête de grands coups de pied qui lui arrachaient de lamentables hurlements.

Chaque soir, en rentrant de leurs tournées, les mendiants se hâtaient de se débarrasser de leur camouflage. Le « manchot » enlevait le moignon qui était attaché à son épaule et faisait désangler son bras valide, mais tout engourdi, qu'une courroie, passée plusieurs fois autour de son corps, avait maintenue, durant de longues heures, étroitement plaqué à son côté. Les faux aveugles jetaient leurs lunettes noires et les bâtons à l'aide desquels ils se dirigeaient en tâtonnant à travers les rues de la ville. Les culs-de-jatte quittaient leurs chariots et goûtaient le plaisir de détendre leurs deux jambes longtemps repliées sous eux.

ABONNEMENTS : France.. 45 francs. Six mois. France.. 23 francs. Étranger. 63 francs. Étranger. 32 francs. Compte chèques postaux : 259-10

LE MARDI, LE JEUDI ET LE DIMANCHE

Direction, Administration : 3, rue de Rocroy, Paris (X^e).

Les abonnements sont augmentés de **15 fr.** *par an pour les pays n'ayant pas accepté le tarif postal réduit.* (Se renseigner à la poste.)

AVIS IMPORTANT : Nos lecteurs habitant : L'Allemagne, l'Autriche, la Belgique, le Danemark, l'Esthonie, la Finlande, l'Italie, le Luxembourg, la Norvège, les Pays-Bas, le Portugal, la Suède, la Suisse et la Tchéco-Slovaquie, peuvent s'abonner (s'ils habitent une localité possédant un bureau de poste) à notre journal en payant seulement le prix fixé pour la France. Ces abonnements poste ne peuvent être souscrits qu'à partir du 1er janvier ou du 1er juillet de chaque année. **Se renseigner à la poste.**

« Je me contenterais facilement de la moitié. J'ai fait une fichue journée. »

Après quoi, redevenus de solides garnements aux membres solides, ils se payaient à cœur joie du plaisir et des douceurs dans le bar du sieur Ramon. Là, on pouvait boire, manger et danser jusqu'à une heure avancée de la nuit, en compagnie de quelques belles filles complaisantes, voire même de quelques beautés plus mûres qui, pour se consoler de leur jeunesse envolée étaient devenues des ferventes du vin et du whisky.

Il y avait environ un mois qu'une jeune femme assez jolie, aux allures timides, aux grands yeux tristes et fiévreux, fréquentait assidûment ce bouge mal famé. On la voyait toujours assise à côté d'une vieille habituée du lieu connue sous le nom de « Sophie l'empanachée », parce qu'elle arborait toujours de fantastiques chapeaux garnis de volumineuses plumes d'autruche qui devaient dater de l'époque lointaine de ses vingt ans.

Affalée sur sa banquette, la jeune femme demeurait le plus souvent silencieuse, regardant évoluer, sans presque paraître les voir, les couples qui « chaloupaient » autour d'elle. De temps en temps, elle était prise de quintes de toux qui la secouaient atrocement. Et, après ces crises, elle ne sortait de sa torpeur que pour commander au garçon un verre de whisky qu'elle avalait d'un seul trait.

Lorsqu'elle buvait par trop, sa voisine qui l'observait à la dérobée d'un air apitoyé lui disait amicalement:

— Voyons, ma petite Fanny, sois donc raisonnable ! Ne bois pas comme cela, alors que déjà ta santé n'est pas très brillante.

Mais elle haussait les épaules d'un mouvement plein de lassitude et murmurait :

— Au point où j'en suis, qu'est-ce que cela peut faire? Pour le peu de temps qu'il me reste à vivre, j'ai besoin de m'étourdir pour oublier mes misères.

Touchée de cette détresse physique et morale qu'elle ne pouvait secourir, Sophie essuyait furtivement une larme, puis, elle grondait doucement :

— Mais c'est cet alcool qui va te tuer le plus sûrement, ma pauvre petite ! Tu ferais mieux d'aller te coucher, tu grelottes de fièvre.

Fanny ne répondait pas. Elle serrait simplement de sa main brûlante la main couverte de bagues de pacotille de son amie pour lui faire tacitement comprendre qu'il était inutile d'insister ni d'essayer de la raisonner.

Certain jour, Sophie lui suggéra :

— Ecoute... je sais bien, n'est-ce pas, la secrète torture qui te ronge... Pourquoi ne t'adresserais-tu pas à Charley le manchot? Il pourrait te venir en aide. C'est un garçon qui a un excellent cœur, et, ce qui ne gâte rien, du foin dans ses bottes. Je suis certaine que si tu lui racontais ton histoire, il ne refuserait pas de faire quelque chose pour toi et pour ta petite.

A ce moment même Charley rentrait, suivi de son chien comme de coutume et traversait le bar en saluant les camarades à la ronde.

Fanny le suivit de ses prunelles ardentes et angoissées. Certes, il avait l'air très sympathique, très bon, mais elle ne lui avait jamais encore adressé la parole; elle lui était complètement inconnue ; voudrait-il seulement l'écouter et la croire? Son histoire était si banale en même temps que si lamentable... Elle ne cessa de le regarder jusqu'à ce qu'il eût disparu dans l'arrière-boutique où le sinistre « homme aux yeux blancs » ne tarda pas à aller le rejoindre. Avec un profond soupir, il se laissa tomber sur un escabeau, tandis que Charley se débarrassait de sa veste et de son moignon et libérait son bras de la sangle qui l'enserrait.

— Bonne recette? interrogea le père Tom avec le plus aimable intérêt.

— Excellente, mon brave ami, répondit gaiement Charley. Les « clients » ont été particulièrement généreux. Je rapporte exactement trente-six-dollars et, après déduction des vingt pour cent qui reviennent au patron, ce qui m'en restera est loin d'être à dédaigner.

Baxter, qui observait sournoisement Charley sous le bord de son chapeau rabattu, grogna aigrement :

— Je me contenterais facilement de la moitié, moi ! J'ai encore fait une fichue journée.

— Aussi, pourquoi t'es-tu « mis » aveugle, plutôt que béquillard, manchot ou cul-de-jatte? blagua Charley tout en recomptant soigneusement sa recette? Crois-moi, les passants sont moins généreux quand ils savent... ou croient savoir qu'on ne peut les contrôler.

— Possible. Mais si je pouvais seulement avoir un cabot comme le tien, pour les apitoyer, les affaires iraient mieux ! Veux-tu me le céder ? Je t'en offrirais un bon prix...

— N'y compte pas, mon vieux, répliqua Charley. Mon cabot, comme tu dis, mon brave Dick, n'est pas à vendre. A aucun prix, je ne consentirais à me séparer de mon cher, de mon plus fidèle compagnon.

Le père Tom, cependant, s'empressait d'emplir une cuvette et de préparer une serviette pour le « manchot » qui avait coutume de faire chaque jour ; en rentrant de sa fructueuse tournée, une minutieuse toilette. Charley plongea avec délices son visage dans l'eau fraîche et réclama ensuite du barbier un bon coup de peigne.

La gaieté, l'insouciance de l'homme qui excitait sa haineuse jalousie, achevèrent d'exaspérer Baxter. Profitant de ce qu'on ne faisait plus attention à lui, il enleva brusquement entre ses bras Dick qui, allant et venant à travers la pièce, avait commis l'imprudence, malgré les coups qu'il en avait maintes fois reçus, de passer à sa portée.

— Toi, sale clebs, marmonna-t-il entre ses dents, tu payeras pour ton maître, ce sera toujours ça !

Le muselant en même temps d'une poigne solide, il se dirigea à pas de loup vers l'orifice d'une cave dont, au fond de l'atelier, la trappe était ouverte. Et, une fois là, d'un geste violent, il précipita la pauvre bête sur les marches de pierre. On entendit un choc lourd, un gémissement plaintif. Charley se retourna, bondit en avant et se précipita dans l'escalier au bas duquel gisait Dick, qui, les côtes fracassées, achevait de mourir.

Le « manchot » eut alors un tel cri que les clients du bar firent irruption dans l'atelier. Fanny les avait suivis. Elle vit Charley qui, lentement, remontait du sous-sol, portant, pressant contre son cœur son chien pantelant, son unique ami perdu à jamais, et son visage avait une expression si douloureuse qu'elle ne put retenir ses larmes.

Charley remarqua cette femme qui pleurait et qui, seule peut-être, parmi cette foule qui se pressait là, le comprenait. Mais il vit Baxter aussi qui, affectant de demander ce qui se passait, essayait néanmoins de se dissimuler. Le désignant d'un doigt menaçant, il s'écria avec un sanglot dans la gorge :

— Mon pauvre chien était le seul être au monde qui m'aimait, et ce misérable l'a tué !

Tremblant de peur, l'autre protesta :

— Tu sais bien, le manchot, que je n'y vois pas clair ! Je t'assure que je ne l'ai pas fait exprès ! Ton Dick m'a échappé des mains. Je ne me doutais pas que la trappe fût ouverte... Pour un peu, je serais tombé moi-même au travers !

Charley transporté de colère s'élança avec l'intention d'assommer « l'homme aux yeux blancs », mais, constatant que celui-ci ne bougeait pas à son approche, il s'arrêta net, et Fanny l'entendit murmurer comme pour lui-même :

— Non, ce serait lâche de frapper un aveugle.

II

Une sorte de fraternité était née entre Fanny Hirch et « Charley le manchot », depuis le jour où celui-ci l'avait vue verser des larmes sur la mort de son pauvre chien. La jeune femme n'osait cependant s'ouvrir à son nouvel ami de la lamentable situation, en laquelle seul, un cœur très noble et très généreux aurait pu lui venir en aide, et elle continuait à passer ses soirées au bar Ramon, y usant le peu qui lui restait encore de santé. Le moment ne tarda guère à arriver où minée par la maladie, sentant ses forces l'abandonner de plus en plus, elle se trouva forcée de garder la chambre.

Inquiète de ne pas la voir depuis deux ou trois jours, son amie Sophie alla s'enquérir de ses nouvelles. Elle la trouva à tel point affaiblie, que, très alarmée, elle prit sur elle d'aller immédiatement chercher un médecin. Celui-ci n'eut pas besoin d'un bien long examen pour lui confier que la malheureuse était perdue, que sa vie n'était plus qu'une question de jours, d'heures peut-être.

A la mine consternée que Sophie essayait en vain de masquer sous un sourire de commande, Fanny devina sans peine l'arrêt qui venait d'être prononcé. Elle ne s'en frappa point : il ne constituait pas pour elle une surprise, car il y avait plusieurs semaines déjà qu'elle se sentait irrémissiblement condamnée. Mais elle implora son amie d'aller immédiatement à la recherche de Charley et de le lui envoyer de toute urgence.

Aussitôt informé, ce dernier n'hésita pas à se rendre à l'appel de la mourante.

Avec une infinie reconnaissance, Fanny le remercia d'être venu ; toute pâle, toute menue dans le fauteuil où elle était à demi étendue, un triste sourire sur ses lèvres, elle se recueillit quelques instants, puis :

— Je vous ai fait appeler, monsieur Charley, fit-elle, parce que je vais mourir... Ne protestez pas, de grâce, n'essayez pas de me leurrer, je le sais. Mais, avant de rendre le dernier soupir, j'ai un immense service à vous demander...

Écoutez d'abord le récit de ma lamentable existence :

Et elle conta son banal et douloureux roman... le triste roman des filles-mères abandonnées, réduites par la lâcheté, par l'égoïsme des hommes à la pire misère à la pire détresse, et, fatalement à tomber de plus en plus bas.

— Avant la triste aventure dans laquelle j'ai laissé, hélas ! toutes mes illusions, continuait-elle à expliquer, j'étais une petite ouvrière, j'étais heureuse de vivre, et je n'aspirais qu'à un paisible bonheur auprès de l'homme qui m'aimerait et auquel je consacrerais tout mon cœur et tout mon dévouement. Comme tant d'autres, j'ai été grisée par des paroles enjôleuses, abusée par une promesse de mariage qui n'a jamais été tenue. Après la naissance de ma petite Marysette, je me suis trouvée toute seule dans la vie avec elle et, pour ainsi dire, privée de toutes ressources. Vainement j'ai cherché du travail. Il semblait que par un fait exprès, toutes les portes se fermaient devant moi. Épuisée par les privations, je ne pouvais nourrir moi-même mon enfant. Durant quelque temps, j'ai pu végéter et la faire végéter grâce à la compassion de quelques voisines, grâce à quelques petits travaux de couture ou de ménage qu'elles arrivaient très irrégulièrement à me procurer. Et puis un jour est arrivé où je me suis vue devant un tiroir vide de la plus petite pièce de monnaie. J'avais vendu, peu à peu, les quelques hardes que je possédais. Je savais que je ne pouvais plus faire appel à personne et, comme une folle, je me suis dirigée vers une crèmerie voisine, j'ai supplié que l'on me cédât un litre de lait, proposant de me livrer en échange à n'importe quelle besogne. On m'a répondu que l'on n'avait besoin de personne... et que l'on ne faisait pas de crédit... J'ai erré à travers les rues la tête perdue puis, en passant devant une épicerie, cédant à une impulsion plus forte que ma volonté, j'ai volé à l'étalage, une boîte de lait condensé... volé pour que mon enfant ne mourût pas, vous comprenez?... Mon geste fut surpris, je fus arrêtée et condamnée à un mois de prison, malgré mes larmes, malgré mes supplications. Tandis qu'on m'incarcérait, ma petite était envoyée aux enfants assistés. Lorsque, libérée, je voulus la reprendre, on m'en refusa le droit, sous prétexte que je n'avais aucun répondant et que je ne pouvais justifier d'aucun moyen de l'élever... Et j'étais sa mère... sa mère, pourtant ! Je l'ai crié... on m'a brutalement repoussée... Depuis lors, brisée, déchirée, je me suis laissée aller à la dérive, pour échouer enfin dans ce misérable bar où vous m'avez rencontrée. Et elle, ma pauvre enfant, n'a plus de nom, plus de mère, plus de foyer. Elle n'est plus qu'un numéro matricule, dans le grand livre des deshérités... Pour l'amour de Dieu, monsieur Charley, vous qui avez un cœur généreux et compatissant, délivrez-la, recueillez-la, chérissez-la. Exaucez la supplication que vous adresse une mourante !

Elle conta son banal et douloureux roman.

Si profondément ému qu'il se sentît, Charley estima impossible d'accéder à cette touchante prière... Comment, dans le métier qu'il exerçait, pourrait-il prendre la charge d'une enfant? C'était vraiment une responsabilité qu'il ne pouvait encourir. Il le dit à Fanny qui, pâle et défaite, insista cependant :

— Je vous en conjure, répéta-t-elle à bout de souffle, ne l'abandonnez pas au triste avenir qui serait le sien. Elle ne vous gênera pas beaucoup... Vous apprendrez à l'aimer mieux encore que vous n'aimiez le fidèle compagnon que vous avez perdu et sur lequel nous avons pleuré ensemble. Vous éprouverez la douceur de la dorloter, et, le soir, lorsque vous rentrerez chez vous, elle vous accueillera avec un gentil sourire en vous tendant ses petits bras.

La douleur poignante de cette mère le bouleversait jusqu'aux entrailles. Plus mollement, il objecta cependant :

— Encore, si c'était un garçon... Mais une fille... vous n'y pensez pas, ma pauvre amie.

La jeune femme se pencha vers lui désespérément.

— Oh ! ne refusez pas, sanglota-t-elle presque. La mort qui vient ne me fait pas peur, mais ce serait trop terrible de m'en aller en laissant mon enfant là-bas... Si vous saviez combien elle était gentille, si vous saviez combien je vous bénirai, si vous saviez combien je prierai pour vous là-haut, si Dieu, après tout ce que j'ai souffert, daigne m'accueillir auprès de lui.

Il réfléchit durant quelques instants. Mais déjà son siège était fait. Il se sentait incapable de résister à ce vœu suprême qui lui était exprimé, il ne se sentait pas la force de refuser à cette mère l'apaisement qu'elle sollicitait de lui. Il vit ses yeux qui, ardemment, se fixaient sur les siens, pour y deviner l'arrêt qu'il allait prononcer et, gravement, mesurant bien toute la portée de l'engagement qu'il prenait, il dit enfin :

— C'est bien, soyez satisfaite, je vous promets de veiller sur elle.

Fanny se sentit étouffer presque d'une joie depuis bien longtemps elle n'avait pas connue. Elle se laissa glisser aux genoux de Charley, elle s'empara de ses mains qu'elle porta à ses lèvres tout en lui prodiguant ses remerciements éperdus. Puis comme si, au souvenir de ses misères passées, de sa lamentable déchéance une crainte soudain se présentait à son esprit, elle recommanda :

— Surtout, faites qu'elle ne devienne pas une pauver petite dévoyée, comme sa misérable maman !

Doucement il la releva et il l'assura qu'il élèverait la petite Marysette comme sa propre fille... qu'il l'adopterait en fait et en droit.

Elle retomba épuisée sur son fauteuil et son visage émacié témoignait d'un immense apaisement.

Le lendemain, la pauvre créature s'éteignit doucement. Charley et Sophie l'accompagnèrent seuls jusqu'à sa dernière demeure.

Deux semaines plus tard, et après avoir accompli toutes les formalités nécessaires, après aussi s'être assuré des services d'une brave femme, la « mère Mary », qu'il connaissait de longue date et qui tiendrait désormais chez lui l'emploi de « gouvernante », Charley rentra un jour au logis tenant entre ses bras l'enfant que lui avait confiée la morte. Elle s'était endormie contre son épaule. Avec mille précautions, il la déposa sur le lit préparé à son intention. C'était une ravissante fillette de trois ans, toute blonde, toute rose et toute fraîche. Déjà conquise, la « mère Mary », à qui incombait désormais la tâche de veiller sur elle, sourit.

— La chère mignonne !...

Il rentra au logis tenant, entre ses bras l'enfant...

Comme elle dort bien... et comme je vais la câliner.

— Je l'espère bien, appuya Charley, et faites en sorte qu'elle ne se trouve pas trop dépaysée à son réveil... Inutile de vous occuper de moi pour le dîner... Je ne rentrerai que très tard... Je vais « travailler » nuit et jour s'il le faut pour qu'elle ne manque de rien.

Il effleura de ses lèvres les boucles blondes de la fillette et s'en fut d'un pas allègre.

Au club des mendiants, cependant, la nouvelle de cette adoption s'était répandue comme une traînée de poudre. L'acte admirable du « manchot » était vivement commenté et, il faut l'avouer, plutôt ironiquement apprécié. Aussi, lorsqu'il apparut le soir fut-il accueilli par les quolibets variés..

— Bonsoir, papa Charley, clama une jeune habituée de l'établissement. Vous voilà changé en père nourricier. Félicitations. Comment va la môme ?

— La charité, s'il vous plaît, pour un bébé qui n'a plus de mère ! grimaça un pâle voyou en tendant sa casquette graisseuse à la ronde.

Sophie s'avança au devant de Charley, la bouche en cœur, pour le féliciter de sa bonne action. Mais, assez énervé, il lui coupa assez brusquement la parole.

— Si vous aviez tenu votre langue, vieille radoteuse, tous ces imbéciles ne seraient pas en train de se payer ma tête !

Une horrible vieille, complètement édentée et à moitié ivre, brandit un grand verre de gin et glapit d'une voix éraillée, aux éclats de rire de toute l'assistance :

— Eh ! le manchot, si tu as besoin d'une nourrice sèche, pense à moi.

Il haussa dédaigneusement les épaules.

— Je me moque pas mal de vos stupides plaisanteries à tous, entendez-vous ? Ce ne sont pas elles qui me feront regretter ce que j'ai fait... Si, un jour, je deviens millionnaire, j'achèterai cette boîte pour en faire une pouponnière ou un orphelinat.

Le faux aveugle « l'homme aux yeux blancs » n'avait encore rien dit. Il empoigna la vieille ivrognesse à bras le corps et s'esclaffa :

— Tu l'entends, Nénette, une pouponnière, il veut fonder une pouponnière... et peut-être aussi un hospice pour chiens perdus... Il n'y a pas à dire, tu es rigolo, le manchot !

— Hospice ou pouponnière, ce n'est pas toi, en tous cas que je prendrai comme gardien ! riposta Charley.

Et il se retira écœuré sans vouloir discuter avec tous ces gens qui, dans leurs vils instincts, dans leur égoïsme, étaient incapables de le comprendre.

A quelque temps de là, entièrement sous le charme des grands yeux bleus et du joli sourire de Marysette, il se dit que le triste logement dont il s'était contenté jusque-là, et dont les deux seules fenêtres ouvraient sur une cour que jamais n'égayait le moindre rayon de soleil, n'était pas fait pour abriter la fragile et délicate créature qu'était sa fille adoptive. Il voulait en même temps, et sans donner congé pour cela des deux pièces qu'il occupait depuis si longtemps à New-York, faire perdre la trace de l'enfant à toute la coterie du club des mendiants.

Déplaçant une partie de ses économies, il acheta, en en payant moitié comptant, dans une riante banlieue un coquet petit chalet, la « Villa des Roses » entourée d'un jardin tout fleuri ; il le fit garnir de meubles clairs et gais et lorsque l'installation fut complètement terminée, il annonça joyeusement à sa gouvernante :

— Nous déménageons, Mary, et ce sera vite fait, car nous n'emportons rien de ce qui se trouve ici ; je veux que, pas plus tard que demain, Marysette quitte cette vieille masure dans laquelle elle finirait par étouffer. Je veux qu'elle ait de l'air, du soleil et des fleurs.

III

Des années passèrent.

Bien des cheveux avaient blanchi, bien des fronts s'étaient ridés. L'étrange clientèle du bar Ramon n'avait pas changé.

Les faux estropiés, manchots, culs-de-jatte ou aveugles, continuaient à s'y réunir. D'aucuns avaient fait fortune et n'en persévéraient pas moins dans leur misérable métier. D'autres, moins chanceux ou trop portés à gaspiller au fur et à mesure les recettes de leurs journées, ne faisaient que végéter. Parmi ces derniers, William Baxter « l'homme aux yeux blancs » ne cessait de se plaindre de la rigueur des temps. De plus en plus envieux, de plus en plus sournois, il était en même temps le plus fainéant de toute la bande. Le fait seul d'aller s'installer au coin d'une rue et de tendre la main à la charité des passants constituait pour lui un « travail », et par cela même le rebutait. Il passait la majeure partie de ses journées soit à demeurer vautré sur son grabat, soit à boire au comptoir du bar Ramon ce qu'il avait pu récolter en deux ou trois heures de faction.

Durant ces mêmes années « Charley le manchot », avait opiniâtrement continué l'exercice de l'étrange « profession » qu'il s'était choisie. Du matin au soir, à part deux jours par semaine, qu'il consacrait uniquement à sa fille adoptive, et souvent jusqu'aux heures les plus avancées de la nuit, il était à son poste, sébile en main, soit sur les marches des églises, soit à la sortie des théâtres, soit en certains points déterminés des quartiers opulents où il était parvenu à se faire une véritable « clientèle » peu avare de ses aumônes. Celles-ci pleuvaient et, à ce métier, le mendiant était devenu un véritable capitaliste. Très sobre, très économe, il ne dépensait presque rien pour lui-même et ses dépôts en banque, ses placements avaient progressivement pris une importance considérable. Il lui était arrivé même de risquer quelques opérations de Bourse dont les résultats avaient été fructueux. Et, cependant, il continuait à faire appel à la charité publique en pensant à Marysette pour qui, sou par sou, il voulait amasser chaque jour davantage.

Il la chérissait comme si elle eût été sa propre enfant. Il lui avait fait donner, à domicile, une éducation des plus soignées et, d'accord avec Mary Wolf, il avait toujours pris de minutieuses précautions pour qu'elle ignorât le métier auquel il se livrait.

La fille de la malheureuse Fanny Hirch avait grandi, choyée et heureuse à la « Villa des Roses ». Elle était devenue la plus ravissante des jeunes filles. N'ayant, en réalité, jamais connu sa mère, ni sa misérable naissance, elle s'était tout naturellement laissé convaincre qu'à la mort de ses parents, elle avait été recueillie et adoptée par un intime ami de ceux-ci, M. Charles Vanhern et que, si ce dernier ne pouvait demeurer constamment auprès d'elle, c'est qu'il était trop absorbé, par les importantes affaires financières qu'il brassait.

De toute son âme elle lui rendait la tendresse qu'il lui témoignait, les deux soirées, les deux journées qu'il lui consacrait chaque semaine étaient pour elle de véritables fêtes. Afin de lui faire honneur, elle se faisait plus belle que d'habitude ; gaie comme un pinson, elle allait le guetter, bien avant l'heure où il avait coutume d'arriver à la grille du jardin. Aussitôt qu'elle apercevait au loin sa svelte silhouette, elle courait au-devant de lui, se jetait dans ses bras et lui prodiguait ses plus tendres baisers.

Mais l'affection filiale qu'elle lui portait n'occupait pas exclusivement son cœur.

Chez d'aimables voisins de la villa des Roses, elle avait eu occasion de faire la connaissance d'un jeune avocat, Philippe Peyton, encore au début de sa carrière, et dont l'avenir s'annonçait très brillant. Elle avait dès le premier moment produit sur lui la plus vive impression et de son côté Marysette, sans se rendre compte de la véritable nature des sentiments qui s'éveillaient en elle, avait été très sensible au délicat et respectueux empressement dont il témoignait vis-à-vis d'elle. Après l'avoir rencontré à plusieurs reprises chez leurs amis communs, elle avait, certain jour, trouvé l'occasion de le présenter à son père adoptif. Et, depuis lors, avec la permission de celui-ci, Philippe Peyton avait pris la douce habitude de venir de temps en temps, rendre visite à Marysette à la villa des Roses. C'était alors pour les deux jeunes gens, sous la discrète et maternelle surveillance de Mary Wolf, des minutes exquises, durant lesquelles, sans qu'aucune parole d'amour fût encore prononcée, ils sentaient, aussi délicieusement l'un que l'autre, leurs deux cœurs battre à l'unisson.

Certain après-midi « Charley le manchot », abrégeant sa tournée, rentra au club des mendiants bien avant son heure habituelle ; il passa tout de suite dans l'officine du père Tom qui, bien que très vieilli, était toujours solide au poste.

— Vite, cher ami, lui dit-il, aide-moi à quitter mes défroques et à me débarrasser de cet affreux moignon... Je suis très pressé. On m'attend ce soir à dîner... où tu sais.

Le barbier s'activa, dessangla les courroies et délivra le bras comprimé du « manchot ». A sa demande, il se mit en devoir de le raser. L'opération achevée, et tandis que Charley procédait à sa toilette avec un soin tout particulier, un jeune commissionnaire chargé de boîtes et de paquets pénétra à son tour dans l'atelier et déposa ses colis à terre avec précaution.

— Qu'est-ce que c'est que tout cela? interrogea le père Tom tout éberlué... pas possible, tu dois te tromper d'adresse, mon garçon, tout ce que tu apportes là ne peut pas être pour nous.

Charley se retourna.

— Mais si, c'est pour nous, au contraire, ou plutôt pour moi.

Il tendit un généreux pourboire au commissionnaire, et lorsque celui-ci se fut éloigné, il confia à l'oreille du vieux barbier :

— Ne t'ai-je pas dit que c'est ce soir l'anniversaire de ma petite Marysette... Le dix-septième... et ce sont les cadeaux que je vais lui offrir que tu vois là. Mais, pas un mot, n'est-ce pas. Toi seul connais mon secret. Toi seul dois le connaître ici.

Les deux hommes se serrèrent la main affectueusement et, quelques instants après, Charley, vêtu du plus élégant des complets, s'en fut par une porte dérobée afin de n'être pas vu des camarades que l'on entendait brailler et chanter dans le bar. Il monta avec ses paquets dans un taxi que son excellent ami avait été appeler.

A peu près à la même heure, à la villa des Roses, Marysette attendait avec impatience l'arrivée de son père adoptif... et aussi celle de Philippe Peyton qui lui avait promis sa visite.

« Tu l'entends? Il veut fonder une pouponnière! »

Elle était jolie à ravir, dans la fragile robe blanche, dont elle s'était parée pour ce jour de fête et, elle courait à tout instant jusqu'à la grille du jardin, pendant que, dans la cuisine « maman Mary » s'activait en personne à la confection de succulentes pâtisseries.

L'auto de Philippe stoppa enfin devant la villa. La jeune fille qui, pour passer le temps, était en train de cueillir quelques fleurs, s'élança toute joyeuse à sa rencontre.

Philippe garda un long moment dans la sienne la petite main qu'elle lui tendait. Puis, tout en lui exprimant ses vœux, il tira de sa poche un écrin et ajouta :

— Vous me feriez le plus grand plaisir, si vous vouliez me permettre, à l'occasion de votre anniversaire, de vous offrir ce modeste souvenir.

Elle ouvrit l'élégante boîte de maroquin et poussa une exclamation d'admiration à la vue d'un ravissant collier de petites perles du plus bel orient.

— C'est beaucoup trop beau, fit-elle, et je ne sais si je dois accepter ce bijou de prix... Papa Charley ne serait peut-être pas content.

Le front de Philippe s'était soudain assombri.

— Il doit donc venir? demanda-t-il.

— Certainement, et il est même en retard. Je commence à m'inquiéter. J'espère qu'il ne lui est pas survenu au dernier moment quelque empêchement... Mais entrez, je vous en prie.

Lorsque les deux jeunes gens se trouvèrent dans le salon, Philippe après un moment de silence, demanda, quelque peu nerveux :

— Vous l'aimez beaucoup... votre père adoptif?

— Comment pourrait-il en être autrement? Il est tellement bon. Un vrai papa ne pourrait être meilleur pour moi, ni me combler de plus tendres attentions.

Il reprit, et non sans quelque anxiété cette fois :

— Et moi, petite Marysette, m'aimez-vous aussi?

Elle rougit, toute confuse. C'était la première fois que Philippe lui posait pareille question. Il n'y avait jusqu'alors eu entre eux qu'une sorte de petit flirt innocent dans lequel ils n'avaient, ni l'un, ni l'autre, exprimé les doux sentiments qui étaient nés en eux. Comme elle gardait le silence, il implora :

— Je vous en prie, Marysette, répondez-moi. M'aimez-vous assez pour devenir ma femme, quitteriez-vous pour me suivre, celui qui vous a tenu lieu de père? Je vous chéris autant et peut-être plus qu'il ne vous chérit lui-même, et je sens qu'il me serait impossible de vivre sans vous désormais.

Tout en parlant, il l'avait attirée à lui, et elle était tout émue, presque tremblante dans les bras de ce grand garçon qui était très loin de lui être indifférent. Et il insistait :

— Dites, Marysette chérie... Vous voyez bien que c'est mon existence entière, que c'est mon bonheur qui sont entre vos mains. Dites, m'aimez-vous?

— Oui, murmura-t-elle dans un souffle, je vous aime...

Il dessangla les courroies.

« Me trouvez-vous jolie ainsi? ».

Tandis qu'il échangeait avec Philippe quelques mots de politesse...

les magasins pour acheter quelques cadeaux à mon enfant chérie.

Curieuse et ravie, la jeune fille s'empara tout d'abord d'un grand carton qu'il tenait à la main et, tandis qu'il échangeait avec Philippe quelques mots de politesse, elle en détacha les rubans et découvrit un délicieux petit feutre vert Nil qui portait la marque d'une des modistes les plus réputées de New-York. Elle s'en coiffa immédiatement, puis, allant à son père adoptif, saisissant à deux mains les revers de son pardessus, elle se dressa sur la pointe des pieds et demanda avec espièglerie :

— Me trouvez-vous jolie ainsi?

— Jolie entre toutes, répondit-il en lui donnant un long baiser.

Ennuyé de ces épanchements trop tendres à son gré, Philippe jeta un coup d'œil à sa montre et, inventant sur-le-champ un prétexte pour se retirer :

— Excusez-moi, monsieur Vanhern, dit-il soudain, si je me trouve obligé de vous quitter aussitôt votre arrivée. J'étais venu tout exprès pour présenter mes vœux à Marysette, et j'espère qu'elle ne m'en voudra pas non plus si je lui fausse déjà compagnie : un rendez-vous urgent m'appelle à New-York.

La jeune fille prit une petite mine boudeuse qui signifiait claire-

mais je ne pourrais jamais quitter papa Charley; N'exigez pas cela de moi.

Au moment du doux aveu qu'avaient formulé les lèvres de la jeune fille, Philippe éperdu de joie, l'avait d'un grand élan pressée contre son cœur. Mais, au dernier mot qu'elle prononça il ne réprima qu'à grand'peine un mouvement de contrariété.

Mary Wolf, qui était entrée sur ces entrefaites, avait tout entendu. Marysette l'aperçut. Elle se dégagea et, alla se blottir contre sa poitrine en disant :

— Je vous en prie, essayez de faire comprendre à M. Philippe qui, je crois, est un vilain jaloux, qu'il me serait impossible d'abandonner papa Charley... Il en peut pas savoir tout ce qu'il a été, tout ce qu'il est encore pour moi.

La brave femme n'eut pas le loisir de répondre. Charles Vanhern arrivait. Marysette alla joyeusement se jeter à son cou et, après lui avoir prodigué ses plus tendres baisers, elle lui demanda sur un petit ton de reproche, pourquoi il ne venait que si tard.

— Pourquoi? répondit-il, mais tout simplement parce qu'il m'a fallu courir

ment qu'elle lui en voulait tout au contraire quelque peu de partir si vite, et il ajouta en souriant :

— J'espère que vous me prouverez dimanche prochain que vous ne me tenez pas rigueur... car il est toujours entendu, n'est-ce pas, que vous viendrez prendre le thé chez ma sœur?

— Mais certainement. Papa Charley m'a même promis qu'il m'accompagnerait.

— Alors, au revoir, Marysette, à bientôt.

Il se retira en faisant effort pour ne pas laisser deviner sa mauvaise humeur. L'amour qu'il portait à la jeune fille était si profond, si exclusif aussi qu'il prenait ombrage, qu'il souffrait presque de l'affection qu'elle témoignait à son père adoptif. Il eût voulu occuper à lui seul son cœur et sa pensée. Au moment de franchir la porte du jardin, il se sentit le désir impérieux de retourner, malgré tout, auprès de celle qu'il aimait. Mais il se fit violence, remonta dans sa torpédo et s'éloigna.

IV

La présence de « papa Charley » consola vite Marysette de la décep-

Philippe garda un long moment dans la sienne la petite main qu'elle lui tendait.

tion que lui avait causée le départ de Philippe. Elle s'empressa d'ouvrir tous les autres paquets qu'il avait apportés. Dans une longue boîte elle trouva une « adorable » robe de crêpe de Chine ; dans une autre, un élégant sac à main marqué à son chiffre. Et puis, encore nombre de fanfreluches et de coquets petits riens, tous choisis avec le goût le plus sûr. Enfin, tout heureux de la joie qu'elle manifestait à chaque nouvelle découverte, Charley lui tendit un minuscule écrin sous le couvercle duquel scintillait une bague ravissante.

Ce furent encore des remerciements, de tendres effusions, puis Marysette déclara qu'elle voulait essayer sur-le-champ sa nouvelle toilette et elle se sauva dans sa chambre.

Vanhern avait été un peu surpris du brusque départ de Philippe. Il profita de la brève absence de la jeune fille pour demander à Mary Wolf si elle en connaissait le véritable motif ; il avait été frappé en effet de l'air, malgré tout un peu embarrassé, avec lequel ce dernier avait provoqué le prétexte d'un rendez-vous urgent.

Les deux poings sur les hanches, la brave femme vint se camper devant lui.

Les deux poings sur les hanches, la brave femme vint se camper devant lui et, avec le franc parler dont elle avait contracté l'habitude, elle articula :

— Vous êtes donc aveugle? Vous ne voyez pas que M. Philippe est tout simplement jaloux de vous? Il est follement épris de notre Marysette, et elle vient de lui déclarer nettement tout à l'heure que, pour rien au monde, elle ne consentirait à vous quitter... Pour ce qu'elle vous voit, tout juste deux fois par semaine, elle y a du mérite d'ailleurs... N'empêche que ça lui a jeté un froid, à ce garçon !

— Alors, réellement, ces deux enfants s'aiment, Mary?

— Cette question ! Pour sûr qu'ils s'aiment ! Il y a bien longtemps que je l'avais deviné et ils étaient bien touchants il y a un instant, lorsqu'ils se les ont avoué pour la première fois, l'un à l'autre. Je les ai entendus et j'en étais toute remuée.

Vanhern demeura profondément rêveur. Une ou deux minutes s'écoulèrent sans que la vieille gouvernante osât maintenant s'aventurer à le distraire de sa méditation. Soudain, Marysette apparut, toute rieuse, et véritablement éblouissante sous la robe dont la teinte délicate mettait encore en valeur sa beauté. Lorsqu'elle se fut bien fait admirer, elle se décida à montrer à son père adoptif, et non sans quelque timidité, le collier que lui avait offert le jeune avocat.

— C'est Philippe qui m'a apporté, qui a tenu à me laisser ce joli collier, expliqua-t-elle. Mais je lui ai bien dit que je ne savais si je devais l'accepter. Je ferai, papa Charley, exactement comme vous me direz.

Il examina le bijou en connaisseur, peut-être pour se laisser le temps de répondre. Puis, soudain, prenant son parti et poussant un soupir, il attacha lui-même le collier au cou gracile de Marysette et il dit simplement :

— Tu peux, ma chérie, accepter et garder ce présent. Il signifie pour moi que, d'ici un an, lorsque tu auras atteint ta dix-huitième année, tu seras la femme de celui que tu aimes, car tu aimes Philippe, n'est-ce pas?

Les joues de la jeune fille s'empourprèrent. Elle ne répondit pas, mais elle laissa aller sa tête sur l'épaule de celui qu'elle chérissait et vénérait à l'égal d'un véritable père et, dans le regard qu'elle levait sur lui, il put lire tout le bonheur qui était en elle. Elle se souvenait des tendres aveux qu'elle avait échangés au cours de l'après-midi et elle se disait que tout s'arrangerait, et que, pour suivre l'irrésistible impulsion de son cœur, elle ne se trouverait pas dans la triste obligation de quitter, d'abandonner « papa Charley ». Et, celui-ci, de son côté, se représentait qu'il venait de se donner un an de répit, que, durant un an encore, il aurait « son enfant » bien à lui. Après... après... il serait temps d'aviser à ce qu'il adviendrait de lui-même...

Le dimanche suivant, Philippe Peyton vint chercher Marysette pour la conduire au thé dansant que donnait sa sœur, Mme Marmont, dans son élégant hôtel de la Cinquième avenue. Fidèle à la promesse qu'il s'était laissé arracher par la jeune fille, son père adoptif s'était décidé à l'accompagner. Il prit place avec elle dans la voiture de l'avocat.

Vêtu d'une jaquette de coupe impeccable, coiffé d'un éblouissant « huit reflets », les mains finement gantées, personne n'eût reconnu en lui le misérable « manchot » du bar Ramon. Mendiant à certaines heures, homme du monde à d'autres, il était impossible de discerner le double rôle qu'il jouait avec une égale maîtrise. Aux approches de la cinquantaine, il était demeuré élancé, et si ses traits réguliers étaient un peu plus accusés qu'autrefois, si ses tempes commençaient à grisonner, son allure et sa démarche étaient demeurées celles d'un jeune homme.

Ils durent tous trois mettre à pied à terre à une trentaine de pas de la porte de l'hôtel de Mme Marmont, devant lequel stationnait déjà une longue file de voitures. En longeant le trottoir, ils passèrent devant un misérable individu qui, assis sur les marches d'un perron, tendait sa sébile et implorait d'une voix plaintive :

— La charité, s'il vous plaît, pour un pauvre aveugle.

Marysette s'arrêta apitoyée.

— Oh ! le malheureux vieillard, murmura-t-elle.

Et elle ouvrit son sac à main pour y prendre quelque monnaie.

Charles Vanhern, et pour cause, ne prêtait jamais guère attention aux mendiants « ses confrères ». Il tressaillit lorsqu'il reconnut en celui qui venait d'exciter la commisération de Marysette « l'homme aux yeux blancs ». Puis, il se ressaisit à se dire que celui-là, *heureusement*, était un *véritable* aveugle, et, pour faire comme elle, il laissa tomber lui aussi son obole.

Le mendiant marmonna une litanie de remerciements et de bénédictions ; mais aussitôt que ceux qu'il en comblait se furent éloignés, il ricana :

— Eh ! eh ! le manchot, le voilà donc le mystère que tu caches si soigneusement depuis tant d'années... Monsieur joue au gentleman, et promène des poulettes qui, par ma foi, sont assez bien tournées pour qu'on arbore en leur honneur un tuyau de poêle et des gants beurre frais.

Désireux d'en savoir davantage sur la vie intime de celui qu'il se reprenait à ce moment à jalouser, à envier, à haïr plus qu'à aucun moment, il se rapprocha de la porte de l'opulente demeure où il l'avait vu pénétrer, et se posta tout à côté. Il espérait glaner sur le compte de ce « faux frère » quelques renseignements dont il ferait son profit. Mais il en fut pour ses frais. Un agent, au bout de quelques minutes, lui signifia assez brutalement d'avoir à aller implorer ailleurs la charité des passants. Il s'éloigna, non sans gémir, pour la forme, sur la dureté dont on faisait preuve vis-à-vis « d'un pauvre aveugle, qui depuis la veille n'avait pas mangé ». Lentement, du pas hésitant auquel il s'était habitué depuis le temps qu'il jouait la cécité, frappant devant lui le trottoir de son bâton, faisant appel à quelque passant compatissant pour traverser les rues, il regagna le bar Ramon. Mais en même temps il réfléchissait, l'esprit toujours tendu vers le même objet. De déductions en déductions, il en arriva à conclure qu'il y avait de fortes présomptions pour que la jeune personne avec laquelle « le manchot » se promenait en de si beaux atours ne fût autre que l'enfant qu'il avait recueillie jadis et dont personne, depuis lors, n'avait plus entendu parler. Il se promit d'élucider à tout prix le problème. Dans son âme vile, il transformait déjà du tout au tout et de la plus odieuse façon, le rôle que Charley tenait vis-à-vis de sa « soi-disant » fille adoptive. Il se promettait bien, pour peu qu'il se trouvât sûr de son fait, de le faire « chanter ». Et, à cette seule perspective ses regards en apparence éteints se ravivaient pour laisser filtrer des lueurs mauvaises.

Ce jour-là Charley ne parut pas au bar Ramon, mais le lendemain matin, lorsqu'il pénétra dans l'atelier du père Tom, Blaxter s'y trouvait déjà, le guettant sournoisement : il attendait le moment où celui-ci opérerait sa transformation pour fureter dans les poches de ses vêtements qu'il avait coutume de jeter sur un siège avant de les enfermer, au moment de partir, dans une armoire dont il gardait soigneusement la clef. Il comptait bien y découvrir quelques papiers, quelques indices qui pourraient lui être utiles.

Le hasard le servit. Charley venait de quitter son veston, lorsqu'il fut appelé un instant dans le bar. Très affairé de son côté, le barbier ne prêtait nulle attention au faux aveugle qui put ainsi se livrer, presque à loisir, à son investigation. Dans un portefeuille dont il passa rapidement en revue le contenu, il trouva une photographie dans laquelle il reconnut les traits de la ravis-

Elle semblait redouter, en le laissant partir, de le perdre à jamais.

sante personne qui lui avait fait l'aumône la veille, et qui portait cette dédicace : « A papa Charley, tendre souvenir de sa Marysette ». Il découvrit également un carnet de dépôts en banque, au nom de M. Charles Vanhern, villa des Roses, à Long-Island, et quelques chiffres suffirent à lui confirmer que le « manchot » était, décidément, un très riche capitaliste. Entendant celui-ci revenir, il se hâta de tout remettre en place.

Mais à travers la porte entr'ouverte Charley avait, sans que Baxter s'en doutât le moins du monde, surpris son geste. Il fut stupéfait de devoir en tirer la conclusion que « l'homme aux yeux blancs » n'était en aucune façon aveugle et que, depuis des années, il avait su habilement le leurrer, ainsi que tous les camarades. Quand il entra dans l'atelier, l'autre avait déjà eu le temps d'aller s'asseoir sur un escabeau comme si de rien n'était.

— Eh bien, ça va? lui demanda ironiquement le « manchot », tu parais tout guilleret, ce matin.

— Guilleret, moi. Je n'en aurais, ma foi, guère de motif. La santé va à peu près, je ne dis pas, mais ce sont les affaires qui ne marchent pas fort... Les temps sont bien changés et le métier ne rend plus comme autrefois... Qu'est-ce que tu en dis, toi? Est-ce que la chance te favorise toujours?

— Tu dois le savoir mieux que moi, vieux farceur, puisque tu as eu l'indiscrétion de fourrer le nez dans mes papiers tout à l'heure... Le diable t'a donc rendu la vue? Allons, avoue en même temps que tu m'as vu hier dans la Cinquième avenue.

Sous un air narquois, Charley dissimulait à peine son irritation et aussi son inquiétude à savoir que le secret qu'il avait jusqu'alors si soigneusement gardé, se trouvait désormais à la merci du sinistre individu. Furieux de son côté de s'être si stupidement laissé prendre après des années et des années de précaution et de dissimulation, Baxter abandonna toute feinte et ricana :

— Parfaitement, je t'ai vu, et avec la gosse à Fanny Hirch encore, que tu caches précieusement à Long-Island.

Impérieusement, Charley lui imposa silence.

— Tais-toi. Je te défends de prononcer le nom de cette enfant.

— Et pourquoi, s'il te plaît? Ce que j'en dis n'est pas pour te blâmer. Je te comprends au contraire, je t'envie même, car moi non plus, tu sais, je ne déteste pas « les petits poulets de grain ».

Charley ne put en supporter davantage. Ses poings s'abattirent sur la face du vil individu. Baxter poussa un hurlement de douleur. Protégeant de son mieux sous son bras replié le haut de son visage, il criait.

— Attention, espèce de brute... *pas sur les yeux*. A force de faire l'aveugle, je commence à ne plus y voir qu'à peine !

Mais Charley ne l'écoutait pas, et, exaspéré, il continuait à lui administrer une sévère correction devant toute la clientèle accourue sur les lieux. Le tumulte attira un agent qui battait le pavé devant l'établisse-

ment et il dut arracher Baxter aux mains de son adversaire qui continuait à s'acharner contre lui.

— Il faut être le dernier des lâches, grommela-t-il, lorsqu'il eut séparé les deux hommes, pour frapper un malheureux aveugle incapable de se défendre.

— Aveugle, riposta vivement Charley. Il ne l'est pas plus que vous et moi.

— Et lui, grogna hargneusement « l'homme aux yeux blancs » vous avez pu constater qu'il n'est pas si manchot que lorsqu'il s'en va avec son faux moignon essayer d'apitoyer les passants.

Depuis très longtemps de service dans le quartier, l'agent n'était pas sans se douter plus ou moins de tous les trucs qu'employaient ces prétendus estropiés. Mais, comme il n'y avait jamais eu d'histoires ni de rixes sanglantes au bar Ramon, il n'avait jamais eu non plus à intervenir. Il se demanda un instant ce qu'il convenait de faire maintenant qu'il ne pouvait plus douter des moyens qu'ils employaient pour exploiter la charité publique. A cause de Charley avec qui il avait eu à plusieurs reprises occasion d'échanger quelques mots, et dont la physionomie ouverte lui avait toujours inspiré une certaine sympathie, il se décida de ne pas donner d'autres suites à l'affaire pour le moment, et se contenta d'inviter sévèrement les deux adversaires à se tenir tranquilles et à éviter que le bruit de leurs querelles n'arrivât jusqu'à la rue.

Baxter, pour se remettre un peu de la sévère raclée qu'il avait reçue, alla se commander une large rasade de gin au comptoir du bar et ses camarades l'entourèrent aussitôt pour le féliciter de les avoir si longtemps dupés : pour y être arrivé avec des malins comme eux, il fallait être de première force.

Quant à l'agent, avant de sortir, il prit Charley à part et lui glissa ces paroles qui parurent profondément l'impressionner :

— Vous m'avez toujours fait l'impression d'être au fond un brave type. Comment n'avez-vous pas honte de vivre d'un métier pareil?

Le « manchot » courba un instant la tête pour dire :

— Vous avez raison, c'est une honte !

Puis il ajouta avec énergie :

— Mais c'est fini, bien fini, je m'en fais le serment. J'ai assez d'une pareille existence et j'y renonce à jamais.

V

Charles Vanhern tint parole. Il ne reparut plus au bar Ramon et, quelques jours plus tard, grande fut la joie de Marysette lorsqu'il lui annonça qu'il s'octroyait quelques semaines de vacances et que son intention était de les passer à la villa des Roses, où à l'ombre des beaux arbres, il se reposerait un peu du tracas des affaires.

Ils firent ensemble mille beaux projets, mais une ombre ne tarda pas à tomber sur tout le bonheur qu'ils

12 — LE FILM COMPLET

se promettaient : l'installation de Vanhern à la villa, les affectueuses attentions dont la jeune fille le comblait, eurent vite fait de raviver et de pousser à l'extrême la jalousie de Philippe Peyton. Il pressa à plusieurs reprises Marysette de prendre une détermination.

— Puisque vous m'avez fait le doux aveu de votre amour, ma chérie, répétait-il, puisque vous savez que, de mon côté, je vous ai donné toute mon âme, pourquoi différer le moment où nous serons unis? Je ne serai véritablement heureux que le jour où je vous aurai emmenée loin d'ici, où je vous aurai entièrement à moi, où je serai seul à vous entourer de ma tendresse et à être l'objet de la vôtre.

La jeune fille se débattait entre les deux affections qui lui étaient chères. Sans oser le formuler, elle n'arrivait pas à comprendre pourquoi Philippe ne voulait pas admettre l'idée qu'elle pût devenir sa femme sans quitter pour cela l'homme si bon, au cœur si généreux, à qui elle devait tout. N'auraient-ils pas pu vivre ensemble, heureux, réunis tous les trois sous le même toit? Cette pensée, elle ne l'exprimait pas, et, elle répondait, le cœur oppressé :

— Je vous l'ai déjà dit, Philippe, je ne puis abandonner ainsi celui qui, depuis tant d'années, me prodigue une paternelle sollicitude et un dévouement de tous les instants. Je ne puis lui causer ce chagrin affreux.

— C'est donc que vous l'aimez plus que moi?

— Plus? Non, Philippe, mais autrement ; je l'aime comme une fille peut aimer le père le plus tendre, le plus digne d'être chéri et vénéré. De ce sentiment, pourquoi prendre ombrage?

Ces discussions se renouvelaient sous une forme ou sous une autre, à peu près chaque jour, et elles laissaient le jeune homme presque maussade et la pauvre enfant, véritablement torturée.

Le hasard fit qu'un jour Charles Vanhern en perçut involontairement l'écho. Il se trouvait accoudé à un balcon du premier étage de la villa, tandis qu'au dessous de lui, dans le jardin, et sans se douter qu'il les entendait, Philippe et Marysette revenaient de ce qui était devenu le thème ordinaire de leurs entretiens. L'ancien mendiant connaissait déjà par ce que lui en avait dit une fois Mary Wolf, l'étrange jalousie dont Philippe Peyton était animé à son égard. Il n'eût fait qu'en rire comme d'un simple enfantillage s'il eût été un homme comme la plupart des autres, digne de sa propre estime. Il se fût dit qu'il n'y avait là que l'égoïsme d'un amoureux passionnément épris et qui, sa première flamme jetée, se montrerait à coup sûr moins exclusif. Mais, depuis qu'il avait déserté le bar Ramon, il mesurait chaque jour davantage la profondeur de ce que, durant de si longues années, avait été sa déchéance. De celle-ci, il sentait grandir en lui la honte. Lorsqu'il entendit Marysette vanter une fois de plus la noblesse de son âme et répéter qu'à aucun prix elle ne se résignerait à l'abandonner, il sentit ses yeux se mouiller de larmes. Il se dit qu'il devait d'autant moins être un obstacle à son bonheur qu'il se sentait moins digne, sinon de la tendresse, du moins de la vénération qu'elle avait pour lui. Et, sur-le-champ, sa détermination fut prise.

Le jour suivant, il se présenta à New-York au cabinet du jeune avocat. Et, résolu à se sacrifier au bonheur de sa fille adoptive, il alla, après les salutations d'usage, droit au but :

— Monsieur Peyton, vous avez su gagner ma confiance et mon estime dès les premiers jours où je vous ai connu. J'ai, si pénibles qu'elles soient pour moi, certaines révélations à vous faire, que je confierai à votre honneur et à votre discrétion... Et d'abord, vous aimez Marysette, n'est-ce pas?

Quelque peu surpris de cet étrange préambule, le jeune homme n'en affirma pas moins avec chaleur :

— Je l'aime de toute mon âme, en effet, et je n'aspire à d'autre bonheur que d'obtenir sa main.

— Elle est digne, la chère enfant, des sentiments que vous lui portez. Mais, avant de vous engager davantage, il est nécessaire que vous sachiez exactement qui est l'exquise créature à laquelle vous voulez donner votre nom.

Sur ces mots, et avec une entière franchise, Charles Vanhern conta la triste naissance de Marysette, la fin lamentable de sa mère et le serment qu'il avait fait à celle-ci, presque à son lit de mort, serment qu'il s'était fait un pieux devoir de tenir.

Philippe avait écouté avec émotion tout ce récit. Et, à mesure que parlait son visiteur, il sentait fondre en soi la sotte jalousie qu'il avait si longtemps nourrie contre lui. Il l'admirait maintenant, il comprenait toute la tendre gratitude qui attachait Marysette à lui, et lorsqu'il eut terminé il lui saisit chaleureusement la main pour dire :

— Votre conduite en tout cela a été simplement admirable. Je n'ai pas besoin de vous dire qu'après ce que vous venez de me révéler, je souhaite que davantage encore me vouer au bonheur de Marysette, et je m'unis à elle dans le tendre respect filial qu'elle vous porte... Vous m'annonciez tout à l'heure des révélations pénibles pour vous. Nulles au contraire, autant que celles que vous venez de me faire, ne sauraient être à votre honneur !

Vanhern secoua la tête. Il demeura un instant silencieux comme pour puiser en lui-même le courage d'aller jusqu'au bout de ce qu'il s'était juré de dévoiler. Puis :

— Ne vous hâtez pas de me juger avec tant de bienveillance, dit-il. Vous venez de me serrer la main pour la dernière fois et dans un instant vous ne m'en jugerez plus digne et vous aurez raison. Marysette a droit à votre amour et à votre respect. Mais moi... moi, vous ne savez pas encore qui je suis !

Et comme le jeune homme le regardait maintenant stupéfait, il poursuivit d'une voix sourde :

— ... Vous connaissez Charles Vanhern, le riche brasseur d'affaires, l'heureux et estimé propriétaire de la villa des Roses. Mais vous ne connaissez pas encore « Charley le manchot », le faux infirme, le mendiant qui vit depuis des années et des années de mensonge, en exerçant toutes ses facultés, toute son adresse à largement exploiter la crédulité publique. Sachez qu'ils ne font qu'un seul et même personnage et que plus d'une fois, lorsque je vous faisais accueil chez moi à Long Island, je venais à peine de quitter, en ville, mon infâme accoutrement.

Philippe se demandait s'il n'était pas en train de rêver ou si plutôt son interlocuteur n'inventait pas cette fantastique histoire afin d'éprouver la sincérité de ses sentiments à l'égard de Marysette. Mais à le regarder plus attentivement, à voir son visage empreint d'une inexprimable tristesse, ses épaules qui s'étaient soudain voûtées comme sous le poids de sa propre déchéance, il ne douta plus que ce qu'il venait d'entendre là ne fût l'expression d'une inconcevable vérité. Charles Vanhern ne le laissa pas longtemps à toutes les pensées qui venaient se heurter dans son cerveau. Il reprit :

— ... Voilà la confession que ce qui peut me rester d'honneur, s'il m'est encore permis de me servir de ce mot, m'obligeait à vous faire. Marysette ignore tout de ce que je viens de vous confier. J'ai une suprême prière à vous adresser : jurez-moi que jamais, quoi qu'il puisse advenir, vous ne le lui dévoilerez. Jurez-moi que vous demeurez résolu à vous vouer à son bonheur... et je vous promets, en échange, que je ne vous mettrai pas dans le cas d'avoir à rougir de moi : je suis décidé à disparaître... pour longtemps ; à m'en aller très loin... en Australie... par le premier bateau. Je me suis informé. Il y a un départ dès demain.

Le jeune avocat ne savait plus quelle contenance tenir. L'aveu de la sincérité duquel il ne lui était plus permis de douter l'avait laissé sidéré. Il se sentait incapable de mépriser complètement cet homme, à qui l'instant d'auparavant il avait exprimé son admiration et qui venait de lui faire la plus cruelle des confessions, cet homme qui, pour assurer le bonheur de l'enfant qu'il avait recueillie, élevée et chérie, s'abaissait devant lui, lui révélait une honte qu'il aurait pu toujours lui laisser ignorer, et stoïquement se sacrifiait ; il ne voulait pas le juger ; il se sentait incapable de le condamner, mais incapable aussi de l'absoudre. Il se sentait moins entraîné au mépris que saisi de pitié. Mais son amour pour Marysette demeurait inchangé et il fit, sans commentaires, le serment qui lui était demandé.

C'était là tout ce qu'avait voulu obtenir de lui « Charley le manchot ». Il se retira la conscience allégée en disant qu'il allait sans tarder annoncer son départ à sa chère enfant.

Mélancoliquement Marysette se laissait bercer aux douces paroles d'amour.

Il fit quelques courses en ville, puis, rentré à la villa des Roses, il commença par mettre Mary Wolf au courant de sa résolution ; et sans souci de sa stupéfaction, de ses timides remontrances, il la pria de lui préparer ses bagages sans tarder. Marysette survint sur ces entrefaites. Lorsqu'elle apprit de la bouche même de son père adoptif le projet de ce voyage en Australie, elle ne put retenir ses larmes :

— Oh ! papa Charley, reprocha-t-elle dans un sanglot, vous voulez m'abandonner?

Si bouleversé qu'il fût, il s'efforça de la rassurer, de la consoler, de plaisanter même.

— T'abandonner? Tu sais bien, ma chérie, que j'en serais incapable. Que vas-tu chercher là, petite folle? En voilà un désespoir pour un simple voyage d'affaires, qui ne me retiendra certainement pas plus de trois ou quatre mois loin de toi. Hâte-toi de sécher tes pleurs ; n'auras-tu pas Philippe pour te consoler de mon absence?... Philippe qui t'aime de tout son cœur, qui viendra te voir dès demain, et qui n'aspire qu'à se consacrer à ton bonheur.

Ces derniers mots ramenèrent un sourire sur les lèvres de la jeune fille. Et durant tout le reste de la journée, durant toute la soirée il ne fut plus guère question que de l'avenir des deux amoureux dont le mariage serait célébré dès le retour du voyageur.

Mais le lendemain matin, le moment de la séparation venu, le cœur de Marysette se déchira. Elle s'élança entre les bras de Vanhern et s'agrippa à lui comme si elle eût redouté, en le laissant partir, de le perdre à jamais. Ce ne fut qu'à grand'peine, sentant lui-même son courage faiblir, qu'il put s'arracher à son étreinte.

Une quinzaine de jours plus tard, Philippe Peyton trouva dans son courrier une lettre expédiée de Southampton et que lui adressait le commandant du *Melbourne*, le transatlantique à bord duquel s'était embarqué Charles Vanhern. En quelques mots le marin l'informait que son passager était tombé à la mer en vue du port et qu'on l'avait vu disparaître dans les flots malgré tous les efforts tentés pour le sauver. On avait trouvé dans sa cabine un carnet sur lequel on avait relevé cette indication : *En cas d'accident prière de prévenir Mr. Philippe Peyton*, 369, *Broadway, à New-York.*

Le jeune homme se sentit profondément ému. Il se demandait, ainsi que cela paraissait être d'ailleurs l'avis du capitaine, si le malheureux n'avait pas mis volontairement fin à ses jours afin que son indignité passée ne pût jamais être un obstacle au bonheur de l'enfant qu'il avait recueillie et élevée.

Avec des ménagements infinis, il annonça à Marysette le tragique accident dans lequel son père adoptif avait trouvé la mort. C'était pour elle, hélas ! la réalisation des funestes pressentiments qui l'avaient assaillie au moment où il lui faisait ses adieux. Il est impossible de dépeindre ce que fut sa douleur.

Durant plusieurs semaines, Mary Wolf et le jeune avocat qui l'entouraient à l'envi de leur tendre sollicitude tremblèrent, tant elle demeurait déprimée, pour sa propre santé. Puis peu à peu le temps fit son œuvre, sa peine perdit de son acuité. Mélancoliquement Marysette se laissait bercer aux douces paroles d'amour que lui murmurait Philippe. N'était-il pas tout pour elle désormais?

Un terrible corps à corps s'engagea.

Au printemps suivant les fiançailles des deux jeunes gens furent officiellement célébrées, dans une fête intime, chez M**ᵐᵉ** Marmont qui avait pris en profonde affection la chère petite, deux fois orpheline. A certains moments, une ombre de tristesse voilait les beaux yeux de Marysette... sa pensée allait vers « papa Charley ». Philippe devinait ce qui se passait en elle ; il respectait les souvenirs qu'il sentait se réveiller en son cœur, tout en lui répétant encore, avec une délicatesse infinie, les plus tendres serments.

Durant toute la période qui venait de s'écouler, il s'était trouvé en proie, sans rien en dire à qui que ce fût, à un vif débat de conscience : Charley Vanhern, par un testament déposé chez un notaire la veille de son départ, avait désigné sa fille adoptive comme héritière de tous ses biens. De cette fortune Philippe connaissait la source indigne et il s'était d'abord révolté à la pensée que sa fiancée pût la lui apporter en dot. Mais il s'était représenté d'autre part qu'il lui était impossible en même temps de lui conseiller, de lui imposer de refuser ce legs sans en arriver fatalement par là même à trahir le serment prêté à Vanhern. Et il s'était résigné à ne pas intervenir, bien résolu en même temps à ne profiter jamais en rien de cette fortune. Celle qu'il possédait en propre, l'argent qu'il commençait à gagner largement dans l'exercice de sa profession, lui suffisaient d'ailleurs amplement à assurer le très large bien-être de son futur ménage.

Bien qu'annoncée par les principaux journaux, la nouvelle du prochain mariage de Mr. Philippe Peyton avec miss Mary Vanhern passa complètement inaperçue dans le quartier où, durant un si grand nombre d'années, avait vécu « le manchot » et où, pendant très longtemps, « le père Tom », mort depuis peu, avait été seul à connaître son véritable nom.

Mais Baxter « l'homme aux yeux blancs » veillait sournoisement dans l'ombre.

Il n'avait jamais pardonné à celui dont il était parvenu à surprendre le secret, la rude correction qu'il en avait reçue. Étonné tout autant que ses camarades de ne plus le voir apparaître au bar Ramon, il s'en était allé au bout de deux ou trois jours rôder aux alentours de la villa des Roses et là, en prêtant attentivement l'oreille de droite et de gauche à tous les bavardages des uns et des autres, en allant même frapper à la porte de la villa pour implorer la charité, il avait très vite connu la nouvelle du départ de Vanhern, puis peu après celle de sa disparition en mer. Mais s'il avait fait part à toute la clientèle du bar de la mort du « manchot », il n'avait pas soufflé mot par contre des fiançailles de la fille de Fanny Hirch dont il avait également eu vent avant même qu'elles aient été officiellement annoncées. Il avait reporté sur la jeune fille toute la haine dont il avait été animé naguère contre son père adoptif et il attendait l'occasion de l'assouvir. Il estima que le moment était venu d'agir lorsqu'il sut que le mariage était définitivement fixé à une date peu éloignée.

Certain après-midi il fit triomphalement son entrée dans le bar en brandissant un journal qui jouissait d'ailleurs de la triste réputation d'être à l'affût de tous les scandales et de ne vivre que de chantage. Dès le seuil il annonça :

— Écoutez tous, les amis. Voici de quoi vous faire rigoler.

A haute voix il lut ces quelques lignes qui s'étalaient en première page :

Plusieurs de nos confrères ont annoncé le prochain mariage d'un de nos jeunes et plus brillants avocats. Mais ils se sont bien gardés de donner aucun détail sur la charmante fiancée qui n'est autre que la fille adoptive d'un mendiant de la basse pègre. Très prochainement nous servirons à nos fidèles lecteurs, à ce sujet, de savoureux détails.

Puis il ricana :

— Eh bien quoi? Vous n'avez pas l'air de comprendre on dirait que vous tombez de la lune ! Vous n'avez pas encore deviné que c'est du « manchot » qu'il s'agit là, et que la « charmante fiancée » est tout simplement la môme Fanny Hirch?

Ce fut aussitôt un concert d'exclamations stupéfaites. Enchanté de son petit effet, le faux aveugle se vanta :

— J'avais une dent sérieuse contre cette brute de Charley, et maintenant qu'il a disparu de la circulation et qu'il n'y a rien à craindre de lui, j'aurais eu bien tort de me gêner, n'est-ce pas? C'est moi qui ai éventé la mèche et qui l'ai vendue un bon prix. Et ce n'est pas fini. Je n'ai pas été assez poire pour donner au journal tous mes tuyaux d'un seul coup. La suite au prochain numéro ! Je n'ai pas pu me venger sur ce sale type, je me rattraperai sur sa fille adoptive... laissez-moi rire... et par-dessus le marché ça me rapporte un joli bénéfice.

Un homme était entré depuis quelques instants, auquel nul n'avait prêté attention. Il sortit soudain du coin d'ombre où il s'était dissimulé et surgit devant Baxter. La physionomie de celui-ci refléta aussitôt une inexprimable épouvante. Il eut un mouvement de recul tandis qu'il disait, qu'il balbutiait plutôt d'une voix rauque :

— Le manchot !

Sans prendre garde à la stupeur des assistants, le nouveau venu parut se repaître un instant de la folle terreur qui se lisait sur les traits du misérable puis, menaçant, il prononça :

— ... Oui, le *manchot*... Charley en chair et en os, et non pas un revenant ni un fantôme. Tu me croyais bien mort, n'est-ce pas? Il te faut déchanter. Après l'accident que j'ai simulé, j'ai gagné la côte à la nage, je me suis caché et je suis revenu pour veiller dans l'ombre sur le bonheur de mon enfant. Quand j'ai lu cette infamie, j'ai compris que le coup ne pouvait venir que de toi, et je ne me suis pas trompé, bandit, puisque tu étais en train de t'en glorifier.

Le faux aveugle avait repris quelque assurance. Il siffla :

— Je n'ai pas de raisons de m'en cacher. Qu'est-ce que tu en dis? Ne crains-tu pas que ton ami l'avocat paierait un bon prix pour que les journaux n'en dégoisent pas plus long?

Pour toute réponse, Vanhern lui envoya son poing en pleine face. L'autre, écumant de rage bondit sur lui. Un terrible corps à corps s'engagea. En une minute les deux adversaires eurent le visage ruisselant de sang. Un instant terrassé par Baxter qui après lui avoir traîtreusement donné un croc-en-jambe, le maintenait à terre sous lui et le serrait à la gorge, Vanhern dans un suprême effort, réussit à se dégager. L'écume aux lèvres « l'homme aux yeux blancs » s'élança de nouveau contre lui. Encore haletant, l'ancien « manchot », pour parer son attaque, n'eut que le temps de saisir un tabouret dont il se fit une sorte de bouclier. Emporté par son élan, Baxter alla y donner du front avec la plus grande violence. Il chancela et s'écroula sur le plancher. Il y eut quelques secondes de tragique silence et puis, péniblement, le misérable se releva sur les genoux. Il avait les yeux grands ouverts, presque exorbités, et ce n'était plus la rage et la haine qui crispaient ses traits, mais une tragique angoisse. Il bégaya :

— Que se passe-t-il donc?... On dirait qu'il fait nuit...

Il demeurait immobile, comme figé et tout autour de lui courut un murmure épouvanté. Il en comprit la signification et il eut un hoquet qui n'avait presque rien d'humain. Sous le choc qu'il venait de subir, ses yeux déjà affaiblis s'étaient éteints à jamais... Il n'aurait plus à contrefaire l'aveugle... il ne l'était plus désormais que trop réellement. L'horrible catastrophe qui s'abattait sur lui remua tout son être, chavira ses

La mariée venait d'apparaître.

sentiments, éteignit ses haines. Il frémissait de terreur à la pensée que c'était le châtiment qui commençait, le châtiment de sa fourberie, de ses lâches et perfides machinations, de toutes les mauvaises actions qu'il avait très longtemps accumulées... A tâtons, ses mains s'agrippèrent aux jambes de Vanhern, montèrent presque jusqu'à la ceinture de celui-ci. De ses yeux morts, des larmes se mirent à couler, lourdement, et il supplia, il gémit :

— Oh! par pitié. ne me quitte pas, Charley. J'ai été bien coupable vis-à-vis de toi, mais cette fois, Dieu m'a puni, je n'y vois plus !

Alors, doucement, la main du « manchot » se posa sur l'épaule de l'ennemi terrassé qui implorait son assistance, sa protection. Il l'aida à se relever et au milieu de l'émotion générale il prononça :

— Appuie-toi sur moi... rassure-toi, je ne t'abandonnerai pas.

***

A proximité des marches d'une des plus élégantes églises de New-York, deux hommes misérablement vêtus se trouvaient mêlés à la foule des badauds qui attendaient la sortie d'un grand mariage. L'un, la sébile à la main et indifférent à tout, regardait sans voir de ses yeux éteints à jamais. L'autre, de taille élancée, se dissimulait de son mieux derrière son compagnon ; il tenait ses regards fixés sur le porche dont les lourds battants venaient de s'écarter, laissant entendre les échos triomphants d'une marche nuptiale.

Un grand remous se produisit parmi la foule. La mariée, toute jeune, et d'une délicate beauté, venait d'apparaître et commençait à descendre les degrés, doucement appuyée au bras d'un jeune homme sur la physionomie duquel pouvait se lire l'expression du plus vif bonheur. Une somptueuse limousine les attendait.

— Ma petite Marysette... murmura l'un des deux pauvres hères.

Il y avait des sanglots dans sa gorge, des larmes dans ses yeux.

— Que dis-tu? demanda l'aveugle d'une voix morne en se retournant vers son compagnon d'infortune. Pourquoi me serres-tu si fort le bras?

— Rien... Ce n'est rien.

Les deux mariés disparurent dans leur automobile. Alors Charley le manchot — nos lecteurs l'ont déjà reconnu — ferma les yeux comme en proie à quelque éblouissement. Il chancela presque. Mais faisant effort sur lui-même il s'éloigna le front lourd, à pas lents, avec « l'homme aux yeux blancs ».

La tentative de chantage amorcée par ce dernier n'avait pas eu de lendemain. Toujours Marysette devait ignorer que « papa Charley » lui avait tout sacrifié, sacrifié non seulement tout son bonheur sur terre, mais encore sa vie : ne demeurait-il pas en effet volontairement mort à ses yeux, mort aussi à tout espoir d'avenir !

Redevenu « Charley le manchot », courbé sous le poids du destin, n'ayant plus aucun but à atteindre puisque sa chère enfant était heureuse, sans énergie pour réagir, il s'en allait avec l'aveugle vers le bar Ramon... parmi les « hommes oubliés ».

Fin

Yves MIROËL.

The Street of Forgotten Men: From Story to Screen and Beyond

Japanese magazine page – 1926

Swedish movie poster – 1926

German promotional piece – 1926

French movie poster – 1927

AROUND THE WORLD

Film exhibition practices during the silent era differ from those of today. For example, not every film played everywhere around the world. And what's more, those films which did show abroad might open a year or two or even three after they first played in the United States. Films were also promoted, advertised, shown, cut, and censored differently – based on the local language and local practices. Notably, such differences might well go beyond an alternative or foreign language title to include differing subtitles, differing lengths, and more.

Under its American title, documented screenings of *The Street of Forgotten Men* took place in Australia (including Tasmania), Bermuda, Canada, China, Hong Kong, Ireland, Jamaica, Korea, New Zealand, Panama, South Africa, and the United Kingdom (namely England, Isle of Man, Northern Ireland, Scotland, and Wales). Elsewhere around the world, *The Street of Forgotten Men* was shown under the title *L'école des mendiants* (Algeria); *Die Straße des Grauens* (Austria); *De School der Bedelaars* (Belgium); *O mendigo elegante* and *Um mendigo elegante* (Brazil); *La calle del olvido* (Chile); *La calle del olvido* (Cuba); *Ulice zapomenutých mužu* (Czechoslovakia); *Tiggerkongen* (Denmark); *De Straat der Ellendigen* (Dutch East Indies); *De Straat der verlaten Wezens* (Dutch Guiana); *Varjojen lapsi* (Finland); *L'école des mendiants* – primarily, but also on a few occasions as *Le roi des mendiants* and *La rue des hommes perdus* (France); *Die Straße des Grauens* (Germany); *Konungur Betlaranna* (Iceland); 或る乞食の話 or *Aru kojiki no hanashi* (Japan); *L'école des mendiants* (Luxembourg); *La calle del olvido* (Mexico); *De School der Bedelaars* and *De Vakschool der bedelaars* (The Netherlands); *Varjojen lapsia* (Norway); *Vidas Perdidas* (Portugal); *La calle del olvido* (Spain); *Skuggornas barn* (Sweden), and Улица забытых людей (U.S.S.R.).

The Street of Forgotten Men played in North Africa, parts of Asia, Australia and the Pacific, and much of Latin America. In Cuba, for example, a Havana newspaper, *Diario de la Marina*, reported large crowds turned out for what it described as a "masterful film," (5-31-1926), an "intense drama" (6-9-1926), and a "great attraction" (6-17-1926) during the film's extended run in the Caribbean city.

The Street of Forgotten Men was well received in Europe. In the United Kingdom, one of the major trade journals, *Kinematograph Weekly*, reported business was brisk wherever the film was shown. Glasgow, for example, was said to have had "a very good week," as did Barnsley, despite the fact many local picturegoers were out of work due to a coal dispute. (6-3-1926) The film also went over big in Liverpool, despite three films showing locally which starred the recently deceased Rudolph Valentino. At the time, in September, 1926, an ad in the *Liverpool Echo* proclaimed "Crowds were still wanting a seat." *Kinematograph Weekly* summed-up the film's U.K. run, stating "The success of this picture served to illustrate that there has been a strong advancement in public taste since the days of *The Miracle Man*, of which the new Paramount film is somewhat reminiscent." (9-31-1926) Later, in Leeds, *The Street of Forgotten Men* followed up its first-run success "with splendid results … where business over three days was the best experienced in some time." (10-14-1926)

The Street of Forgotten Men also went over well in Ireland. Herbert Brenon was born in Dún Laoghaire, and the celebrated director of *Peter Pan* was given the honor of having this newest work shown at Dublin's La Scala theatre, then the largest cinema house in the country, where it played in July of 1926.

On the continent, the Austrian trade journal *Paimann's Filmlisten* praised the film, writing "The subject is rich in poignant moments, though strongly influenced by its largely gloomy milieu. The acting is very good in all roles, especially Percy Marmont who gives a remarkable performance. The photography is good, as well as the presentation." (6-11-1926) Austria's *Der Filmbote* agreed, declaring *Die Straße des Grauens* a "gripping film that is downright masterful in its portrayal of its milieu." (6-19-1926) Elsewhere on the continent, the Paris newspaper *Le Soir* thought the film "among the best of recent years." (5-7-1927)

CITIZENS OF AUCKLAND
WHERE IN THIS CITY IS
"THE STREET OF FORGOTTEN MEN?"

Among the first overseas screenings of *The Street of Forgotten Men* was this showing at the Olympia in Stockholm, Sweden where the film played under the title *Skuggornas barn* (*The Children of the shadows*). This page shows three different advertisements for that showing, including two on the right announcing the film's local premiere. The ad to the left feature snippets from the film's local reviews. One Swedish reviewer said it was an "unusually strong film, captivating and gripping throughout." Another thought it a work of masterful realism, suggesting Brenon a disciple of Chaplin. Stockholm, Sweden – January-February 1926

O MENDIGO ELEGANTE

FILM DA "PARAMOUNT" COM A SEGUINTE DISTRIBUIÇÃO

Charley, "O Fura-Vidas"	PERCY MARMONT
Mary	MARY BRIAN
Philip Reyton	NEIL HAMILTON
O "Quebra-Trincos"	John Harrington
Dolly	Josephine Deffrey
Fancy	Juliet Brenon
Diamond Mike	Riley Hatch
Adolphe	Agostino Borgato
Nannie Mac Gee	Dorothy Walters
Jim M	Albert Riccard

No bairro dos pobres, em Nova York, no tempo das anquinhas e dos bondes por tracção animal, o logar de reunião favorito da gatunagem era o botequim da Folia, do velho Diamond Mike.

Uma "Fabrica de Aleijões" funccionava na Sala dos Fundos, transformando corpos sadios e perfeitos, em invalidos capazes de inspirar compaixão.

Adolpho, o inventor genial dos "aleijados" que tanto lucro dão á fabrica, trabalha alli em sua arte e quando os estropeados deformados e desfigurados mendigos sahem do "estabelecimento" promptos para pedir esmolas durante o dia, elle lhes entrega para distribuirem aos transeuntes, cartões com os seguintes dizeres:

"Quem dá aos pobres empresta a Deus, porque a esmola livra os infelizes de um infortunio constante."

Exasperado por não poder obter esse animalsinho, o supposto cego atira-o para a rua e um barril de cerveja, que naquelle momento estava sendo descarregado de uma carroça, esmaga o pobre cão, matando-o instantaneamente.

A colera de Charley quasi o obriga a bater no cégo, mas convencido de que elle não tinha feito aquillo de proposito sua ira transforma-se em dôr pungente.

Fancy, uma "sereia" que frequentava muito o botequim da Folia e que talvez por ser mãi de uma menina de seis annos, é dotada de nobres sentimentos, assiste á morte do "Figaro". Pobre e doente, Fancy sente que tambem está prestes a morrer, sem achar um protector que possa tomar conta de sua filhinha depois da sua morte.

Uma ideia se apodera d'ella. Pedir a Charley para ser o tutor de sua filhinha.

— Charley, nunca tiveste uma amizade pela qual fosses capaz de passar por soffrimentos e privações? Se a tivesse, ficasse sendo o tutor da minha filhinha. Tens bom coração, tens dinheiro e não te embriagas! Quem protege a infancia, terá todas as bençãos do céu na velhice. Não terás que gastar com ella muito mais do que gastavas com teu cachorrinho! Não te has de arrepender. Minha filha Mary, é muito bôasinha.

— Eu, nunca servi de "ama secca", mas prometto tomar conta da tua filha, se por desgraça morreres.

— Eu te peço que tomes conta de minha filha.

A velha ama viu que Mary recusava aceitar a proposta de casamento de Reyton.

Charley, "O Fura-Vidas", recebe mais esmolas em um dia do que todos os seus collegas em um mez e sua sorte é invejada por um collega o "Quebra Trincos", que se considera mais habil do que seus companheiros de officio, porque todos pensam que elle é cégo, tal a perfeição com que imita um homem privado da vista. O unico, que conhece seu segredo, é Adolphe, o dono da "fabrica".

A unica affeição de Charley é seu cachorrinho "Figaro" e o "Quebra-Trincos" ao voltar para casa em um dia de poucas esmolas, diz-lhe:

— Charley, és tu? Recebeste muitas esmolas?

— Sim, "Quebra-Trincos", recebi cento e cincoenta e dois dollares e vinte e sete centavos.

— Eu já me contentava com a metade, mas nem isso recebi! Eu, que sou o Rei dos Mendigos! Podias me ceder teu cachorro "Figaro" para me conduzir pelas ruas. Quanto queres por elle? Garanto-te que não quero que me faças presente d'elle! Quero compral-o!

— Amigo "Quebra-Trincos" não ha bastante dinheiro no mundo para me tentar a vendel-o!

A SCENA MUDA — 6.º ANNO — N. 261

No primeiro impeto de colera, Charley teve a tentação de bater no cego.

Mary apresentou seu tutor com um sorriso feliz.

Uma conferencia com um tabellião, um chamado urgente a um medico e dias depois, Fancy morria de uma syncope cardiaca.

Charley conduz a criança para casa e diz á sua velha criada Nannie:

— Sou muito feliz! Adoptei uma criança!

— Adoptou? Ella não é de facto sua filha?

— Não, mas vai ser! Prometta que me ha de auxiliar a tomar conta d'ella!

— Prometto!

Entretanto, no botequim da Folia, já todos sabiam que Charley estava servindo de "ama secca" e quando elle alli volta é recebido com apupos e chalaças. Envergonhado elle nega ter adoptado a criança.

Decorrem doze annos e depois de terminada a grande guerra, novas leis existiam em Nova York, menos no botequim da Folia.

Charley reside em uma casa de campo com Mary, sua filha adoptiva e a sua velha criada Nannie. Possuidor agora de uma grande fortuna, faz todas as vontades a Mary, cumprindo assim a promessa que fez a Fancy. Continua, porem, a mendigar. Durante o exercicio de seu vil officio, anda sujo e esfarrapado, para depois, ao voltar para a sua casa de campo, trajar mais elegantemente do que o mais rico millionario de Nova York.

(Continúa na pag. 40).

O advogado Philip Reyton apaixonára-se por Mary.

(Above) Paramount films played big in Brazil, the largest and most populous nation in South America. This three-page spread in *A Scena Muda*, one of the country's leading film magazines, features a summary of the film story which includes a rare depiction of Louise Brooks. As such, it is likely one of only two times the actress was included in a published image from the film anywhere in the world. Brazil – March 1926

(Following page) *O mendigo elegante* also received feature coverage in *Cinearte*, the other significant Brazilian film journal. This three-page spread likewise ends with a rather unusual image, a production still of *The Street of Forgotten Men* with a solitary figure standing in the middle of the film's titular street. Brazil – March 1926

O MENDIGO ELEGANTE

No bairro dos pobres, em Nova York, no tempo das anquinhas e dos bondes puxados por tracção animal, o logar de reunião favorito da gatunagem era o Botequim da Folia do velho Diamond Mike.

Uma "Fabrica de Aleijões" funccionava na Sala dos Fundos, transformando corpos sadios e perfeitos, em invalidos que inspiravam compaixão.

Adolphe, o inventor genial dos "aleijados" que tanto lucro dão á "fabrica" trabalha na sua arte.

Charley, "O Fura-Vidas", recebe mais esmolas em um dia do que todos os seus collegas em um mez e a sua sorte é invejada pelo "Quebra-Trincos", que se considera mais habil do que os seus companheiros de officio, p o r q u e todos pensam que elle é cégo, tal é a perfeição com que imita um homem privado da vista. O unico que conhece o seu segredo, é Adolphe, o dono da "fabrica".

A unica affeição de Charley é o seu cachorrinho "Figaro" e o "Quebra-Trincos" ao voltar para casa em um dia de poucas esmolas, diz-lhe:

— Charley, és tu? Recebeste muitas esmolas?
— Sim, uns cento e cincoenta e dois dollars e vinte e sete centavos.
— Charley, eu já me contentava com a metade, mas nem isso ganhei!

O teu cachorro "Figaro" devia ser meu. Poderia conduzir-me pelas ruas. Quanto queres? Garanto-te que não quero que me faças presente delle! Quero compral-o!

— Amigo "Quebra-Trincos", não ha bastante dinheiro no mundo para me tentar a vendel-o!

Exasperado por não poder c o m p r a r o animalsinho, o supposto cégo atira-o para a rua, mas um barril de cerveja que naquelle momento estava sendo descarregado de uma carroça, esmaga o pobre cão matando-o instantaneamente.

A colera de Charley quasi que o obriga a bater no cégo, mas convencido de que elle não tinha feito aquillo de proposito, a sua ira transforma-se em uma dôr pungente.

Fancy, uma "sereia" que frequentava muito o Botequim da Folia e que talvez por ser mãe de uma menina de seis annos, é dotada de nobres sentimentos, assiste á morte do "Figaro". Pobre e doente, Fancy sente que tambem vae morrer, sem achar um protector que pudesse tomar conta da sua filha depois da sua morte.

Uma idéa apodera-se della. Pediria a Charley para ser o tutor da sua filhinha.

— Charley, nunca tiveste uma amizade pela qual fosses capaz de passar por soffrimentos e privações? Se a tiveste, fica sendo o tutor da minha filhinha. T e n s bom coração,

tens d i n h e i r o e não te embriagas! Quem protege a infancia, terá todas as commodidades durante a velhice. Não terás que gastar muito mais do que gastavas com o teu cachorrinho! Não te has de arrepender. A minha filhinha Mary é muito boasinha.

— Fancy, nunca servi de "ama secca", mas prometto t o m a r conta da tua filha depois da tua morte.

U m a conferencia com um tabellião, um chamado urgente a um medico e, dias depois, F a n c y morria de uma syncope cardiaca.

Charley conduz a c r e a n ç a para casa.

Entretanto, no Botequim da Folia, já todos sabiam q u e Charley estava servindo de "ama secca" e q u a n d o elle volta é recebido c o m apupos e chalaças. Para attenuar a troça que todos lhe faziam, nega ter adoptado a creança.

Decorrem doze annos e depois de terminada a grande guerra, novas leis existiam em Nova York, menos no Botequim da Folia.

Charley r e s i d e em uma casa de campo com Mary, a sua filha adopti-

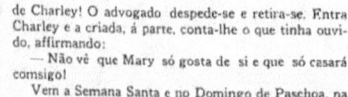

va e a sua velha criada Nannie. Possuidor de uma grande fortuna, faz todas as vontades a Mary, cumprindo assim a promessa que tinha feito a Fancy. Continúa, porém, a mendigar. Durante o seu vil officio, anda sujo e esfarrapado, para depois, ao voltar para a casa de campo, trajar mais elegantemente do que o mais rico millionario de Nova York.

Philip Reyton, um joven e rico advogado, apaixona-se por Mary, a quem diz:

— Ainda não me disse que parentesco existe entre si e Charley?

— Nenhum... elle é meu tutor! Ah, se soubesse como elle é bom e forte!

— Mary, não fale assim! Bem sabe que a amo!

— O amor é um sorriso de luz na treva da vida, mas eu não quero me casar... nunca poderei me separar de Charley! O advogado despede-se e retira-se. Entra Charley e a criada, á parte, conta-lhe o que tinha ouvido, affirmando:

— Não vê que Mary só gosta de si e que só casará comsigo!

Vem a Semana Santa e no Domingo de Paschoa, na Quinta Avenida, onde as classes privilegiadas da sociedade se reunem para demonstrar que conhecem a arte de bem vestir, prestando assim uma justa homenagem á "Sua Majestade a Moda", Charley vae passear com Mary, trajando ambos ao côrte dos ultimos figurinos.

Depois do passeio, Charley leva Mary para casa e sem poder esquecer que ella só seria feliz casando com elle, resolve contar tudo ao advogado Reyton.

— Philip, tenho confiança em si e desejo que saiba quem eu sou! Como sei que deseja casar com Mary, tambem tem o direito de saber que ella é filha de uma

(Continúa no fim do numero).

UMA MONTAGEM DO FILM "O MENDIGO ELEGANTE".

The film, *O Mendigo Elegante*, which translates into English as *The Elegant Beggar*, was the subject of interest in Brazil, as evidenced by the preceding feature stories published in the country's film magazines.

O Mendigo Elegante

(FIM)

mulher de má reputação, mas de bons sentimentos!

Charley, aguas passadas não moem moinhos! Amo Mary e desejo casar com ella!

— Bem, desde já approvo esse casamento, mas antes vae saber quem eu sou! Sou um mendigo profissional que obtem esmolas pelo ardil e pela manha, em n o m e da caridade! Chamam-me Charley, "O Fura-Vidas" e ganho "rios de dinheiro", porque conheço a fundo a psychologia do sentimento! Nasci para esse mistér! É mais forte do que a minha vontade! Não posso viver sem mendigar! Resolvi, portanto, ir para a Australia. Não quero manchar a vida de Mary! Adeus!

Charley, porém, não p a r t e para a Australia, para poder continuar, mesmo de longe, a proteger a mulher que tanto ama. Soffre torturas immensas e para mitigal-as resolve continuar a mendigar. Sujo e esfarrapado, ninguem o reconheceria.

No dia do casamento de Mary com Philip, vae assistir da rua, com o "Quebra-Trincos" que em uma luta tinha ficado realmente cégo, ao enlace da mulher que adora.

— Charley, por que estás apertando o meu braço? O que aconteceu?

— Nada, amigo "Quebra-Trincos"! Estou hoje com saudades do passado!

— Charley, o que vamos fazer agora?

— Vamos continuar a soffrer neste valle de martyrios!

E com os semblantes transfigurados p e l a vehemencia da saudade, os dois mendigos afastam-se lentamente, e m quanto que Mary e Philip, ao sahirem do templo, são mimoseados com uma chuva de flores e confettis.

O MENDIGO ELEGANTE

(THE STREET OF FORGOTTEN MEN)

Film da Paramount

DISTRIBUIÇÃO:

Charley.......... Percy Marmont
Mary............. Mary Brian
Philip Reyton.... Neil Hamilton
O "Quebra-Trincos"........ John Harrington
Dolly............ Josephine Deffrey
Diamond Mike... Riley Hatch

(Left) A bobbed-hair young women standing in the street can be seen in the lower middle of this rare production still. In front of her is a man with a hat – quite possibly director Brenon – holding a megaphone while cast and crew stand alongside. To their right is a large arc lamp. Cutting through the image is part of the studio set. Brazil – March 1926

To sell a somewhat gritty film, this promotional page recalls Mary Brian's tender role in *Peter Pan*, the popular prior film by Herbert Brenon. China – 1926

(Left) The text beneath the names of stars Percy Marmont and Mary Brian speaks of the miserable lives led by the characters, whom, it is noted, live in big cities. Reykjavík, Iceland – February 1928

(Lower left) One of the last documented European screenings of the film took place at the Biografteatern on the Åboland archipelago in southwestern Finland. The words "Förbjudet för barn" notes children were prohibited from seeing the film. Pargas, Finland – April 1929

(Right) A newspaper ad published in *The Beiping chenbao* (北平晨報), a Chinese newspaper published in the capitol. Beiping (or Beijing), China – March 1931

(Above) Aside from the invitation to British troops to visit the Navy Y.M.C.A., this otherwise insignificant clipping from an English-language newspaper is noteworthy on another account, it marks the last documented public screening of *The Street of Forgotten Men* for more than five decades. Shanghai, China – September 1931

Herbert Brenon Productions and *The Street of Forgotten Men* were highlighted in Paramount's promotion of its Greater Forty films of 1925.

CAST, CREDITS & TRIVIA

Studio: Famous-Players Lasky
Distributor: Paramount
Presenter (Producer): Adolph Zukor and Jesse L. Lasky
Director: Herbert Brenon
Writing Credits: George Kibbe Turner (story), John Russell (adaptation), Paul Schofield (screen play)
Cinematography: Hal Rosson (Harold Rosson)
Art Direction (Production Designer): Frederick A. Foord
Format: Silent – black & white
Running Time: 7 reels (6,366 feet), or 76 minutes; elsewhere – Austria: 970 meters, or 6463 feet, in 8 acts. United Kingdom: 6,000 and 6,009 feet.
Copyright: August 22, 1925 by Famous Players-Lasky Corporation (LP21769)
Release Date: August 24, 1925
Premiere: July 19, 1925 (Rivoli Theater, NYC)
Cast: Percy Marmont as Easy Money Charlie; Mary Brian as Fancy (or Mary) Vanhern; Neil Hamilton as Philip Peyton; John Harrington as Bridgeport White-Eye; Juliet Brenon as Portland Fancy; Josephine Deffry as Dutch Dolly; Riley Hatch as Diamond Mike; Agostino Borgato as Adolphe; Albert Roccardi as Adolphe's helper; Dorothy Walters as Widow McGee; Lassie as The Dog cared for Easy Money Charlie (uncredited); Whitney Bolton as a Bum (uncredited); Louise Brooks as a Moll who associates with Bridgeport White-Eye (uncredited); John Kiernan as the streetcar driver (uncredited); Harry Lewis as man in the bar (uncredited); Anita Louise as a flower girl (uncredited); Elizabeth Meehan as woman who encounters a friend (uncredited); Joe Trudden as hearse drive (uncredited); unknown as Officer Quinn (uncredited); unknown as Bertram the Barber (uncredited); unknown as Blind Ben (uncredited); unknown as Dumb Dan (uncredited); unknown as Harry the Hop

(uncredited); and unknown as Legless Lew (uncredited). According to both *Exhibitors Herald* and *Motion Picture News*, Raymond Hatton had an unknown (though unconfirmed) role in the film.

Two other individuals who made uncredited behind-the-camera contributions to the film were **Harold C. Hendee** (head of the research department at Paramount's Long Island studio), and **H. M. K. Smith** (head of the costume department). Each were mentioned in reportage from the time as having assisted in the production.

Another individual involved in the making of the film was mendicant officer **John D. Godfrey** (1863-1950). According to the studio Press Sheet, this veteran of the Brooklyn Bureau of Charity served as a technical adviser regarding beggars and begging and for the scenes shot inside the backroom of the bar, the so-called "cripple factory." Notably, Godfrey's involvement with the film was repeatedly mentioned in his hometown paper, the *Brooklyn Daily Times*.

A production still showing Herbert Brenon (standing right, with a white brimmed hat), John D. Godfrey (seated), and some of the uncredited background players. *Author collection*

Herbert Brenon (1880-1958) was an Irish-born film director, actor and screenwriter who worked much of his life in the United States. Though not especially well known today, Brenon was among the first great names behind the camera, a gifted director once spoken of alongside D.W. Griffith and Cecil B. DeMille. Not only did Brenon direct dozens of films – perhaps more than 100 – between 1912 and 1940, he also acted in them, oversaw their cinematography, and was their sometime writer and sometime editor.

Born near Dublin, Brenon emigrated to the United States in 1896. He began as an office boy, working his way up to stage actor and scriptwriter, and for a time, manager of a small-town nickelodeon. He directed his first film, a one-reeler, in 1911. Two years later, he directed a lavish four-reel *Ivanhoe* and an acclaimed two-reel *Dr. Jekyll and Mr. Hyde*; both feature King Baggot. He followed these successes with the seven-reel *Neptune's Daughter* (1914), a fantasy starring swimming star Annette Kellerman that shattered attendance records at the time. In 1915, Brenon directed Theda Bara in four features. A year later, he made *War Brides*, which marked the screen debut of theater great Alla Nazimova. Other significant early works include another Annette Kellerman vehicle, *A Daughter of the Gods* (1916) – from which his name was removed over a dispute with the studio, and *Empty Pockets* (1918).

Herbert Brenon is now busy with the business of directing "The Street of Forgotten Men," featuring Percy Marmont and Mary Brian

Brenon hit his stride in the 1920s. *The Spanish Dancer* (1923), starring Pola Negri, stands out. As do the two films characteristic of the "Brenon style" – *Peter Pan* (1924) and *A Kiss for Cinderella* (1925). Each were theatrical adaptions of J.M. Barrie fantasies, and each proved hugely popular. Brenon's most accomplished dramatic effort is *Beau Geste* (1926), starring Ronald Colman. It won the *Photoplay* Medal of Honor, one of the industry's first awards recognizing the best picture of the year. Brenon made three more significant pictures that same year:

God Gave Me Twenty Cents with Lois Moran and Lya De Putti, *Dancing Mothers* with Alice Joyce and Clara Bow, and *The Great Gatsby*, the first adaption of F. Scott Fitzgerald's era-defining novel of the Jazz Age. *Sorrell and Son* (1927) earned a Best Director nomination at the first Academy Awards. The following year, he directed film great Lon Chaney in *Laugh, Clown, Laugh* (1928), Brenon's last silent release.

Among the sound films that followed are *The Case of Sergeant Grischa* (1930) and *Lummox* (1930), the later based on the novel by Fannie Hurst. Brenon's film career began to lose its luster with the transition to sound, but revived somewhat when he moved back to England in the mid-1930s. There, he made a number of pictures at Elstree and other studios, including the well-regarded *The Housemaster* (1938). He completed his last film, *The Flying Squad*, in 1940, and later retired to Hollywood.

Noted for his imaginative use of light, Hal Rosson, or **Harold Rosson** (1895-1988) was one of the most celebrated cinematographers of his time. Awarded an Honorary Oscar for the color cinematography seen in *The Garden of Allah* (1936), Rosson was also nominated for his work in five other films, *The Wizard of Oz* (1939), *Boom Town* (1940), *Thirty Seconds Over Tokyo* (1944), *The Asphalt Jungle* (1950), and *The Bad Seed* (1956). Notably, in 1933, he married actress Jean Harlow.

Rosson began his film career in 1908 as an actor at the Vitagraph Studios in Brooklyn. Eventually, he quit acting to become an assistant to director of photography Irvin Willat. Moving on to Famous Players in 1912, he served as a jack-of-all-trades, working as an assistant, extra, and even handyman. Among his first films as a cameraman are *David Harum* (1915), and *Oliver Twist* (1916). Early on, he also worked for the Kalem Company and Essanay before his career was interrupted by the first World War, during which he served in the army.

After demobilization, Rosson got a job as assistant cameraman on *The Dark Star* (1919), which featured Marion Davies. He worked for Davies' production company, Cosmopolitan Productions, before being signed by Mary Pickford to shoot movies starring her brother, Jack Pickford.

Rosson shot eight films for Allan Dwan between 1915 and 1929, and another with Brenon, *The Little French Girl* (1925). Other notable early films shot by Rosson include *Zaza* (1923) with Gloria Swanson, *Evening Clothes* (1927) with Adolphe Menjou and

Louise Brooks, and *Rough House Rosie* (1927) with Clara Bow, as well as *Gentlemen Prefer Blondes* (1928) and *The Docks of New York* (1928). Eventually, he rejoined Metro (which became Metro-Goldwyn-Mayer), and that is where he made his name. His later films include *Tarzan the Ape Man* (1932), *Red-Headed Woman* (1932), *Red Dust* (1932), *The Scarlet Pimpernel* (1934), *Treasure Island* (1934), *As You Like It* (1936), *Captains Courageous* (1937), *Duel in the Sun* (1946), *On the Town* (1949), and *Singin' in the Rain* (1952). He came out of retirement to film Howard Hawks' *El Dorado* (1966), which starred John Wayne.

Motion Picture News, 1930

John Russell (1885-1956) started out as a journalist, short story writer, and novelist before getting into screenwriting. In 1910, his novel *The Society Wolf* was published under a pseudonym, Luke Thrice. A collection of short fiction, *The Red Mark and Other Stories* (later retitled *Where the Pavement Ends*) was published in 1919, followed by *In Dark Places* in 1923, *Far Wandering Men* in 1929, and other books.

Russell began working as a screenwriter in the early 1920s, sometimes adapting his own work. Among his significant credits are *The Iron Horse* (1924), the first major film from director John Ford, *Lord Jim* (1925), Victor Fleming's version of the Joseph Conrad novel starring Percy Marmont, and the fantasy film *The Sorrows of Satan* (1926), from director D. W. Griffith. Russell was also an uncredited contributor to the classic horror film, *Frankenstein* (1931). Besides adapting George Kibbe Turner's magazine story, Russell's other credits in association with Herbert Brenon include *The Little French Girl* (1925), *Beau Geste* (1926), and *God Gave Me Twenty Cents* (1926).

John Russell, who prepared the scenarios of "The Little French Girl" and "The Street of Forgotten Men," in which Mary Brian appeared for Paramount, is on his way to Alexandria Bay and Thousand Islands after returning to New York. Miss Brian met him in California for the first time just an hour before he started his trip, after he had adapted Conrad's "Lord Jim."

Exhibitors Herald, July 25, 1925

A handful of Russell's original stories and novels were turned into films. Among them are *Where the Pavement Ends* (1923), which was adapted and directed by Rex Ingram, *The Red Mark* (1928) directed by James Cruze, and *The Pagan* (1929), a Ramon Novarro film directed by W.S. Van Dyke. Other films adapted from Russell's fiction include *Side Street* (1929), *Girl of the Port* (1930), and *The Sea God* (1930) and its Spanish-language version, *El Dios del mar* (1930).

Russell's name continued to show-up in the trades through the mid-1930s. He was signed to write screenplays, original stories, or provide continuity for various studios including Fox (*The Painted Lady*, 1930), MGM (*The Half-Caste*, 1934), and RKO Radio Pictures (a series of mystery adventure films in 1932 with Merian C. Cooper), but all of these projects seem to have changed hands or not come about.

John **Paul Schofield** (1894-1963) was a well-regarded screenwriter during the silent and early sound era. He began his career as a newspaperman, initially as a reporter for the *Washington Herald* and then as editor and general manager of the *Frederick Post* in Maryland. Following a stint in the United States Army, Schofield relocated to Hollywood to convalesce after contracting influenza. There, according to a profile in July 16, 1927 issue of *Moving Picture World*, he met members of Tom Ince's company. Schofield submitted a couple of stories to Ince, which were rejected; nevertheless, the veteran journalist was brought on as a staff writer.

Schofield signed a contract with Ince Studios in October 1919. He remained with the company for fifteen months, all the while honing his craft. After leaving Ince, Schofield established himself as a free-lance writer, working on scripts for Fox, First National, Universal, Warner Bros. and others. In 1924, he wrote and produced *East of Broadway* for Associated Exhibitors. In 1925, Schofield wrote the scenario for *The Street of Forgotten Men* after signing a contract with Famous Players-Lasky. (In the scenario, Schofield is credited with providing the "continuity". On the film print, he is credited with writing the "screen play".) Like others associated with the film, he would work with Brenon on other projects including *The Song and Dance Man* (1926), *Beau Geste*

(1926), and *Beau Ideal* (1931). Among his more than 40 writing credits are John Ford's *Just Pals* (1920), Allan Dwan's *Night Life of New York* (1925), D.W. Griffith's *That Royle Girl* (1925), *Subway Sadie* (1926), *Just Another Blonde* (1926), and *Scandal* (1929). Schofield also reportedly wrote an early draft of the Paul Whiteman vehicle, *King of Jazz* (1930). Among his later efforts are *Sensation Hunters* (1933), Frank Lloyd's

Wells Fargo (1937), and *Mystery Plane* (1939), his last credit.

Schofield continued writing for newspapers, magazines, and radio. In 1941, Edward G. Robinson and Ona Munson starred in Schofield's radio play, *Behind the Garden Wall*, which was broadcast over the Columbia CBS network. During the second World War, he served in the United States Signal Corp.

The English-born actor **Percy Marmont** (1883-1977) was a major film star in the 1920s. Tall and debonair, Marmont first acted on stage in 1900. He made his screen debut in 1916 while touring South Africa with a theatrical troupe. From there, the troupe went to Australia, where Marmont appeared in a second film, and then in 1918 to the United States, where his film stardom took hold. Before his return to England in 1928, Marmont made nearly fifty films, working with some of the leading directors of the time (Clarence Badger, Frank Borzage, Victor Fleming), while appearing alongside many leading stars (Betty Compson, Corrine Griffith, Leatrice Joy, Alma Rubens).

PERCY MARMONT—can you believe it! These sunken eyes and hollow cheeks and broken teeth and drab gray locks are his in his new Paramount picture, "The Street of Forgotten Men." He plays the part of a beggar.

Who's Who on the Screen (1920) noted, "His first screen appearance in America was with Elsie Ferguson in *Rose of the World* and his popularity with lovers of the silent drama has grown steadily through his masterful characterizations in Goldwyn, Famous Players, and Vitagraph productions as well as by his work opposite Norma Talmadge with whom he recently finished *The Branded Woman*."

Marmont's role as Mark Sabre in *If Winter Comes* (1923) was widely praised. (That film included *Street* actor Riley Hatch in a supporting role, while another of Marmont's 1923 films, *Broadway Broke*, included Lassie, the dog Marmont's character looks after in *Street*.) Other films include *The Enemy Sex* (1924), *Lord Jim* (1925), with Marmont in the title role, *Fine Clothes*

(1925), *Aloma of the South Seas* (1926) with Gilda Gray, and most famously *Mantrap* (1926), starring Clara Bow.

In *Silent Players*, Anthony Slide quotes Marmont regarding *The Street of Forgotten Men*: "I came back from California to New York to make that with Herbert Brenon. He directed. Brenon was very efficient, a very difficult man, very temperamental. We became very good friends, but you had to be very tactful with Herbert Brenon. He had a lot of Irish blood in him, and you had to be very careful that you didn't tread on the tail of his coat. I trod on it several times, but we got over it."

Marmont left Hollywood in 1928; he returned to England and the British stage and also found parts in British films. *The Squeaker* (1930), written and directed by Edgar Wallace, was his first talkie. Other highlights of his U.K. work include supporting roles in two Alfred Hitchcock films, *Secret Agent* (1936) and *Young and Innocent* (1937). Marmont had a small part in the Hammer sci-fi film, *Four Sided Triangle* (1953), and played opposite Vivien Leigh in her last British stage appearance, *La Contessa* (1965).

Mary Brian (1906-2002) was considered one of Hollywood's prettiest actresses, an ingénue once described as "The Sweetest Girl in Pictures" and "The Girl of a Thousand-and-One Boy Friends." Brian entered films after losing a beauty contest. One of the contest judges, actress Esther Ralston, insisted Brian be given a consolation prize – an interview or screen test with Famous Players-Lasky. Brenon interviewed Brian, gave her a screen test, and soon cast her as Wendy Darling in his about-to-be filmed *Peter Pan* (1924). Brenon would go on to direct Brian in *The Little French Girl* (1925), *The Street of Forgotten Men* (1925), and *Beau Geste* (1926).

Brian was named a WAMPAS Baby Star in 1926. She was loaned out to MGM for *Brown of Harvard* (1926), opposite William Haines, and appeared with Wallace Beery in four films, *Behind the Front* (1926), *Partners in Crime* (1928), *The Big Killing* (1928), and

Mary Brian, who plays a featured role in Paramount's forthcoming picture, "The Street of Forgotten Men."

River of Romance (1929). Brian was also in three films with W.C. Fields, *Running Wild* (1927) and *Two Flaming Youths* (1927), and as Fields's daughter in *The Man on the Flying Trapeze* (1935). Other early films include Buster Keaton's *Battling Butler* (1926), and with Richard Dix in *Knockout Reilly* (1927), which included Lassie, the dog in *The Street of Forgotten Men*.

Brian made a successful transition to sound, and was featured in three classic talkies, *The Virginian* (1929) with Gary Cooper, *The Royal Family of Broadway* (1931), directed by George Cukor, and Lewis Milestone's adaptation of *The Front Page* (1931). Paramount chose not to renew her contract in 1932, and after that, she worked for both major and poverty row studios, including once again Paramount, for whom she made two films in 1934, *College Rhythm* and *Private Scandal*. Brian also worked in the U.K., and played opposite Cary Grant in *The Amazing Quest of Ernest Bliss* (1936). After stepping way from films in 1937, Brian appeared in stage productions, and during the second World War, helped entertain the troops. She appeared in a handful of lesser films in the 1940s, and worked briefly in television in the mid-1950s.

Neil Hamilton and Mary Brian play the young couple. *Author collection*

As Mary Brian was pretty, **Neil Hamilton** (1899-1984) was handsome. He began his career as a model, and most notably, was the famed model for Arrow Collars as drawn by the celebrated artist Joseph Leyendecker. In fact, Hamilton was so popular that he received fan mail, and modeled for other noted illustrators such as James Montgomery Flagg, Charles Dana Gibson, and Norman Rockwell.

Interested in acting, Hamilton joined several stock companies. He received his first film role in 1918, and received his first big break when he was cast in D. W. Griffith's *The White Rose* (1923). After performing in two more Griffith films, *Isn't Life Wonderful* (1924) and *America* (1924), Hamilton was signed by Paramount and soon became one of the studio's popular leading men. He appeared in a handful of Brenon films, *The Side Show of Life* (1924), *The Little French Girl* (1925), *The Street of Forgotten Men* (1925), *Beau Geste* (1926), and *The Great Gatsby* (1926).

Hamilton appeared opposite stars such as Bebe Daniels, Clara Bow, Esther Ralston, and Colleen Moore, and in films by significant directors including Allan Dwan, Dorothy Arzner, Clarence Badger and William DeMille. A busy actor during the Twenties, he also played in John Ford's *Mother Machree* (1928), Ernst Lubitsch's *The Patriot* (1928), and other well-regarded films.

Over the years, Hamilton's good looks and sophisticated manner kept him steadily employed, and at one time or another, he worked for just about every studio in Hollywood, from MGM to PRC on Poverty Row. Just as busy in the 1930s, Hamilton played in everything from *The Dawn Patrol* (1930) to *The Return of Dr. Fu Manchu* (1930), as well as *Tarzan the Ape Man* (1932) and *What Price Hollywood?* (1932).

When television came along, Hamilton co-starred in the short-lived sitcom *That Wonderful Guy* (1949–50) with Jack Lemmon, and did guest roles on numerous series of the 1950s and 1960s such as *Perry Mason*, *77 Sunset Strip*, *Maverick*, *Mister Ed*, and *The Outer Limits*. Despite his many accomplishments, Hamilton is today best known for his role as Police Commissioner Gordon in the *Batman* TV series and 1966 movie.

John Harrington (1882-1945) was already a veteran of the New York stage when he appeared in *The Street of Forgotten Men*, his first film. Harrington's stage career began in 1902, and he acted in numerous plays over the years including *Cameo Kirby* (1909), *The Bad Man* (1920), and *The Dove* (1925) – a David Belasco production starring Judith

Anderson which included *Street* actor Josephine Deffry. It was while Harrington was appearing in *The Dove* that he was seen by Brenon, with whom he had worked in the past. Brenon recruited Harrington for the role of Bridgeport White-Eye. *The Street of Forgotten Men* was made and released around the same time as another of Harrington's films, *The Man Who Found Himself* (1925). It starred Thomas Meighan, as did Harrington's next film, *Tin Gods* (1926). Other credits include parts in *Lulu Belle* (1926), *Local Boy Makes Good* (1931), *Young Sinners* (1931), *Mutiny on the Bounty* (1935), *Counterfeit Lady* (1936), *Swing Time* (1936), and *Step Lively, Jeeves!* (1937).

(Left) A newspaper clipping from May, 1925 and (Right) another from November, 1925.

Juliet Brenon (1885-1979) was the niece of director Herbert Brenon. Despite the fact each of her four films, *The Eternal Sin* (1917), *The Lone Wolf* (1917), *The Street of Forgotten Men* (1925), and *A Kiss for Cinderella* (1925), were directed by her uncle, Juliet was a talent in her own right. By the time she was cast in *The Street of Forgotten Men*, she had already acted in a number of stage plays (including *Nice People* with Tallulah Bankhead, in 1921) and garnered positive notices. In 1926, the *Los Angeles Times* reported Brenon was to be cast in another of her uncle's films, *The Great Gatsby* (1926), but that seems not to have come about.

Juliet Brenon was at the heart of an illustrious family. Her father was Algernon St. John-Brenon, esteemed music critic of the N.Y. *Morning Telegraph*. Her sister, Aileen, made a name for herself writing about the movies – while Aileen's husband was the noted art critic Thomas Craven. Juliet was married to Cleon Throckmorton, himself a noted American painter, theatrical designer, producer, and architect considered one of the most prolific set designers of the Jazz Age. During the 1930s, their Greenwich Village apartment became a salon for actors, artists, and intellectuals such as e.e. cummings, Noël Coward, Norman Bel Geddes, and notably, playwright Eugene O'Neill. Later, she contributed articles recounting her early life to *Yankee* magazine.

Josephine Deffry and Juliet Brenon in an early scene from the film. *Author collection*

The Missouri-born **Josephine Deffry** (1875-19??) started on the stage, touring the United States and appearing in various productions as early as 1899. In 1905, she scored successes starring in *A Broken Heart*, *A Deserted Bride*, and *A Wicked Woman* in Tacoma, Washington. Praised wherever she played as an "emotional" actress, she was soon heading the 10-member Josephine Deffry Company, staging *The Empire Against a Woman* and similar works in Nevada, Utah, Montana and elsewhere around the American West. When she performed in Roseville, California, the local newspaper stated, "Josephine Deffry is a pleasing actress and only lacks the reputation to be placed in the same class with Florence Roberts." (1-21-1909) In early 1925, she was seen in *The Dove*, a David Belasco production starring Judith Anderson which also included *Street* actor John Harrington.

In 1925, when *The Street of Forgotten Men* (her only known film credit) was shown in Twin Falls, Idaho, the local newspaper ran a story headlined, "Former Twin Falls Favorite in *Street of Forgotten Men*." The paper noted that Deffry, who many "will remember from her appearance here with her own stock company," added "to the characterization of the 'Old Bowery'." In 1926, she was in the supporting cast of *Love 'Em and Leave 'Em* when it was staged in Detroit. In 1928, she was among the cast of *Manhattan Mary*, a George White production which starred Ed Wynn. Deffry continued to act and tour throughout the 1930s, with her last known credit in 1939.

Like others in the cast of *The Street of Forgotten Men*, William **Riley Hatch** (1862-1925) acted both on stage and in the movies. His Broadway debut came in *The Burgomaster* (1900), followed by *Paid in Full* (1908), *Sherlock Holmes* (1910), *The Squaw Man* (1921), and *The Nervous Wreck* (1923), perhaps his best regarded role. Beginning in 1913, Hatch began appearing in films including a reprise of his celebrated role as Capt. Williams in *Paid in Full* (1914); there were also supporting roles in the Pearl White vehicles *The Exploits of Elaine* (1914) and *Hazel Kirke* (1916), *The Lone Wolf* (1917) – directed by Brenon, *Peck's Bad Girl* (1918), *Little Miss Rebellion* (1920), *The Conquest of Canaan* (1921), *Little Old New York* (1923), and Alan Dwan's *Zaza* (1923), and *Night Life of New York* (1925). Among his other credits are *If Winter Comes* (1923), which starred Percy Marmont, and D.W. Griffith's *America* (1924) which starred Neil Hamilton. Hatch died in September, 1925, shortly after the release of *The Street of Forgotten Men*.

Agostino Borgato (1871-1939), who plays Adolphe, was an Italian actor and director before moving to the United States. Borgato started on the stage, and later acted in and/or directed some 15 films in his native Italy between 1913 and 1922.

According to newspaper accounts from the time, Borgato once played opposite Eleanora Duse, and later managed her stage show and toured with the famed actress in Europe.

Agostino Borgato as Adolphe, and Percy Marmont as Easy Money Charlie, shown emptying his pockets in the back room of the Dead House, also known as the "cripple factory." *Author collection*

In 1925, Borgato immigrated to the United States, where he began his film career with *The Street of Forgotten Men*. Borgato's career in America lasted fourteen years, during which time he appeared in numerous films. He had parts in *Fashions for Women* (1927), Clara Bow's *Hula* (1927) with fellow Italian émigré Arnold Kent, *The Maltese Falcon* (1931), *Murders in the Rue Morgue* (1932), *Christopher Strong* (1933), *Daughter of Shanghai* (1938), and *The Three Musketeers* (1939), among others.

Albert Roccardi (1864-1934), who plays Adolphe's helper, was another Italian actor of the silent era. Along with a modest stage career, Roccardi appeared in more than 60 films between 1912 and 1933, among them American productions such as *The Virtuous Model* (1919) and *Partners in Crime* (1928). The

> While George Kibbe Turner's "The Street of Forgotten Men" at the Paramount Long Island studio, Herbert Brenon was obliged to use four languages. In addition to English he employed French and Italian in giving instructions to A. Bargato and Albert Roccardi, who appear in the "cripple factory" scenes and he used the fourth. Technical language, when speaking to the electricians and other artisans.

latter co-starred Mary Brian. *Sunken Silver* (1925) was a ten-part serial from Pathé which included Roccardi and Jean Bronte, Lassie's canine sibling. *Romance of the Rio Grande* (1929), a Western which starred Warner Baxter and Antonio Moreno, included both Roccardi and Agostino Borgato in supporting roles.

Dorothy Walters (c. 1877-1934) began her stage career performing a novelty act as a whistler in Vaudeville. Some 15 years later, she received her first role on Broadway in *Paris by Night* (1904), the play Stanford White was attending when he was shot. As her theatrical career progressed, Walters became known for her various character roles, including parts in stage productions of *Irene* (1919), *Paradise Alley* (1924), *Kosher Kitty Kelly* (1925) *Manhattan Mary* (1926), *Whirlpool* (1929), *Mr. Gilhooley* (1930), and as the cook in *Dinner at Eight* (1932). Among the prominent actresses she supported were Helen Hayes, Ethel Barrymore, and Mrs. (Minnie Maddern) Fiske. When she died in 1934, Walter's *New York Times* obituary noted she "had not missed a performance of a play in which she was appearing during her entire career until . . . she was forced by her illness to remain at home. She had played both performances of *Big-Hearted Herbert*, at the Biltmore Theatre, on Saturday." (4-18-1934)

Walter's film career, which ran from 1918 to 1930, included mostly small parts in some 22 films. Among the highlights are *The Woman Who Gave* (1918) with Evelyn Nesbit, *Good References* (1920) with Constance Talmadge, *Light in the Dark* (1922) with Hope Hampton, two Thomas Meighan films, *Pied Piper Malone* (1924) and *The Confidence Man* (1924), and the Brenon film *A Kiss for Cinderella* (1925), which included *Street* actors Mary Brian and Juliet Brenon.

Louise Brooks (1906-1985) started as a dancer, performing locally in her native Kansas before joining the Denishawn Dance Company and later George White *Scandals* and then Ziegfeld *Follies*. After that, she appeared in a string of Paramount productions including *The American Venus* (1926) with Esther Ralston, *A Social Celebrity* (1926) with Adolphe Menjou, *The City Gone Wild* (1927) with Thomas Meighan, *Beggars of Life* (1928) with Wallace Beery, and *The Canary Murder Case* (1929) with William Powell. However, the three films Brooks made in Europe, *Pandora's Box* (1929), *Diary of a Lost Girl* (1929), and *Prix de beauté* (1930), define her career – and her legend. In the 1930s, Brooks returned to dance, and appeared in lesser parts in a handful of lesser films, the highlight being *God's Gift to Women* (1931), directed by Michael Curtiz.

In early 1925, Brooks was a featured dancer in the Ziegfeld *Follies*. The Broadway revue was widely celebrated, and all manner of notables turned out to see shows. Some made a bee-line to the performer's dressing rooms. Among those who visited Brooks was producer Walter Wanger, then a Paramount talent scout. According to various sources, Wanger had heard Edmund Goulding (the British-born screenwriter and director) rave about her, and so Wanger and Townsend Martin (a Paramount screenwriter and another dressing room visitor) arranged to test Brooks for a role in *The Street of Forgotten Men*, which was already filming at the Astoria Studios on Long Island. Brooks' screen test was overseen by Allan Dwan. It went well, with the result being the Ziegfeld dancer was assigned a bit part in *The Street of Forgotten Men*, which was already in production.

In his celebrated profile of Brooks in *The New Yorker*, Kenneth Tynan quoted Brooks on her time at the Astoria studio. "The stages were freezing in the winter, steaming hot in the summer. The dressing rooms were windowless cubicles. We rode on the freight elevator, crushed by lights and electricians. But none of that mattered, because the writers, directors, and cast were free from all supervision. Jesse Lasky, Adolph Zukor, and Walter Wanger never left the Paramount office on Fifth Avenue, and the head of production never came on the set. There were writers and directors from Princeton and Yale. Motion pictures did not consume us. When work was finished, we dressed in evening clothes, dined at The Colony or '21' and went to the theater."

Brooks, a dancer by training, was a newcomer to film acting when she appeared in *The Street of Forgotten Men*; during her short time on screen, she plays her bit part large, vamping over Bridgeport White-Eye (John Harrington) and then dashing across the screen once a fight breaks out between White-Eye and Easy Money Charlie. Brooks wrote in her diary, "I ran around like Carol Dempster, being very frightened and graceful and having a lovely time."

In 1928, after she became an established star, film magazines carried a piece about her debut and her reaction to praise sent by a fan. "Louise Brooks must have been very satisfied when she received her first fan letter from a girl in Brooklyn who said she saw her in *The Street of Forgotten Men*, because after reading it, she immediately took a photograph of herself that she had hanging in her dressing room and sent it to the girl in thanks."

***Motion Picture* magazine, August 1925**

Another uncredited role went to **Anita Louise** (1915-1970), who at the age of 10 is thought to have played a flower girl in the wedding scene near the end of the film. Though internet sources claim Louise played a bit part – which seems to be the case, no source from the time has yet been found which mentions the fact. However, based on images of Louise as a child from around this time, the future film star is likely one of the two girls shown here.

Louise made her Broadway debut at age seven. Also at age seven, she had an uncredited bit part in the film *Down to the Sea in Ships* (1922), which included Clara Bow. She received her first screen credit at age nine in *The Sixth Commandment* (1924), which featured Neil Hamilton, followed by uncredited or small parts in F.W. Murnau's *4 Devils* (1928) and the Greta Garbo-John Gilbert film, *A Women of Affairs* (1928).

Pretty, and noted for her delicate features and blonde hair, Louise was named a WAMPAS Baby Star in 1931. She had noted roles in *The Florodora Girl* (1930), *Madame Du Barry* (1934), *A Midsummer Night's Dream* (1935), *The Story of Louis Pasteur* (1935), *Anthony Adverse* (1936), *Marie Antoinette* (1938), and *The Little Princess* (1939).

By the 1940s, her career started to slow, but revived somewhat in the 1950s and 1960s with television appearances on *The Loretta Young Show* (1953), *Ethel Barrymore Theater* (1956), *My Friend Flicka* (1956-1957), and *Playhouse 90* (1957). Later, she was in *Mannix* (1969) and *Mod Squad* (1970).

Anita Louise is one of two flower girls seen at the end of the film, as the young newlyweds, played by Neil Hamilton and Mary Brian, exit the Little Church Around the Corner. The 10-year-old actress may be the youngster on the right. Cropped screen capture *Courtesy of San Francisco Silent Film Festival*

The Dog in the film was played by canine performer **Lassie** (c. 1917-19??), a long-haired cross between a bull-terrier and a cocker spaniel guided by Emery B. Bronte (c. 1868-1939). Though little known today, Lassie was one of the more popular animals performing in films during the silent era. A profile in *National Humane Review* stated, "In filmdom, Lassie is something more than a dog. She is a personage." (8-1920)

Reportedly, Lassie made her screen debut at the age of eight months in *Rosie O'Grady* (1917), also known as *Her Brother's Champion*, a John H. Collins-directed Edison film starring Viola Dana. Lassie's big break occurred by chance when a dog was needed for a scene, and Bronte, who was cast in the film, suggested his puppy.

Lassie was featured in two Dell Henderson films starring George Walsh, *The Shark* (1920) and *The Dead Line* (1920); three films starring Richard Barthelmess including *Tol'able David* (1921), the Henry King directed *Sonny* (1922), and *The Beautiful City* (1925); Lassie credits also include two Percy Marmont vehicles, *Broadway Broke* (1923), and *The Street of Forgotten Men* (1925). Her last known appearances include D.W. Griffith's *Sorrows of Satan* (1926), and Malcolm St. Clair's *Knockout Reilly* (1927), which starred Richard Dix and Mary Brian. According to various articles from the time, some of the other stars in whose films Lassie appeared included Marion Davies, Mabel Normand, Alice Brady, Elsie Ferguson, Irene Castle, Olive Thomas, Alma Rubens, Tom Moore, and Glen Hunter.

Lassie was starred in her own film, the still extant Bronte-directed "scenic" *Fish for Two* (1925). [It can be seen on YouTube.] This half-reel short features the dog, a boy, and a fish. *Exhibitor's Trade Review* called it an "interesting little picture featuring a very intelligent dog and his boy pal." In 1926, it was announced that Max Fleischer's Red Seal Pictures would distribute 13 Bronte featurettes featuring Lassie and Jean, Emery Bronte's other dog (and Lassie's reported "understudy"). According to a *New York Times* article – which described Lassie as a "Clever screen actress" who had been "spoken of by some directors as possessing more intelligence than some of the human players" – the 10-year-old animal was earning a remarkable $15,000 a year. (1-16-1927)

By all accounts, Lassie was a well-behaved, good dog who enjoyed performing. She lived with Bronte in Englewood, New Jersey. Nothing is known of her life after 1927, at which time she was supposed to have gone to Hollywood.

Lassie

Dog Used in The Street of Forgotten Men Not Killed

Did you see The Street of Forgotten Men at Loew's State last week? So realistic was the death of a dog in the picture, that the Paramount Long Island studio has received protests from individuals, Societies for the Prevention of Cruelty to Animals and all sorts or organizations in all parts of the country against the supposed cruelty to the dog.

It was a bit of realism, however, which was achieved without the slightest injury or inconvenience to the dog. On the other hand, the pup seemed to have a lot of fun out of the incident. The scenario of The Street of Forgotten Men called for a dog to be killed by having a heavy barrel roll over it. Lassie the fine actor-dog of Emery Bronte of New York, was selected. Lassie appeared "in person" before the camera as the barrel started to roll, but when the barrel reached what seemed to be the prostrate body of Lassie a dummy dog was substituted and the "dead dog" picked up after the barrel had passed over it also was a dummy, so that Lassie received not a scratch.

And just that everybody who felt sorry for Lassie and thought the producers of the picture cruel, the following affidavit has been obtained, duly sworn to, by Emery Bronte.

"This is to certify that my dog, Lassie Bronte, was not injured in any way in making the scenes for The Street of Forgotten Men, a Paramount picture. Those who see this picture must remember that Lassie is a dog actress and can simulate as well as the other players in the picture. Lassie has appeared in many productions and has never been injured, although she has done many hazardous stunts. Every precaution was taken to safeguard Lassie's life in The Street of Forgotten Men and I am happy to make this affidavit to assure the public that no harm came to her during the filming of this picture.

(Signed) EMERY BRONTE (L.S.)
"Sworn to before me this 25th day of August, 1925.
WILLIAM J. MARK.

Syndicated article from September 1925

The Movies

SECRETS OF THE MOVIES REVEALED.

Q.—In what picture was a scene showing the killing of a dog so realistic that the company making the story received hundreds of letters from individuals and societies protesting against the supposed cruelty?

A.—So realistic was the death of a dog in "The Street of Forgotten Men" that the studio has received protests from individuals, societies for the prevention of cruelty to animals and all sorts of organizations in all parts of the country against the supposed cruelty to the dog. It was a bit of realism, however, which was achieved without the slightest injury or inconvenience to the dog. As a matter of fact, the pup seemed to have a lot of fun out of the incident. The scenario called for a dog to be killed by having a heavy barrel roll over it. Lassie appeared "in person" before the camera as the barrel started to roll, but when the barrel reached what seemed to be the prostrate body of Lassie a dummy dog was substituted and the "dead dog" picked up after the barrel had passed over it, also was a dummy, so that Lassie received not a scratch.

Syndicated article from October 1925

Emery B. Bronte and his dogs

Magazine clipping from 1926

Journalist **Whitney Bolton** (1900-1969) played a forgotten man, an unnamed bum in an uncredited role. A bit in *Billboard* magazine stated, "Whitney Bolton, of *The New York Herald Tribune*, has been assigned to a part in *Headlines*, a St. Regis picture being filmed in New York. Bolton, who resembles Norman Kerry, recently worked in *The Street of Forgotten Men*, being made by Herbert Brenon at the Paramount Long Island Studio." (5-30-1925)

Bolton started out as a sports reporter in Spartanburg, South Carolina before moving to New York City in 1924, where he worked for the *Herald Tribune* and later *Morning Telegraph*. In 1925, a wire service story noted in addition to his newspaper work, Bolton found time to take "minor roles on the silver screen." During the next few years, Bolton maintained a professional and social connection to the movie world. A 1927 bit in a Walter Winchell column mentioned Bolton had accompanied actress Josephine Dunn to a newspaper ball, and a 1929 article noted his presence among the illustrious of the stage and screen at a meeting of the Theatre Guild in New York City. As a celebrated critic and "star reporter," Bolton took a stab at Hollywood, where he worked as an occasional screenwriter; his best-known efforts were contributions to *If I Had a Million* (1932), *Apartment House Love* (1932), *42nd Street* (1933), and *The Spirit of Culver* (1939). Bolton also continued working as a journalist and later-on, syndicated columnist.

In four different pieces dating from the 1950s and 1960s, Bolton recalled his entry into films. In a 1958 remembrance of director Herbert Brenon, who had recently died, Bolton detailed how the two met. "At a party given for Miss Negri, I was sitting out a waltz when this gentleman came along, sat alongside and we started to talk. He asked me what I did and I told him I was waiting for an opening on *The Herald Tribune*. He said it might be a long wait, and how about acting in a movie he was about to make for Paramount? I said, well, now, that was a nice thing to suggest but I was not an actor and didn't know anything about acting. He said: I wish heartily some of the so-called actors were as candid."

In 1963, Bolton wrote in another syndicated column, "When I first came to New York and was trying to get a job on a newspaper, I paid the rent and put scoff on the table by being a movie actor in two films, *The Unguarded Hour* and *The Street of Forgotten Men*."

Percy Marmont and Whitney Bolton, flanked on either side by two unknown extras. *Courtesy of New York Public Library*

Before getting into films, **Elizabeth Meehan** (1894-1967) was a sometime beauty contestant who also appeared on stage (under the name Betty Williams) in plays and Ziegfeld productions, including most notably the original production of *Sally* (1920), as well as its 1923 revival. Like other Ziegfeld performers, she supplemented her income by working in films. According to a profile of Meehan in *Screenland*, "... somebody suggested I try pictures. I started playing bits at the Paramount Studios in Long Island, but it wasn't long before the production end began to fascinate me, and I resolved to try and break into the scenario game. After serving an apprenticeship as a script girl I had my chance to work into continuity." (2-1929) According to another profile of Meehan published that same month in *Smart Set*, Meehan played an uncredited bit in *The Street of Forgotten Men* in a scene which was likely part of the missing second real.

Around the time she appeared in *The Street of Forgotten Men*, Meehan began to develop an interest in how films were made, particularly screenwriting. She tried her hand at scripting *Beau Geste*, whose story she reportedly heard Brenon was considering as a film. According to the profile of Meehan in *Smart Set*, the aspiring screenwriter secured an interview with Brenon, who "impaled her with a glittering eye. 'You worked in *The Street of Forgotten Men*, didn't you?' he asked. 'Guilty as charged,' answered Elizabeth expecting hanging at the very least. 'Do you want to get on as an actress?' he continued. Miss Meehan, gulping, confessed that writing successful scenarios was really her ultimate aim and hope. 'Well,' smiled the director, 'I'm glad you're not taking acting too seriously. Frankly, my dear, you're a pretty girl but you certainly are a rotten actress'." (2-1929)

The Isle of Wight-born Meehan went on to a rather remarkable career in Hollywood. She wrote or contributed to twelve Brenon films, including *Beau Geste* (1926, uncredited), *The Great Gatsby* (1926), *God Gave Me Twenty Cents* (1926), *Sorrell and Son* (1927), *The Telephone Girl* (1927), *Laugh, Clown, Laugh* (1928), *The Rescue* (1929), *Lummox* (1930), *The Case of Sergeant Grischa* (1930), *Beau Ideal* (1931), *Transgression* (1931), *Girl of the Rio* (1932), and *The Housemaster* (1938). Her other non-Brenon credits include the screenplays for *West of Singapore* (1933) and *Oliver Twist* (1933), and contributions to later films such as *Mystery of Room 13* (1938), *Storm Over Lisbon* (1944), and Allan Dwan's *Northwest Outpost* (1947). Meehan's last three writing credits, for television, date to the early 1950s. Meehan's daughter, Frances, was also an actress.

Cast, Credits & Trivia

According to an article in *Exhibitors Herald*, **Harry Lewis** (1886-1956) also played an uncredited bit part as a saloon patron.

Lewis was famed as a boxer, having been the Welterweight Champion of the World from 1908 to 1911. Lewis, who also boxed in the lightweight and featherweight divisions, fought around the world, including a losing match to French boxing great Georges Carpentier in Paris in 1911. Today, Lewis is rated the sixth-greatest welterweight of all time; he was inducted into the International Jewish Sports Hall of Fame in 2002, and into the International Boxing Hall of Fame in 2008.

Like other sports celebrities of the time, including Carpentier, Lewis took a stab at acting. A bit in *Exhibitors Herald* read, "Harry Lewis, former middleweight boxer, who acted as a comedy taxicab driver in Richard Dix's *Manhandled* and in Brenon's *Street of Forgotten Men*, is again behind the meter in W.C. Field's latest starring picture, *The Potters*, just being completed at the Paramount Long Island studio under the direction of Fred Newmeyer." (12-25-1926)

(Left) Boxer Harry Lewis, pictured early in his career. *Courtesy of Wikipedia* **(Right) Actor Harry Lewis, pictured far right wearing a cap, and two other background players during the fight scene near the end of** ***The Street of Forgotten Men.*** *Courtesy of San Francisco Silent Film Festival*

The Church of the Transfiguration, also known as the **Little Church Around the Corner** (built 1850), was the real-life setting for a scene at the end of *The Street of Forgotten Men*, where the characters played by Mary Brian and Neil Hamilton are married. In actuality, the building is an Episcopal church located at 1 East 29th Street, between Madison and Fifth Avenues in New York City.

In 1931, a book about the church was published under the title *Through the Lich-Gate: A Biography of the Little Church Around the Corner*. The book detailed the congregation's rich history, and noted the time when a film was made there, just six years before. "One of the most picturesque wedding parties that ever passed through the lich-gate was a cinema group being filmed for *The Street of Forgotten Men*. The 'bride' was Mary Brian and she was followed by a group of bridesmaids. Percy Marmont stood outside the lich-gate as a beggar with his tin cup. He was so realistic in the role that he had difficulty in keeping people from dropping coppers in his cup."

The Little Church Around the Corner got its nickname not long after the Civil War. At the time, actors and other performers and entertainers were considered morally suspect in some quarters. According to the Church's website, in 1870, Joseph Jefferson, an actor renowned for his portrayal of Rip Van Winkle, approached the rector of a nearby church to request a funeral for his friend and fellow actor, George Holland. Upon learning that the deceased was an actor, the rector refused to hold services. Jefferson persisted, and asked if there was a church in the area that would hold a funeral for his friend. The rector answered, "I believe there is a little church around the corner where it might be done." Jefferson replied, 'If that be so, God bless the little church around the corner!" [According to an article in the *New York Tribune*, Herbert Brenon once met Jefferson in the late 1800s, while both were in stock theater, with Jefferson the veteran, and Brenon the newcomer.]

To this day, the church has maintained various ties with the theatre and acting world. In 1898, stained glass windows were placed in the building memorializing Edwin Booth, who is widely considered the greatest American actor of the 19th century. [His achievements, unfortunately, are often overshadowed by his younger brother, actor John Wilkes Booth, assassin of President Abraham Lincoln.] Notably, as well, many prominent people, including a number of actors associated with both stage and screen, have visited or been married in this picturesque parish church.

Among them was novelist and Broadway lyricist P. G. Wodehouse, who was married there in 1914 and subsequently set his fictionalized weddings at the church.

Since 1923, the church has served as the national headquarters of the Episcopal Actors' Guild. Over the years, its officers and council members have included Basil Rathbone, Tallulah Bankhead, Peggy Wood, Joan Fontaine, Rex Harrison, and Charlton Heston. In the 1970s, the Church hosted the Joseph Jefferson Theatre Company, which gave starts to actors such as Armand Assante, Tom Hulce, and Rhea Perlman. In 1986, the Church was featured in an episode of *The Equalizer* (the original TV series), as well as in the Woody Allen film, *Hannah and Her Sisters*.

In 1967, the Church of the Transfiguration was designated a New York City landmark, and in 1973, it was listed on the National Register of Historic Places.

Mary Brian and Neil Hamilton Were Married in New York in the Little Church Around the Corner!

But not really, you know—just a screen wedding for "The Street of Forgotten Men." There's a very charming Mrs. Hamilton already; we'll give you a picture of the two, next month if you'd like it. And Mary Brian is much too young even to be engaged

A clipping from *Motion Picture* magazine, September 1925.

(Above) A view of the Little Church Around the Corner, from around the time the film was to have taken place, c. 1900. (Below) A vintage postcard view of the Church, from around the time the film was made, c. 1925. Notably, the skyscrapers of modern New York can be seen in the background.

The street car depicted in an early scene in the film was driven by **John J. Kiernan** (1871?-1933). As the Queens *Daily Star* noted, "Back in '92, John Kiernan used to drive a horse car from Greenpoint to Erie Basin. For two days this week he drove one of the same cars back and forth across the studio floor in the filming of *The Street of Forgotten Men*. On Monday John will again hold the reins from the front platform of the car as a feature of the second annual safety parade." (5-9-1925)

The Queens newspaper was referring to an event held on May 11, 1925. One syndicated article, which ran in newspapers across the country, reported on the happening. "Among the most interesting exhibits of New York's safety day parade were three contributed by the movies. These exemplify the development of transportation. First was a rude cart drawn by oxen which was seen in Richard Dix's *Too Many Kisses*. Second was a gold coach of the time of Louis the 15th of France and used in Valentino's *Monsieur Beaucaire*. The other was an old horse car now being used in Herbert Brenon's production, *The Street of Forgotten Men*." (5-29-1925)

Easy Money Charlie steps off a horse drawn street car driven by John Kiernan. *Author collection*

Some of the film's many colorful characters. (Top) Saloon keep Diamond Mike (Riley Hatch) overlooks his busy bar room; among the dozen beer drinking patrons is a modestly dressed woman wearing spectacles – the second figure from the left. She stands out, and seems out-of-place. But who is she? (Bottom) Diamond Mike and Bridgeport White-Eye's unnamed moll (Louise Brooks) – seen wearing a cloche hat with a question mark pin, observe the bar room brawl as other patrons of the Dead House take-in the raucous scene. *Courtesy of San Francisco Silent Film Festival*

More background players, as just about every scene in the Bowery is crowded with the down-and-out denizens of the street of forgotten men. (Top) Easy Money Charlie (Percy Marmont) greets his beloved dog (played by Lassie), as the bearded, downward-looking Adolphe (Agostino Borgato) assists some of the cripple factory's other "fake beggars". (Bottom) An injured Bridgeport White-Eye (John Harrington) staggers past uncredited actor Harry Lewis and along the bar of the Dead House as other forgotten men look on. *Courtesy of San Francisco Silent Film Festival*

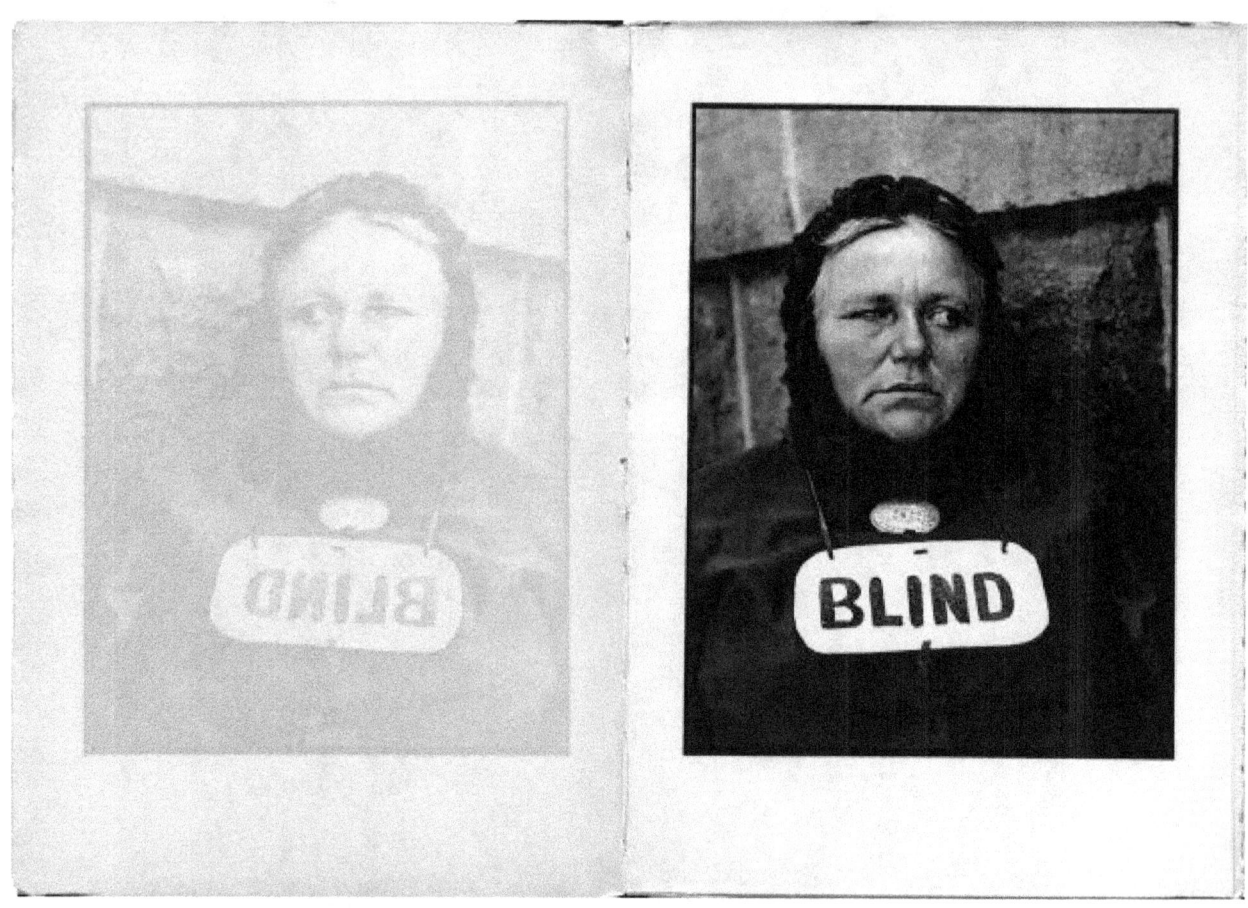

In 1916, photographer & filmmaker Paul Strand shot this evocative image of a blind woman, which was published the following year in Alfred Stieglitz's seminal journal, *Camera Work*. The woman is wearing a New York City peddler's license, number 2622, similar to those seen in the film. *Courtesy of New York Public Library*

A GLOSSARY

The world has changed a great deal since 1925. And so has the language used to describe it. There are enough unusual terms, usages, and names in George Kibbe Turner's story, in John Russell's notes, in the film scenario, in the Paramount Press Sheet, and in some of the other articles and reviews included in this book to warrant this small glossary, an extension of the previous chapter.

Beezer: a slang term referring to a person's nose.

Billie-cock: a hard felt hat with a rounded crown, better known as a bowler, derby, bob hat or billycock; such hats were popular with American working classes during the second half of the 19th century. Easy Money Charlie is seen sporting such a hat.

Billy McGlory's Saloon: referenced in the press sheet, a Hester Street drinking establishment owned by William McGlory (1850–1927), an American saloon keeper and underworld figure during the mid-to late 19th century. McGlory owned a number of popular establishments throughout the city which sometimes served as hangouts for members of the underworld.

Birds: a slang term for a promiscuous woman or prostitute. Both Dutch Dolly and Portland Fancy are described as "bedraggled birds of the night." In John Russell's notes on the characters, Dutch Dolly is described as a prostitute.

Bowery: a street and a neighborhood in New York City. Historically, the Bowery has been considered a part of the Lower East Side of Manhattan. Following the Civil War, the neighborhood fell on hard times, and once respectable homes and businesses gave way to low-brow concert halls, saloons, brothels, pawn shops, and flophouses.

The Bowery was also the home turf of one of America's earlier street gangs, the Bowery Boys. Notably, the Bowery is the setting of a number of literary works and films. They include Stephen Crane's *Maggie: A Girl of the Streets* (1893), about a poor family living in the neighborhood, and Theodore Dreiser's *Sister Carrie* (1900), which closes with the suicide of one of the main characters in a Bowery flophouse. One other early film set in the Bowery is Mary Pickford's *Little Annie Rooney* (1925).

Bungstarter: a tool for opening beer barrels by removing the bung, or stopper.

Cheese it: slang term meaning to run away or flee.

The City that Never Sleeps: a now lost 1924 drama directed by James Cruze. The film concerns a saloon run by a widow, whose husband was killed by a thug. Feeling that such an establishment is not a good place to raise a child, she gives up her daughter to another. On a few occasions, the film was compared to *The Street of Forgotten Men*, with which it shares plot points.

Emanced: as used in the Press Sheet, this term is used to refer to an emancipated woman, and is likely satirical.

John D. Godfrey: a once well-known mendicant officer for the Brooklyn Bureau of Charity who advised Herbert Brenon during the making of the film. He was considered an authority on beggars and begging.

McGurk's Suicide Hall: referenced in the Press Sheet, a notorious Bowery saloon known as a haven for debauchery, brawling and for the frequents deaths and "suicides" which occurred there.

Leg O'Mutton sleeves: in 1925, such sleeves were considered old-fashioned; they feature fullness around the shoulder-bicep area but are fitted around the forearm and wrist; leg o'mutton sleeves were worn by some of the women in the film and helped establish its historical setting.

A Glossary

Mendicant officer: a mendicant is a beggar, and a mendicant officer were members of a city agency meant to regulate their conduct.

The Miracle Man: a now mostly lost 1919 drama directed by George Loane Tucker. The film concerns a group of con men who use a faith healer to swindle money from the sympathetic and unsuspecting. Hugely popular, the film was the second highest-grossing film of the year of its release, and helped make stars out of leads Thomas Meighan, Betty Compson, and Lon Chaney. (The latter played a character who pretends to be severely handicapped, similar to Percy Marmont's role in *The Street of Forgotten Men*.) In 1920, this Paramount distributed film was voted the #1 fan favorite in a poll conducted by *Photoplay* magazine.

Near beer: a type of beer produced so as to have a very low or no alcohol content; it was the only type of beer that could be produced and sold legally in the United States during Prohibition. By law, near beer could not contain more than one half of one percent alcohol by volume.

A Night in Chinatown: a one act musical play by Loney Haskel set in the Bowery and dating from around the turn of the 20th century; it is described in the Press Sheet as a "perennial favorite," and was performed in 1903 by the Bowery Burlesquers.

O. Henry: noted American short story writer (1862-1910) who is referenced in the Press Sheet to evoke the popular fiction of a by-gone era. Notably, a number of O. Henry's best-known stories are set among the working classes. Two other writers of the time also mentioned alongside O. Henry were **Laura Jean Libby** (1862-1924), a popular author of 82 novels and 120 plays whose bestselling book was *The Pretty Young Girl* (1889), and **Bertha M. Clay**, a literary pseudonym first used by Charlotte Mary Brame (1836-1884), her daughter, and at least a dozen male writers in the production of a series of dime novels, the most famous of which is *Dora Thorne* (1877).

Prohibition: a period in American history, between 1919–1933, when the manufacture, storage, transportation, sale, possession, and consumption of alcoholic beverages was illegal. The action in the first part of the film dates to before Prohibition, the action in the later part during Prohibition, with changing signage in the saloon reflecting the period in which scenes are taking place.

Stevepost: a shortening of the title *Saturday Evening Post*. A few articles and reviews incorrectly credited the popular magazine with having printed George Kibbe Turner's short story, "The Street of the Forgotten Men." In fact, the story appeared in the *Saturday Evening Post's* competitor, *Liberty*.

Schooner: a type of glass (rounded with a short stem), often used in drinking beer.

Spieler: a social dance in which a couple spin around seemingly out of control; the dance was considered sometimes lewd because of the "easy familiarity" with which the men handled their female partners.

Steve Brodie's Place: Steve Brodie's Place is mentioned in the Press Sheet along with The Glass Barrel, The Silvan Divan, The Slide and other drinking establishments, or saloons, of the time. Steve Brodie (1861–1901) claimed to have jumped off the Brooklyn Bridge and survived. The actual jump, which was disputed, brought Brodie considerable fame and made his saloon a thriving enterprise. Brodie's fame was such that he became a symbol of the Bowery, and his name a term for jumping from a structure. Characters based on Brody have appeared in later films, including a portrayal by George Raft in the 1933 film, *The Bowery*.

Tinpan: a term in the Press Sheet referring to music from Tin Pan Alley, a street in New York which was home to numerous music publishers; the term also refers to a style of American popular music that arose in the late 19th century and was considered in some quarters as somewhat old-fashioned by 1925.

Tony Pastors: a well-known entertainment venue home to early vaudeville. Tony Pastors is mentioned in the Press Sheet along with The People's Theater and The Atlantic Gardens and other entertainment venues of the time.

A Glossary

Volstead: National Prohibition Act of 1919, sometimes called the Volstead Act, led to the banning of alcoholic drinks in the United States.

It is hard to know what to make of this piece by Douglas Hodges, which appeared in *Exhibitor's Herald* five weeks after the film's debut. Is it summary, satire, suggestion for a stage play, or something else?

The Street of Forgotten Men: From Story to Screen and Beyond

Actress Mary Brian on the cover of *Brooklyn Life and Activities of Long Island Society* at the time *The Street of Forgotten Men* was showing at Loew's Metropolitan.

FURTHER READING

Agel, Jerome and Walter D. Glanze. *Cleopatra's Nose the Twinkie Defense & 1500 Other Verbal Shortcuts in Popular Parlance.* Prentice Hall Press, 1990.

Brownlow, Kevin. *Behind the Mask of Innocence.* New York: Knopf, 1990.

Brownlow, Kevin. *The Parade's Gone By.* New York: Knopf, 1968.

Calhoun, Ada. *St. Marks Is Dead: The Many Lives of America's Hippest Street.* W.W. Norton & Company, 2016.

Chalmers, David Mark. *The Social and Political Ideas of the Muckrakers.* New York: Citadel Press, 1964.

Cowie, Peter. *Louise Brooks: Lulu Forever.* New York: Rizzoli, 2006.

Cullen, Frank et al. *Vaudeville Old & New: An Encyclopedia of Variety Performers in America.* New York: Routledge Taylor & Francis Group, 2007.

Day, Dorothy and Robert Ellsberg. *By Little and by Little: The Selected Writings of Dorothy Day.* New York: Knopf, 1983.

Derr, Mark. *A Dog's History of America: How Our Best Friend Explored, Conquered, and Settled a Continent.* New York: North Point Press, 2004.

Eliot, T. S. *Selected Essays 1917-1932.* New York: Harcourt Brace and Company, 1932.

Everson, William K. *American Silent Film.* Oxford University Press 1978.

Fox, Charles Donald and Milton L Silver. *Who's Who on the Screen.* New York: Ross Pub. Co., 1920.

Fuller-Seeley, Kathryn. *Hollywood in the Neighborhood: Historical Case Studies of Local Moviegoing.* University of California Press, 2008.

Gladysz, Thomas. *Around the World with Louise Brooks.* PandorasBoxPress, 2024.

Gladysz, Thomas. *Louise Brooks: The Persistent Star.* PandorasBoxPress, 2018.

Gladysz, Thomas. "The Street of Forgotten Men." San Francisco: *San Francisco Silent Film Festival* program, 2022.

Graham, Ian. 2017. *Herbert Brenon: An American Cinema Odyssey.* Ian Graham, 2017.

Koszarski, Richard. *The Astoria Studio and Its Fabulous Films: A Picture History with 227 Stills and Photographs.* New York: Dover Publications, 1983.

Koszarski, Richard. *An Evening's Entertainment: The Age of the Silent Feature Picture 1915-1928.* University of California Press, 1994.

Koszarski, Richard. *Hollywood Directors: 1914-1940.* London: Oxford University Press, 1976.

Koszarski, Richard. *Hollywood on the Hudson: Film and Television in New York from Griffith to Sarnoff.* New Brunswick, N.J.: Rutgers University Press, 2008.

Lodge, Jack. "The Career of Herbert Brenon." *Griffithiana*, 1996.

MacAdam, George. *The Little Church Around the Corner.* New York: G.P. Putnam's Sons, 1925.

McClure, Arthur F. *The Movies: An American Idiom: Readings in the Social History of the American Motion Picture.* Fairleigh Dickinson University Press, 1971.

Mencken, H. L. *The American Language. Supplement 1.* A. A. Knopf, 1945.

Muscio, Giuliana. *Napoli/New York/Hollywood: Film Between Italy and the United States.* New York: Fordham University Press, 2019.

Paris, Barry. *Louise Brooks.* New York: Knopf, 1989.

Parish, James Robert. *Hollywood Players the Thirties.* New Rochelle: Arlington House, 1976.

Pierce, David. *The Survival of American Silent Feature Films 1912-1929.* Council on Library and Information Resources and the Library of Congress, 2013.

Ray, Randolph. *My Little Church Around the Corner.* New York: Simon and Schuster, 1957.

Ross, Ishbel. *Through the Lich-Gate: Biography of the Little Church Around the Corner.* New York: William Farquhar Payson, 1931.

Sandburg, Carl and Arnie Bernstein. *"The Movies Are": Carl Sandburg's Film Reviews and Essays, 1920-1928.* Chicago, Illinois: Lake Claremont Press, 2000.

Further Reading

Sante, Luc. *Low Life: Lures and Snares of Old New York*. New York: Farrar Straus Giroux, 1991.

Segrave, Kerry. *Begging in America, 1850-1940: The Needy, the Frauds, the Charities and the Law*. Jefferson, NC: McFarland, 2011.

Shlaes, Amity. *The Forgotten Man: A New History of the Great Depression*. HarperCollins, 2008.

Slide, Anthony. *Silent Players: A Biographical and Autobiographical Study of 100 Silent Film Actors and Actresses*. Lexington, KY: University Press of Kentucky, 2002.

Swados, Harvey (editor). *Years of Conscience, the Muckrakers: An Anthology of Reform Journalism*. Cleveland: World Publishing Co., 1962.

Thompson, Frank. *The Compleat Beau Geste*. Asheville, NC: Men with Wings Press, 2023.

Tynan, Kenneth. *Show People: Profiles in Entertainment*. Simon and Schuster, 1979.

Wakeman, John (editor). *World Film Directors: Vol. 1 1890-1945*. New York: H. W. Wilson Company, 1987.

Weinberg, Arthur and Lila Weinberg. *The Muckrakers*. New York: Simon & Schuster, 1961.

At the end of the film, Bridgeport White-Eye's sign changes from "I am blind" to "I <u>am</u> blind." *Courtesy of San Francisco Silent Film Festival*

Please Cheer Up, Percy

Bluefield, W. Va.

Just one little brickbat, although I am not meaning to hurt anyone's feelings. Yesterday I saw the worst picture I have ever seen—"The Street of Forgotten Men." I know several people who are sick and tired of seeing Percy Marmont as the downcast, the one who bears the brunt of everything. It may be his nature, but I know he could act better parts if he were put in them. I would rather not see him at all than as he is.

BILLY FRANKLIN.

A still pensive Percy Marmont, still "alone" on the street of forgotten men. The actor was both praised and mocked for his many downbeat roles. "Please, Cheer Up Percy" was a letter to the editor published in *Photoplay* in December, 1925. A later *Photoplay* feature, from May 1926, titled "Poor Percy: The most persecuted person in pictures," used words like "agony," "tortured," "pitiful," "suffering," and "heartbroken" in describing his various roles. *Courtesy of SilentHollywood.com*

INDEX

Page numbers in bold refer to images and their captions, and sidebars
Page numbers in italics refer to John Russell's notes or the scenario, or if underlined, the <u>Press Sheet</u>

4 Devils, 309
5th Avenue (also Fifth Ave.), *12, 14, 16,* 111, **112**, 116, **131**, <u>*151*</u>, 308
21 (club), 308
35th Street, 112
42nd Street, 312
77 Sunset Strip, 301
"400", *75*

Ablemarie theater (Brooklyn, New York), 242
Academy Awards, 294
Adolphe (Adolf the face artist / Adolphe the Disguiser / Adolphe the Frenchman), *13-14, 18, 30-36, 40, 52-53, 56-60, 78-80, 82-85, 104,* 115, <u>*143*</u>, <u>*149*</u>, **160**, 291, 304, **305**, **321**
Adolphe's assistant, *18,* 291, 306
"Adestes Fideles", 169
Advertising Price List, <u>*157*</u>
AFI catalogue, xvi
Africa, 279
Agel, Jerome B., 261
Alba, Maria, 3
Albany, New York, 136
Aldine Concert Orchestra, **204**
Alger, Horatio <u>*145*</u>
Algeria, 279
"All Alone", 168, 169
Allan, Dot, 258
Allen, James, 240
Allen, Kelcey, 109

Allen, Woody, 317
"The" Allens, <u>*147*</u>
Allison, May, 3
Allvine, Glendon, 136
Aloma of the South Seas, 299
Amazing Quest of Ernest Bliss, The, 300
America (film), 301, 304
American Agriculturist, 179
American Jewish Times-Outlook, 245, 256
American Language, The, 240
American Magazine, 1
American Mercury, 256
American theater (Oakland, California), **211**
American theater (Wautonan, Wisconsin), 229-230
American Tragedy, 253
American Venus, The, xxii, 307
Amusements (column), 109
Anderson, Judith, 301-302, 304
Andino, Julián, 169
Anthony Adverse, 309
Apartment House Love, 312
Appeal to Reason, 1
Arcadia Theatre (Wilmington, Deleware), **227**
Ariza, 185
Arrow Collars, 301
Art Institute of Chicago, 260
Aru kojiki no hanashi (*The Street of Forgotten Men*), 279
As You Like It, 295

333

Asbury, Herbert, 256
Ash, Paul, **174**, 198-199, 202
Asia, 278
Asimov, Isaac, 261
Asphalt Jungle, The, xx, 294
Assante, Armand, 317
Associated Exhibitors, 297
Astoria Studio (Paramount Long Island studio), 111, 112, 113, 115, 117, 121, 124, 126, 129, 134, *148*, *155*, 163, 307, 312, 313, 315
Atkins Theater (Yuba City, California), 235
Atlanta, Georgia, 224, **243**-244
Atlantic City, New Jersey, 259
Atlantic Gardens, *152*, 326
Atlantic Monthly, 2
Atoka, Oklahoma, **228**
Auckland, New Zealand, **280**
Austria, 263, 279, 291
Australia, 279, 298
Avalon theater (Bellingham, Washington), 235

B., M., 182
Baby Peggy, 247
Bad Man, The, 301
Bad Seed, The, 294
Badger, Clarence, 301
Baggot, King, 293
Baguez, Salvador, 243
Baker, Montana, 231
Baltimore, Maryland, 221
Baltimore Daily Post, **226**
Baltimore Evening Sun, 226
Bankhead, Tallulah, 302, 317
Batman, 301
Bara, Theda, 293
Borgato, Agostino, 196, 291, 304-306, **321**
Barnsley, England, 280
Barrie, J.M., xix, 194, 293
Barry, Wesley, 247
Barrymore, Ethel, 306
Barthelmess, Richard, 310
Battling Butler, 300
Baxter, Warner, 3, **211**, 306

"Be a Brave Girl", 169
Beau Geste, xix, xxiii, xxvii, 293, 297, 299, 301, 314
Beau Ideal, 297, 314
Beautiful City, The, 310
Beery, Noah, **211**
Beery, Wallace, xvii, **211**, 231, 299, 307
Beggars of Life, xxvi, 307
Beggar on Horseback, The, 233, 234
"Begging – A $100,000,000 A Year American Industry", **250**
Behind the Front, 231, 299
Behind the Garden Wall, 298
Beiping chenbao, The, (Beijing, China), **289**
Belasco, David, 192, 301, 304
Belgium, 263, 279
"Belle of Avenue A, The", *147*, 165
Berlin, Irving, 168, 169
Bermuda, 279
Bernie, Ben, 172-173, **174**, **189**, 196, 198
Ben-Hur, 177
Bertram the Barber, 115, 291
Beyond Trivia, 261
Bible, The, **238**
Big-Hearted Herbert, 306
Big Killing, The, 299
Big Parade, The, 177
Billboard, 109-110, 113, 127, 312
Billings, Montana, 231, 237
Billy McGlory's (saloon), *147*, 323
Biltmore Theatre (New York, New York), 306
Binder, Otto, **255**
Biography of a Million Dollars, The, 2
Biografteatern theater (Pargas, Finland), **289**
Birmingham, Alabama, **205**
Birmingham News (Birmingham, Alabama), 226
Bleeker Street, 142, *147*
Blind Ben, 115, 291
Blondell, Joan, 240
Bloom, C. H., 245
Blue, Monte, 3
Bluefield, West Virginia, **332**
Bogota, New Jersey, 229
Bolton, Whitney, 126-127, **160**, 291, 312-**313**

Boom Town, 294
Booth, Edwin, 316
Booth, John Wilkes, 316
Borgato, Agostino, 291, 304-306, **321**
Boston, Massachusetts, 221
Boston Tech (film stock), 22, *24*
Borzage, Frank, 298
Botkin, B.A., 257
Bow, Clara, xix, 177, 294, 295, 299, 301, 306, 309
Bowery, xxiii, *12*, *15*, *19*, *25*, *27*, *46*, *47*, 110, 113, 117, 121, 127, *145*, *146*, *147*, *150*, *152*, *154*, *155*, 164, 165, 169, 185, 188, 190, 191, 192, 193, 194, 200, 222, 223, 224, **225**, 230, 239, 241, **246**, 254, 257, 259, 260, 261, **321**, 323-324, 325
"The Bowery", 163, 164, 168, 169
"The Bowery and Afterward", 194
"Bowery Boy", *27*
Bowery Burlesquers, 325
Bowery Cinderella, *143*
"Box Office Reports", 230-231
Boyd, Herbert, 218
Boyd, William, 3
Bradford, James C., 168
Brady, Alice, 310
Brady, Nicholas F., **111**
Brame, Charlotte Mary (Bertha M. Clay), 325
Branded Woman, The, 298
Brazil, 279, **284**, **287**
Brenon, Aileen, 302
Brenon, Algernon (Algernon St. John-Brenon), 110, 302
Brenon, Herbert, xvi, xvii, xviii, xix, xxiii, 11, 109-110, **111**, 112-113, 115, 116, 117, 118-120, 121-122, 123, 124, 125, 126-127, 129, 134, 139, 141, *143*, *145*, *147*, *148*, *149*, *150*, *151-152*, *153*, *154*, *155-156*, 166, 169, 177, 178, 179, 181, 182, 184-185, **186**, 187, 188, 190, 191, 192, 193-194, 195, 196, 198, 200, 202, 218, 222, 223, **226-227**, 230, 231, 239, 240, 241, 249, 251, **252**, 253, 259, 280, **281**, **287**, **288**, **290**, 291, **292**, 293-294, 296, 297, 299, 301, 302, 304, 307, 312, 314, 315, 316, 319, 324, **352**
Brenon, Juliet, 110, 113, 129, **158**, **159**, 179, 180, 185, 191, 192, 196, 219, **238**, **247**, 291, 302-303, 307
Brent, Evelyn, **215**
Brian, Mary, **ix**, **10**, 11, *18*, 109, **130**, 142, *143*, *144*, *149*, *151*, *153-154*, **161**, 165, 166, 180, 181, 182, 185, **186**, 190, 192, 195, 200, 201, **211**, 218, 226, 229, 230, **288**, **289**, 291, 299-**300**, 301, 306, 307, **309**, 310, 316, **317**, **328**, **352**
Bridgeport, Connecticut, 198
Bridgeport White-Eye (Whitey), **xiv**, **xxx**, *18*, *19*, 21, *33-34*, 121, **123**, 124, **125**, 129, **130**, **132**, 138, *143-144*, *149*, 180, 196, 263, 291, 302, 308, **320**, **321**, **331**
Briegleb, G. A., 242-243
Brinkley, Nell, **133**,
Broadway, 164, 191, 304, 306, 307, 309, 317
Broadway Broke, 298, 310
Broadway Lady, The, 215
Broadway temple (New York, New York), 241
Brodie, Steve, 326
Broken Blossoms, 202
Broken Heart, A, 303
Bronson, Betty, xviii
Bronte, Emery, 128, 310, **311**
Bronte, Jean, 306, 310
Brooklyn, New York, 136, 139, 190, 241-242, 251, 294, 308
Brooklyn Bridge, 326
Brooklyn Bureau of Charity, *148*, *149*, 292, 324
Brooklyn Daily Eagle, 112, 188, 191, 241
Brooklyn Daily Star, 129,
Brooklyn Daily Times, 188, 292
Brooklyn Life and Activities of Long Island Society, 328
Brooks, Louise, xix, xxii, xxiii, xxiv, xxvi, xxvii, 110, **123**, 124-125, **133**, 219, 263, 284, 291, 295, 307-308, **320**
Brooks Brothers, 126
Brownlow, Kevin, xvi-xx

Brown of Harvard, 299
Die Büchse der Pandora (see also *Pandora's Box*), 124
Buffalo, New York, 136, 221
Buffalo Express (Buffalo, New York), 249
Burgomaster, The, 304
Burney, Donald, 188
Burroughs, Wesley Ray, 169
B*Utterfield 8*, 258
Butterfield Church (Butterfield, Minnesota), 245
Byrne, Robert, xxii-xxiv, 22

C., H.P., 202
C., S.L., 226
California, 188
California saengerfest, **210**
Calle de los Olvidados, La (*The Street of Forgotten Men*), 185
Cameo Kirby, 301
Cameo Thematic Music Co., 168
Camera Work, **322**
Cameraphone or East Liberty Cameraphone (Pittsburgh, Pennsylvania), **204**
"Campus Scout", 256
Canada, 198, 279
Canary Murder Case, The, xxvi, 307
Capitol theater (New York, New York), 198
Captains Courageous, 295
Captain Marvel, 254, **255**
"Captain Marvel and the Street of Forgotten Men", 254-**255**
Capt. Williams, 304
Card, James, xviii
Carpentier, Georges, 315
Caribbean, 280
Caribbean Quarterly, 256
Carrier, Willis, 187
Carroll, Carroll, 178
Case of Sergeant Grischa, The, 294, 314
Castle, Irene, 310
Castro theater, xxii, **225**, **354**
Cather, Willa, 1
Catholic Advance, 178

Catholic Church, 191
Catholic Telegraph, 178
Catholic Worker, The, 247
Catholic Worker's Movement, 245-246
Cavat, Nika, 260-261
Central Congregational Church (Atlanta, Georgia), **243**-244
Century, The, 256
Champaign, Illinois, **236**, 237
Chaney, Lon, xx, 177, 178, 223, **226**, **227**, 251, 294, 325
Char-Bell theatre (Rochester, Indiana), 229
Charlie's Aunt, 139
Charlie Chaplin, 119, **216**, **281**
Charleston (dance), **174**
Charlotte, North Carolina, **213**
Chase, Canon, 139
Chat, The, (Brooklyn, New York), 241
"Cheerful Churches by a Layman", 241
Chelsea Methodist Episcopal Church (New York, New York), 240
Cherryvale, Kansas, 221
Chicago, Illinois, **ix**, 2, 169, **174**, 198, 201, 202, 218, 228, 253, 254, **255**, 260
Chicago American, 202
Chicago Daily Journal, 202
Chicago Daily News, 201
Chicago Evening Post, 199
Chicago Herald and Examiner, 200
Chicago Tribune, 200, 202
Chicago Stick, *149*
Chickie, 202
Child Welfare Magazine, 178
Children of the Shadows, **281**
Chile, 279
China, 279, **288**
Chinatown, 257
Chivalrous Charley, xvi
Christian Advocate, 245
Christian Herald, 245
Christian Science Monitor, 256
Christopher Strong, 306
Church Publicity: the modern way to compel them to come in, 241

Index

Church as a Social Center, The, 241
Church of Christ (Sayre, Pennsylvania), 245
Church of Our Father (New York, New York), 242
Church of the Transfiguration (Little Church Around the Corner), 316-**318**
Cincinnati, Ohio, 178, **209**
Cine-Mundial, 186
Cinearte, **285**
Cinema World, 185
City Gone Wild, The, xxii, xxiv, 307
"City of Chicago: A Study of the Great Immoralities, The", 2
City That Never Sleeps, The, 181, 194, 324
Civil War, 316, 323
Clarion-Ledger (Jackson, Mississippi), 241
Clark Street (Chicago, Illinois), 253
Clarke, Eric T., 232-234
Clay, Bertha M., *145*, 325
Cleopatra's Nose: The Twinkie Defense, and 1500 Other Verbal Shortcuts in Popular Parlance, 261
Cleveland, Ohio, 198, **206**, 223
Cleveland Plain Dealer, 222
College Rhythm, 300
Collins, John H., 310
Colman, Ronald, 293
Columbia (radio network), 298
Columbia (records), 256
Columbia City, Indiana, 231
Columbia theatre (Columbia City, Indiana), 230
Columbia University, 261
Columbus, Ohio, **174**
Columbus Citizen, **226**
Common Ground, 178
Commonweal, 245
Compson, Betty, 3, 298, 325
Confidence Man, The, 307
Confidential, xx
Congregational Church (Burlington, Vermont), 244
Congressional Committee on Education, 138-139
Conrad, Joseph, 296

Conquest of Canaan, The, 304
La Contessa, 299
Contre-enquête ("Those Who Dance"), 3
Cooper, Gary, 300
Cooper, Merian C., 231, 244, 297
Cooper-Hewitt, 112
Copp's Guide to New York City, 257
Cosmopolitan Productions, 294
"Could Such Things Be", 133
Counterfeit Lady, 302
Coward, Noël, 303
Cozy theatre (Fayette, Iowa), 229
Crane, Stephen, 324
Craven, Thomas, 303
Cripple Factory, xxiii, 3, *12*, *29-40*, *52-60*, *78-85*, 117, 118, *143*, *145*, *148*, *149*, 193, 251, 292, **305**
Cross Roads, The, 260
"Crosswords", **174**
Cruze, James, 194, 296, 324
Cukor, George, 300
cummings, e.e., 303
Curtiz, Michael, 307
Czechoslovakia, 263, 279

D., H. E., **227**
D., Q. E., **226**
Daily Argus-Leader (Sioux Falls, South Dakota), 246-247, 249
Daily Capital (Topeka, Kansas), 177
Daily Illini (Champaign, Illinois), 256
Daily Star (Queens N.Y.), 166, 320
Dana, Viola, 310
Dancing Mothers, xx, 231, 294
Daniels, Bebe, 301
Dark Star, The, 294
Wendy Darling, 299
Daughter of Shanghai, 306
Daughter of the Gods, A, 293
"The Daughters of the Poor: A Plain Story of the White Slave Trade Under Tammany Hall," 2
David Harum, 294
Davies, Marion, 294, 310

337

Davis, Bette, **257**
Dawn Patrol, The, 301
Day, Dorothy, 191-192, 245-246
DC Comics, 254
Dead House, 3, *12*, *19*, *25-30*, *33-34*, *40-41*, *44*, *46-47*, *50-53*, *57-59*, *99-104*, <u>*152-153*</u>, 165, **305**, **320**, **321**
Dead Line, The, 310
"Dear Beatrice Fairfax", **133**
Deffry, Josephine, 110, **159**, 192, 219, 291, 302, 303-304
DeForest Phonofilm, 172
DeMille, Cecil B., 126, 177, 293
DeMille, William, 301
Dempster, Carol, **216**, **308**
Denishawn Dance Company, 307
Denmark, 263, 279
Deserted Bride, A, 303
Detroit, Michigan, 169, 221, 253, 304
Detroit Free Press, 128, **226**
Detroit Times, 223
Diamond Mike, 3, 11, *12*, *14*, 18, 22, *25-26*, *37*, *57*, *100*, 129, <u>*143*</u>, <u>*149*</u>, <u>*152*</u>, <u>*153*</u>, 165, 291, **320**
Diapason, The, 169
Diario de la Marina (Havana, Cuba), 279-280
Diary of a Lost Girl, xxvi, 307
Dickstein, Martin, 112, 188
Dieterle, William, 3
Dinner at Eight, 306
El Dios del mar (The Sea God), 296
Disney, xix
Dix, Richard, 3, 300, 310, 315, 319
Docks of New York, The, xx, 295
Dodge, Witherspoon, 244
"Dog Used in *The Street of Forgotten Men* Not Killed", **311**
Don Q, 177
Donne, John, xxvii
Donnelly, Mr., 136
Dora Thorne, 325
Dove, The, 192, 301-302, 304
Dove, Billie, **211**
Down to the Sea in Ships, **309**

Dr. Jekyll and Mr. Hyde, 293
Dreiser, Theodore, 253, 324
Duel in the Sun, 295
Dumb Dan, 115, 119, 291
Dublin, Ireland, 280, 293
Dumont Theater (Hackensack, New Jersey), 237
Dún Laoghaire, Ireland, 280
Dunn, Josephine, 312
Duse, Eleanora, 304
Dutch Dolly (Dutch Molly), *19*, *27*, *28*, *38*, *40*, *45*, *50*, 192, 292, 323
Dutch East Indies, 279
Dutch Guiana, 279
Dwan, Allan, 22, *24*, 124, 294, 297, 301, 304, 307, 314

Eagle, The, 177
East 29th, 111, 316
East of Broadway, 297
"East Side, West Side", 142, <u>*147*</u>, 165
"Easter Sunday" (musical composition), 169
Eastman House, xix
Eastman Theatre, 232-234
Easy Money Charlie (Easy Money Charley / Charles Vanhern), **xv**, **xxx**, 3, 11, *12*, *14-16*, *18*, 21, *24*, *28*, *30-94*, *98-107*, 114, 115, 121, 123, **125**, **128**, **132**, 138, 142, <u>*143-144*</u>, <u>*149*</u>, <u>*153*</u>, <u>*154*</u>, 168, 180, 184, 190, 191, 192, 195, **196**, 201, 223, 224, **226**, 264, 291, 308, **319**, **321**, 323
Easy Money Charlie's dog, 195
Ed the Flop, <u>*149*</u>
Eden Movies theater (Brooklyn, New York), 242
Edge, William, 258
Edison (studio), 310
Edwards, Gus, 165
El Dorado, 295
El Paso, Texas, 253
El Paso Herald (El Paso, Texas), 251
Az Elfelejtett Emberek Utcája (The Street of Forgotten Men), **189**
Eliot, T.S., 165

Ellarcotte, Roy, **226**
Ellis, Robert, xvi
Elstree, 294
Empire Against a Woman, The, 303
Empty Pockets, 293
Enemy, The, 242
Enemy Sex, The, 298
"Engagement is Surprise", **132**
England, **132**, 165-166, 279, 294, 298, 299
Englewood, New Jersey, 310
English, Joe, 231
Episcopal Actors' Guild, 317
Equalizer, The, 317
Erie Basin (New York City), 319
Essanay, 294
Estonia, 263
Eternal Sin, The, 302
Ethel Barrymore Theater, 309
Europe, 115, 280, 304, 307
Evans, Dorothy, 224
Evening Clothes, xxii, 294
Evening Journal (Wilmington, Delaware), **227**
Evening's Entertainment, An, 168
Everson, William K, xviii
"Evolution", 172, **173**
Exceptional Photoplays, 139
Exhibit Supply Co., **ix**
Exhibitors Herald, 116, 182-183, 228-230, 292, **296**, 314, 315, **327**
"An Exhibitor's Problems in 1925", 232
"An Exhibitor's Problems in 1926", 233-234
Exhibitor's Trade Review, 134, **135**, 177, 182, 310
Exploits of Elaine, The, 304
Eye Institute, xvii

F., F.W., 180
Fallon County Times, 231-232
Famous Players-Lasky (Famous Players), xvi, 111, 112, 125, 134, 136, **138**, 187, 230, 291, 294, 297, 299, 300
Fauchey, Paul, 169
Fairbanks, Douglas, 177
Far Wandering Men, 295
Faries, John C., 249

Farragut theater (Brooklyn, New York), 242
Fashions for Women, 306
Fawcett Publications, **255**
Fayette, Iowa, 229
Federal Arts Project, 259
Federal Motion Picture Commission, 139
Feldkamp, Frances V., 224
Fields, W.C., **216**, 231, 300, 315
Ferguson, Elsie, 298, 310
Fifth Avenue (see 5th Ave.)
Film Complet, Le, **262**-277
Film Daily, 123, 181, **227**
Film Mercury, 180
Film Progress, 139, 182
Film Till Now, The, xviii
Financial World, 256
Filmbote, Der, 280
Fine Clothes, 298
Finland, 263, 279, **289**
"Fight Scene in *The Street of Forgotten Men* a Bear For Realism—Never Before Equaled in Motion Pictures", 123
First Presbyterian church (Waterloo, Iowa), 244
First National, 3, 231, 297
Fish for Two, 310
Fiske, Mrs. (Minnie Maddern), 306
Fitzgerald, F. Scott, 127, 294
Flagg, James Montgomery, 301
Flaherty, Robert J., 231
Fleischer, Max, 310
Fleming, Victor, 296, 298
Flint, Leslie, xvi
Florodora Girl, The, 309
Flying Squad, The, 294
Fontaine, Joan, 317
Foord, Frederick A., 291
For Heaven's Sake, 231
Ford, John, 296, 297, 301
Forgotten Man, and other Essays, The, 239
"*Forgotten Men* Roles Assigned", 109
Forman, Milos, 261
Fort Worth, Texas, **212**
Fort Worth Star-Telegram, 212

Fourth Avenue South (New York City), 254
Forverts (Jewish Forward), **189**
Fotosho theater (Miami, Florida), 235
Fox (studio), 172, 236, 297
France, xxvi, 246, 263, **278**, 279, 319
Frank Brothers, 126
Franklin, Billy, **332**
Fred (*Variety* critic), 1854-185
Frederick Post (Frederick, Maryland), 297
Freshman, The, 139, 177, 233
"From a Camera Platform in the Astoria Studio", 117, 163
Front Page, The, 300
Futter, Walter, 260

Galveston, Texas, 1
"Galveston: A Business Corporation", 1
Gance, Abel, xviii
Gangs of New York, The, 256
Garden of Allah, The, 294
Geddes, Norman Bel, 303
Gentlemen Prefer Blondes, 295
George White *Scandals*, 304, 307
German bands, *152*, 165
Germany, 263, **278**, 279
Gibson, Charles Dana, 301
Gibson girl, 200
Gilbert, John, 309
Gillaspey, A. F., 225
Girl in the Glass Cage, The, 3
Girl in Every Port, A, xxvi
Girl of the Port, 296
Girl of the Rio, 314
Gish, Dorothy, 22
Glass Barrell, *147*, *152*
Glasgow, Montana, 228
Glasgow, Scotland, 258, 280
Go West, 177
God Gave Me Twenty Cents, 294, 296, 314
God's Gift to Women, 307
Godfrey, John D., *148*, *149*, *151*, 251, **252**, 292, 324
Gold Coast (New York City), **111**
Gold Coast and the Slum: A Sociological Study of Chicago's Near North Side, The, 253
Gold Diggers of 1933, 240
Gold Lay on the Streets, The, 257
Gold Rush, The, 177, **216**
"Gold Rush and the Street of Forgotten Men", The, 242-243
Goldwyn (studio), 295, 298
Goulding, Edmund, 307
Good References, 307
Grace Lutheran Church (Rochester, New York), 244
Granada theater (San Francisco, California), 227
Grand Theater (Pierre, South Dakota), 228
Grant, Cary, 300
Grantland Rice Sportlight, 172
Grantsville Theatre (Grantsville, West Virginia), 230
Grantsville, West Virginia, 229
Grass, 231
Gray, Gilda, 299
Great Depression, 240, 245
Greater Forty **290**, **353**
Great Gatsby, The, 294, 301, 302, 314
Greater Movie Season, **205**, **206**, **207**, **211**, 222, **225**
Greenpoint (New York City), 319
Greenwich Village, 303
Garbo, Greta, 309
Grieg, Edvard, 168
Griffith, Corrine, 298
Griffith, D.W., xix, 112, 126, **216**, 293, 296, 297, 301, 304, 310

Hagar's Hoard, 2
Haines, William, 299
Haldeman-Julius, E., 1
Half-Caste, The, 297
Hall, Mordaunt, 194
Halstead, Henry, **174**
Hamilton, Neil, 109-110, **111**, **130**, *143*, *144*, *149*, *154*, **161**, 180, 181, 182, 190, 192, 195, 200, 201, 202, **211**, 218, **226**, 291, **300**, 301, 304, **309**, 316

Index

Hampton, Hope, 307
Handsome Harry, *149*
Hannah and Her Sisters, 317
Harding, Warren, **204**
Harlow, Jean, xx, 294
Harper's Weekly, 239
Harrington, John, xxiv, **xxx**, 110, 117, **120**, 121-122, 124, **130**, *151-152*, 179, 180, 181, 182, 185, 190, 191, 192, 195, **199**, 219-219, **220**, 223, 230, 291, 301-302, 304, 308, **321**
Harris, Genevieve, 199-200
Harrison, P.S., 183-184
Harrison, Rex, 317
Harrison's Reports, 183
Hawks, Howard, 295
Harry the Hop, 115, 291
Haskel, Loney, 325
Hastings News (Hastings-on-Hudson, New York), 236
Hastings-on-Hudson, New York, 236
Hat on the Bed, The, 259
Hatch, Riley, 22, 110, **120**, **125**, 185, 196, 291, 298, 304, **320**
Hartford Courant (Hartford, Connecticut), **117**
Hatton, Raymond, 231, 292
Havana (Cuba), 279
Hayes, Helen, 306
Hazel Kirke, 304
Headlines, 312
Heaps, Allison Ray, 241
Hearst (newspaper), **133**
Held in Trust, 2
Helena, Montana, **213**
Hendee, Harold C., 292
Henderson, Dell, 310
Henry, O., 142, *145*, 258, 325
Her Brother's Champion, 310
Herbert, Victor, 169
"Herbert Brenon had the best of advice", 121
"Herbert Brenon Proves a Versatile Director", 115, 121
Herzog, Dorothy, 173, 188, 191
Hester Street (New York, New York), *147*, 323

Heston, Charlton, 317
Hickman, Dr., 232-233
Hilton, Violet and Daisy, **205**
Hitchcock, Alfred, 299
Hodges, Douglas, 183, **327**
Holiday, 256
Holland, George, 316
Hollywood, California, xviii, 3, 11, *155*, 200, 218, 294, 297, 299, 301, 310, 312, 314
Hollywood, Kansas, 228
Hollywood Congregational Church (Los Angeles, California), 243
Hollywood Filmograph, 256
Holt, Jack, 202
"Homeless at Home", 261
Hong Kong, 279
Honolulu Advertiser, **227**
Hook, xix
Hope Star (Hope, Arkansas), 254
House of David Band, **175**
Housemaster, The, 294, 314
Houston Chronicle (Houston, Texas), 177
"How 'FAKE' Cripples FOOL Holiday Crowds", **248**, 249
Howe, James Wong, xvii, xx
H.R. 4094 and H.R. 6233, 138-139
Hughes, Gareth, xvii
Hulbert, George Murray, **133**
Hulce, Tom, 317
Humpty Joe, *14, 19, 31, 32*
Hunger March, 258
Hunter, Glen, 310
Hurst, Fannie, 294
H., H.S., 221-222
Hula, 306
Hunchback of Notre Dame, The, 139
Hunter's Point, 129,
"Hunter's Point Undertaker Drives Hearse As 'Philadelphia Kitty' Is Buried—On Astoria Movie Lot", 129

I Am a Fugitive from a Chain Gang, 240
Iceland, 279, 289
Idwal Jones, **225**

If I Had a Million, 312
If Winter Comes, 118, 200, 202, 298, 304
"I'll See You in My Dreams", 168
Imperial theater, **211**
In Dark Places, 295
"In the Good Old Summer Time", 165
Ince, Tom, 297
Ince Studios, 297
Ingram, Rex, 296
Inisfada, 111
Institute of Crippled and Disabled Men, 249
International (studio), 172
International Boxing Hall of Fame, 315
International Jewish Sports Hall of Fame, 315
Irene [Lentz], 231
Ireland, 279, 280
Irene, 306
Irish Advocate, 256
Iron Horse, The, 295
Isle of Man, 279
Isle of Wight, 314
Isn't Life Wonderful, 301
Italy, xvi, 263, 304
Ithaca, New York, **217**
It's the Old Army Game, xxvi, 231
"It Was Not Like that in the Olden Days!", *156*, 163
Ivanhoe, 293

Jacobi, Eli (or Elias), 259-260
Jamaica, 279
Japan, **278**, 279
Jazz Age, xxvii
Jekyll-Hyde, 226
Jefferson, Joseph, 121, 316
Joseph Jefferson Theatre Company, 317
"Jolly Minstrel, The", 168
Jones, Isham, 168
Jonesport Neighbors, 257
Joy, Leatrice, 298
Joyce, Alice, xix, **186**, 294
Judge, 178
Jungle, The, 1
Just Another Blonde, 297

Just Pals, 297
K., K. T., **226**
Kalem Company, 294
Kansas, 138, 308
Kansas Board of Review, 138
Kansas City, Missouri, **207**
Keaton, Buster, 177, 300
Kellerman, Annette, 293
Kent theater (Philadelphia, Pennsylvania), 235
Kent, Arnold, 306
Kentucky Derby, xx, 124
Kerry, Norman, 312
Kiernan, John, 291, 319
"Killing Love by Suspicion", **133**
Kinematograph Weekly, 280
King City, California, 229
King, Edwin C., 134
King, Henry, 310
King of Jazz, 297
Kino, xix
Kinograms, 172
Kiss for Cinderella, A, xviii, 194, 293, 302, 307
Knockout Reilly, 300, 310
Kodak, xvii
Kodascope Library, xvii
Konungur Betlaranna (The Street of Forgotten Men), 279
Korea, 279
Kosher Kitty Kelly, 307
Kozarski, Diane, 124
Kozarski, Richard, 124, 168
Krumwiede, Walter, 244

Lake, Mr., 231
Lake Theater (Baker, Montana), 231-232
Lancaster, Pennsylvania, **215**
La Scala theatre (Dublin, Ireland), 280
Lash, James, 243
Lasky, Jesse L., 291, 308
Lassie, 110, 127-128, **196**, 291, 298, 300, 306, 310-**311**, **321**
Last Christian, The, 2
Last Laugh, The, 234
Laugh, Clown, Laugh, xx, xxiii, xxvii, 294, 314

Index

Libby, Laura Jean, *145*, 325
Rocque, Rod La, 22
"L'Ecole des Mendiants" (*The Street of Forgotten Men*), 263, **265-277**, **278**, 279
Leeds, England, 280
Legless Lew, *14*, *19*, *31*, 115, 292
Leigh, Vivien, 299
"Leonard School Notes", **215**
Leonard, Texas, 229
Lee, Lila, 3
Le Soir, 280
Lemmon, Jack, 301
Levant, Oscar, 172
Lewis, Harry, 291, 314-315, **321**
Lewis Avenue Congregational Church (Brooklyn, New York), 241-242
Leyendecker, Joseph, 301
Libby, Laura Jean, *145*, 325
Liberty, **xxxi**, 3, 11, 109, *143*, *150*, *154*, 178, 185, 193, 200, 326
Liberty Theater (Leonard, Texas), 229
Library of Congress, xxiii, xxvii, 142
LIFE, 256
Light in the Dark, 307
Light that Failed, The, 202
Lincoln, Abraham, 316
Lincoln, Caryl, 236
Link, Stanley, 254
Little Annie Rooney, *147*, 165, 177, 324
Little Church Around the Corner, 11, *17*, *98*, *104-106*, 111, **112**, **132**, 165, **309**, 316-**318**
Little French Girl, The, *143*, *145*, *149*, 181, **186**, 187, 193, 194, 294, 296, 299, 301
Little Miss Rebellion, 304
Little Neck Hills, 111
Little Old New York, 188, 304
Little Princess, The, 309
Liverpool Echo, 280
Liverpool, England, 280
Lloyd, Alice, 165-166
Lloyd, Frank, 297
Lloyd, Harold, 231, 233
Lloyd, Marie, 165-166
Local Boy Makes Good, 302

Loew's Aldine (Pittsburgh, Pennsylvania), **204**
Loew's Metropolitan, (Brooklyn, New York), 188, **328**
Loew's Temple (Birmingham, Alabama), **205**
Lombard, Carole, 240
Lombardo, Carmen, 256
Lombardo, Guy, 256
London, xvii
London Tip, *149*
Lone Wolf, The, 302, 304
Long Island, *60*, *98*, 109, 111, 115, 121, 124, 126, 134, *148*, *155*, 190, 195, 292, 307, 312, 313, 315
Lord Jim, 296, 298
Loretta Young Show, The, 309
Los Angeles, California, **209**, 218, 222
Los Angeles Evening Express, 218
Los Angeles Examiner, 218
Los Angeles Herald, 218
Los Angeles *Illustrated Daily News*, 113, 218
Los Angeles Public Library, 11
Los Angeles Record, 218
Los Angeles Times, 218-219, 242, 243, 302
Los que danzan ("Those Who Dance"), 3
Louis the 14th, 110, 124, **186**, 308
Louis the 15th of France, 319
Louise, Anita, 291, 309
Louisville, Kentucky, 124
Love, Bessie, 3
Love Em and Leave Em, xxvi, 304
Lubitsch, Ernst, 302
Lulu (character), xxvi
Lulu Belle, 302
Lulu in Hollywood, 125
Lummox, 294, 314
Luxembourg, 263, 279
Lyric theater (Billings, Montana), 237

M., J., 202
M. Witmark & Sons, 256
Macartney, J.R., 244
Madame Du Barry, 309
Madison Avenue (New York City), 316
Madison street (Chicago, Illinois), 253

Madison, Wisconsin, **212**
Maggie: A Girl of the Streets, 324
Main Stem: The Adventures of Slim and Blondey, The, 258
Majestic theater (Wilmington, Delaware), **227**
Maltese Falcon, The, 306
Man on the Flying Trapeze, The, 300
Man Who Found Himself, The, 302
Manhandled, 315
Manhattan 111, 323
Manhattan Mary, 304, 306
Mannix, 309
"Mansion of Aching Hearts, The", 168
Mantrap, 299
Marie Antoinette, 309
Marion, Ohio, **215**
Marlow, George, 228
Percy Marmont, **ix, xv, xxi, xxx**, **10**, 109, 11, 114, 115, 118, 119, **120**, 121-122, 126, 127, 129, **139**, 141, 1432, *143*, *145*, *149*, *151*, *152*, *154*, *155*, **159**-161, 169, 178, 179, 180-181, 182, 185, 188, **189**, 190, 191, 192, 195, 199, 200, 201, 202, 218, **220**, 222, 223, 224, **226-227**, 229, 230, **234**, **238**, 242, 249, 251, 259, 280, 289, 291, 296, 298-299, 304, **305**, 310, **313**, 316, **321**, 325, **332**
Marks, Ben & Ethel, **174**
Marsh, W. Ward, 222-223
Martin, Townsend, 307
Marysville, California, 253
Marzoni, Pettersen, **205**, **226**
Massachusetts, 179
Maverick, 301
McClure's, 1
McGlory, William (Billy McGlory), 147, 323
McGurk's Suicide Hall, 142, *152*, 324
McLuhan, Marshall, 261
McMahon, Charles A., 178
MacQueen, Scott, xix
McVickers theater (Chicago, Illinois), 198, 199, 201, 202
Medina, New York, **217**
"Meditation," 169
Meehan, Elizabeth, 126, 291, 313-314

Meehan, Frances, 314
Meighan, Thomas, 143, 178, 302, 307, 325
Melba, Nellie, 247
Memphis, Tennessee, 253
Mencken, H. L., 240
Mendelssohn, Felix, 168
Mendicant Squad, 249
Mendigo elegante, O (The Street of Forgotten Men), 279, **282-284, 285-287**
Menjou, Adolphe, xvii, 294, 307
Mennonite, The, 245
Merry Widow, The, 177
Metro (studio), 3, 295
Metropolitan Museum of Art, 260
Metropolitan theater (Baltimore, Maryland) **226**
Metropolitan theater (Los Angeles, California), 218
Mexico, 279
Michigan, **175**
Midsummer Night's Dream, A, 309
Mid-west Free Press, 256
Miles, Connie, 188, 190, 191
Milestone, Lewis, 300
Milo's Minstrels, **174**
Million and One Nights, A, xvi
Minneapolis, Minnesota, **206**
Minneapolis Star Daily, **226**
Miracle Man, **xxv**, 134, *143*, *153*, **174**, 178, 181, 202, 223, 224, **226**, **227**, 229, 230, 280, 325
Miroël, Yves, 263
Missoula, Montana, **217**
Mister Ed, 301
Moana, 231
Mod Squad, 309
Montana, 303
"Montmartre", 172
Moody Monthly, 245
Moore, Colleen, 177, 301
Moore, Tom, 310
Monsieur Beaucaire, 319
Moran, Lois, 294
Moreno, Antonio, 3, 306

Morning News, The (Wilmington, Delaware), **xxviii**
Mother Machree, 301
Motion Picture, **181**, 182, 308, **317**
"Motion Picture Copyright Descriptions Collection, 1912-1977", 142
Motion Picture News, **xxv**, 11, **108**, 113-114, **122**, **205**, 292, **295**
Movie Age, 230
Movie Magazine, 180
Movie Weekly, 180
Moviegoer, The, 193-194
Moving Picture World, 116, 182, 185, 228-229, 297
Mr. District Attorney, 254
Mr. Gilhooley, 306
Mr. Zero, 260
Mt. Baker, 236
Muni, Paul, 240
Munson, Ona, 298
Murders in the Rue Morgue, 306
Murnau, F.W., 309
Museum of Modern Art (MoMA), 260
Musical Courier, 172
Mutiny on the Bounty, 302
My Friend Flicka, 309
My Man Godfrey, 240
Mystery of Room 13, 314
Mystery Plane, 298

Nangle, Roberta, 200
Napoleon, xviii
Nashville, Tennessee, **212**
Nation, The, 1
National Board of Review, 134, 177
National Catholic Welfare Conference, 178
National Humane Review, 310
National Register of Historic Places, 317
Nazareth, Pennsylvania, 229
Nazimova, Alla, 293
Negri, Pola, xvi, 293, 312
Neptune's Daughter, 293
Nervous Wreck, The, 304
Nesbit, Evelyn, 307

Netherlands, The, 263, 279
Nevada, 303
"Never Introduce Your Bloke to Your Lady Friend", 165
New Britain, Connecticut, 243
New Deal, 240
New Janus theater (Shelbyville, Missouri), **215**
New Orleans Times-Picayune, 226
New Platz Normal School, 236
New York, New York (New York City), xviii, xxviii, 22, 136, *148*, *151*, *152*, 169, 172, 173, **186**, 187, **189**, 201, 202, 219, 223, 240, 241, 249, 251, 255, 257, 261, 312, 316, 317, **318**, 319, **322**, 323
New York American, 190
New York Board of Motion Picture Censorship, 134
"New York by Electric Light", 168
New York City Folklore: Legends, Tall Tales, Anecdotes, Stories, Sagas, Heroes and Characters, Customs, Traditions, and Sayings, 257
New York *Daily Mirror*, 173, 188, 191
New York *Daily News*, 109, 188, 190
New York Evening Journal, **132-133**, 173, 190
New York Evening Post, 124
New York Evening World, 188, 190, 191
New York Herald Tribune, 110, 115, 121, 123, 124, 173, 191, 192, 194, 240, 312
New York *Morning Telegraph*, 110, 191, 245, 302, 312
New York Motion Picture Commission, 134, 136-**138**
New York Post, 191
New York Public Library, 22
New York Review, 188, 191
New York Sun, 192-194
New York Telegram, 188
New York Times, 116-120, 121, 163, 164, 166, 194-195, 240, 251, 254, 306, 310
New York *World*, 192
New Yorker, The, 178, 256, 258, 307
New Yorker Volkszeitung, **189**
New Zealand, 279
Newark, Arkansas, 230

Newman theater (Kansas City, Missouri), **207**
Newmeyer, Fred, 315
News and Observer (Raleigh, North Carolina), 239
News Brunswick, New Jersey, **214**
Newsweek, 256, 259
Nice People, 302
Nie, 223-224
Nigger Mike, 129
"A Night at Coffee Dan's", **208**
Night in Chinatown, A, *145*, 325
Night Life of New York, 22, 297, 304
Noonan, Tom, **246**
Normand, Mabel, 310
Norris, Frank, 1
North Congregational Church (Portsmouth, New Hampshire), 244
Northern Ireland, 279
Northwest Outpost, 315
Norway, 263, 279
"Notes on characters in *Street of Forgotten Men*", 11, *18*
"Notice to Motorists", 215
Novarro, Ramon, 296
Nu-Art Picture, 260

Oakland, California, **211**
O'Dare, Kain, 259
Officer Quinn, *19*, 21, *102-104*, **160**, 291
O'Hara, John, 258-259
Ohio, **175**
"Old Chestnuts Waltz", 169
"Old Time New York", 204
Oliver Twist (1916 and 1933 films), 294, 314
Olympia theater (Stockholm, Sweden), **281**
Omaha, Nebraska, 230
Omaha Beach, xix
On the Town, 295
O'Neill, Eugene, 303
Our Navy, **197**
Outer Limits, The, 301
Owensboro, Kentucky, **216**

Pabst, G. W., xxvi

Pacific (region), 279
Pacific Garden Mission (Chicago, Illinois), 260
Paid in Full, 304
Paimann's Filmlisten, 280
Painted Lady, The, 297
Pal Joey, 258
Palace theater (New Britain, Connecticut), 243
Palace theatre (Newark, Arkansas), 229
Palace theater (Washington D.C.), 222
Panama, 279
Pandora's Box, xxvi, 307
Paradise Alley, 306
Paramount, xiv, xvii, xviii, **xxv**, 11, 22, 109, 111, 113, 117, 121, 126, 134, 136, **141**, *143*, *145*, *147*, *148*, *150*, *152*, *154*, *155*, *156*, 164, 169, **170**, 173, **176**, 180, 181, 182, 185, 187, 188, 198, 202, 203, **205**, **206**, **211**, 218, 223, 224, 229, 230, 231, 240, 259, 280, **284**, **290**, 292, 300, 301, 307-308, 312, 313, 315, 323, 325, **352-353**
"Paramount Exploiters", *156*
Paramount theatre (Wyoming, Illinois), 229
Paris by Night, 306
Paris, Charles, 254
Paris, France, 172, 246, 280, 315
Park Row, 115
Parker, Seth, **257**
Parker, South Dakota, 229
Partners in Crime, 299, 306
"Passage to Hong Kong, A", 3
Pathé (studio), 172, 306
Patriot, The, 301
Peck, Frances, 200
Peck's Bad Girl, 304
Peerless theater (Brooklyn, New York), 242
People's Theater (New York, New York), *152*, 326
Perlman, Rhea, 317
Perry Mason, 301
Peter Pan, xviii, xxiii, xxvii, 11, 115, 139, *143*, *145*, *149*, 166, 177, 181, 193, 195, 218, 231, 280, **288**, 293, 299
"Peter Pan (I Love You)", *64*, 167, 169

Pettis, Jack, 172
Peyton, Philip, *19, 60-67, 70, 72-73, 77, 85-89, 92-97, 104-105*, **132**, <u>*144*</u>, 291
Phantom of the Opera, The, 177, **214**
Philadelphia Inquirer, 134, 235
Philadelphia Kitty, 129
Philadelphia, Pennsylvania, 169, 198, 210, 236, 246
Philadelphia Public Ledger, 249
Philadelphia Record, **226**
Philosophy of the Dusk, 258
Photoplay, **116**, *179*, 182, 325, **332**
Photoplay Medal of Honor, xix, 293
Pickford, Jack, 294
Pickford, Mary, xix, 177, 294, 324
Pied Piper Malone, 307
Pierce, David, xviii
Pierre, South Dakota, 228
Pittsburgh Gazette Times (Pittsburgh, Pennsylvania), 177
Pittsburgh, Pennsylvania, 198, **204**
Plastic Age, The, 177
Playhouse 90, 309
"Please, Cheer Up Percy", **332**
Police Commissioner Gordon, 301
Police Gazette, 47
Pollock, Channing, 242
Pomona, California, **213**
Pony Express, The, 177, **211**, 231
"Poor Percy: The most persecuted person in pictures", 332
Pope Francis, 245
Poppy, 112
Popular Mechanics, 256
Portland Fancy, **xxi**, 3, *12, 15, 18,* 21, *27, 38, 41-45, 79, 82, 87-88,* 113, 114, 129, <u>*143*</u>, 168, 180, 291, 323
Portugal, 263, 279
Potters, The, 315
Potterton, Thomas Edward, 242
Pottsville Journal (Pottsville, Pennsylvania), 258
Pottsville, Pennsylvania, 258
Pottsville Republican (Pottsville, Pennsylvania), 258

Pour Vous, 124
Powell, William, 240, 307
PRC (Producers Releasing Corporation), 301
Pretty Young Girl, The, 325
Princess theater (Honolulu, Hawaii), **227**
Princeton University, 308
"Prologue", 169
Press Sheet, 21, 123, **140**, 141, 142, 163, 164, 203, 221, 292, 323, 324, 325,
Print Club of Philadelphia, 259-260
Private Scandal, 300
Prix de Beauté, xxvi, 308
Pulitzer Prize, 201
Purcell, Howard, 254
Purvis, Samuel W., 245
Putti, Lya De, 294
"Putting it Over Right", ***153***

Queen Elizabeth Hall (London, England), xix
Queens, New York, 111, **217**, 319
Quigley, Martin J., 183

R., J., 223
R., W., 192
Raft, George, 326
Ralston, Esther, **186**, 299, 301, 307
Ramsbottom, Harold, 173
Rapée, Ernö, 168
Rathbone, Basil, 317
Raynaud, Armand, 169
Red Badge of Courage, The, xx
Red Book, 2
Red Dust, 295
Red Friday, 2
Red Mark and Other Stories, The, 295, 296
Red-Headed Woman, 295
Red Seal Pictures, 310
Reel Joy theater (King City, California), 229
Regent Theatre (Bogota, New Jersey), 229
Regent theater (Rochester, New York), 232-233
Rehan, Ada, 121
Reisner, Christian F., 240-241
"Remember My Forgotten Man", 240

Republican (Springfield, Massachusetts), 1
Rescue, The, 314
Rescue Society, **246**
Return of Dr. Fu Manchu, The, 301
Revere House, 253
Rex theater (Salmon, Idaho), 230, 232
Reykjavík, Iceland, **289**
Rialto theater, *148*
Rialto theater (Champaign, Illinois), **236**, 237
Rialto theater (Missoula, Montana), **216**
Rialto theater (New York, New York), **186, 189**
Richardson, Charles J., 223
Riders of the Purple Sage, 177, **205**
Riesenfeld, Hugo, **173**
Riis, Jacob, 1
Rin Tin Tin, 177, 196
River of Romance, 300
Riverview Manor, 236
Rivoli theater (New York, New York), 136, 172-173, **186**-191, 193, 196, 198, 240, 291
RKO Radio Pictures (studio), 3, **257**, 297
Roar of the Dragon, 3
Roberts, Bob, 165
Roberts, Florence, 304
Robinson, Edward G., 298
Roccardi, Albert, 291, 306
Rochester, Indiana, 229
Rochester, New York, 136, 170, 233
Rochester Herald (Rochester, New York), 178
Rockefeller, Jr., John D., 2
Rockwell, Norman, 301
Roi des mendiants, Le (*The Street of Forgotten Men*), 279
Rolled Stockings, xxii
Roman Cinè, 263
Romance of the Rio Grande, 306
Rongen, Elif, xvii
Roosevelt, Franklin, 240
Rose, Ted, **174**
Rose of the World, 298
Roseville, California, 303
Rosie O'Grady, 310
Rosson, Arthur, xix,

Rosson, Hal, xix, **130-131, 133**, 291, 294-295
Rotha, Paul, xviii
Rough House Rosie, 295
Royal Family of Broadway, The, 300
Rubens, Alma, 298, 310
Rue des hommes perdus, La (*The Street of Forgotten Men*), 279
Rugged Water, **186, 189**
Running Wild, 300
Russell, John, 11, *12, 18, 20*, 21, 124, **133**, 291, 295-297, 323

Sabre, Mark, 118, 298
Sacramento Union, 224
Sagan, Carl, 261
Sally, 177, 313
Salmon, Idaho, 230
Salvation Army, 134, 136, 151, 259
San Antonio, Texas, **205, 210**
San Antonio Express, **226**
San Francisco, California, xxii, xxviii, 198, **211**, 221, 225, **227**, 228, 253, 258
San Francisco Bulletin, 226, **227**
San Francisco Call & Post, 177, **227**
San Francisco Chronicle, **227**
San Francisco Cinematheque, 260
San Francisco Examiner, **225, 227**
San Francisco News, **227**
San Francisco Public Library, xxvi
Sandburg, Carl, 201-202
Santa Barbara Daily News, 224
Santa Barbara Morning Press, 224
Saturday Evening Post (*Satevepost*), 2, 185, 193, 326
Scandal, 297
Scarlet Pimpernel, The, 295
Scena Muda, A, **282-284**
Schoedsack, Ernest, 231, 244,
Schofield, Paul, 21, 22, *23*, 109, *143, 150*, 291, 297-298
School der Bedelaars, De, (*The Street of Forgotten Men*), 279
Scopes Monkey trial, 172, **173**
Scotland, 279

348

Index

Scott, Leroy, 194
Screenland, 182, 313
Sea God, The, 296
Seattle, Washington, **205**
Secret Agent, 299
Semon, Larry, 237
Sensation Hunters, 297
Seth Parker Fireside Poems, **257**
Sewell, C.S., 182
Shane, Theodore, (T.S.), 178
Shanghai, China, **289**
Shark, The, 310
Sharkey, Jack, 256
Shaw, George Bernard, 259
Shearer, Norma, 196
Shelbyville, Missouri, **215**
Sherlock Holmes, 304
Show Off, The, xxvi
Side Street, 296
Side Show of Life, The, 301
"The Sidewalks of New York" (song), 119, **162**, 163, 164, 168, 169
Silent Players, 299
Silvan Divan, *147*, *152*, 326
Sinclair, Upton, 1-2
Singin' in the Rain, 295
Single, Erwin A., 257
Sister Carrie, 253, 324
Sixth Commandment, The, 309
Skuggornas barn (The Street of Forgotten Men), **278**, 279, **281**
Slave of Fashion, A, 196
Slide, The, *147*, 326
Slide, Anthony, 299
"Slow Motion", 112
"Sleepy Baby", 169
Smart Set, 126, 256, 313, 314
Smith, Al, 164
Smith, Almelia, 217
Smith, Capt. E. R., 94
Smith, H. M. K., 113, 292
Snuggles Joy, xxii, xxiv
Social Celebrity, A, 307

Societies for the Prevention of Cruelty to Animals, 128
Society Wolf, The, 295
Soir, Le (Paris, France), 280
Son of Zorro, 177
Song and Dance Man, The, 231, 297
"Songs that You Have Sung", 172
Sonny, 310
Sorrell and Son, 294, 314
Sorrows of Satan, The, 296, 310
South Africa, 279, 298
South Church (New Britain, Connecticut), 243
Spain, 279
Spain, Mildred, 188, 190
Spanish Cavalier, The, xvi
Spanish Dancer, The, xvi, xvii, xviii, xxiii, 293
Spartanburg, South Carolina, 312
"Speakeasy Equips Beggars as Cripple," 251
Springfield Leader and Press (Springfield, Illinois), 253
Spirit of Culver, The, 312
Squaw Man, The, 304
Squeaker, The, 299
S.T. theatre (Parker, South Dakota), 229
St. Clair, Malcolm, 310
St. Louis, Missouri, **216**
St. Louis Globe-Democrat, 224
St. Louis Post-Dispatch, 224
St. Marks Place (New York, New York), 260
St. Patrick's Cathedral (New York, New York), *151*
St. Paul's Evangelical Lutheran Church (Camden, New Jersey), 244
St. Regis (studio), 312
Stanton theater (Philadelphia, Pennsylvania), **209**
Star theater (Shelbyville, Missouri), **215**
Star theatre (Montevideo, Minnesota), 229
Star, Jimmy, 218
Steffens, Lincoln, 1
Step Lively, Jeeves!, 302
Stereopticon, 244, 246
"Stereoscopik Luna-cy", 217

Steve Brodie's Place, *152*, 326
Stieglitz, Alfred, **322**
Stinson, Eugene, 201
Stockholm, Sweden, **281**
"Stockings on the Line", 165
Stockton, California, **210**
Stone, Lewis, 202
Storm Over Lisbon, 314
Straat der Ellendigen, De (*The Street of Forgotten Men*), 279
Straat der verlaten Wezens, De (*The Street of Forgotten Men*), 279
"Straight From the Shoulder Reports", 228
Strand theater (Seattle, Washington), **205**
Strand theater (Minneapolis, Minnesota), **226**
Strand, Paul, **322**
Straße des Grauens, Die (*The Street of Forgotten Men*), **278**, 279, 280
Strasse vergessener Menschen, Die (*The Street of Forgotten Men*), **189**
Street of Forgotten Men, The, (book), 253
Street of Forgotten Men, The, (poem), **257**
Street of Forgotten Men – a Prologue, The, **327**
Street of Forgotten Women, 260
"Streets of New York", 169
"Street of the Forgotten Men, The" (short story), **xxxi**, 3, 5, 11, 109, **258**, 326
Subway Sadie, 297
Sumner, William Graham, 239, 240
Summers, Dudley G., 3
"Sunday Morning Beggar", 116
Sunday School Times, **246**
Sunken Silver, 306
Swanson, Gloria, 294
Sweden, 263, **278**, 279, 281
Sweet, Blanche, 3
"Sweet Georgia Brown", 172
Swing Time, 302
Switzerland, 263
"Synthetic Cripples Turned Out To Beg On New York Sts.", 251
Syracuse, New York, 136

Tacoma, Washington, 224, 303

Tacoma Daily Ledger (Tacoma, Washington), 177
Tacoma News Tribune (Tacoma, Washington), 225
Tacoma Times (Tacoma, Washington), 177
Taffe, Agnes, 226
Talley, Alma, 180
Talmadge, Constance, 307
Talmadge, Norma, xix, 298
Tanz geht weiter, Der ("Those Who Dance"), 3
Tarbell, Ida, 1
Tarzan the Ape Man, 295, 301
Taskmaster, The, 1
Tasmania, 279
Tchaikovsky, Pyotr Ilyich, 168
Telephone Girl, The, 314
Ten Commandments, The, 139, 177, 202, 231
Ten North Frederick, 258
That Royle Girl, **216**, 231, 297
That Wonderful Guy, 301
"That's an Irish Lullaby", 168
Theatre Guild (NYC), 312
Thematic Music Cue Sheet, 168, **170**
Thirty Seconds Over Tokyo, 294
Thomas, Olive, 310
"Those Who Dance", 3
Three Bees Candy Shop, **217**
Three Musketeers, The, 306
Thrice, Luke, 295
Throckmorton, Cleon, 303
Through the Lich-Gate: A Biography of the Little Church Around the Corner, 316
Thunder the Dog, 236
Tiggerkongen (*The Street of Forgotten Men*), 279
TIME, 178, 253
Tin Gods, 302
Tin Pan Alley, 326
Tinée, Mae, 200, 202
Tiny Tim, 254
Together, 245
Tol'able David, 310
Toledo, Ohio, **175**
Toledo Times, (Toledo, Ohio), **175**
Tony Pastors, *152*, 326

Index

Too Many Kisses, 319
"Tourist and the Maid, The", 165
Tracked in the Snow Country, 177, 196
Transactions of the Society of Motion Picture Engineers, 232, 233
Transgression, 314
Treasure Island, 295
Trip to Chinatown, A, 164
Tristar, xix
Trudden, Joe, 291
Tucker, George Loane, 143, 325
Tully, Jim, 191, 258
Tunnel Saloon, **257**
Turner, George Kibbe, 1-3, 11, 21, *23*, 109, 117, *143*, *145*, *148*, *150*, *152*, *154*, 178, 184, 193, 200, 218, 236, 239, 258, 291, 296, 323, 326
Twin Falls, Idaho, 304
Two Flaming Youths, 300
Tynan, Kenneth, 307

Uj Előre, **189**
Ukraine, 259
Ulice zapomenutých mužu (*The Street of Forgotten Men*), 279
Улица забытых людей (*The Street of Forgotten Men*), 279
Underhill, Harriet, 115, 121, 173, 192, 194
Unguarded Hour, The, 312
Unholy Three, The, 139, 177, **227**
Union League Club, 127
United Kingdom, 279, 280, 291
United States (America), xxix, 133, 134, 136, 156, 165, 187, 198, 203, **206**, **207**, 224, **226**, 237, 244, **248**, 258, 279, 293, 298, 303, 304, 306, 325, 327
United States Congress, 245
United States Copyright Office, 142
United States Army, 297
United States Navy, 197
United States Signal Corp., 298
Universal, 297
Utah, 303

Vakschool der bedelaars, De (*The Street of Forgotten Men*), 279
Valentino, Rudolph, xvi, 177, 280, 319
Valentino Memorial Guild, xvi
Van Winkle, Rip, 316
Vanguard Press, 258
Vanhern, Fancy (Mary, also Fannie), 11, *16*, *18*, 21, **132**, 138, 142, **167**, **247**, 291
Vanishing American, The, 231
Variety, 124, 172, 184, 196, **209**, 227
Varjojen lapsi (*The Street of Forgotten Men*), 279
Vaudeville, 165, 172, 173, **174**, 306
Vannah, Kate, 169
Vernon, Suzy, 3
Victoria theater (previously Loew's Aldine), **204**
Vidas Perdidas (*The Street of Forgotten Men*), 279
Virginian, The, 300
Virtuous Model, The, 306
Vitagraph Studios, 294, 298
Volstead Act, 57, 200, 327

Waifs of New York, The, 235
Wales, 279
Walker, Mickey, 256
Wall Street Journal, 239
Wallace, Edgar, 299
Walsh, George, 310
Walters, Dorothy, 110, 114, **161**, 196, 219, 291, 306-307
WAMPAS, 299, 309
Wanger, Walter, 307, 308
War Brides, 293
War Game, The, xviii
Warner Bros. (studio), 3, 297
Washington theater (Atoka, Oklahoma), **228**
Washington D.C., xxvii, **203**, 221
Washington Herald, 221-222, 297
Washington Post, **226**
Washington Times, 223
Water, John Vande, 253
Watkins, Pete, xviii
Way Back Home, **257**

Wayne, John, 295
"Wedding March", 168
Weekly Film Review, 224
"Weekly Meditation, A", 246-247, 249
Weems, Ted, **174, 204**
Weird Tales, **205**
Wells Fargo, 298
Welterweight Champion of the World, 315
Wendy, *149*, 195, 299
West of Singapore, 314
Westlake Presbyterian Church (Los Angeles, California), 242
"What the Picture Did For Me", 228
Where the Pavement Ends, 295, 296
What Price Hollywood?, 301
Whirlpool, 3076
White, George, 304, 307
White, Pearl, 304
White, Stanford, 306
White Rose, The, 301
White Shoulders, 2
Whiteman, Paul, 297
Whitey (see Bridgeport White-Eye)
"Who Are You Looking At?", 165
Who's Who on the Screen, 298
'Why Did You?", 256
Why Kids Leave Home, 172
Wicked Woman, A, 303
Widow McGee (Widow M'Gee), *19, 47-50, 54-55, 60, 62, 65, 67-69, 71-74, 90-91, 94-95, 106*, **114, 179**, 291
Williams, (policeman), 251
Williams, Betty, (Elizabeth Meehan), 313
William, Capt., 304
Williams, Emlyn, 259
Williams, Kathlyn, xvii
Williams, Margaret, 236
Willis, H. B. K., 218
Willat, Irvin, 294
Winchell, Walter, 312
"With the Moving Picture Organist", 169
Wizard of Oz, The, 294
Wodehouse, P. G., 317
Wolf Fangs, 236

Wood, Peggy, 317
Wood, Polly, 200
Woman Who Gave, The, 307
Woman's Home Companion, 2
Women's Wear (Daily), 109
Women of Affairs, A, 309
Works Progress Administration, 259
World War I, 239, 241, 294,
World War II, 246, 298, 300
WPA Guide to New York, 260
"Writer Mingles with Misfits", 253
Wynn, Ed, 304
Wyoming, Illinois, 229

"Y" theatre (Nazareth, Pennsylvania), 229
Yale University, 239, 308
Yankee magazine, 303
Y.M.C.A., 197, 289
"You'll Like This Tale of Bowery Underworld", 200
Yonkers Herald, 236
Yonkers Statesman, 236
Young, Loretta, xx, 3
Young and Innocent, 299
Young Sinners, 302
YouTube, 172, 260, 310
"Yucca Knolls", 259

Zamecnik, J.S., 168
Zaza, 294, 304
Ziegfeld, (Florenz), 124, 313
Ziegfeld Follies, 110, 126, **186**, 307, 313
Zimmerman, Katherine, 188
Zorbaugh, Harvey Warren, 253
Zukor, Adolphe, 187, 291, 308

One of the trade ads placed by Paramount in trade publications in the summer of 1925. The text in the ad reads, in part, "*The Street of Forgotten Men*. How shall we describe it and what Herbert Brenon has made in this picture? You can offer money back to any one who can see this picture and not feel the thrill of it, the so-hard-to-catch heart tug of it, the powerful punch of its story and scenes. And if you want to hear of a new real star, remember the name Mary Brian." July 1925

The Street of Forgotten Men: From Story to Screen and Beyond

The author (right) and film historians Richard and Diane Koszarski at the Castro Theater during the 2022 San Francisco Silent Film Festival, at which the restoration of *The Street of Forgotten Men* premiered. *Courtesy of Christy Pascoe*

ABOUT THE AUTHOR

Thomas Gladysz is the Director of the Louise Brooks Society™ (www.pandorasbox.com), a pioneering website and online archive which he launched in 1995. The website has been praised by the *New York Times*, *USA Today*, *Wired*, and other publications. In 2018, Jack Garner, the late critic for the *Rochester Democrat & Chronicle* and a friend to Louise Brooks said, "if there exists a No. 1 fan and a No. 1 chronicler of Brooks, it's Thomas Gladysz, the founder and longtime champion of the Louise Brooks Society."

In 2010, Gladysz edited and wrote the introduction to the "Louise Brooks edition" of Margarete Böhme's *The Diary of a Lost Girl*, the book that was the basis for the 1929 film. In 2017, he authored books on two of Brooks' films, *Beggars of Life: A Companion to the 1928 Film*, and *Now We're in the Air: A Companion to the Once "Lost" Film*. And in 2018, he published *Louise Brooks: The Persistent Star*, a collection of his articles, essays, blogs, and interviews.

Gladysz has curated exhibits and spoken on the actress at the San Francisco Public Library, introduced her films at the Detroit Institute of Arts, Niles Essanay Silent Film Museum, San Francisco Silent Film Festival, and Action Cinema in Paris, France, and assisted with the restoration of *Now We're in the Air* and *The Street of Forgotten Men*. His audio commentaries appear on the Kino Lorber releases *Diary of a Lost Girl* and *Beggars of Life*.

In 2019, Gladysz gave the keynote address at the 92nd annual Rudolph Valentino Memorial Service at the Hollywood Forever cemetery, speaking on the little-known connection between Valentino and Brooks. He has authored numerous articles on early film for *Film International*, *Classic Images*, *PopMatters*, *Huffington Post* and other publications and websites. Gladysz has also contributed program notes to the San Francisco and Cleveland silent film festivals, as well as to Ebertfest, Syracuse CineFest, Telluride Film Festival, University of Wisconsin Cinematheque, and Brattle Theater in Cambridge, Massachusetts. More at www.thomasgladysz.com.

www.ingramcontent.com/pod-product-compliance
Lightning Source LLC
Chambersburg PA
CBHW080834230426
43665CB00021B/2839